Waiting for Spring 12

Anashin

Waiting
for Spring
vol.12

Presented by
Anashin

CONTENTS

WAITING FOR SPRING
Harumatsu Bokura

Character & Story

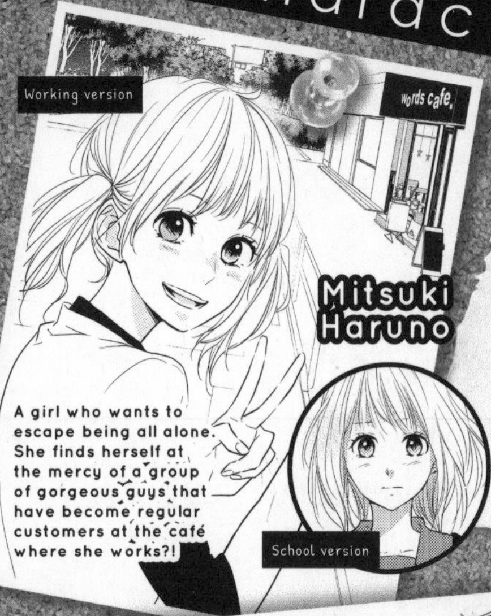

Working version
words cafe.
School version

Mitsuki Haruno

A girl who wants to escape being all alone. She finds herself at the mercy of a group of gorgeous guys that have become regular customers at the café where she works?!

Mitsuki, a loner, is determined to make some real friends in high school. One day, the school celebrities—the Elite Four Hotties of the basketball team—appear at the café where she works! Mitsuki gets caught up in their silly hijinks, but also successfully makes new friends, and gradually falls in love with her classmate Towa. But when Mitsuki is reunited with her old friend Aya-chan, she is stunned to learn that he was actually a boy! What's more, he really wants to date her!! Towa also tells Mitsuki he likes her, but members of the basketball team aren't allowed to date—so she has to put her answer on hold. To get this rule changed, the team must defeat Aya-chan's school, Hōjō, and win the New Team Tournament! At last, Towa and Aya face each other in the Seiryo-Hōjō match. And when Towa gets injured mid-game, Mitsuki rushes to his side and tells him how she feels..!

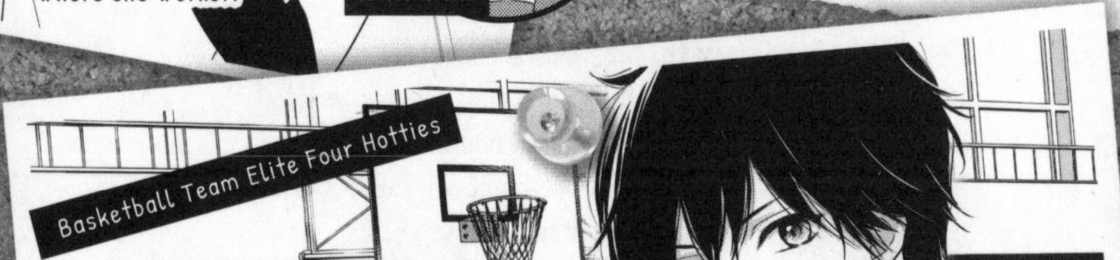

Basketball Team Elite Four Hotties

Towa Asakura

Mitsuki's classmate. He's quiet and a bit spacey, but he's always there to help her.

Rui Miyamoto

A first-year in high school. His innocent smile is adorable, but it hides a wicked heart?!

Kyōsuke Wakamiya

A second-year in high school. Mysterious and always cool-headed, he's like a big brother to everyone.

Ryūji Tada

A second-year. Comes off as a bad boy but is rather naïve. He's crushing on the Boss's daughter, Nanase-san.

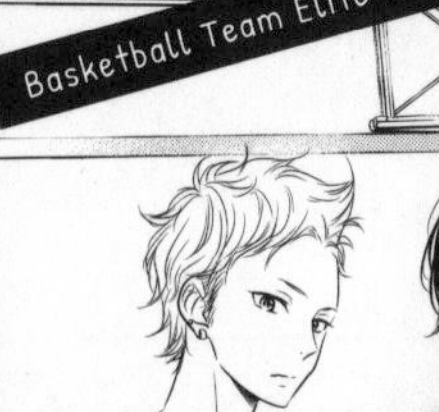

Aya-chan

Mitsuki's best friend from elementary school. When they finally meet again, she discovers he was a boy!

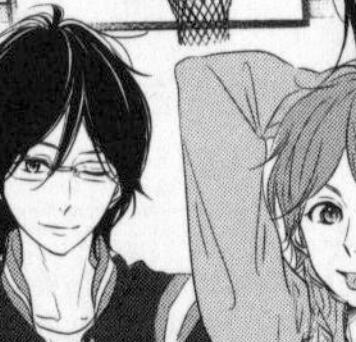

Reina Yamada

Mitsuki's first friend from her class. She has somewhat eccentric tastes?!

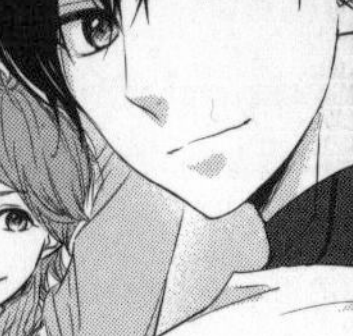

Maki-chan

A first-year on the girls' basketball team who gets along with Mitsuki. Apparently she has a crush on Towa?!

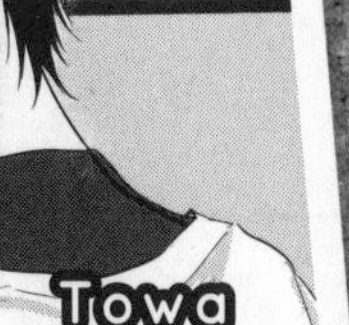

Nana-san

The Boss's daughter. Straightforward and resolute, she is a reliable, big sister type.

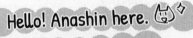

Hello! Anashin here. 🐱✦
Thank you so much
         for picking up Volume 12!

The covers have gone through every character once for
the solo version and once for the two-character version,
and now I've drawn Towa and Mitsuki again. (They should
be a lot closer than they were on the cover for Volume 7,
if you look closely. Like at their hands and stuff...)

So that's the end of the two-character version. I'm just
going to tell you about the next volume...

I'm planning to have all (five) of them on the cover!

Waaah! That's gonna be hard to draw (ha ha)

I hope you enjoy Volume 12! ✧ ◇

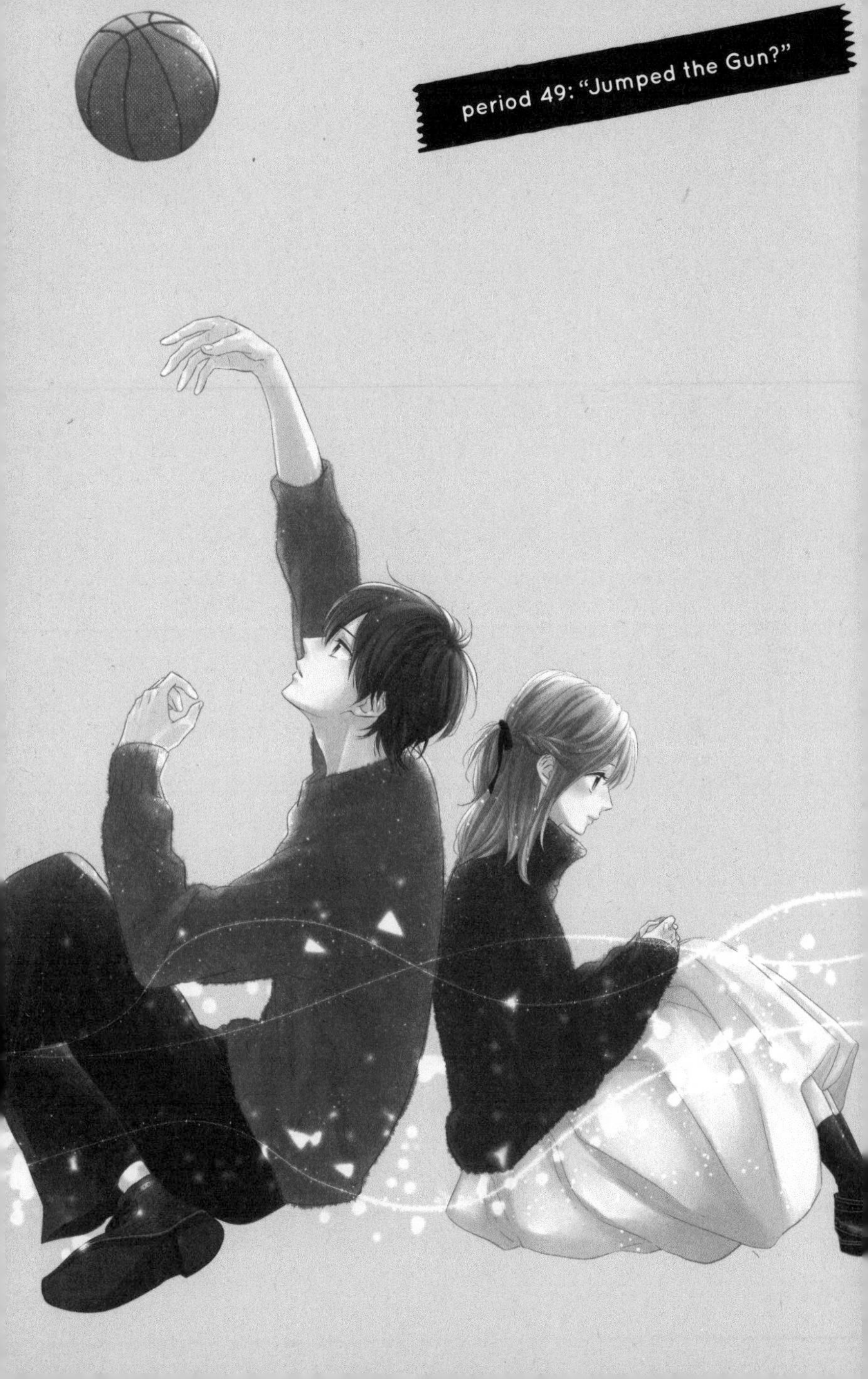
period 49: "Jumped the Gun?"

Waiting for Spring

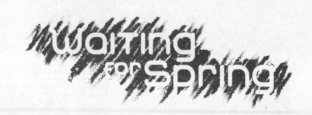

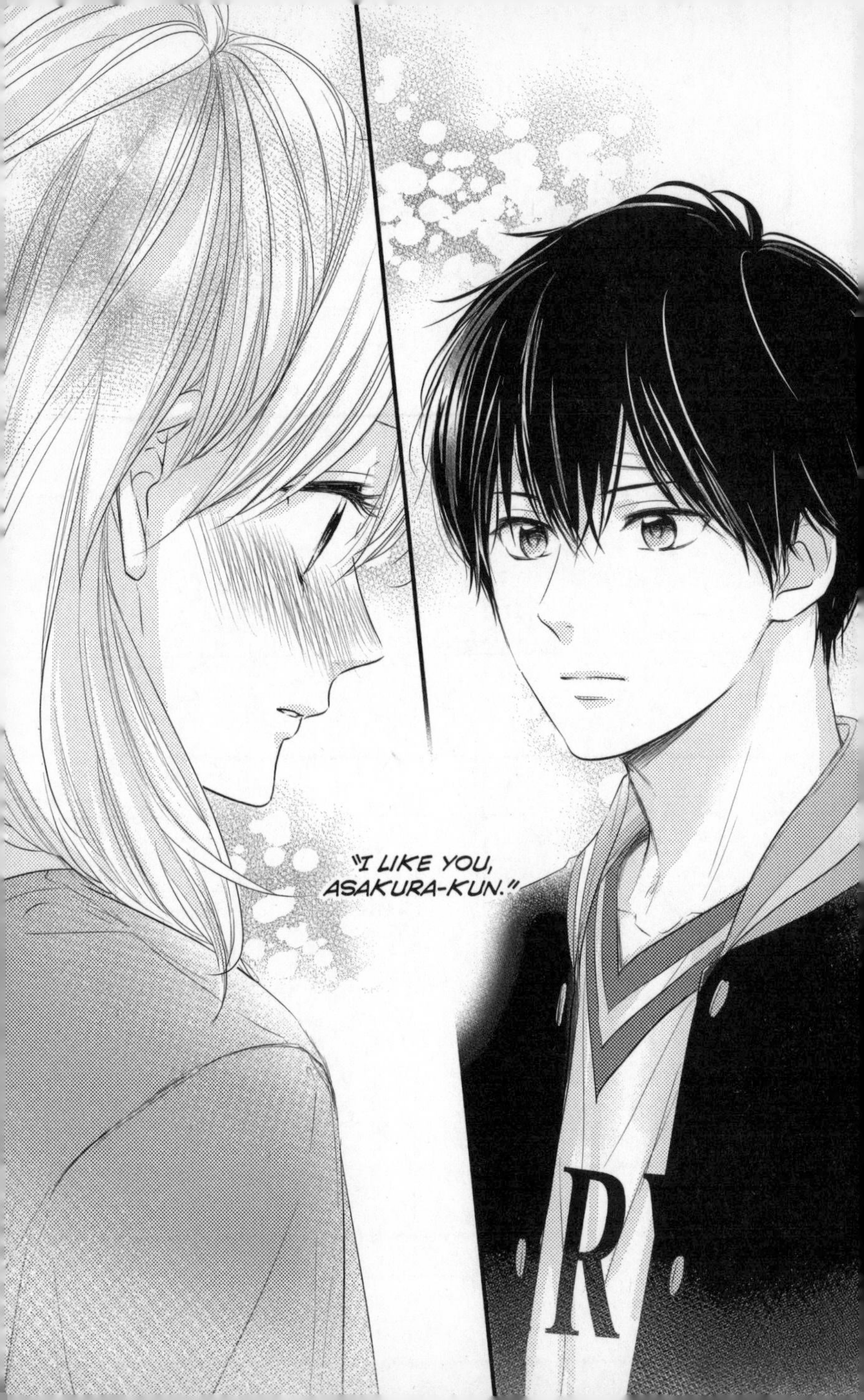
"I LIKE YOU, ASAKURA-KUN."

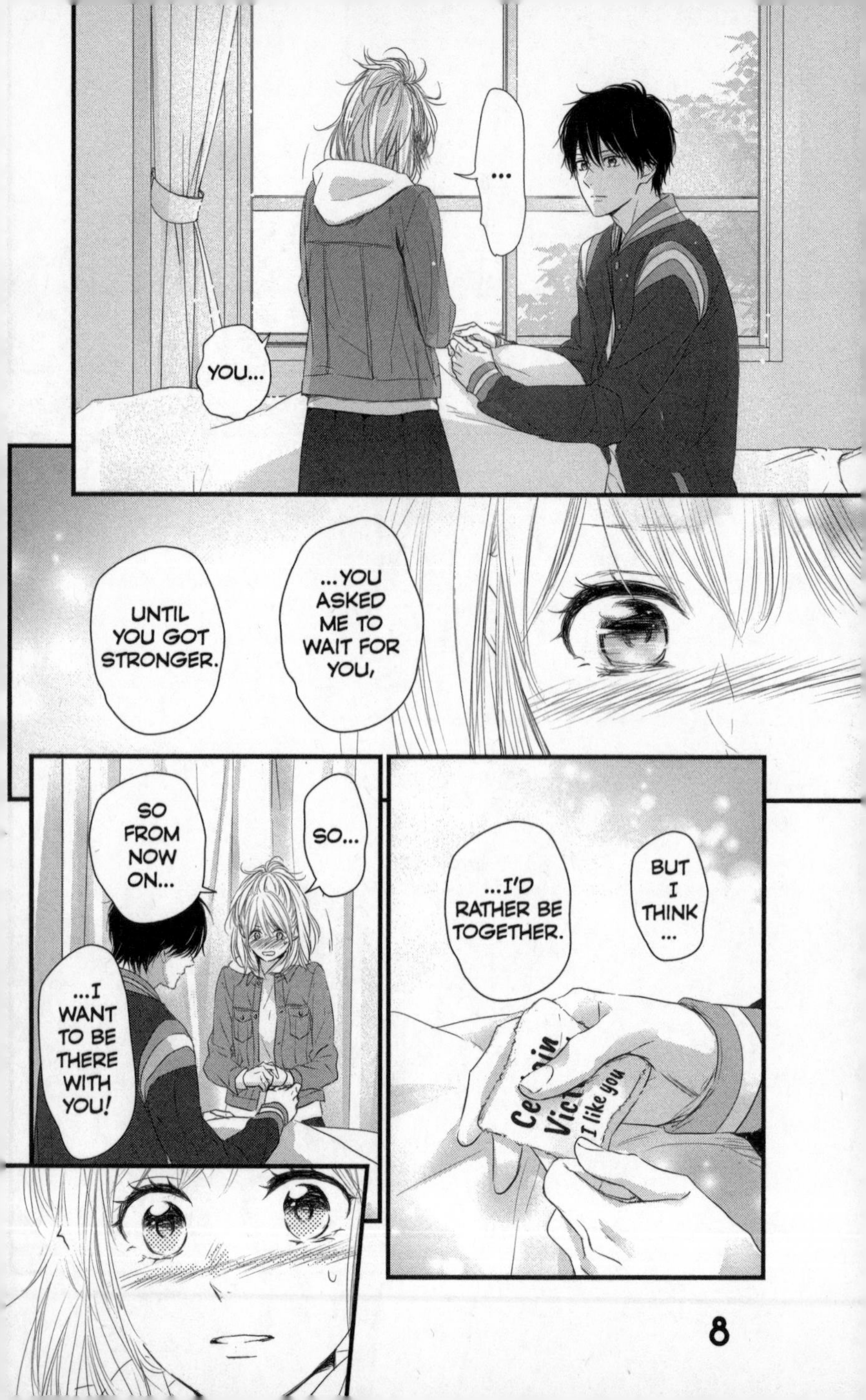
...
YOU...
...YOU ASKED ME TO WAIT FOR YOU,
UNTIL YOU GOT STRONGER.
BUT I THINK...
...I'D RATHER BE TOGETHER.
I like you
SO...
SO FROM NOW ON...
...I WANT TO BE THERE WITH YOU!

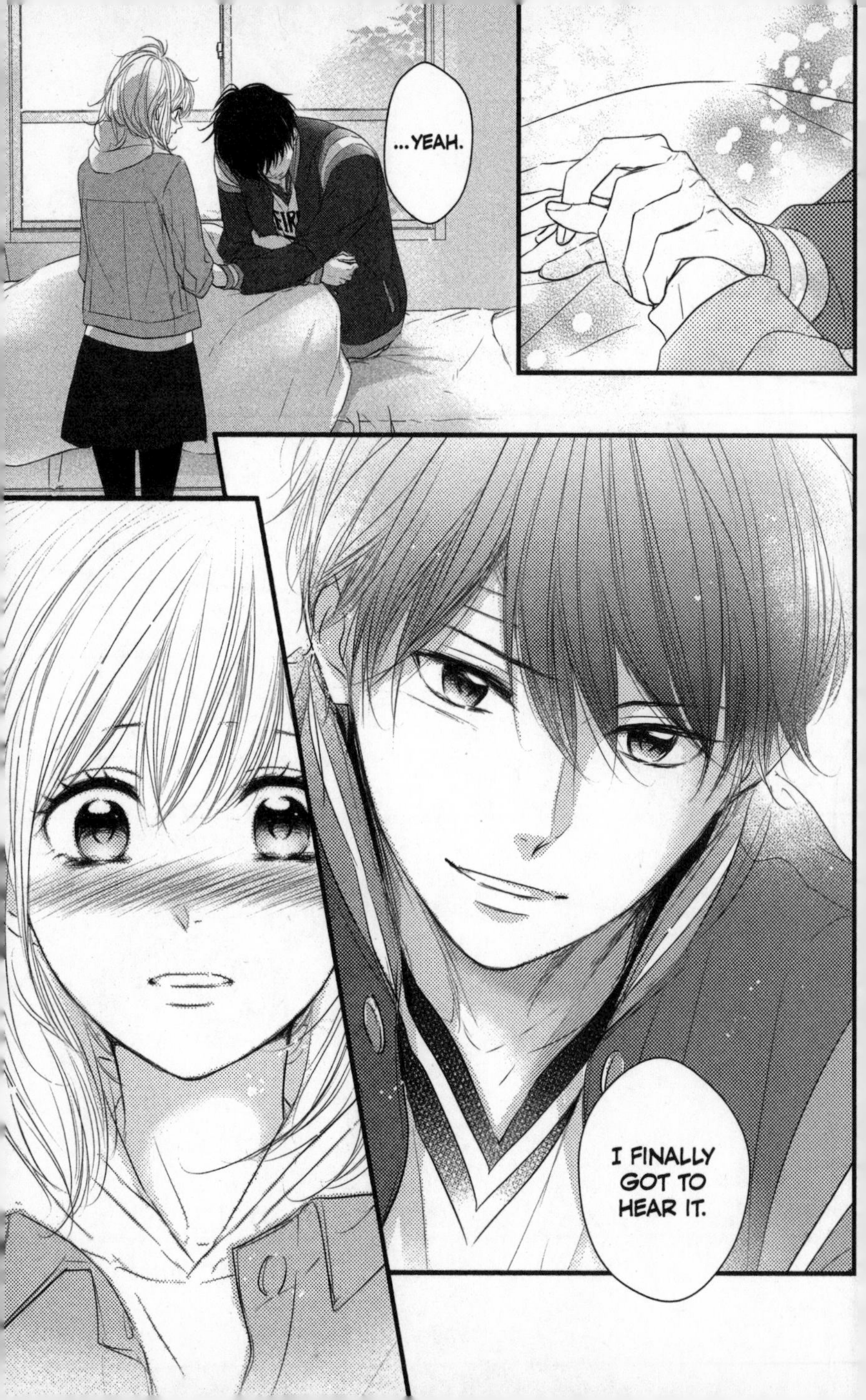
...YEAH.
I FINALLY GOT TO HEAR IT.

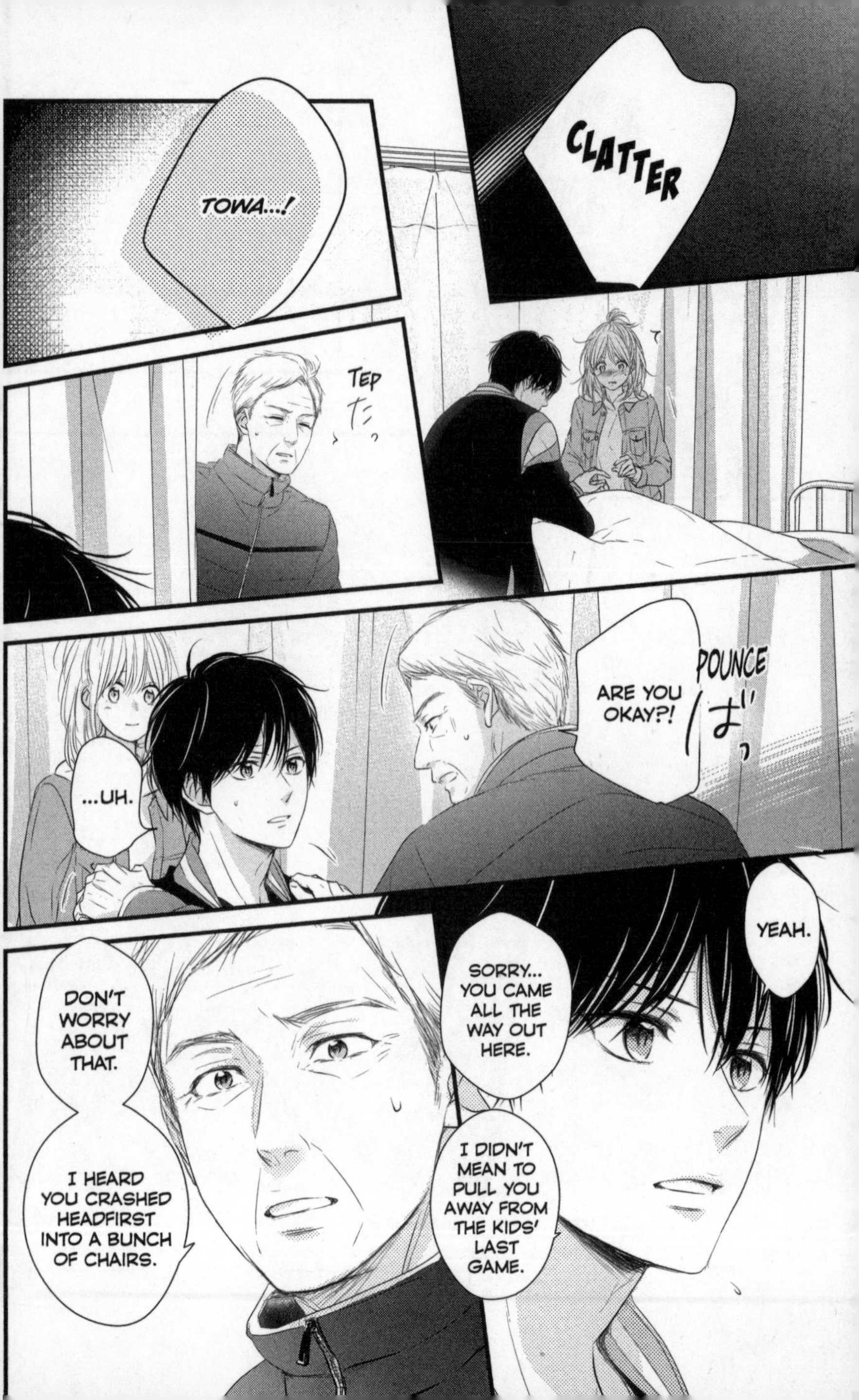
CLATTER
TOWA...!
TEP
たっ
POUNCE
ばっ
ARE YOU OKAY?!
...UH.
YEAH.
SORRY... YOU CAME ALL THE WAY OUT HERE.
I DIDN'T MEAN TO PULL YOU AWAY FROM THE KIDS' LAST GAME.
DON'T WORRY ABOUT THAT.
I HEARD YOU CRASHED HEADFIRST INTO A BUNCH OF CHAIRS.

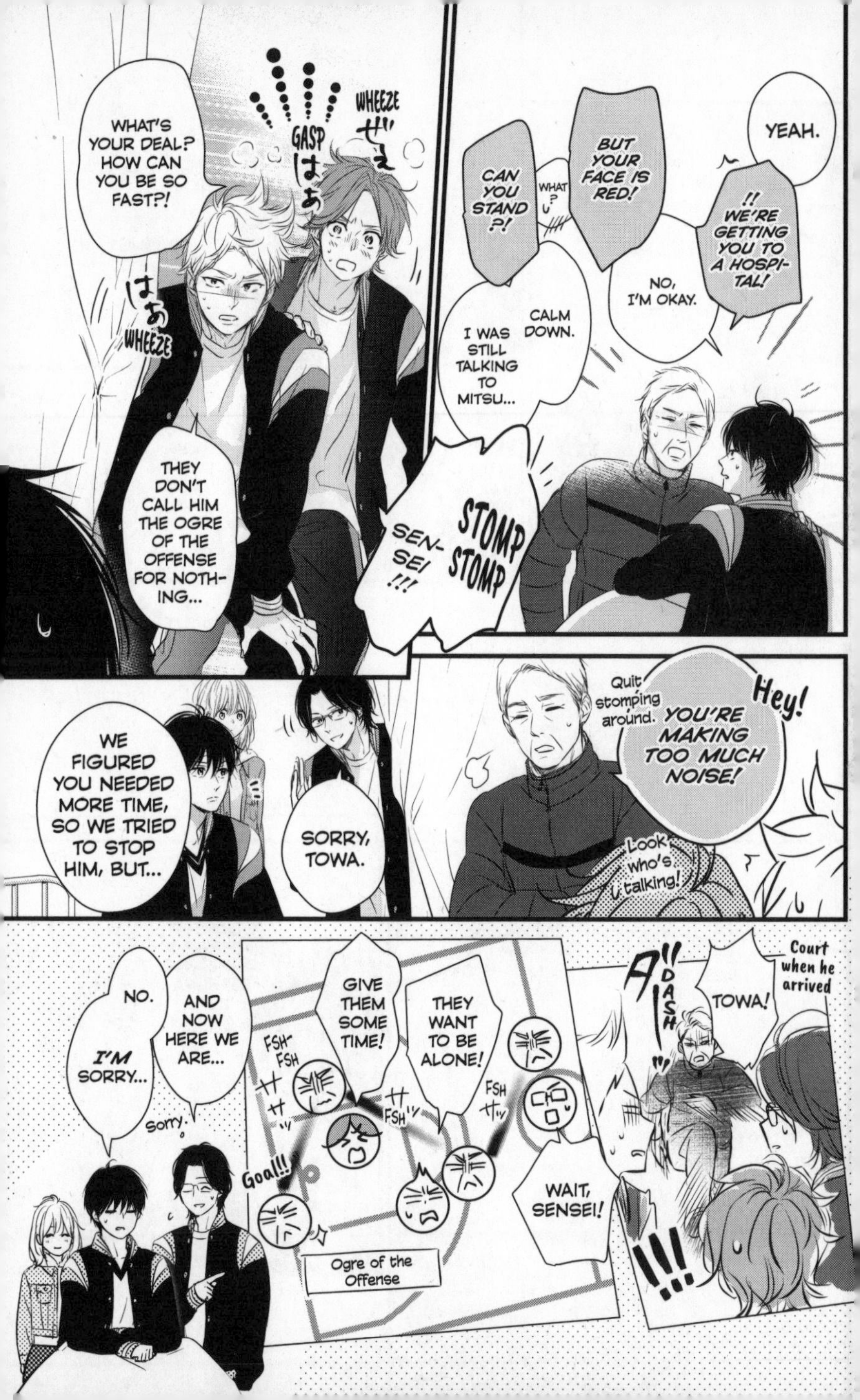
YEAH.
!! WE'RE GETTING YOU TO A HOSPITAL!
BUT YOUR FACE IS RED!
WHAT?
CAN YOU STAND?!
NO, I'M OKAY.
CALM DOWN.
I WAS STILL TALKING TO MITSU...
STOMP STOMP
SEN-SEI!!!
WHEEZE ぜぇ
GASP はぁ
WHAT'S YOUR DEAL? HOW CAN YOU BE SO FAST?!
はぁ WHEEZE
THEY DON'T CALL HIM THE OGRE OF THE OFFENSE FOR NOTHING...
Hey!
YOU'RE MAKING TOO MUCH NOISE!
Quit stomping around.
Look who's talking!
SORRY, TOWA.
WE FIGURED YOU NEEDED MORE TIME, SO WE TRIED TO STOP HIM, BUT...
Court when he arrived
TOWA!
A!! DASH
!!!
WAIT, SENSEI!
THEY WANT TO BE ALONE!
GIVE THEM SOME TIME!
FSH FSH
FSH
FSH
Goal!!
Ogre of the Offense
AND NOW HERE WE ARE...
NO.
I'M SORRY...
Sorry.

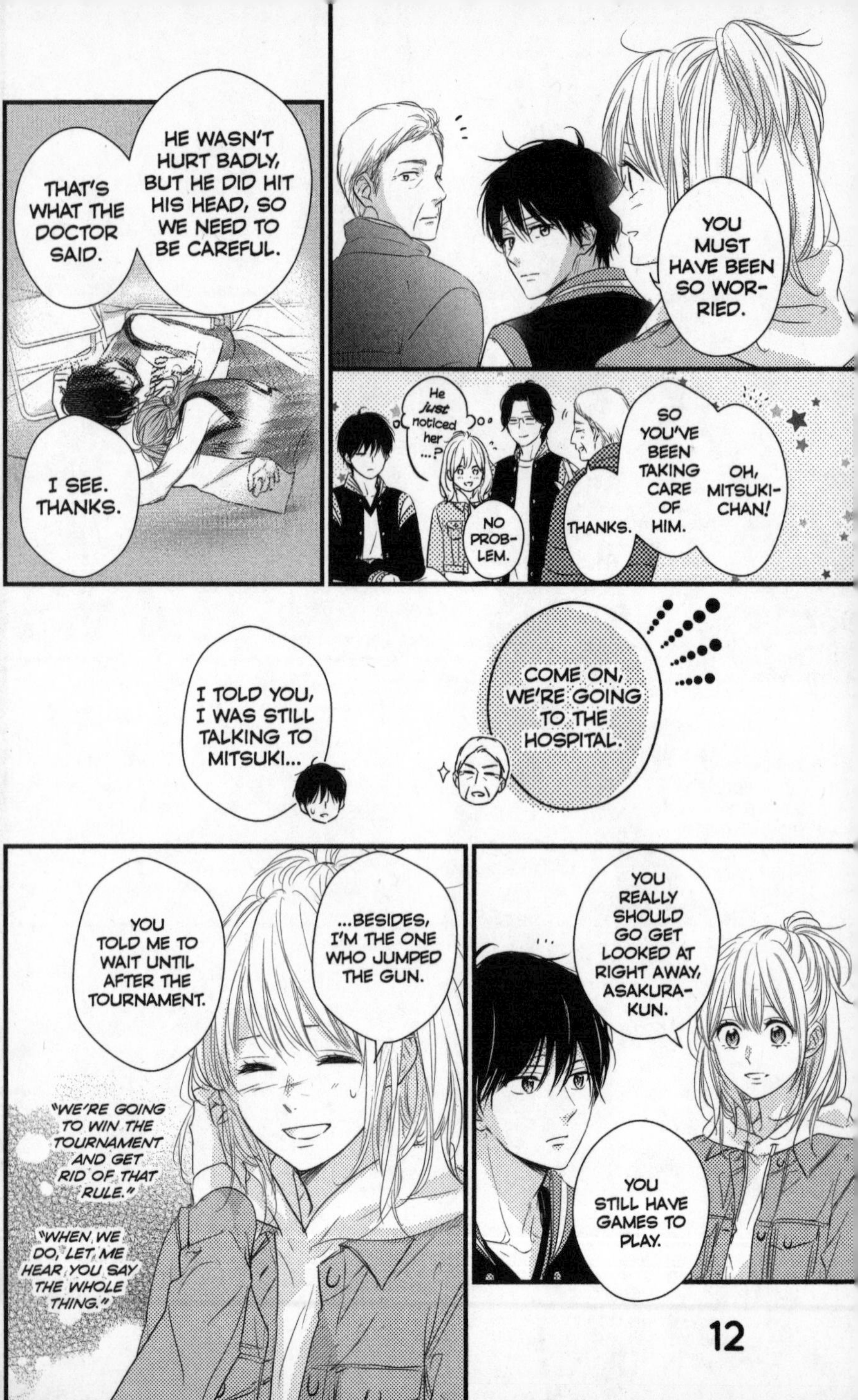
YOU MUST HAVE BEEN SO WOR- RIED.
OH, MITSUKI-CHAN!
SO YOU'VE BEEN TAKING CARE OF HIM.
THANKS.
NO PROB- LEM.
He just noticed her ...?
HE WASN'T HURT BADLY, BUT HE DID HIT HIS HEAD, SO WE NEED TO BE CAREFUL.
THAT'S WHAT THE DOCTOR SAID.
I SEE. THANKS.
COME ON, WE'RE GOING TO THE HOSPITAL.
I TOLD YOU, I WAS STILL TALKING TO MITSUKI...
YOU REALLY SHOULD GO GET LOOKED AT RIGHT AWAY, ASAKURA-KUN.
YOU STILL HAVE GAMES TO PLAY.
...BESIDES, I'M THE ONE WHO JUMPED THE GUN.
YOU TOLD ME TO WAIT UNTIL AFTER THE TOURNAMENT.
"WE'RE GOING TO WIN THE TOURNAMENT AND GET RID OF THAT RULE."
"WHEN WE DO, LET ME HEAR YOU SAY THE WHOLE THING."

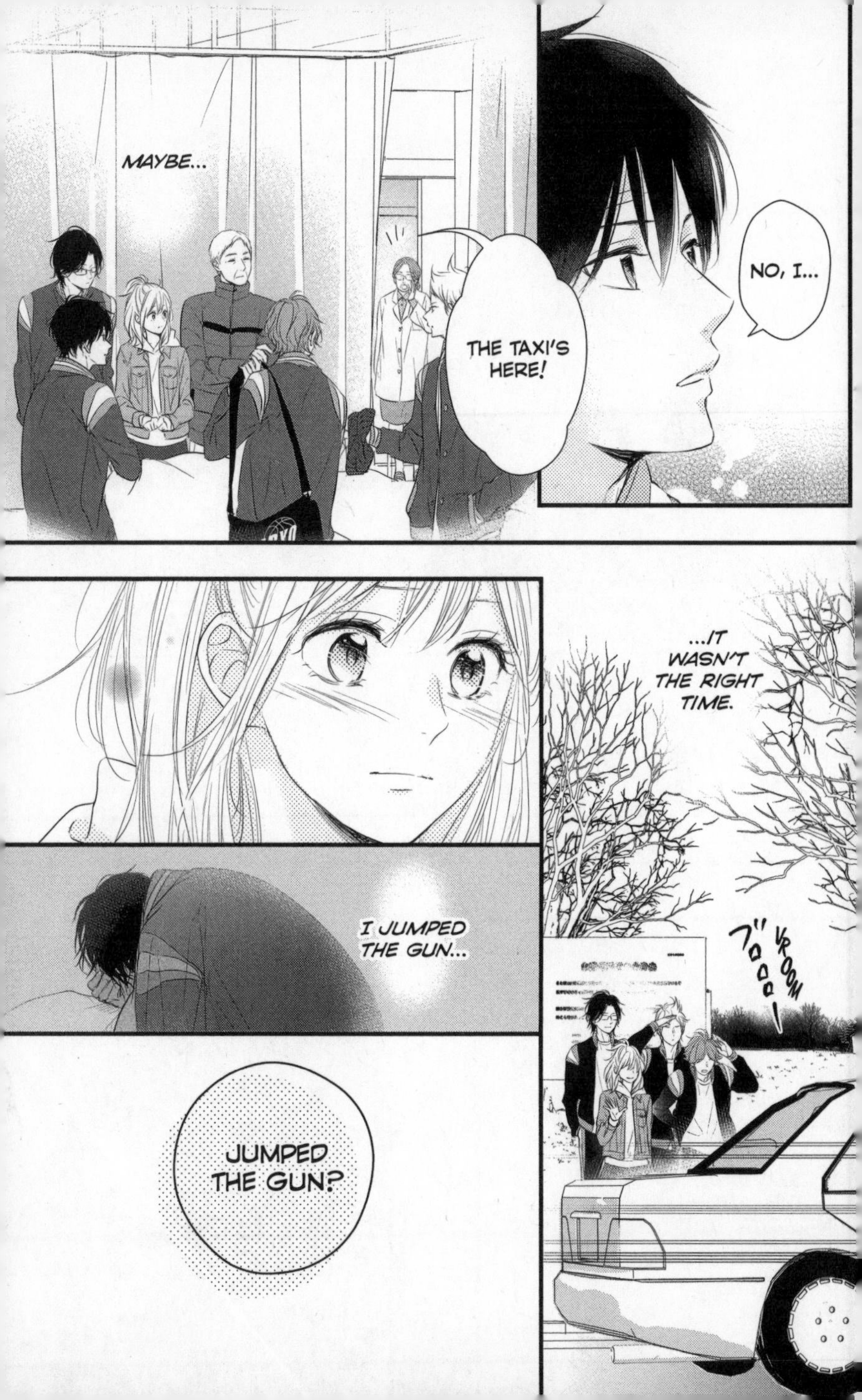

NO, I...
THE TAXI'S HERE!
MAYBE...
...IT WASN'T THE RIGHT TIME.
ブロロロー
VROOM
I JUMPED THE GUN...
JUMPED THE GUN?

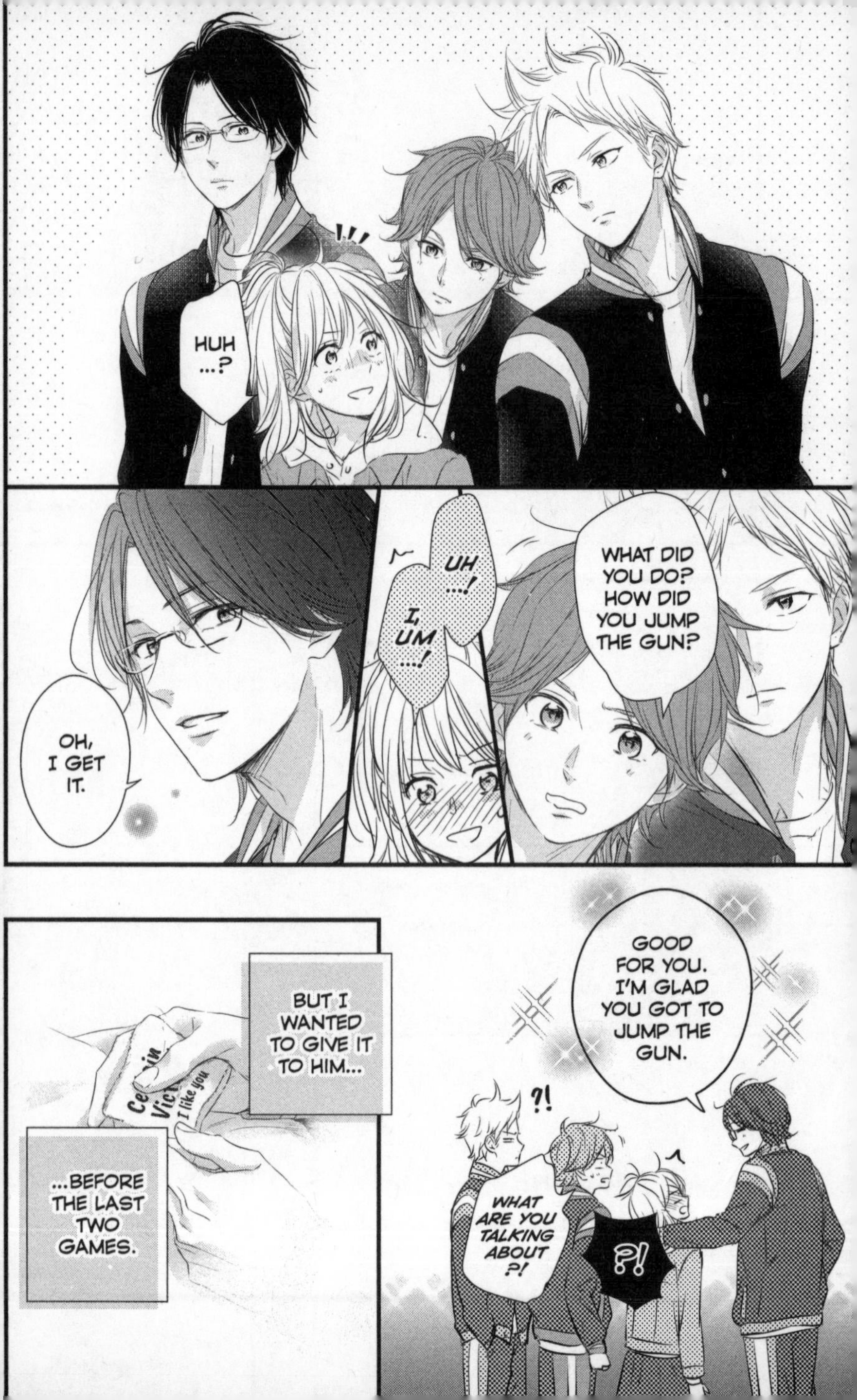
!!
HUH ...?
WHAT DID YOU DO? HOW DID YOU JUMP THE GUN?
UH ...!
I, UM ...!
OH, I GET IT.
GOOD FOR YOU. I'M GLAD YOU GOT TO JUMP THE GUN.
?!
WHAT ARE YOU TALKING ABOUT ?!
?!
BUT I WANTED TO GIVE IT TO HIM...
I like you
...BEFORE THE LAST TWO GAMES.

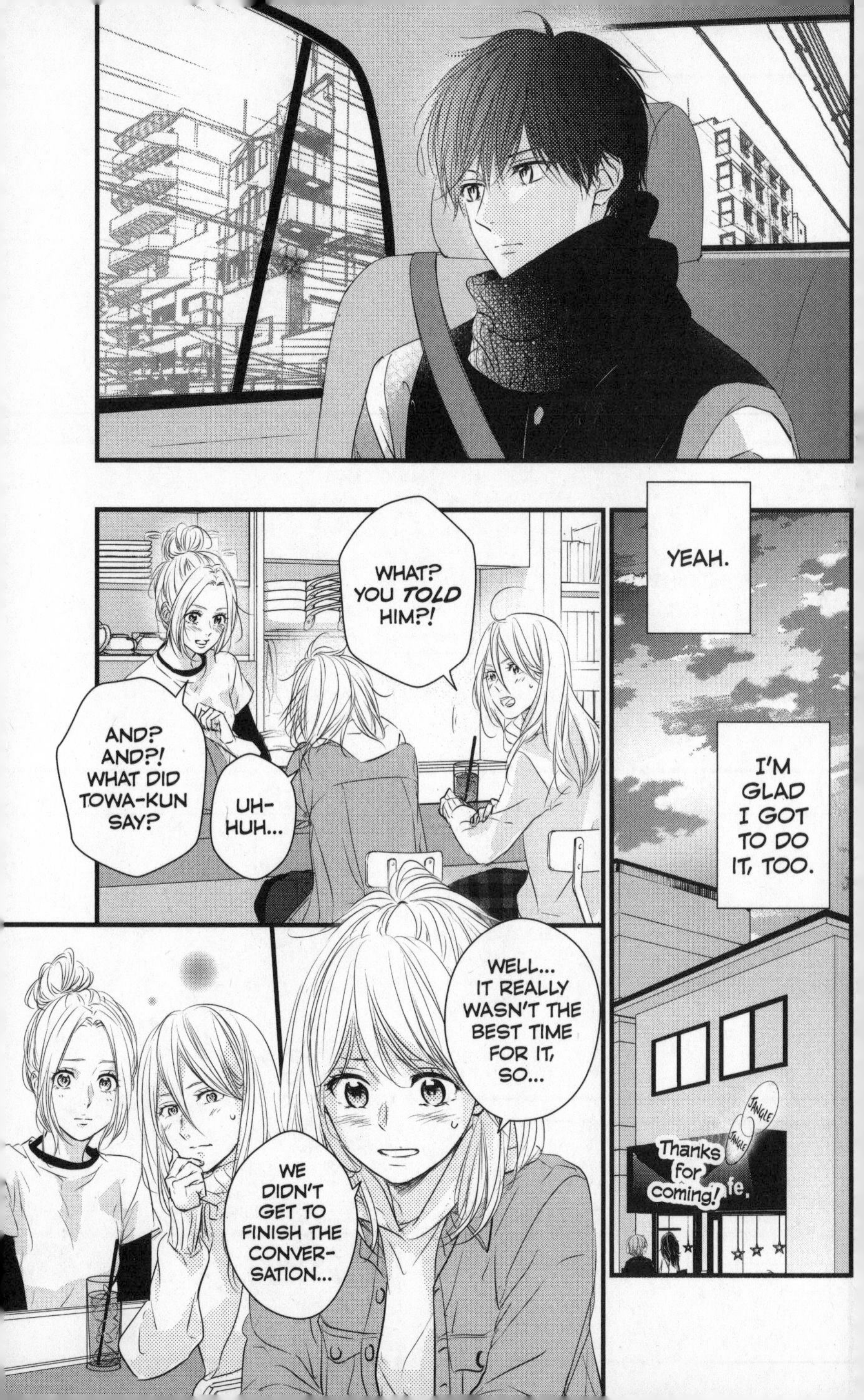
YEAH.
I'M GLAD I GOT TO DO IT, TOO.
JANGLE
JANGLE
Thanks for coming!
WHAT? YOU *TOLD* HIM?!
UH-HUH...
AND? AND?! WHAT DID TOWA-KUN SAY?
WELL... IT REALLY WASN'T THE BEST TIME FOR IT, SO...
WE DIDN'T GET TO FINISH THE CONVER-SATION...

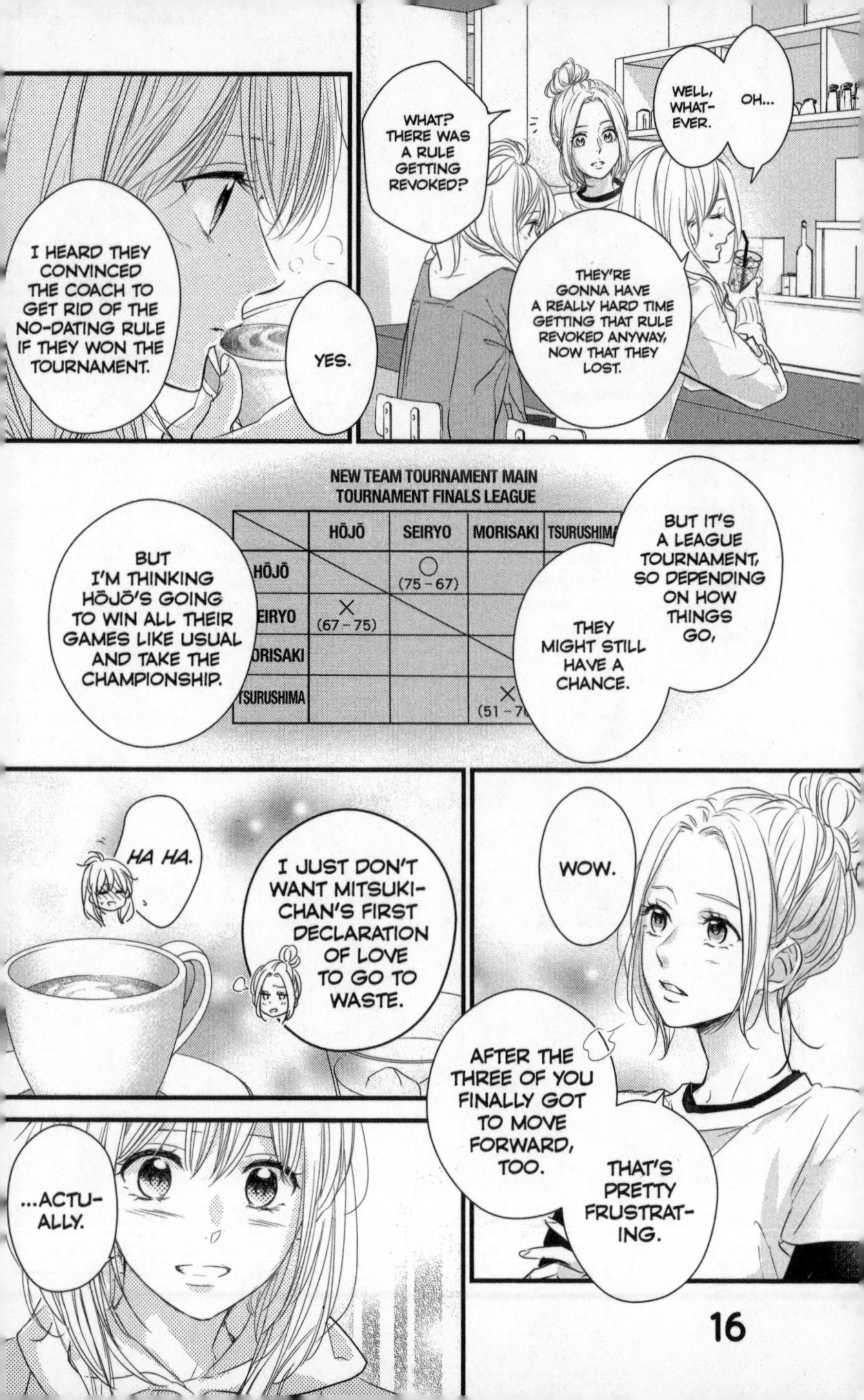
OH...
WELL, WHAT-EVER.
WHAT? THERE WAS A RULE GETTING REVOKED?
THEY'RE GONNA HAVE A REALLY HARD TIME GETTING THAT RULE REVOKED ANYWAY, NOW THAT THEY LOST.
I HEARD THEY CONVINCED THE COACH TO GET RID OF THE NO-DATING RULE IF THEY WON THE TOURNAMENT.
YES.
NEW TEAM TOURNAMENT MAIN TOURNAMENT FINALS LEAGUE
HŌJŌ
SEIRYO
MORISAKI
TSURUSHIMA
HŌJŌ
○ (75 – 67)
SEIRYO
× (67 – 75)
ORISAKI
TSURUSHIMA
× (51 – 7
BUT IT'S A LEAGUE TOURNAMENT, SO DEPENDING ON HOW THINGS GO,
THEY MIGHT STILL HAVE A CHANCE.
BUT I'M THINKING HŌJŌ'S GOING TO WIN ALL THEIR GAMES LIKE USUAL AND TAKE THE CHAMPIONSHIP.
WOW.
AFTER THE THREE OF YOU FINALLY GOT TO MOVE FORWARD, TOO.
THAT'S PRETTY FRUSTRAT-ING.
HA HA.
I JUST DON'T WANT MITSUKI-CHAN'S FIRST DECLARATION OF LOVE TO GO TO WASTE.
...ACTU-ALLY.

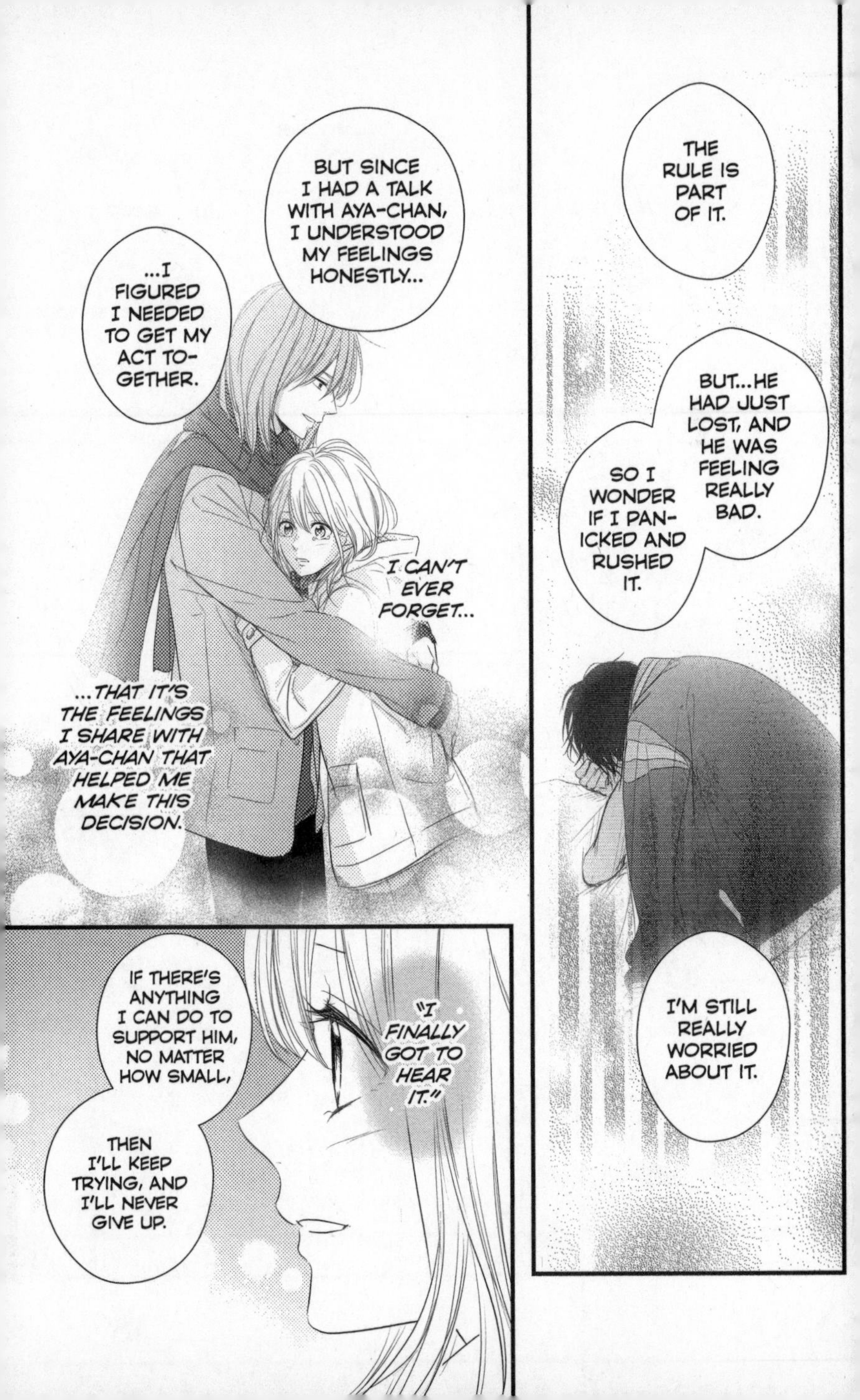
THE RULE IS PART OF IT.
BUT...HE HAD JUST LOST, AND HE WAS FEELING REALLY BAD.
SO I WONDER IF I PANICKED AND RUSHED IT.
I'M STILL REALLY WORRIED ABOUT IT.
BUT SINCE I HAD A TALK WITH AYA-CHAN, I UNDERSTOOD MY FEELINGS HONESTLY...
...I FIGURED I NEEDED TO GET MY ACT TOGETHER.
I CAN'T EVER FORGET...
...THAT IT'S THE FEELINGS I SHARE WITH AYA-CHAN THAT HELPED ME MAKE THIS DECISION.
"I FINALLY GOT TO HEAR IT."
IF THERE'S ANYTHING I CAN DO TO SUPPORT HIM, NO MATTER HOW SMALL,
THEN I'LL KEEP TRYING, AND I'LL NEVER GIVE UP.

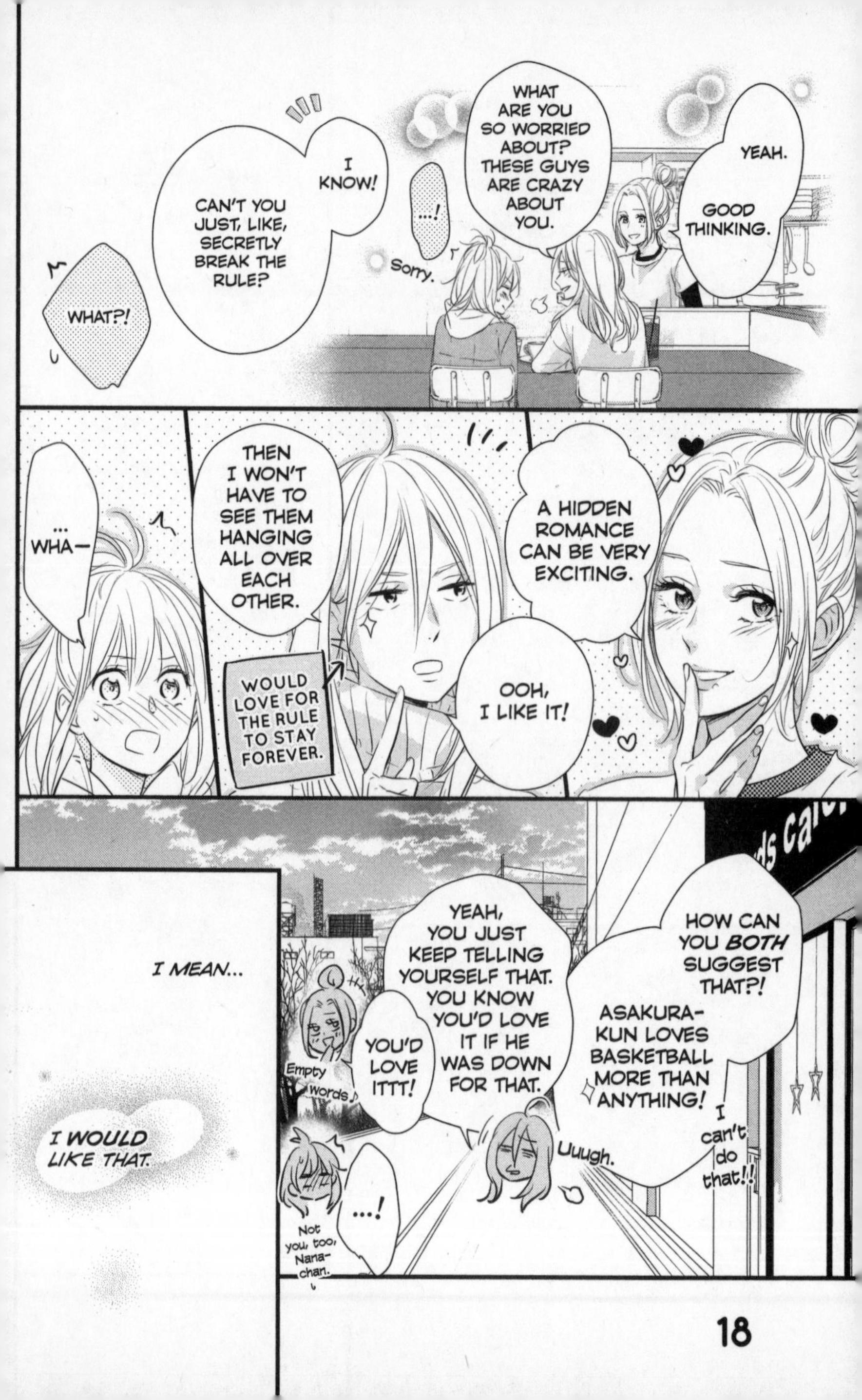
YEAH.
GOOD THINKING.
WHAT ARE YOU SO WORRIED ABOUT? THESE GUYS ARE CRAZY ABOUT YOU.
...!
Sorry.
I KNOW!
CAN'T YOU JUST, LIKE, SECRETLY BREAK THE RULE?
WHAT?!
A HIDDEN ROMANCE CAN BE VERY EXCITING.
OOH, I LIKE IT!
THEN I WON'T HAVE TO SEE THEM HANGING ALL OVER EACH OTHER.
WOULD LOVE FOR THE RULE TO STAY FOREVER.
... WHA—
HOW CAN YOU *BOTH* SUGGEST THAT?!
ASAKURA-KUN LOVES BASKETBALL MORE THAN ANYTHING!
I can't do that!!
Uuugh.
YEAH, YOU JUST KEEP TELLING YOURSELF THAT. YOU KNOW YOU'D LOVE IT IF HE WAS DOWN FOR THAT.
YOU'D LOVE ITTT!
Empty words♪
...!
Not you, too, Nana-chan.
I MEAN...
I WOULD LIKE THAT.

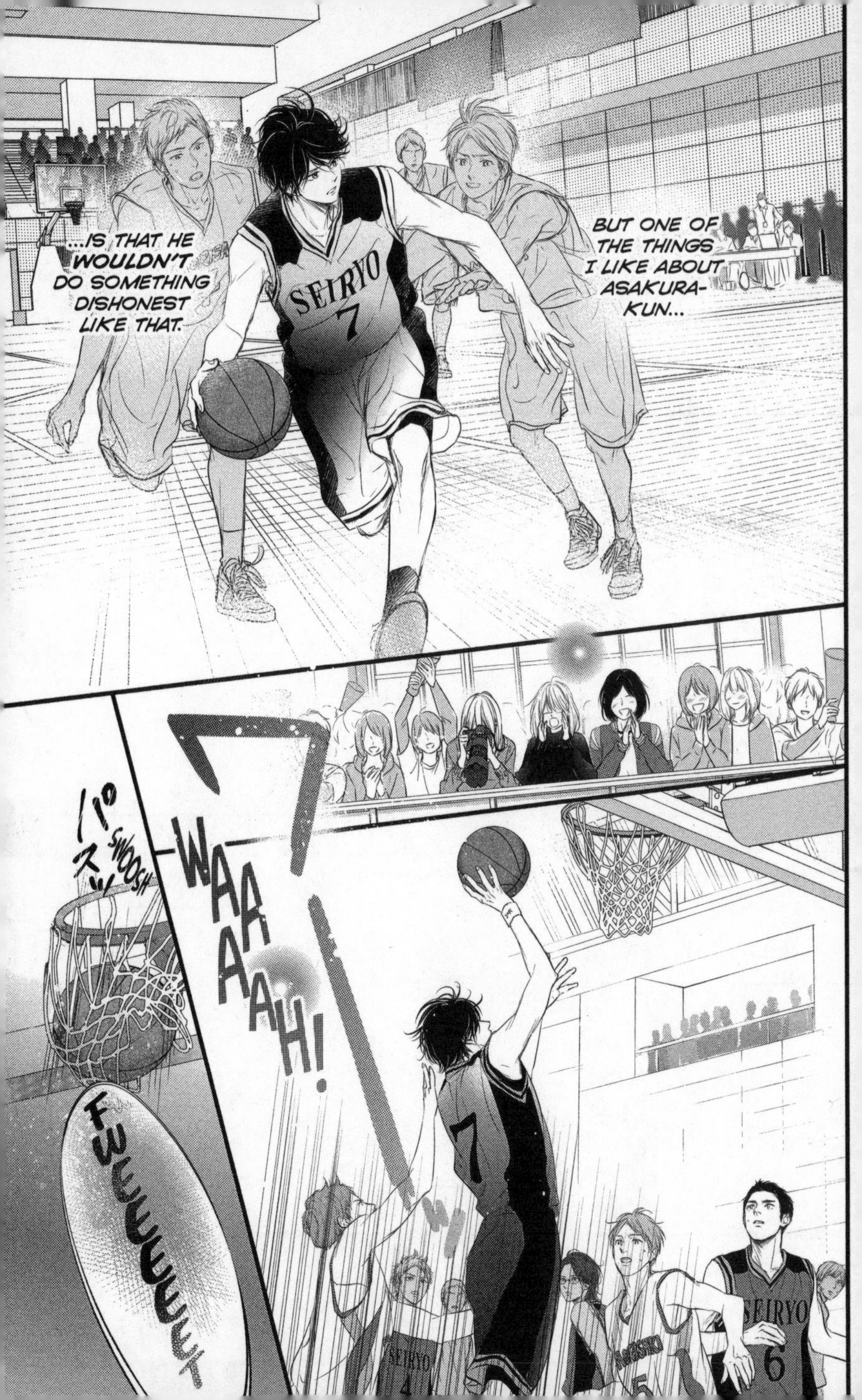
BUT ONE OF THE THINGS I LIKE ABOUT ASAKURA-KUN...
...IS THAT HE WOULDN'T DO SOMETHING DISHONEST LIKE THAT.
WAAAAH!
パスッ
SWOOSH
FWEEEEEET

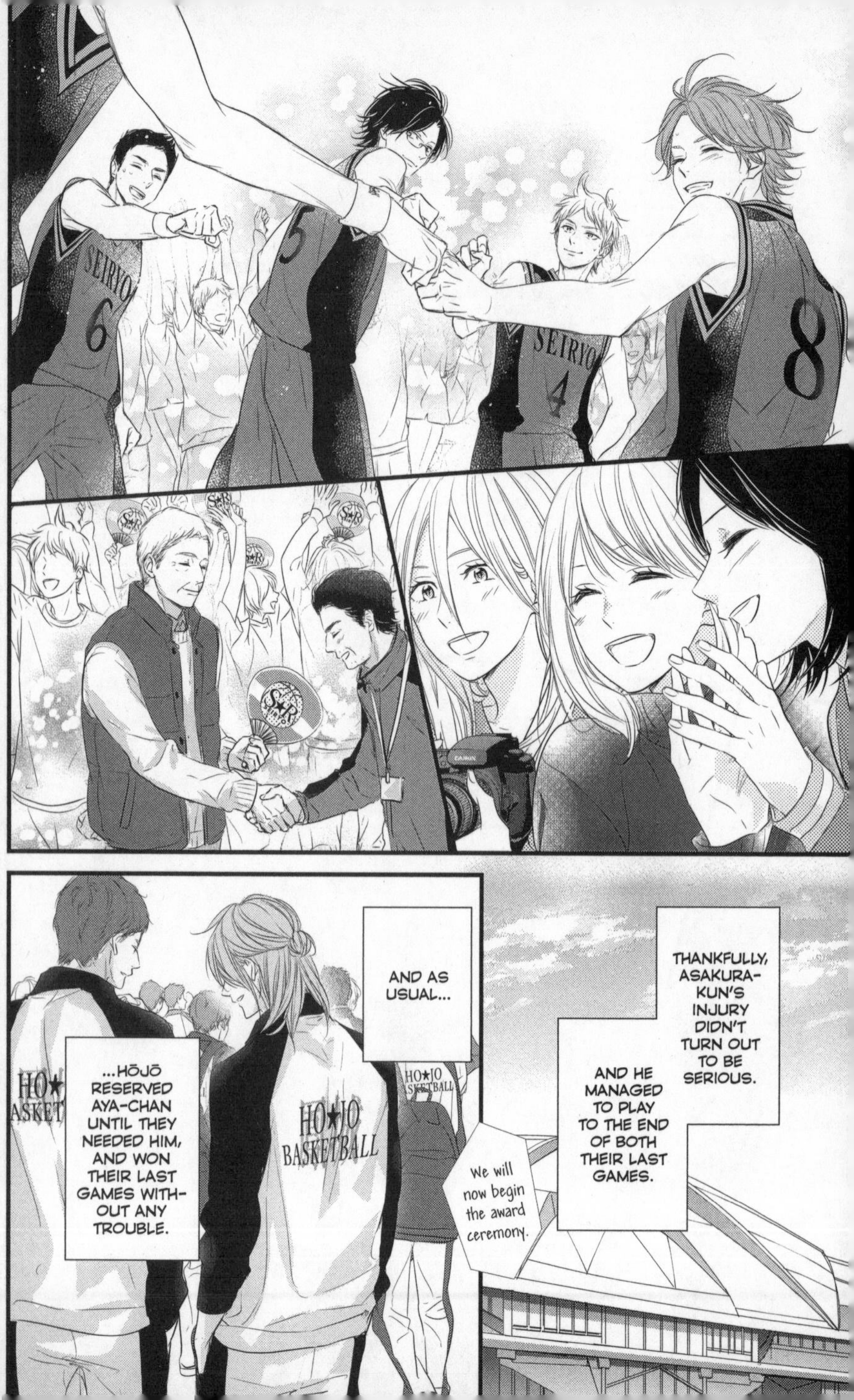
THANKFULLY, ASAKURA-KUN'S INJURY DIDN'T TURN OUT TO BE SERIOUS.
AND HE MANAGED TO PLAY TO THE END OF BOTH THEIR LAST GAMES.
We will now begin the award ceremony.
AND AS USUAL...
...HŌJŌ RESERVED AYA-CHAN UNTIL THEY NEEDED HIM, AND WON THEIR LAST GAMES WITH-OUT ANY TROUBLE.

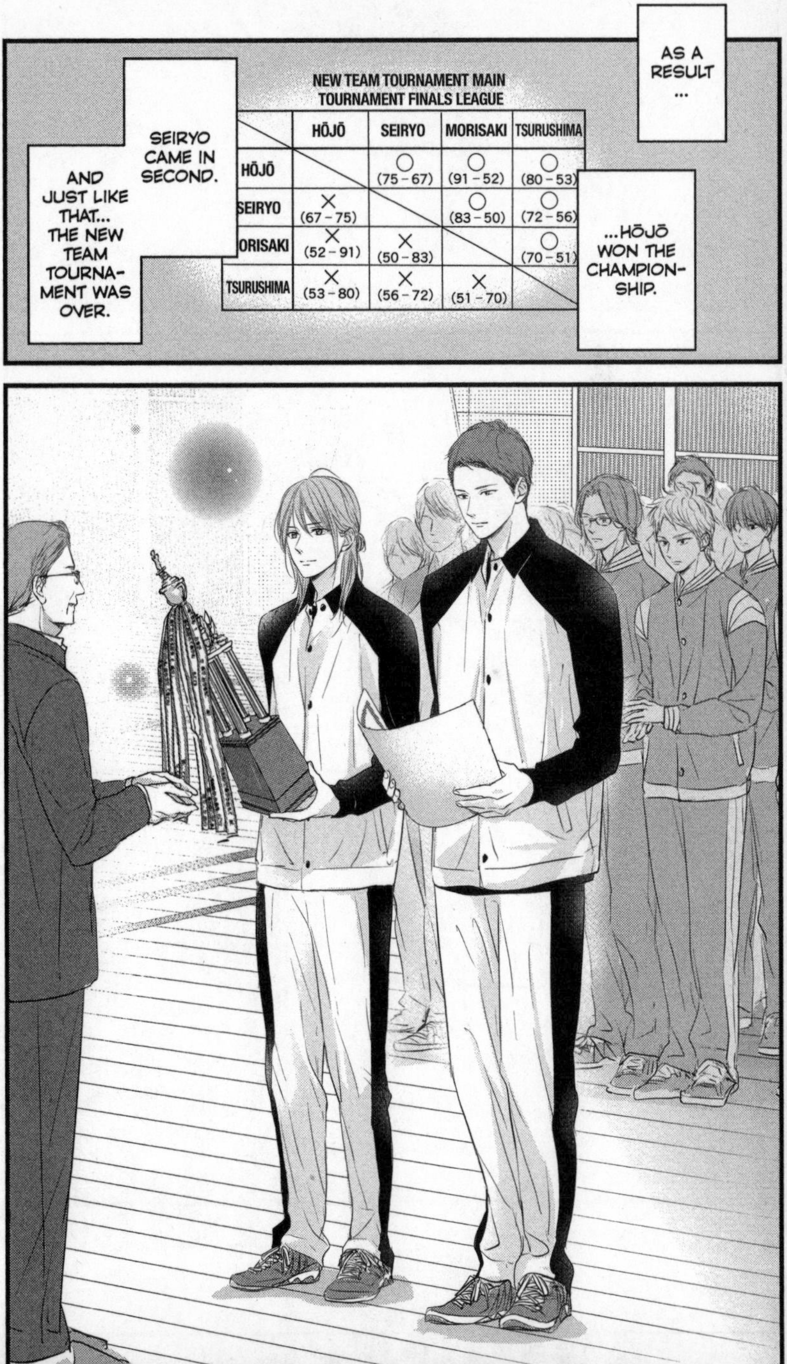
AS A RESULT ...
NEW TEAM TOURNAMENT MAIN TOURNAMENT FINALS LEAGUE

	HŌJŌ	SEIRYO	MORISAKI	TSURUSHIMA
HŌJŌ		○ (75 – 67)	○ (91 – 52)	○ (80 – 53)
SEIRYO	× (67 – 75)		○ (83 – 50)	○ (72 – 56)
MORISAKI	× (52 – 91)	× (50 – 83)		○ (70 – 51)
TSURUSHIMA	× (53 – 80)	× (56 – 72)	× (51 – 70)	

...HŌJŌ WON THE CHAMPIONSHIP.
SEIRYO CAME IN SECOND.
AND JUST LIKE THAT... THE NEW TEAM TOURNAMENT WAS OVER.

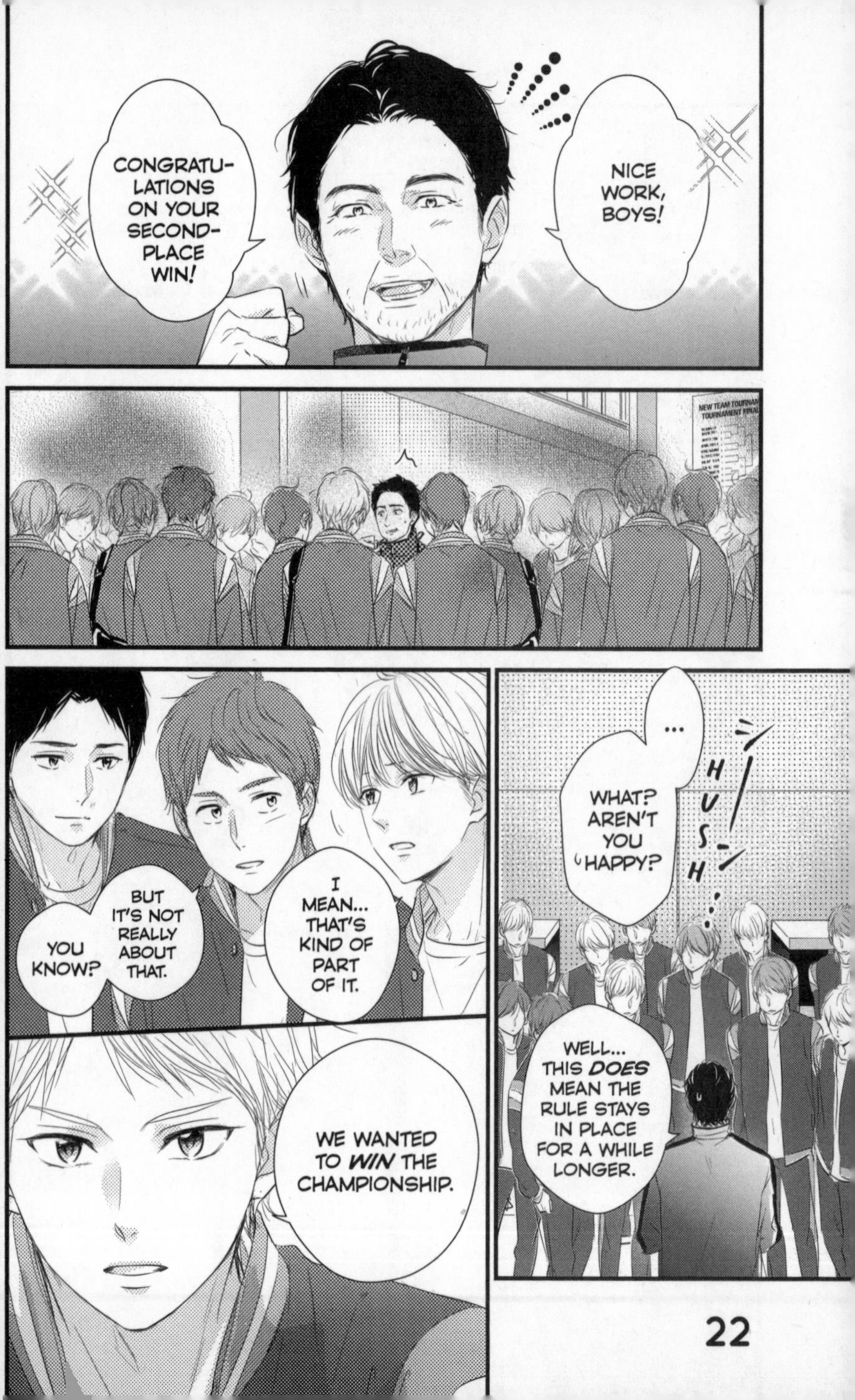
NICE WORK, BOYS!
CONGRATULATIONS ON YOUR SECOND-PLACE WIN!
...
WHAT? AREN'T YOU HAPPY?
HUSH...
WELL... THIS *DOES* MEAN THE RULE STAYS IN PLACE FOR A WHILE LONGER.
I MEAN... THAT'S KIND OF PART OF IT.
BUT IT'S NOT REALLY ABOUT THAT.
YOU KNOW?
WE WANTED TO *WIN* THE CHAMPIONSHIP.

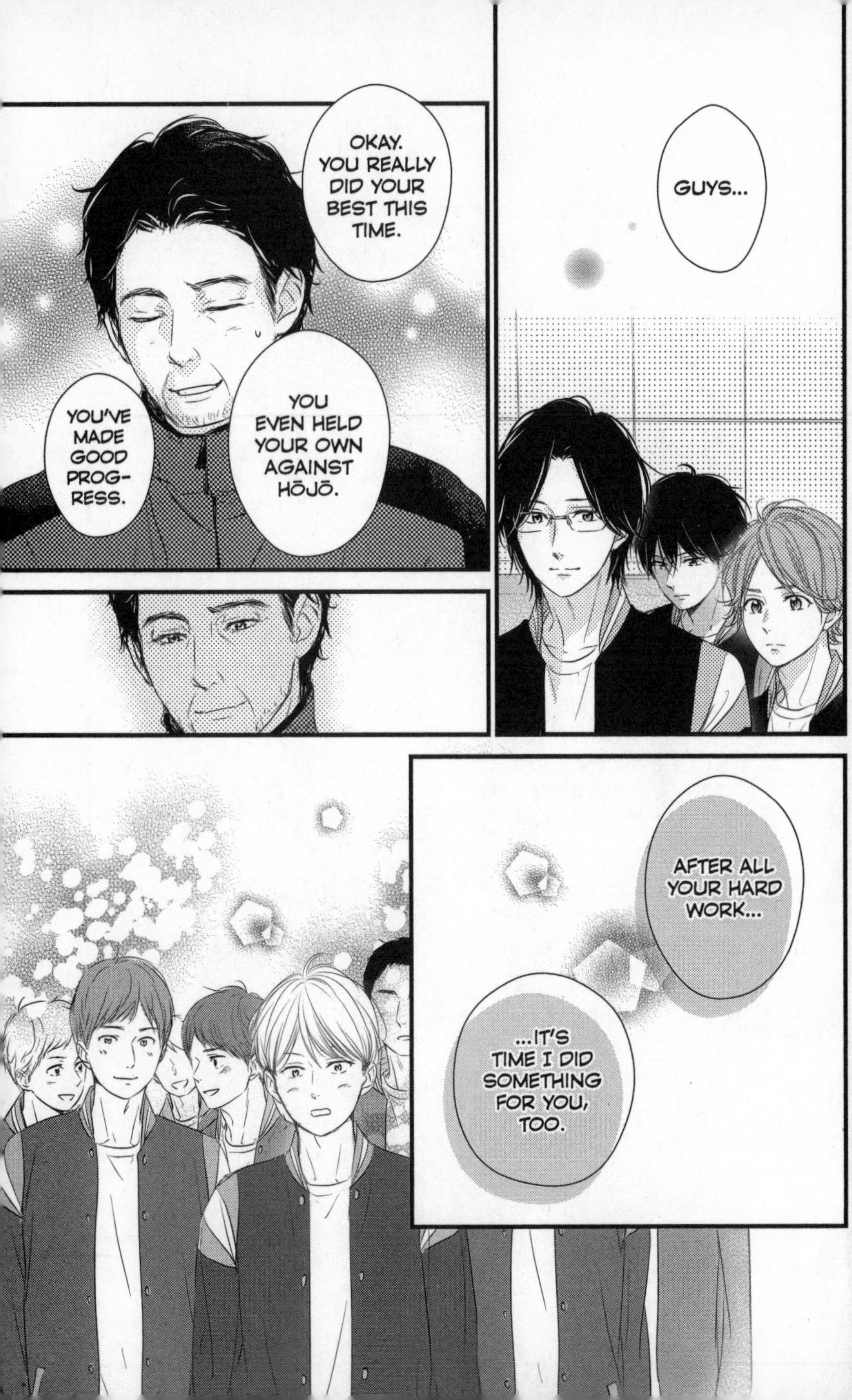
GUYS...
OKAY. YOU REALLY DID YOUR BEST THIS TIME.
YOU EVEN HELD YOUR OWN AGAINST HŌJŌ.
YOU'VE MADE GOOD PROG-RESS.
AFTER ALL YOUR HARD WORK...
...IT'S TIME I DID SOMETHING FOR YOU, TOO.

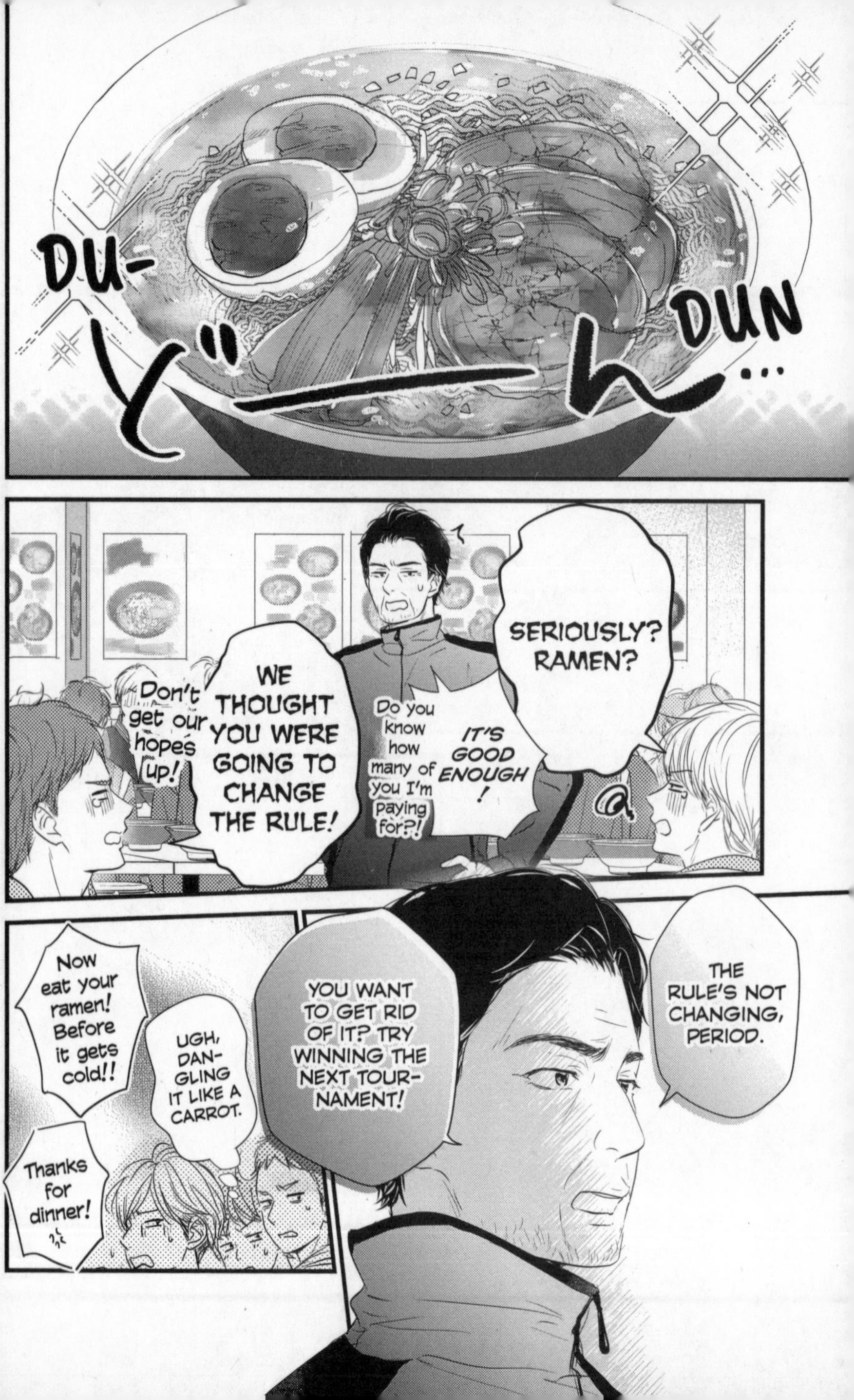
DU-
DUN...
SERIOUSLY? RAMEN?
IT'S GOOD ENOUGH!
Do you know how many of you I'm paying for?!
WE THOUGHT YOU WERE GOING TO CHANGE THE RULE!
Don't get our hopes up!
THE RULE'S NOT CHANGING, PERIOD.
YOU WANT TO GET RID OF IT? TRY WINNING THE NEXT TOUR-NAMENT!
UGH, DAN-GLING IT LIKE A CARROT.
Now eat your ramen! Before it gets cold!!
Thanks for dinner!

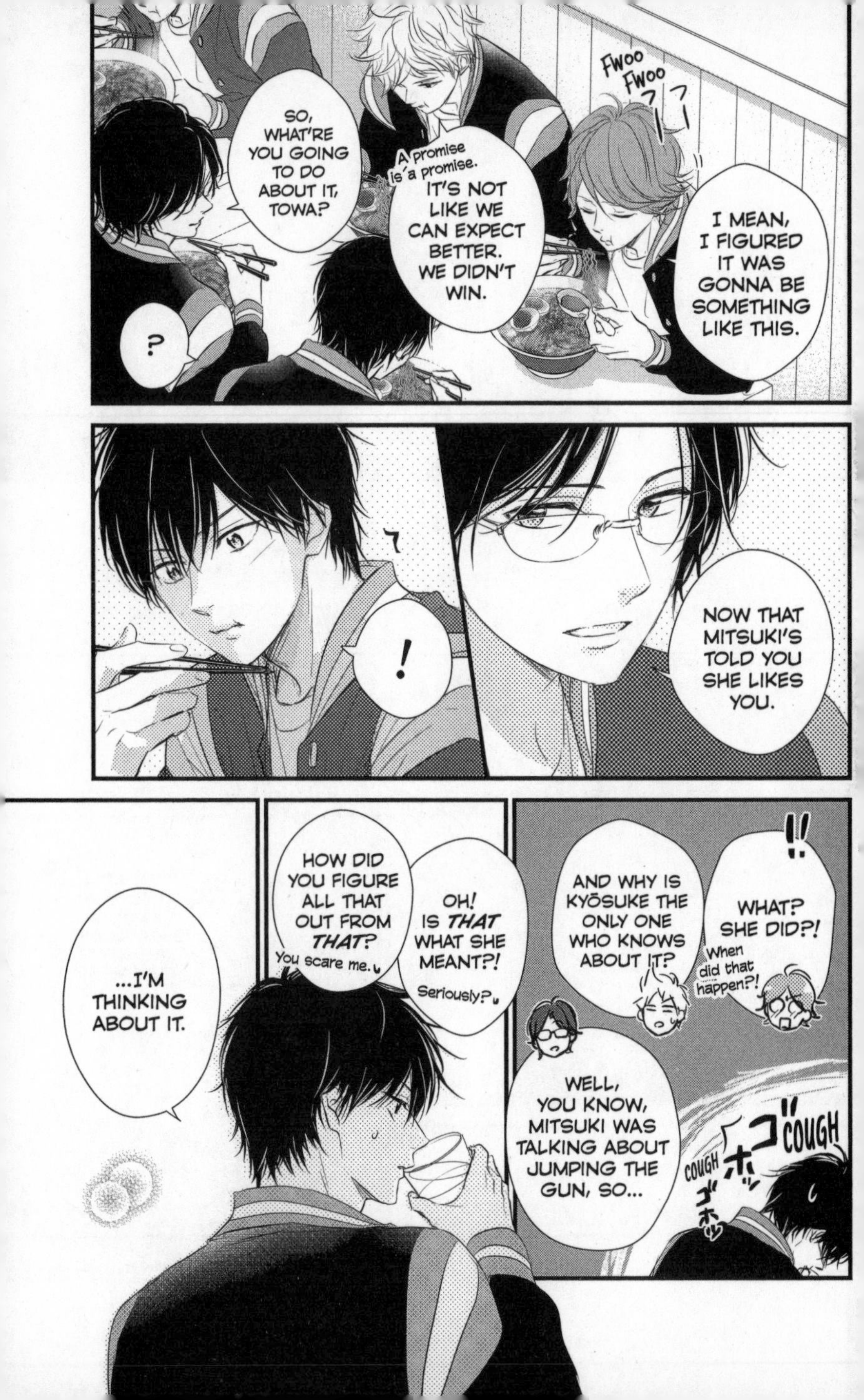
FWOO FWOO
I MEAN, I FIGURED IT WAS GONNA BE SOMETHING LIKE THIS.
A promise is a promise.
IT'S NOT LIKE WE CAN EXPECT BETTER. WE DIDN'T WIN.
SO, WHAT'RE YOU GOING TO DO ABOUT IT, TOWA?
?
NOW THAT MITSUKI'S TOLD YOU SHE LIKES YOU.
!
!!
WHAT? SHE DID?!
When did that happen?!
AND WHY IS KYŌSUKE THE ONLY ONE WHO KNOWS ABOUT IT?
WELL, YOU KNOW, MITSUKI WAS TALKING ABOUT JUMPING THE GUN, SO...
COUGH
COUGH
OH! IS *THAT* WHAT SHE MEANT?!
Seriously?
HOW DID YOU FIGURE ALL THAT OUT FROM *THAT*?
You scare me.
...I'M THINKING ABOUT IT.

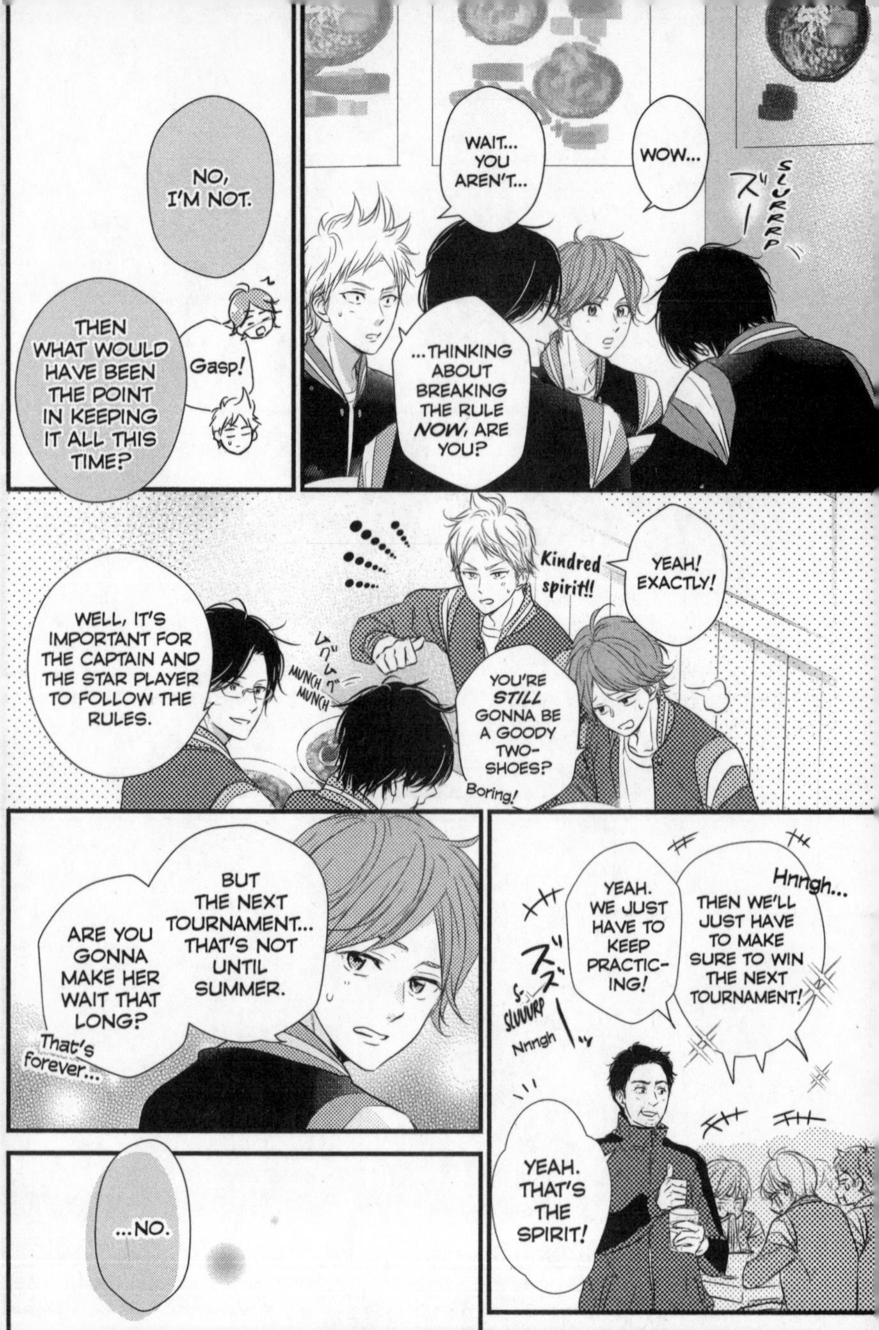
WOW...
SLURRRP
WAIT... YOU AREN'T...
...THINKING ABOUT BREAKING THE RULE *NOW*, ARE YOU?
NO, I'M NOT.
THEN WHAT WOULD HAVE BEEN THE POINT IN KEEPING IT ALL THIS TIME?
Gasp!
YEAH! EXACTLY!
Kindred spirit!!
YOU'RE *STILL* GONNA BE A GOODY TWO-SHOES?
Boring!
MUNCH MUNCH
WELL, IT'S IMPORTANT FOR THE CAPTAIN AND THE STAR PLAYER TO FOLLOW THE RULES.
Hnngh...
THEN WE'LL JUST HAVE TO MAKE SURE TO WIN THE NEXT TOURNAMENT!
YEAH. WE JUST HAVE TO KEEP PRACTICING!
SLUUURP
Nnngh
YEAH. THAT'S THE SPIRIT!
BUT THE NEXT TOURNAMENT... THAT'S NOT UNTIL SUMMER.
ARE YOU GONNA MAKE HER WAIT THAT LONG?
That's forever...
...NO.

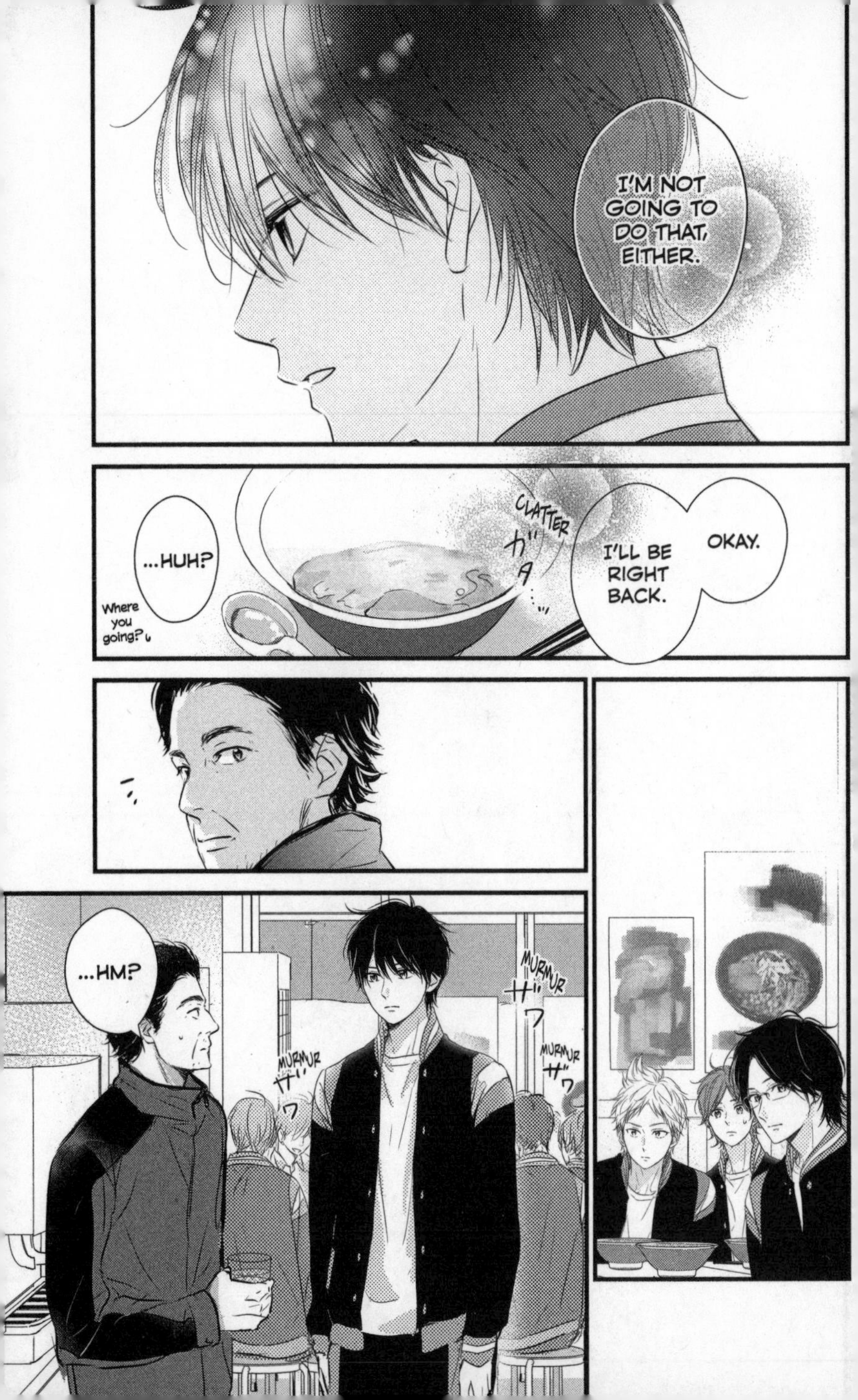
I'M NOT GOING TO DO THAT, EITHER.
OKAY.
I'LL BE RIGHT BACK.
CLATTER
...HUH?
Where you going?
MURMUR
MURMUR
MURMUR
...HM?

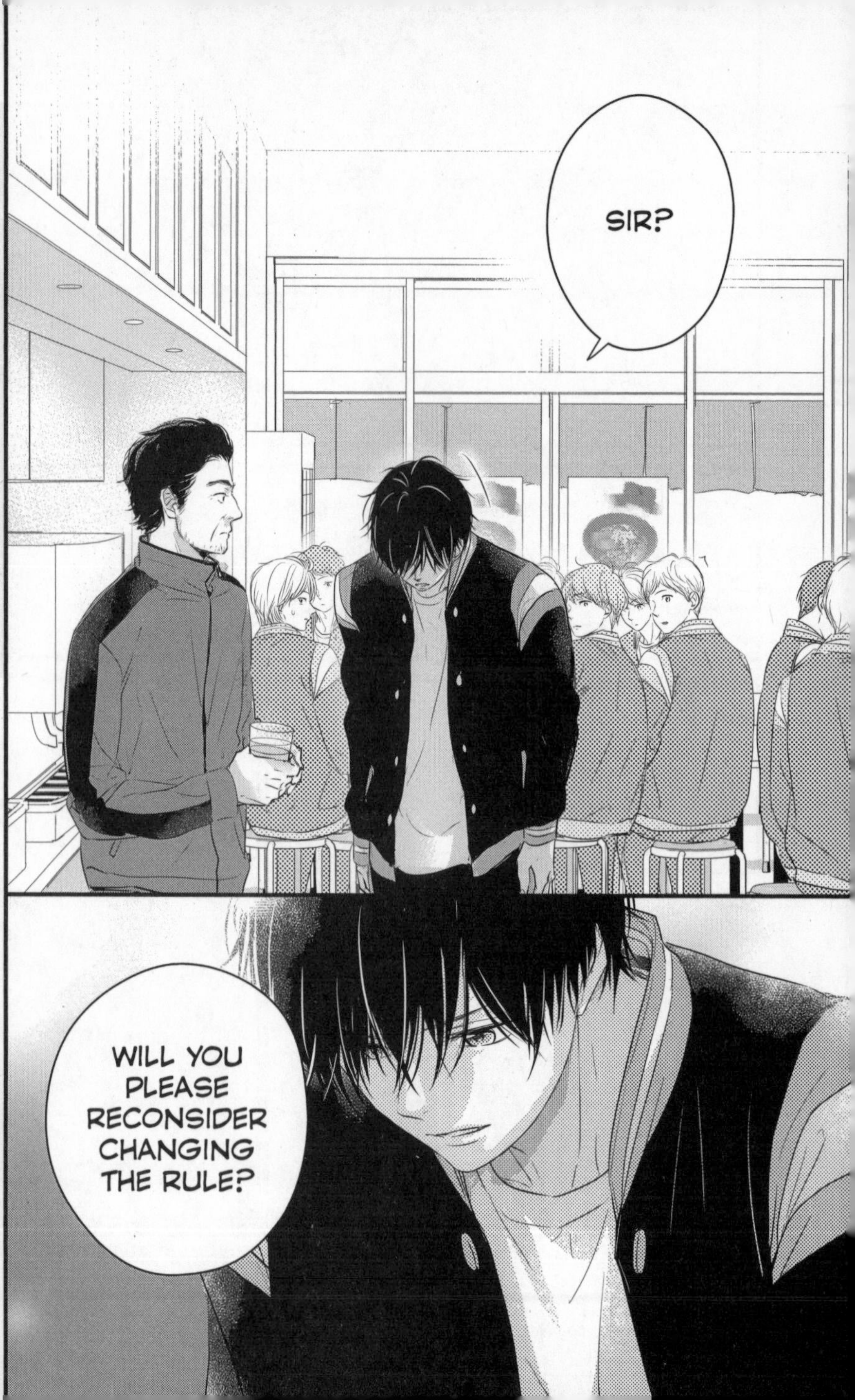
SIR?
WILL YOU PLEASE RECONSIDER CHANGING THE RULE?

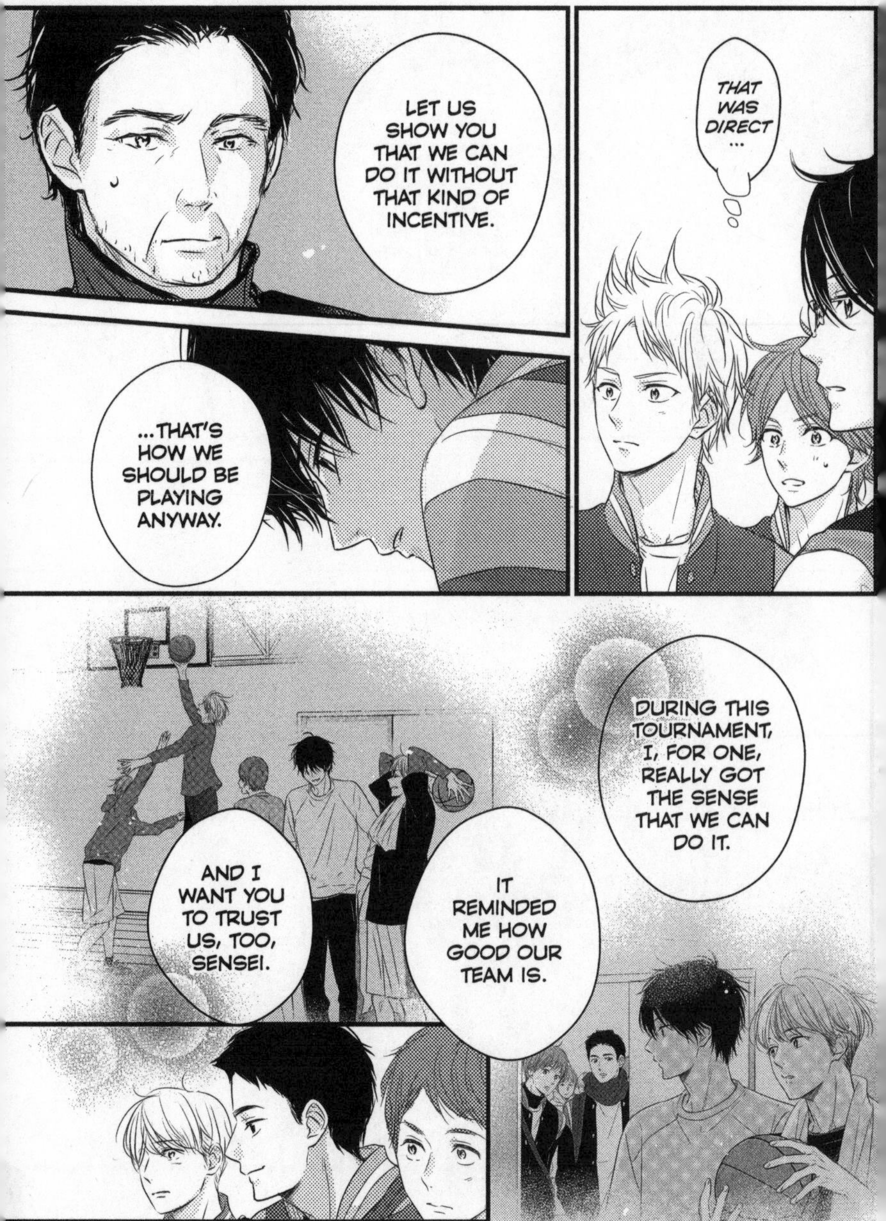
THAT WAS DIRECT...
LET US SHOW YOU THAT WE CAN DO IT WITHOUT THAT KIND OF INCENTIVE.
...THAT'S HOW WE SHOULD BE PLAYING ANYWAY.
DURING THIS TOURNAMENT, I, FOR ONE, REALLY GOT THE SENSE THAT WE CAN DO IT.
IT REMINDED ME HOW GOOD OUR TEAM IS.
AND I WANT YOU TO TRUST US, TOO, SENSEI.

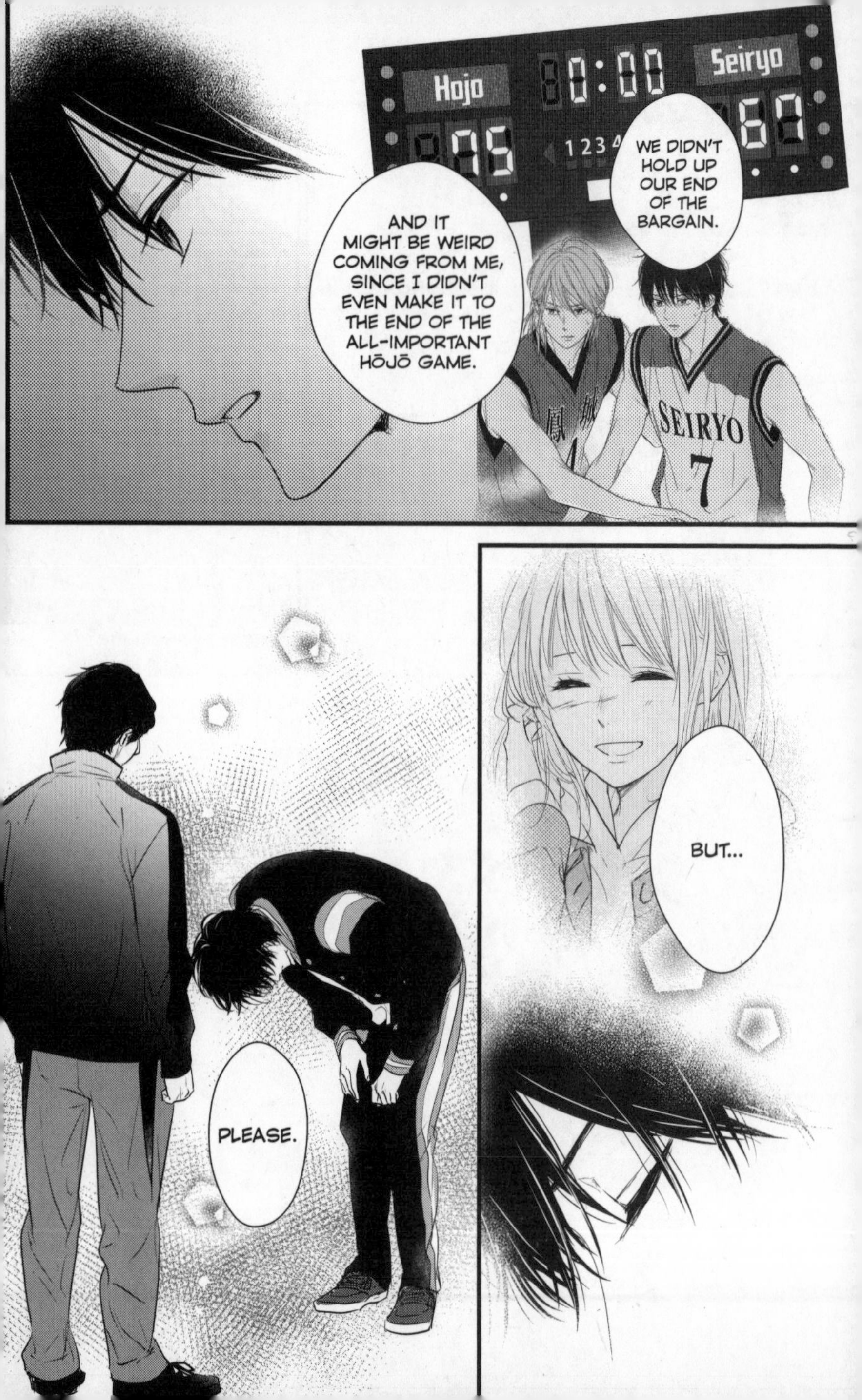
Seiryo
Hojo
WE DIDN'T HOLD UP OUR END OF THE BARGAIN.
AND IT MIGHT BE WEIRD COMING FROM ME, SINCE I DIDN'T EVEN MAKE IT TO THE END OF THE ALL-IMPORTANT HŌJŌ GAME.
SEIRYO 7
BUT...
PLEASE.

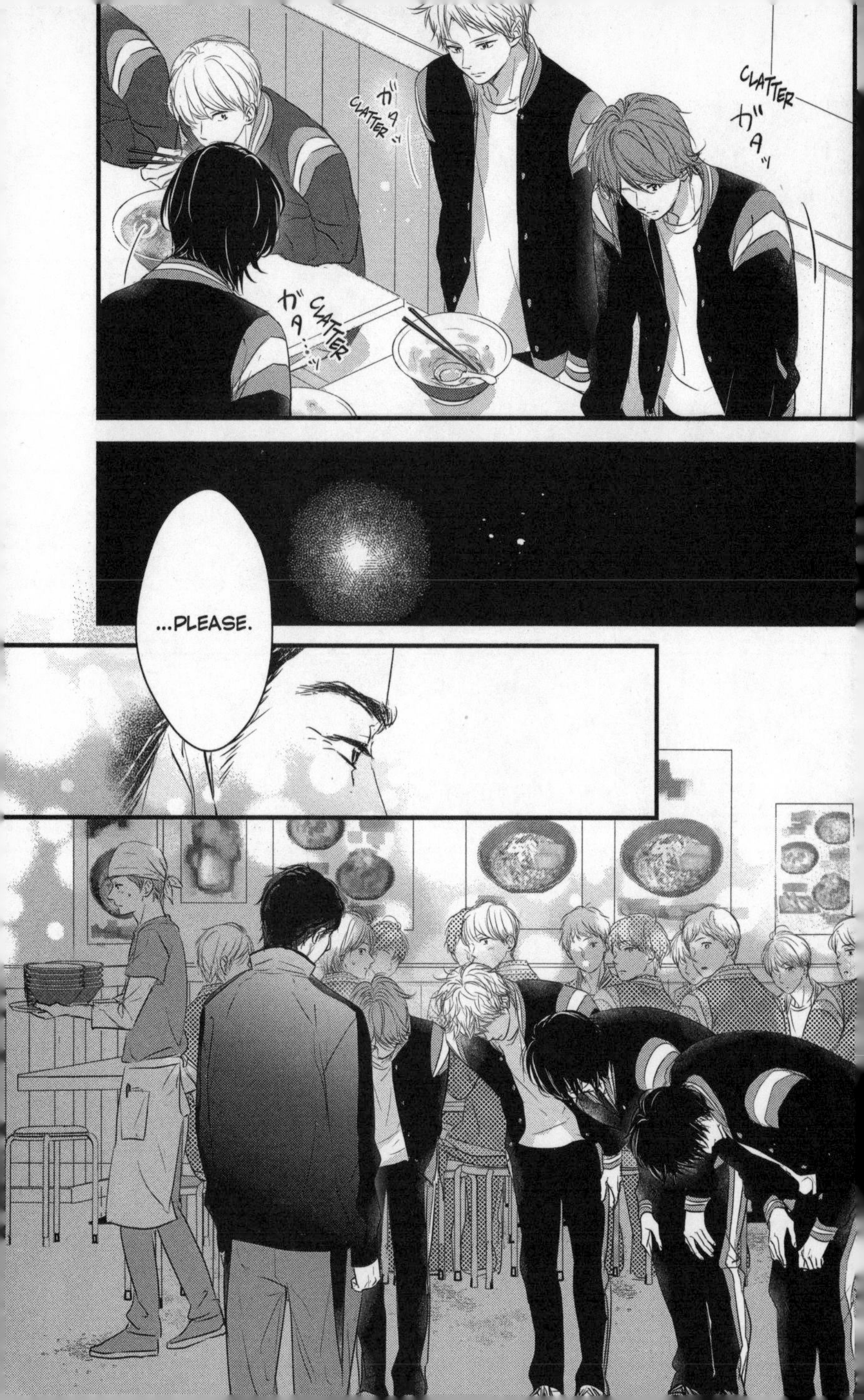
CLATTER
ガタッ
ガタッ
CLATTER
ガタッ
CLATTER
...PLEASE.

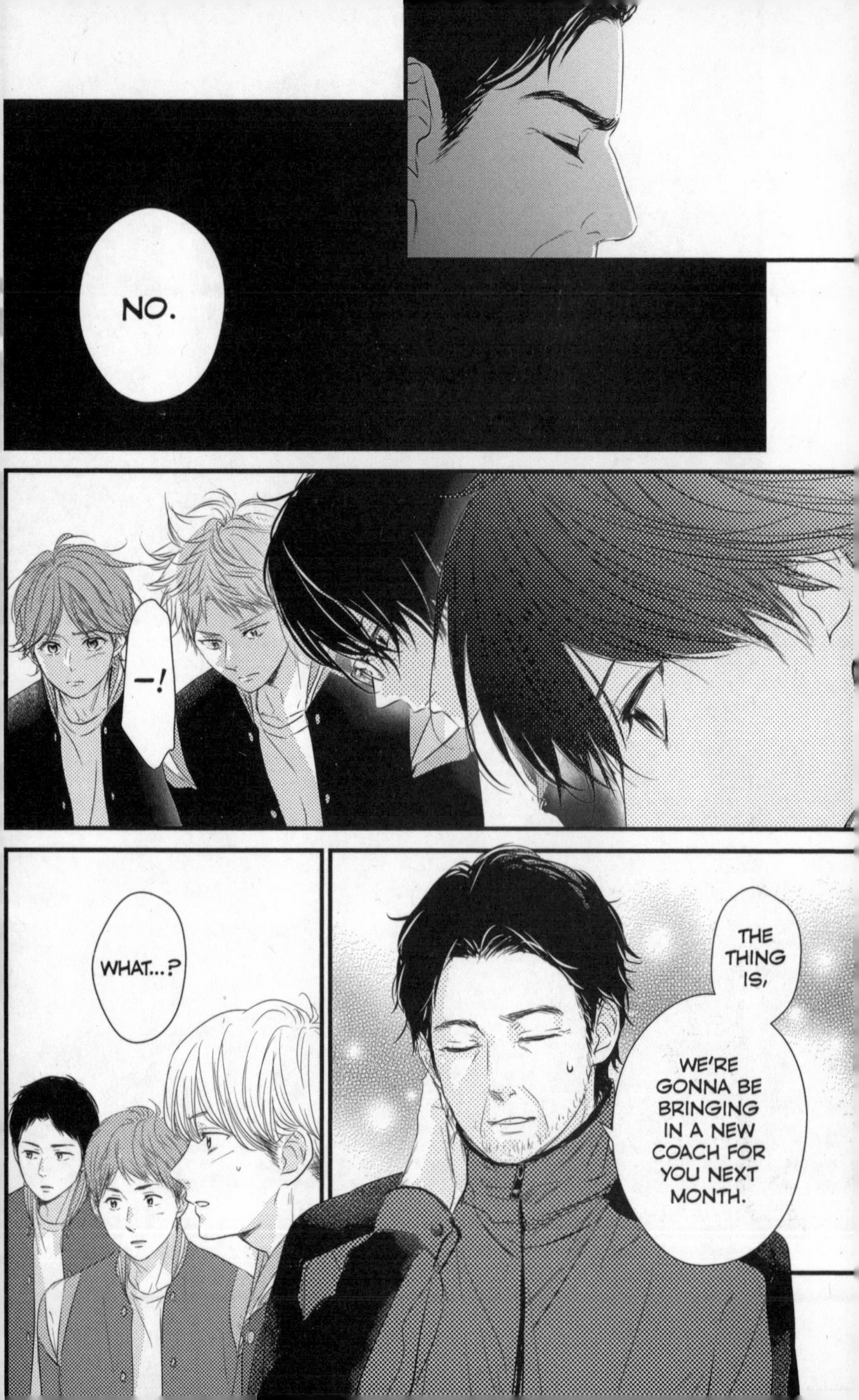
NO.
—!
THE THING IS,
WE'RE GONNA BE BRINGING IN A NEW COACH FOR YOU NEXT MONTH.
WHAT...?

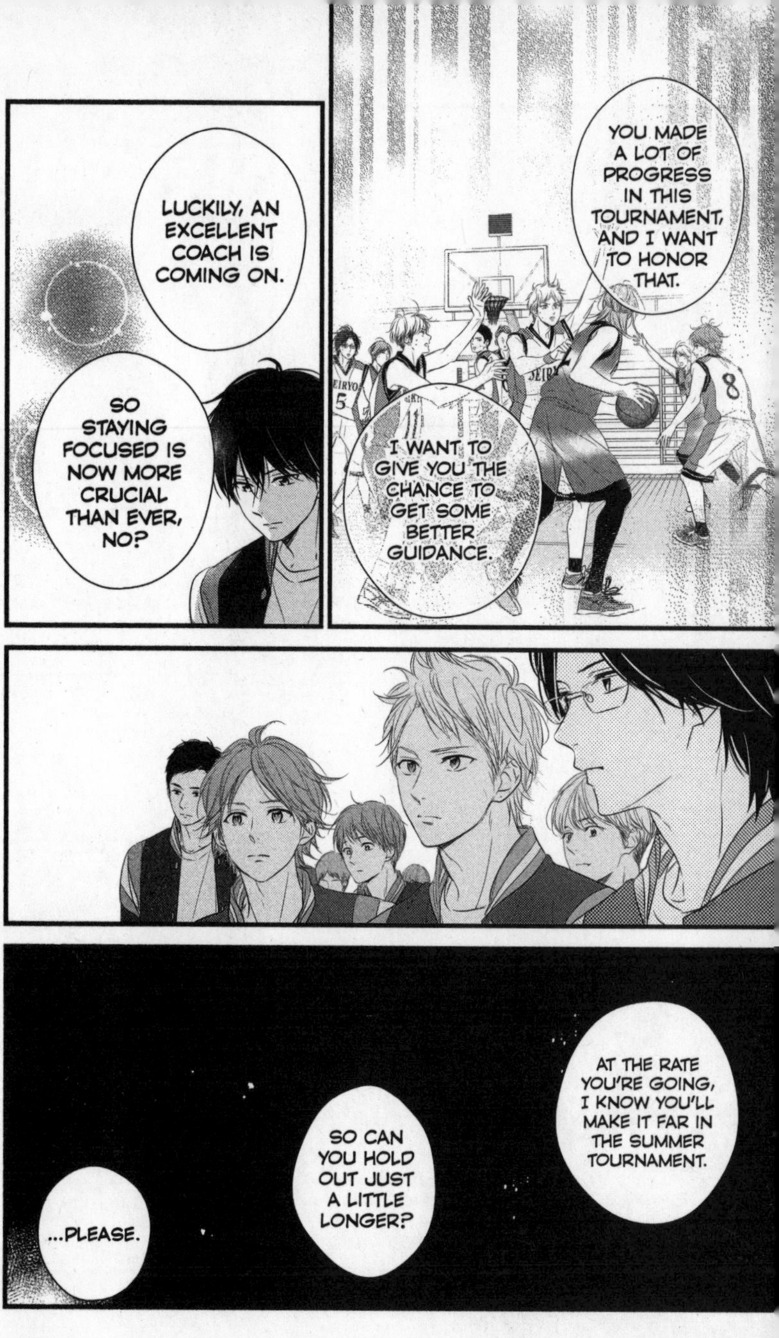
YOU MADE A LOT OF PROGRESS IN THIS TOURNAMENT, AND I WANT TO HONOR THAT.
I WANT TO GIVE YOU THE CHANCE TO GET SOME BETTER GUIDANCE.
LUCKILY, AN EXCELLENT COACH IS COMING ON.
SO STAYING FOCUSED IS NOW MORE CRUCIAL THAN EVER, NO?
AT THE RATE YOU'RE GOING, I KNOW YOU'LL MAKE IT FAR IN THE SUMMER TOURNAMENT.
SO CAN YOU HOLD OUT JUST A LITTLE LONGER?
...PLEASE.

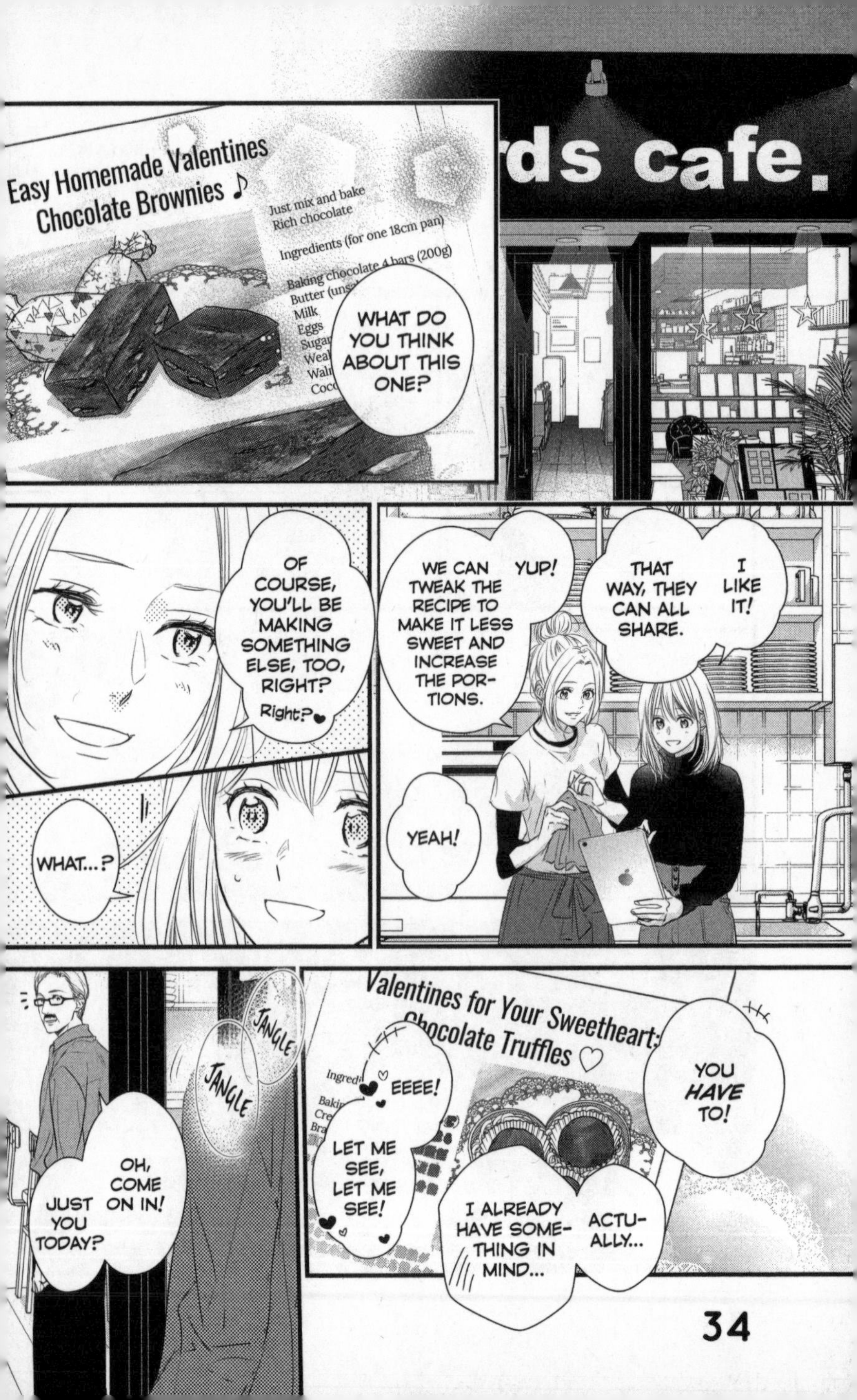
rds cafe.
Easy Homemade Valentines Chocolate Brownies ♪
Just mix and bake
Rich chocolate
Ingredients (for one 18cm pan)
Baking chocolate 4 bars (200g)
Milk
Eggs
WHAT DO YOU THINK ABOUT THIS ONE?
I LIKE IT!
THAT WAY, THEY CAN ALL SHARE.
YUP!
WE CAN TWEAK THE RECIPE TO MAKE IT LESS SWEET AND INCREASE THE POR-TIONS.
YEAH!
OF COURSE, YOU'LL BE MAKING SOMETHING ELSE, TOO, RIGHT?
Right?
WHAT...?
Valentines for Your Sweetheart: Chocolate Truffles ♡
YOU HAVE TO!
EEEE!
LET ME SEE, LET ME SEE!
ACTU-ALLY...
I ALREADY HAVE SOME-THING IN MIND...
JANGLE
JANGLE
OH, COME ON IN!
JUST YOU TODAY?

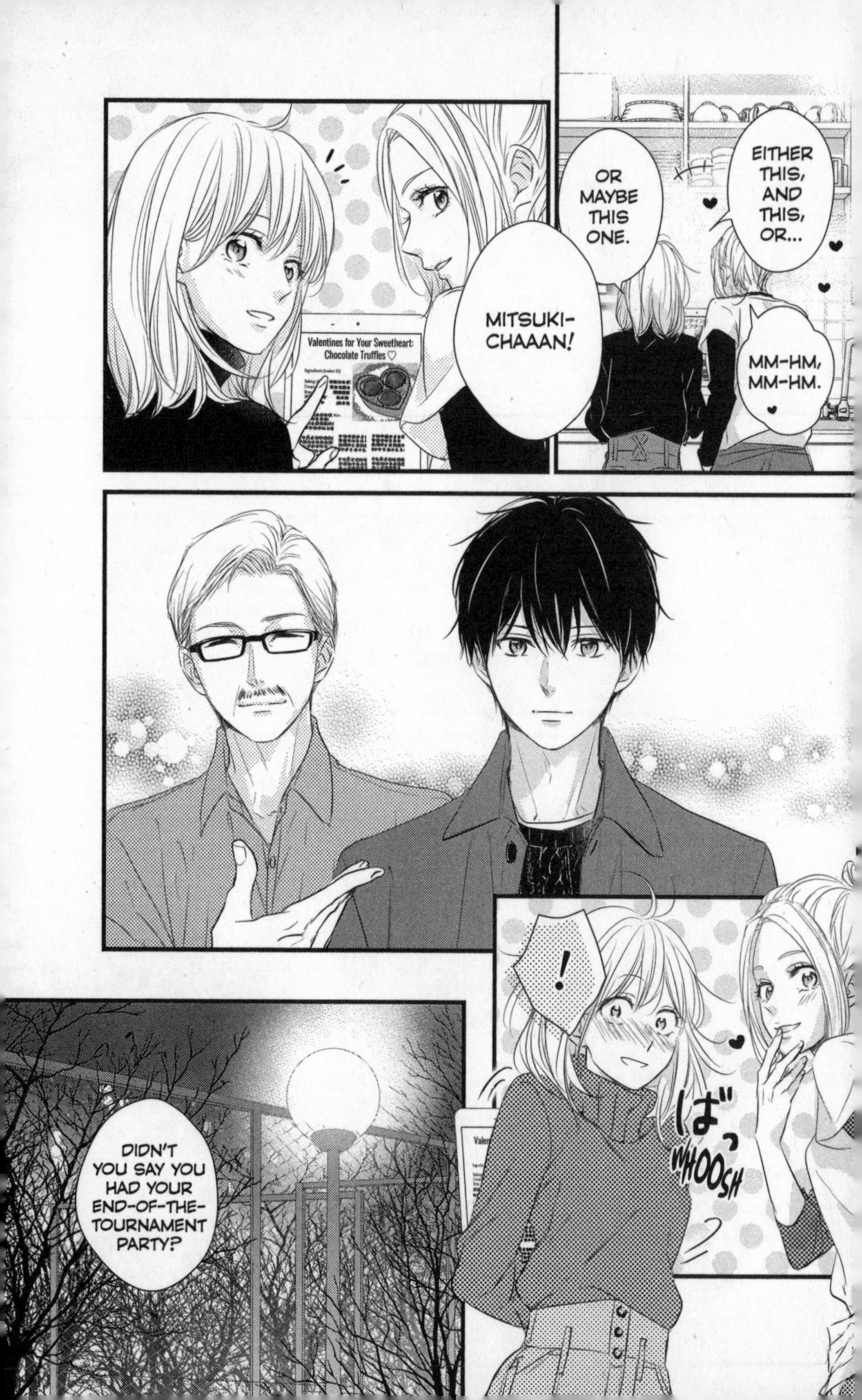
EITHER THIS, AND THIS, OR...
OR MAYBE THIS ONE.
MM-HM, MM-HM.
MITSUKI-CHAAAN!
Valentines for Your Sweetheart: Chocolate Truffles ♡
!
ばっ
WHOOSH
DIDN'T YOU SAY YOU HAD YOUR END-OF-THE-TOURNAMENT PARTY?

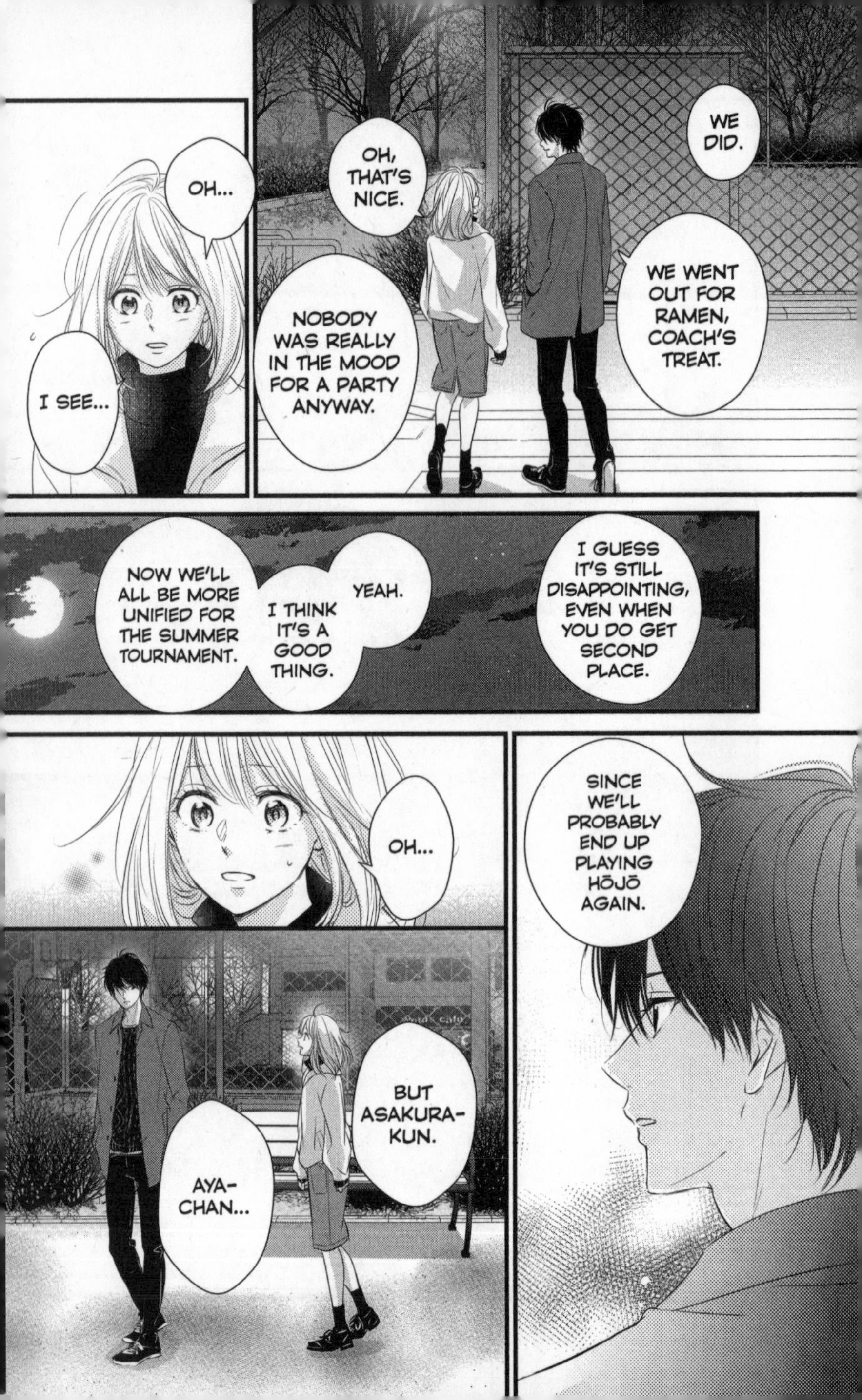
WE DID.
WE WENT OUT FOR RAMEN, COACH'S TREAT.
OH, THAT'S NICE.
NOBODY WAS REALLY IN THE MOOD FOR A PARTY ANYWAY.
OH...
I SEE...
I GUESS IT'S STILL DISAPPOINTING, EVEN WHEN YOU DO GET SECOND PLACE.
YEAH.
I THINK IT'S A GOOD THING.
NOW WE'LL ALL BE MORE UNIFIED FOR THE SUMMER TOURNAMENT.
SINCE WE'LL PROBABLY END UP PLAYING HŌJŌ AGAIN.
OH...
BUT ASAKURA-KUN.
AYA-CHAN...

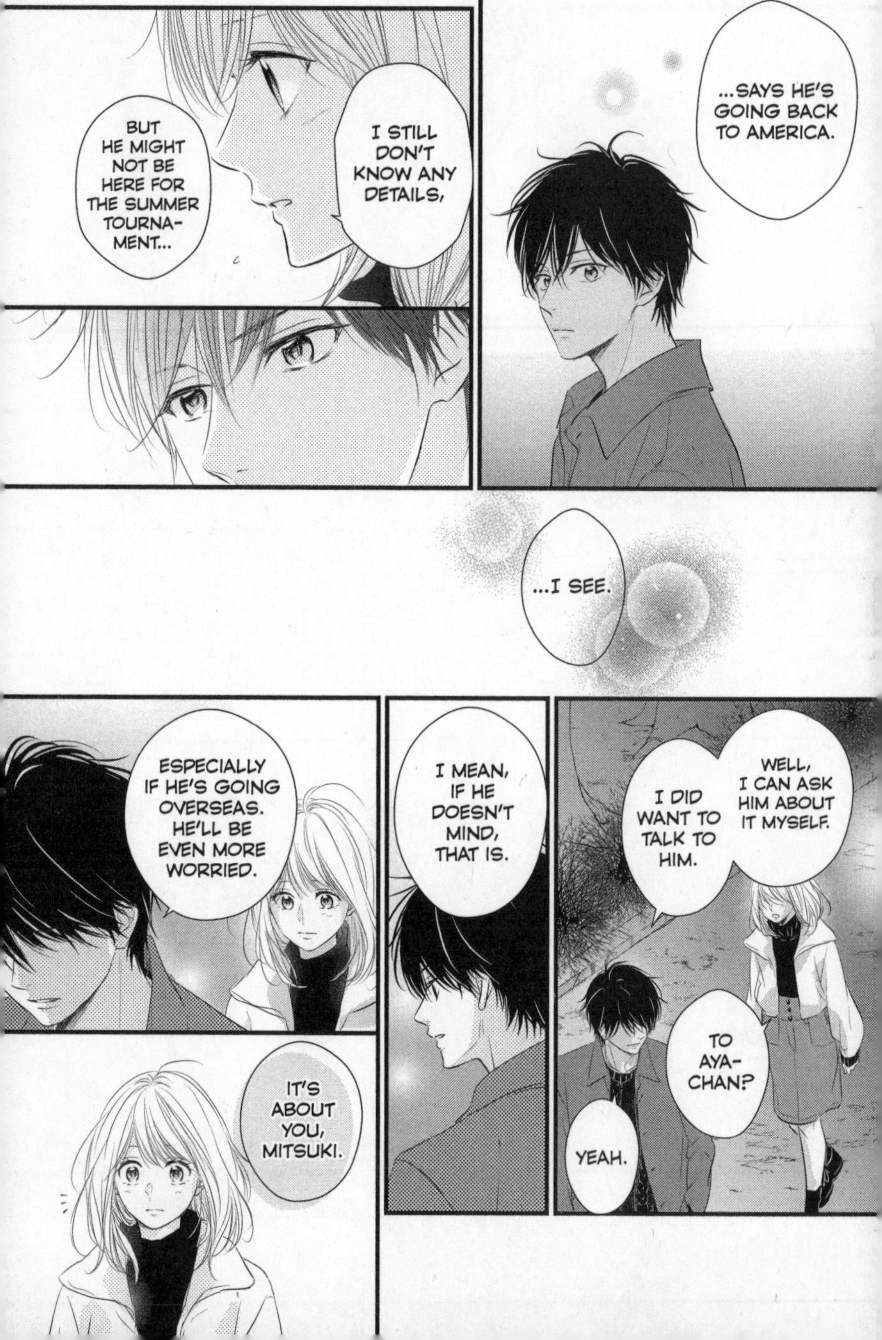
...SAYS HE'S GOING BACK TO AMERICA.
I STILL DON'T KNOW ANY DETAILS,
BUT HE MIGHT NOT BE HERE FOR THE SUMMER TOURNA-MENT...
...I SEE.
WELL, I CAN ASK HIM ABOUT IT MYSELF.
I DID WANT TO TALK TO HIM.
TO AYA-CHAN?
YEAH.
I MEAN, IF HE DOESN'T MIND, THAT IS.
ESPECIALLY IF HE'S GOING OVERSEAS. HE'LL BE EVEN MORE WORRIED.
IT'S ABOUT YOU, MITSUKI.

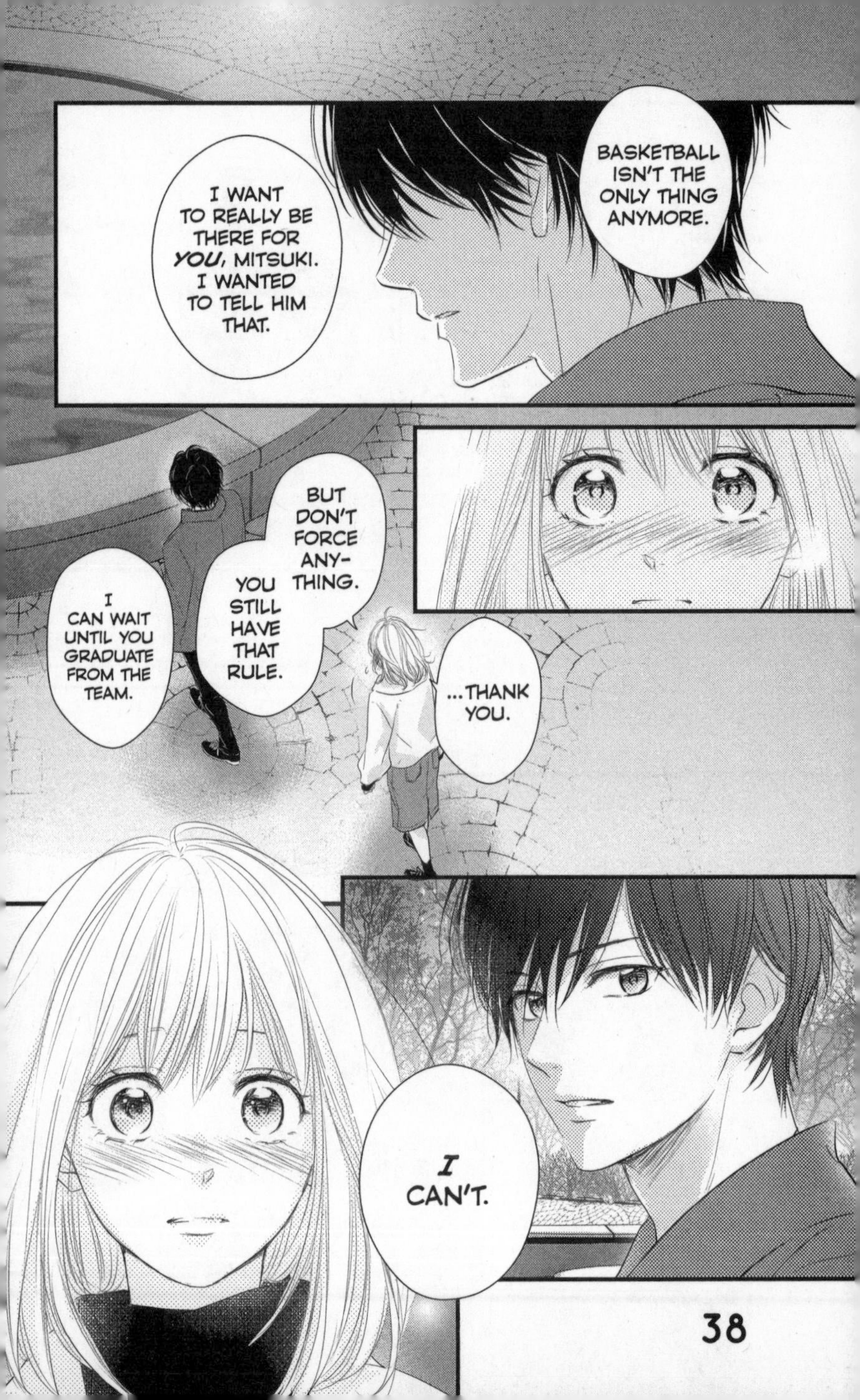
BASKETBALL ISN'T THE ONLY THING ANYMORE.
I WANT TO REALLY BE THERE FOR *YOU*, MITSUKI. I WANTED TO TELL HIM THAT.
...THANK YOU.
BUT DON'T FORCE ANY-THING.
YOU STILL HAVE THAT RULE.
I CAN WAIT UNTIL YOU GRADUATE FROM THE TEAM.
I CAN'T.

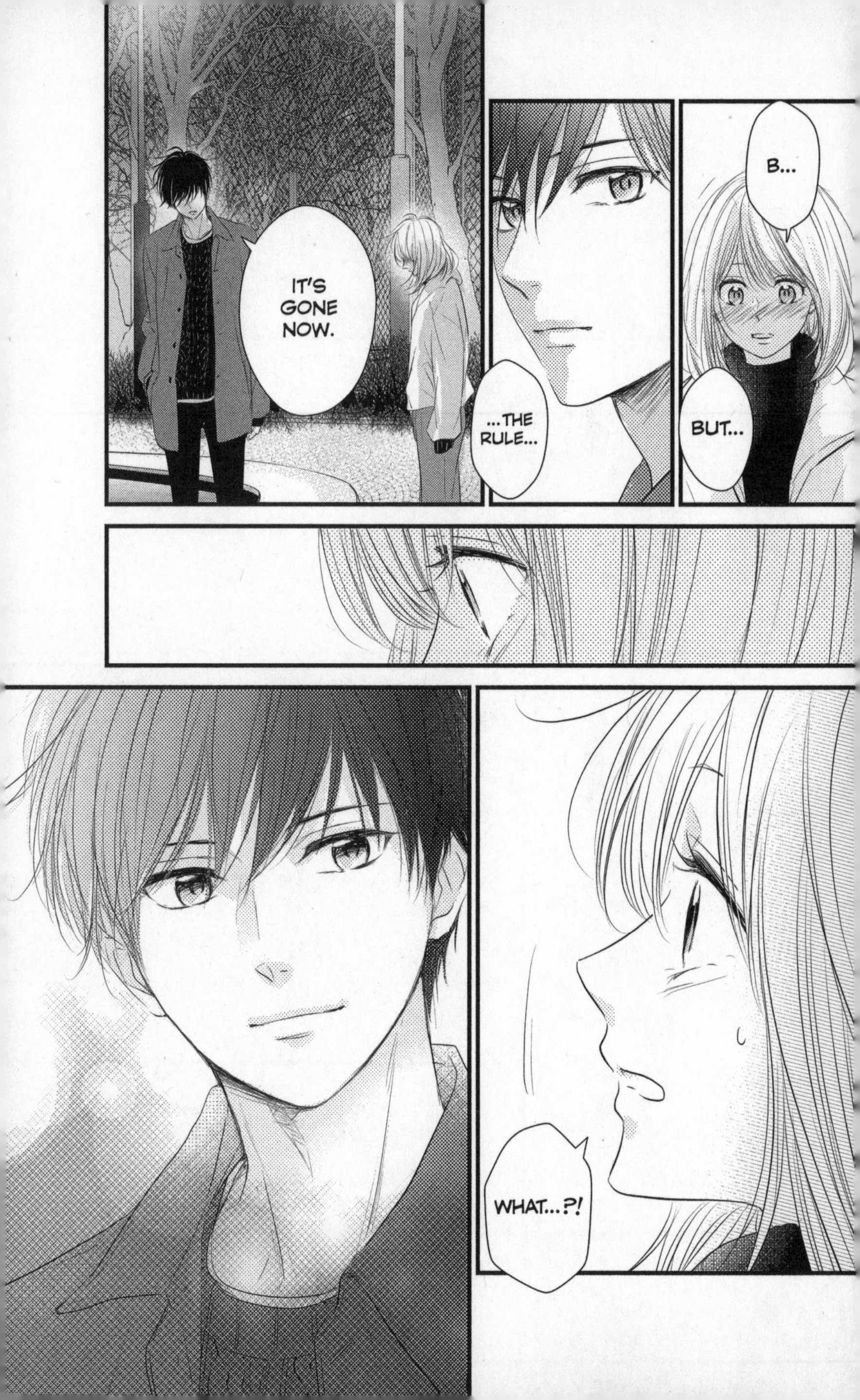
B...
BUT...
...THE RULE...
IT'S GONE NOW.
WHAT...?!

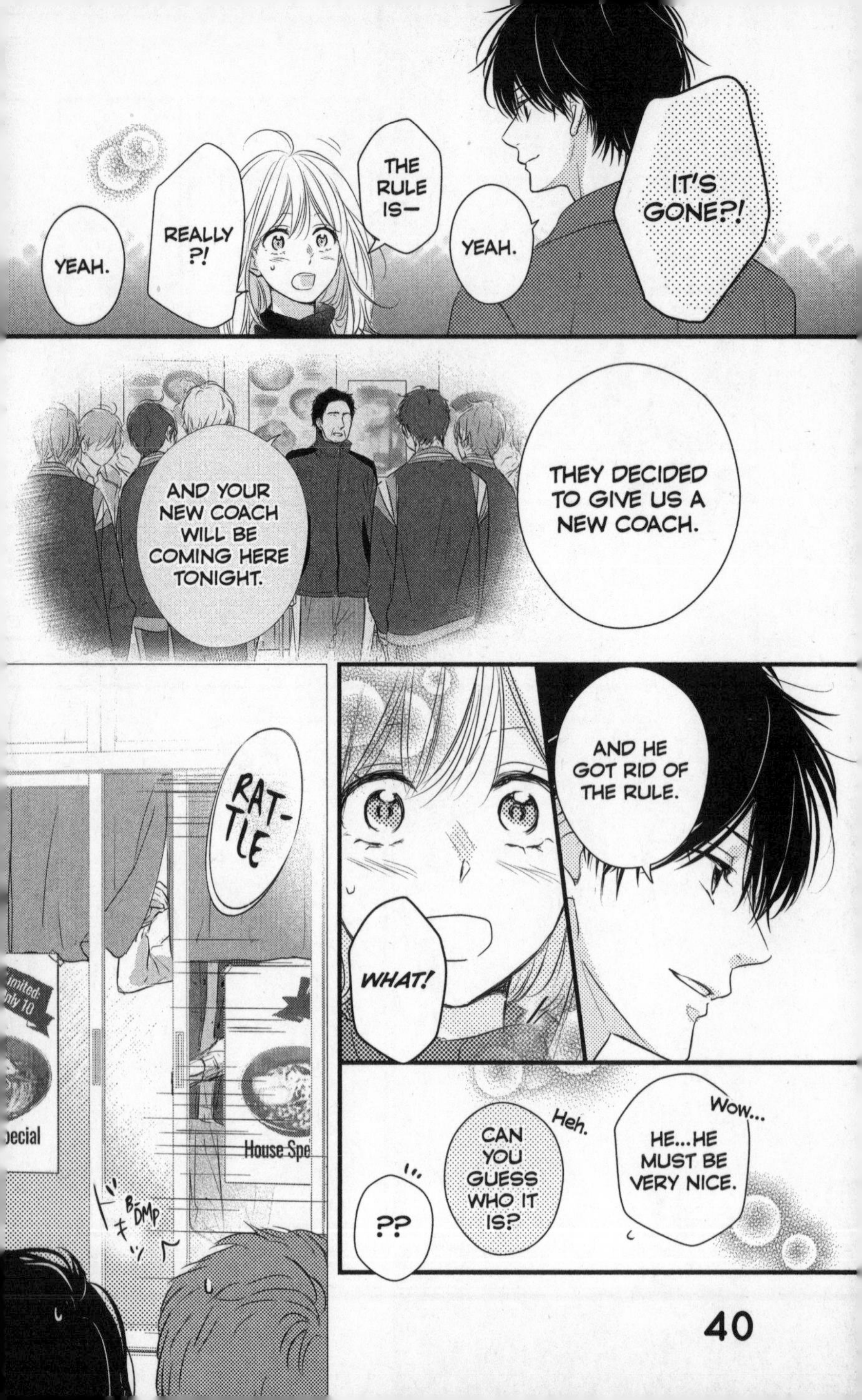
IT'S GONE?!
YEAH.
THE RULE IS—
REALLY?!
YEAH.
THEY DECIDED TO GIVE US A NEW COACH.
AND YOUR NEW COACH WILL BE COMING HERE TONIGHT.
AND HE GOT RID OF THE RULE.
WHAT!
Wow...
HE...HE MUST BE VERY NICE.
Heh.
CAN YOU GUESS WHO IT IS?
??
RAT-TLE
House Spe
B-DMP

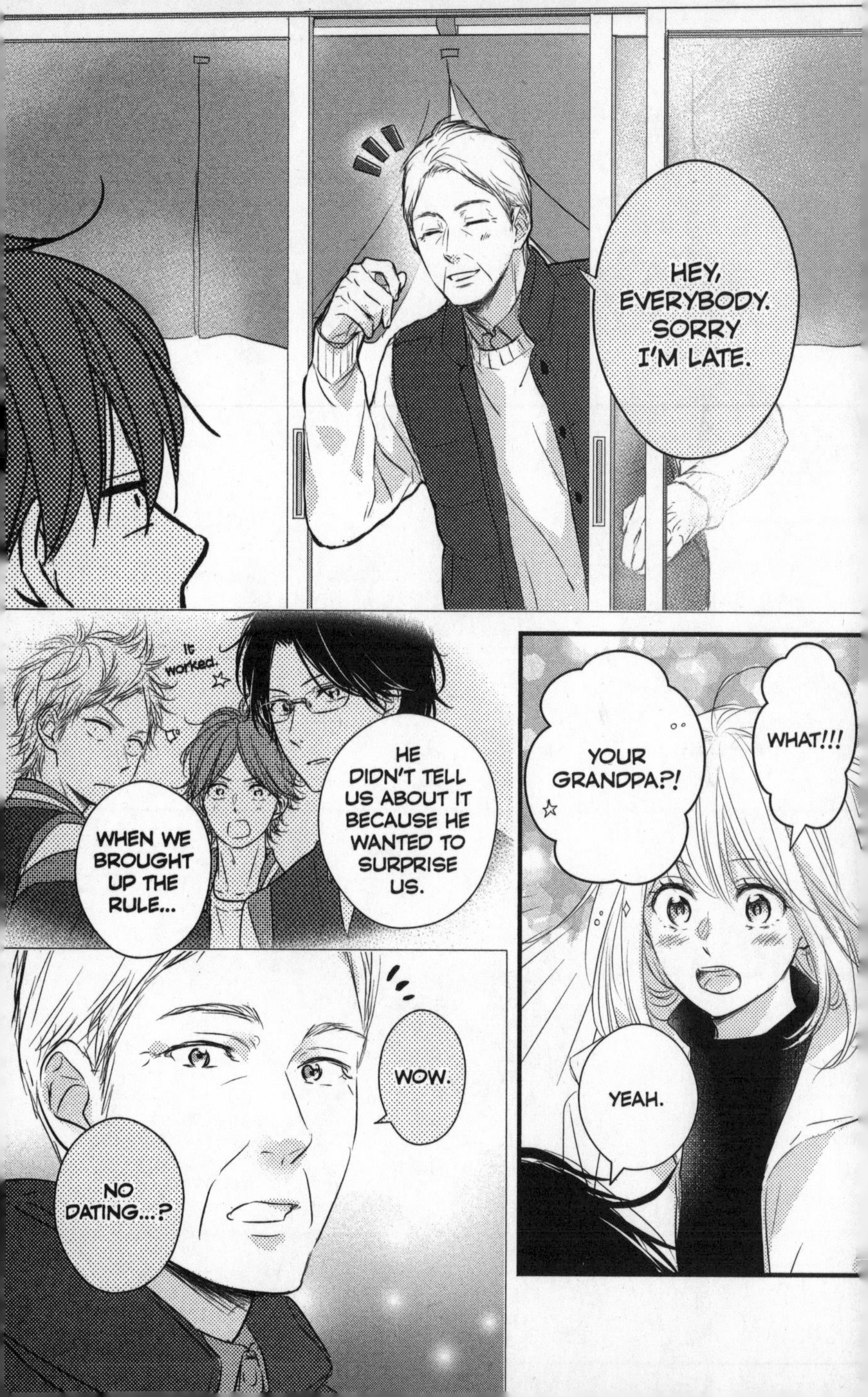
HEY, EVERYBODY. SORRY I'M LATE.
WHAT!!!
YOUR GRANDPA?!
YEAH.
It worked.
HE DIDN'T TELL US ABOUT IT BECAUSE HE WANTED TO SURPRISE US.
WHEN WE BROUGHT UP THE RULE...
WOW.
NO DATING...?

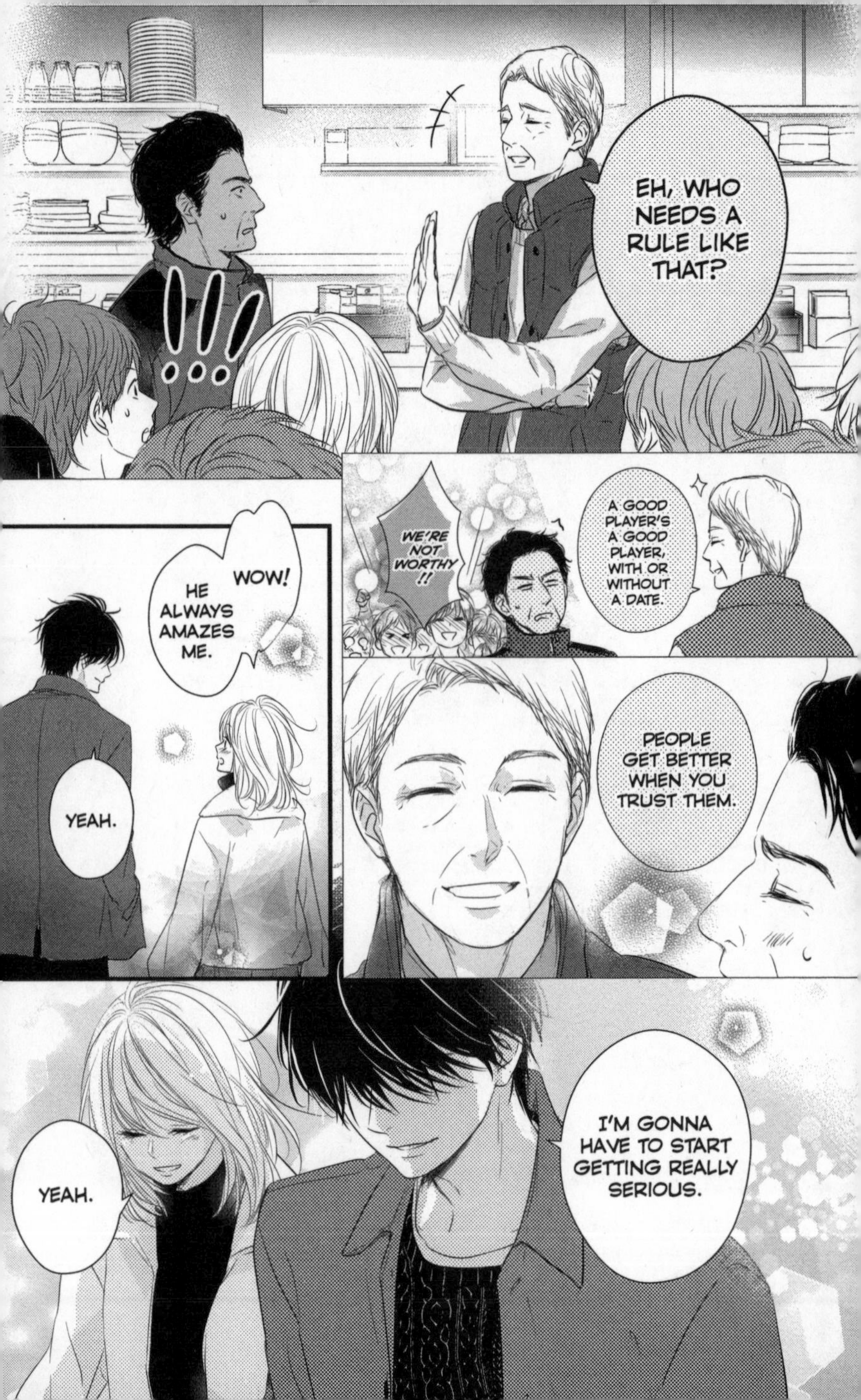
EH, WHO NEEDS A RULE LIKE THAT?
A GOOD PLAYER'S A GOOD PLAYER, WITH OR WITHOUT A DATE.
WE'RE NOT WORTHY!!
PEOPLE GET BETTER WHEN YOU TRUST THEM.
WOW! HE ALWAYS AMAZES ME.
YEAH.
I'M GONNA HAVE TO START GETTING REALLY SERIOUS.
YEAH.

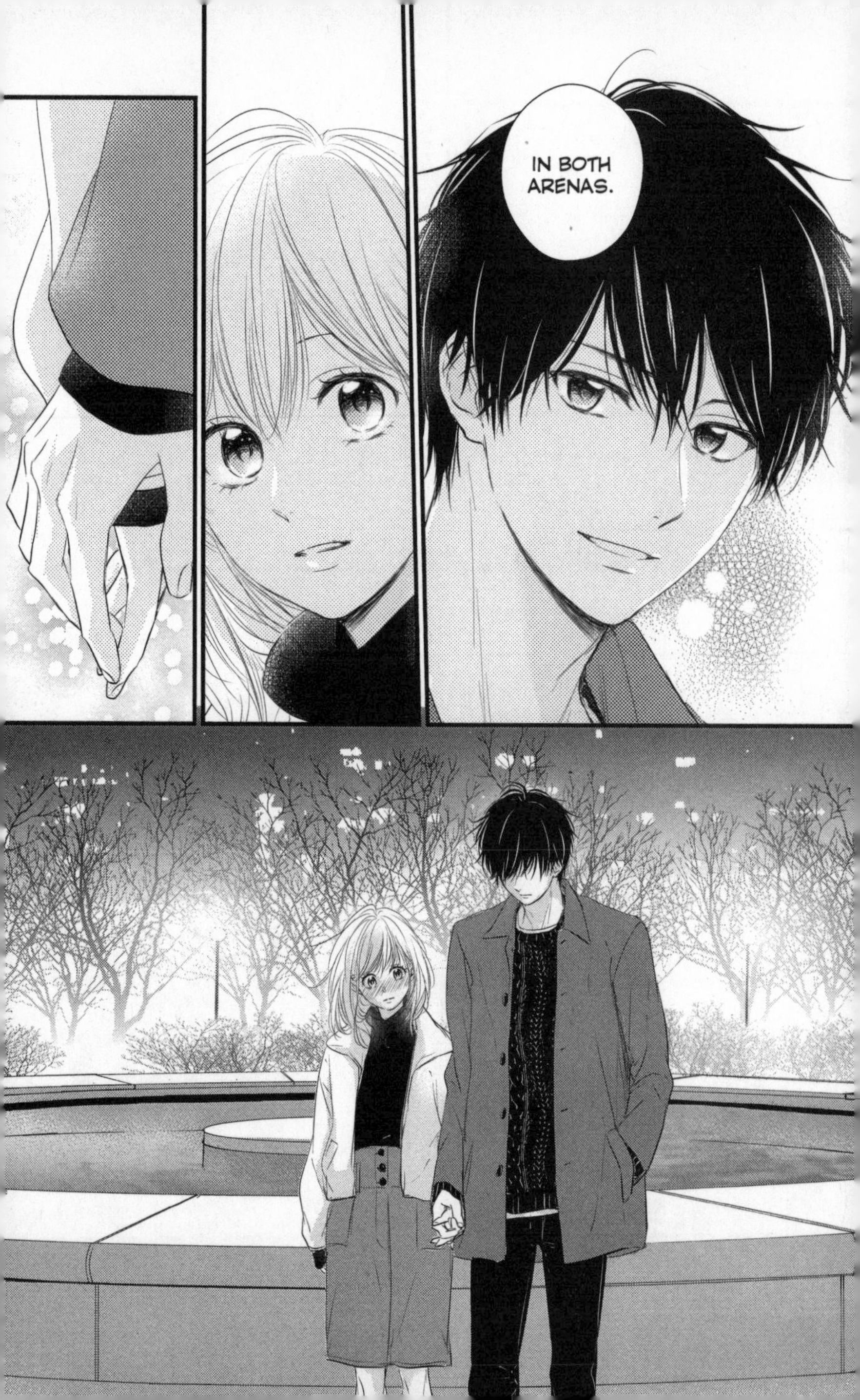
IN BOTH ARENAS.

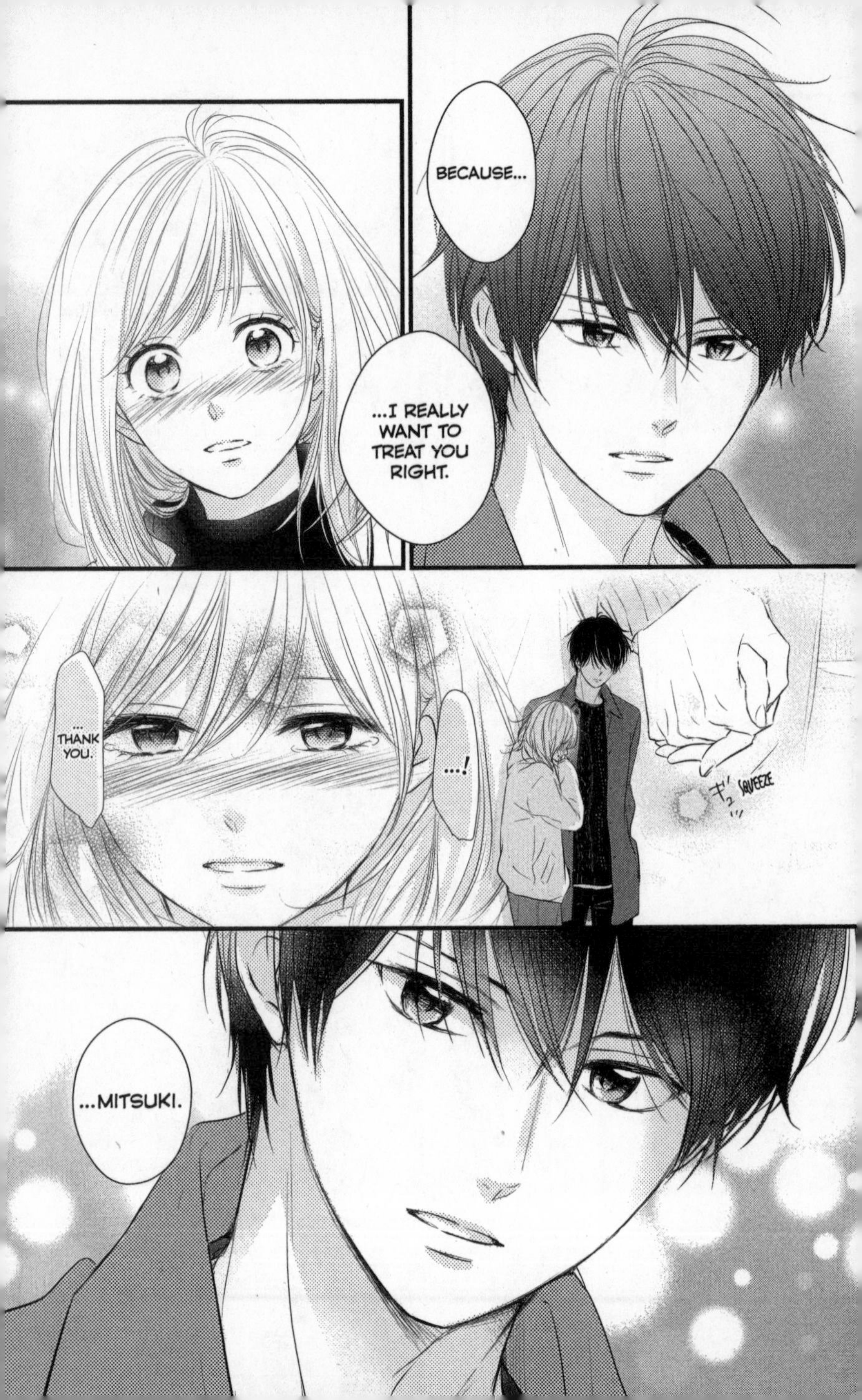
BECAUSE...
...I REALLY WANT TO TREAT YOU RIGHT.
SQUEEZE
...!
...THANK YOU.
...MITSUKI.

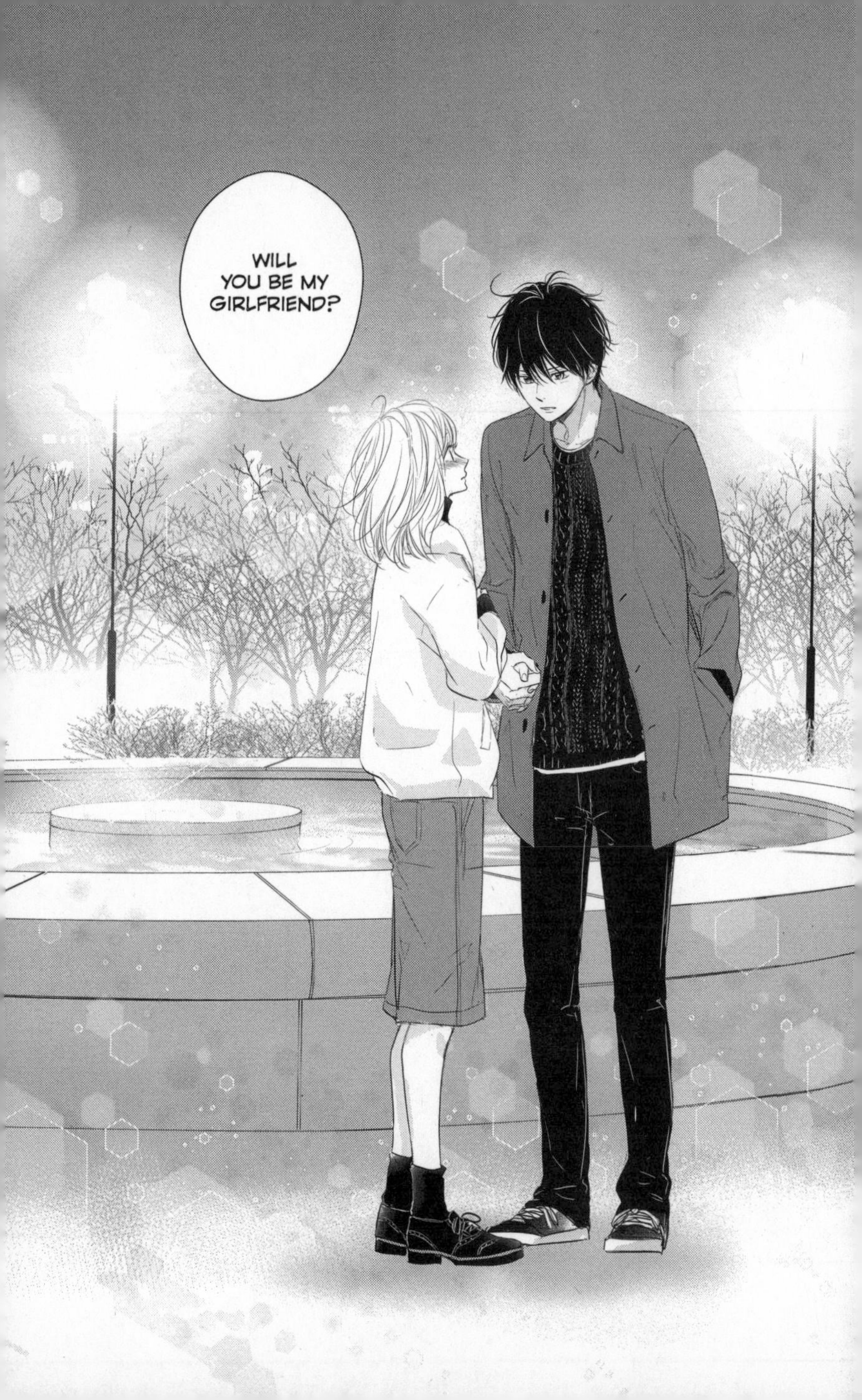
WILL YOU BE MY GIRLFRIEND?

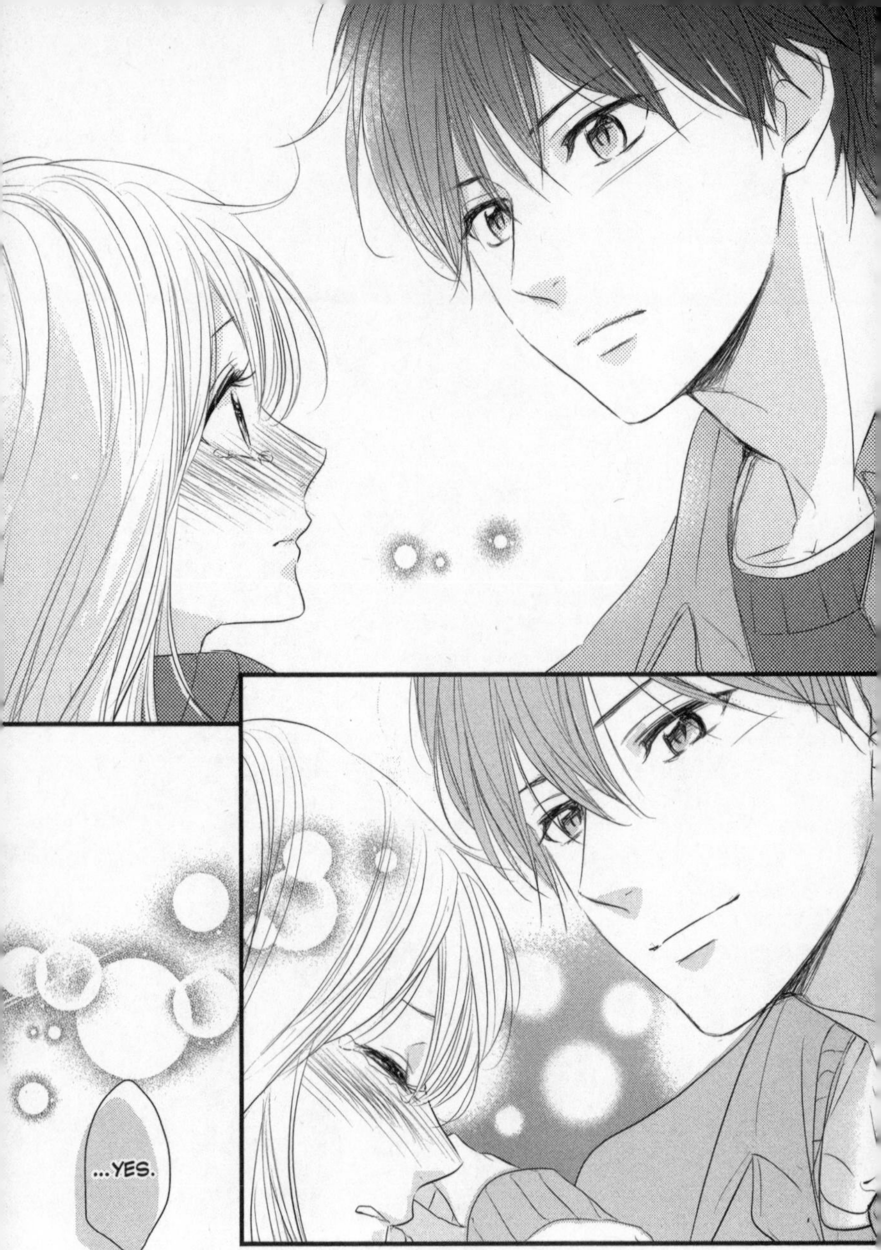
...YES.

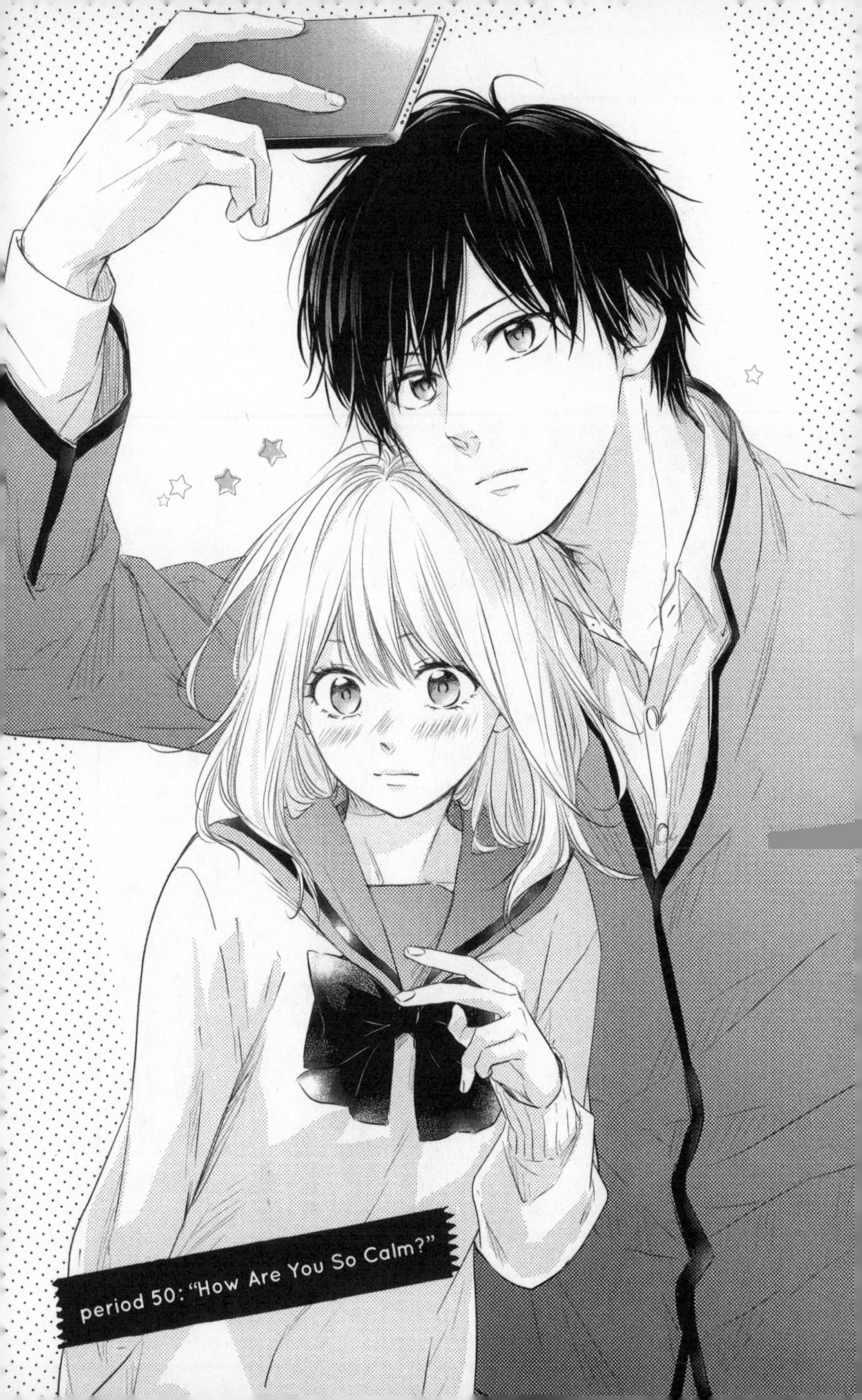
period 50: "How Are You So Calm?"

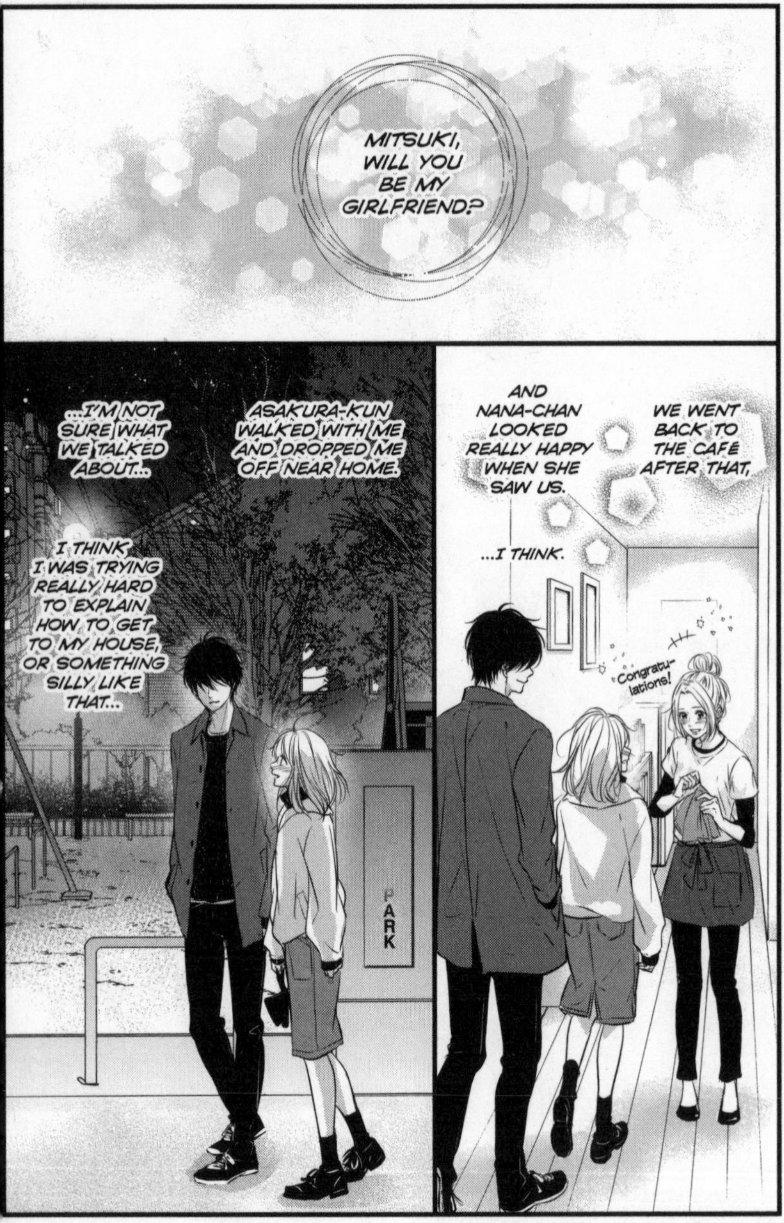
MITSUKI, WILL YOU BE MY GIRLFRIEND?
WE WENT BACK TO THE CAFÉ AFTER THAT,
AND NANA-CHAN LOOKED REALLY HAPPY WHEN SHE SAW US.
...I THINK.
Congratulations!
ASAKURA-KUN WALKED WITH ME AND DROPPED ME OFF NEAR HOME.
...I'M NOT SURE WHAT WE TALKED ABOUT...
I THINK, I WAS TRYING REALLY HARD TO EXPLAIN HOW TO GET TO MY HOUSE, OR SOMETHING SILLY LIKE THAT...
PARK

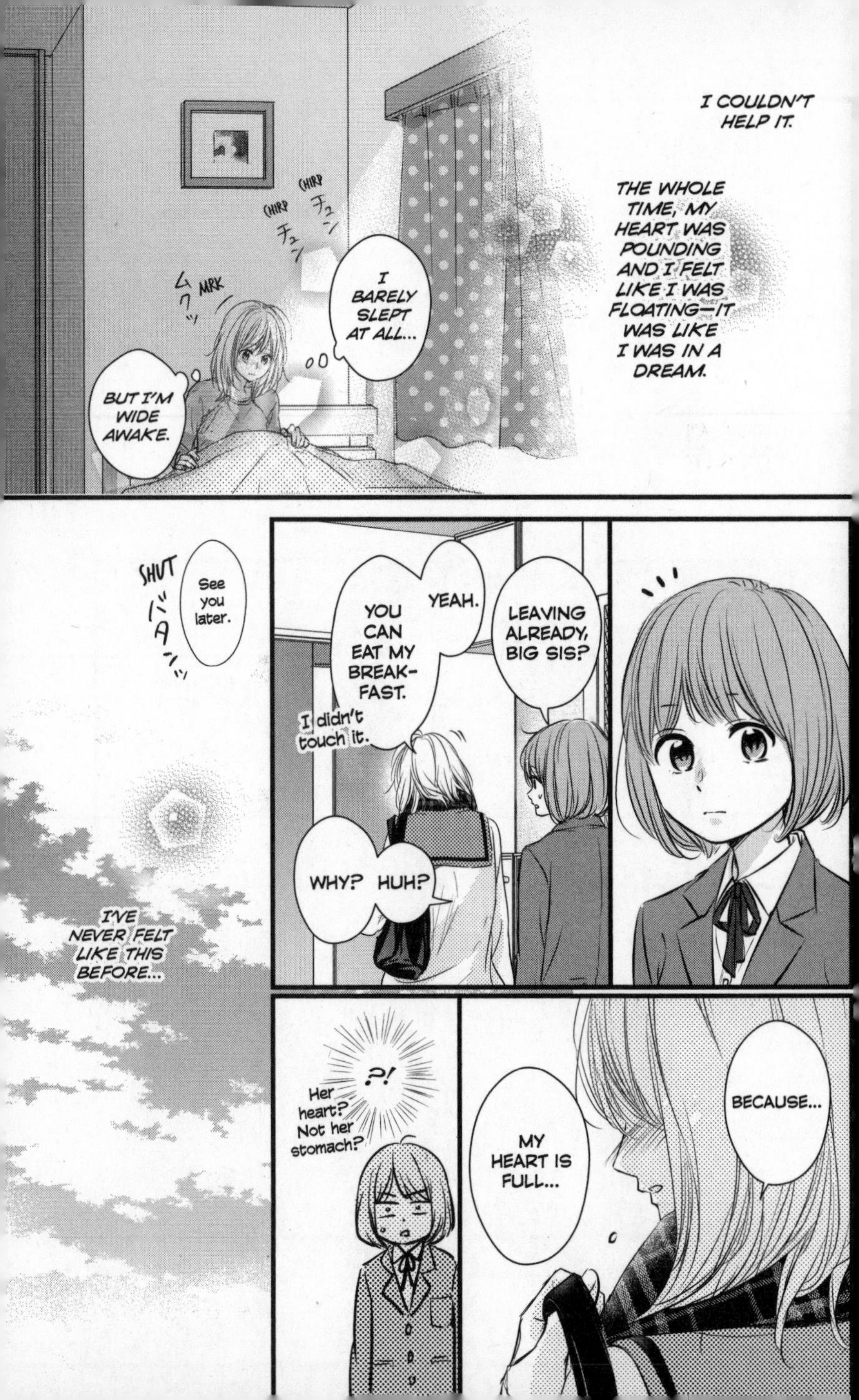
I COULDN'T HELP IT.
THE WHOLE TIME, MY HEART WAS POUNDING AND I FELT LIKE I WAS FLOATING—IT WAS LIKE I WAS IN A DREAM.
I BARELY SLEPT AT ALL...
CHIRP
CHIRP
MRK
BUT I'M WIDE AWAKE.
LEAVING ALREADY, BIG SIS?
YEAH.
YOU CAN EAT MY BREAKFAST.
I didn't touch it.
WHY? HUH?
BECAUSE...
MY HEART IS FULL...
?!
Her heart? Not her stomach?
See you later.
SHUT
I'VE NEVER FELT LIKE THIS BEFORE...

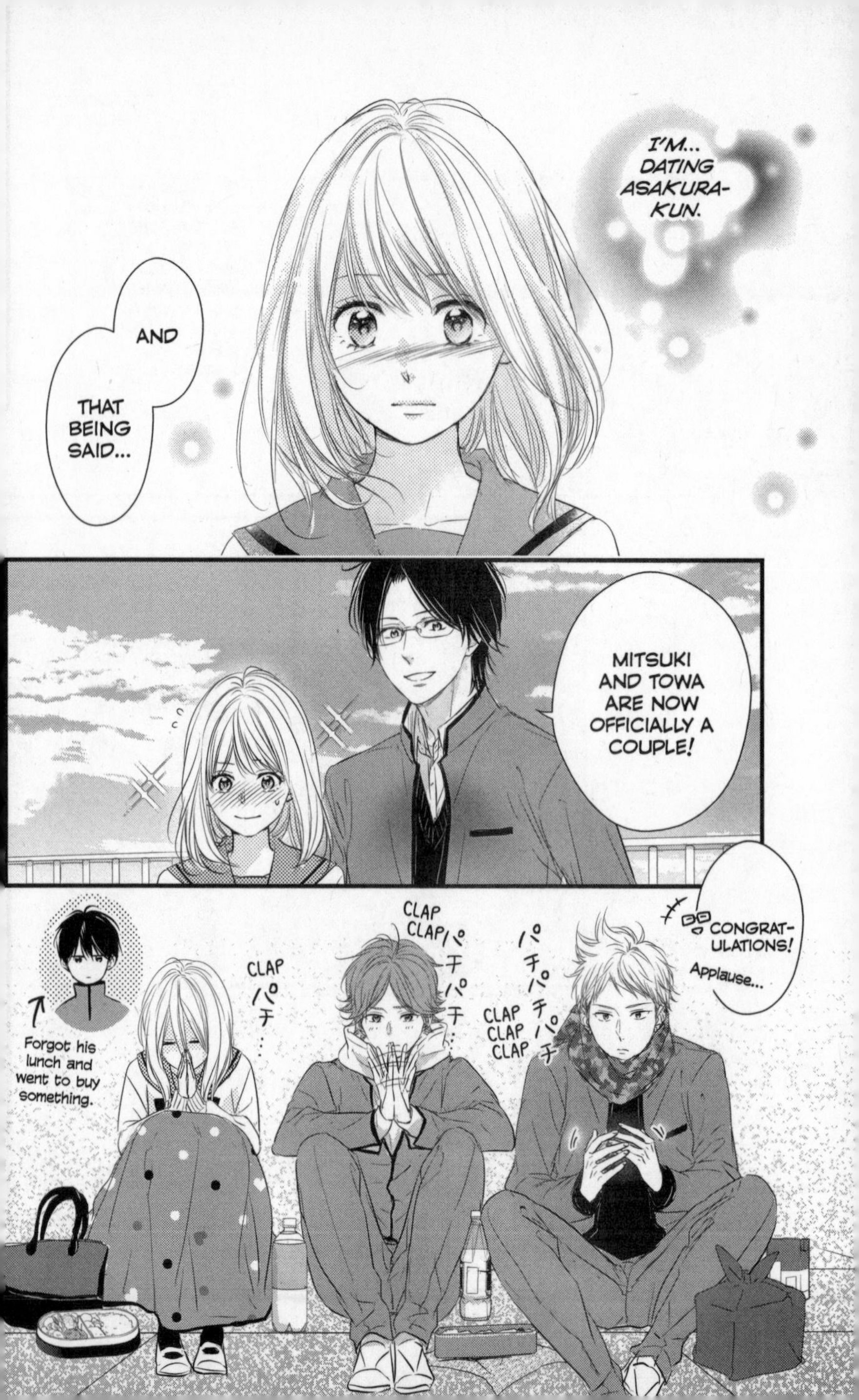
I'M... DATING ASAKURA-KUN.
AND THAT BEING SAID...
MITSUKI AND TOWA ARE NOW OFFICIALLY A COUPLE!
CONGRAT-ULATIONS!
Applause...
CLAP CLAP CLAP
パチパチパチ
CLAP CLAP
パチパチ...
CLAP
パチ...
Forgot his lunch and went to buy something.

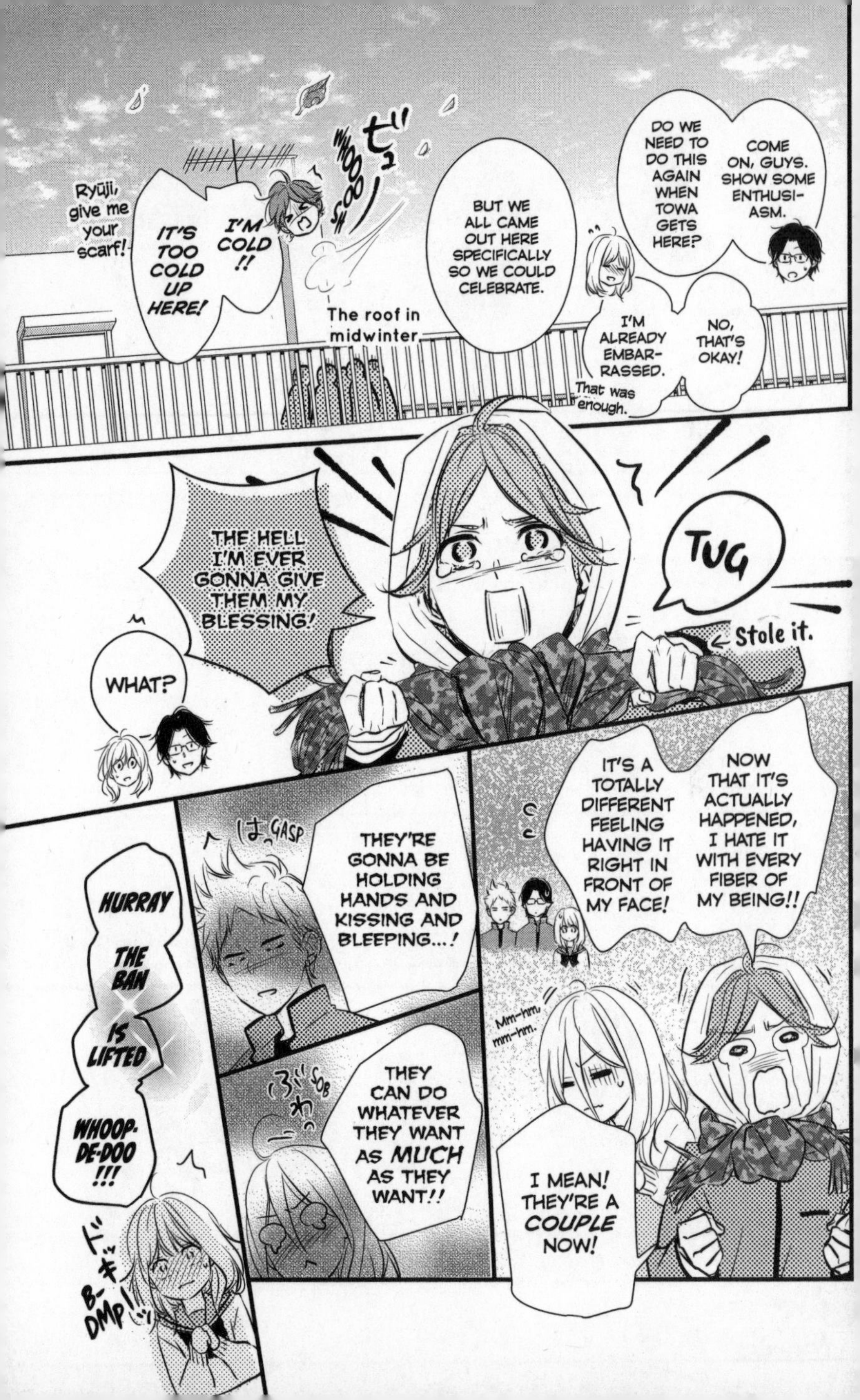
COME ON, GUYS. SHOW SOME ENTHUSI-ASM.
DO WE NEED TO DO THIS AGAIN WHEN TOWA GETS HERE?
NO, THAT'S OKAY!
I'M ALREADY EMBAR-RASSED.
That was enough.
BUT WE ALL CAME OUT HERE SPECIFICALLY SO WE COULD CELEBRATE.
The roof in midwinter
WHOOOOSH
I'M COLD!!
IT'S TOO COLD UP HERE!
Ryūji, give me your scarf!
TUG
Stole it.
THE HELL I'M EVER GONNA GIVE THEM MY BLESSING!
WHAT?
NOW THAT IT'S ACTUALLY HAPPENED, I HATE IT WITH EVERY FIBER OF MY BEING!!
IT'S A TOTALLY DIFFERENT FEELING HAVING IT RIGHT IN FRONT OF MY FACE!
Mm-hm, mm-hm.
I MEAN! THEY'RE A COUPLE NOW!
GASP
THEY'RE GONNA BE HOLDING HANDS AND KISSING AND BLEEPING...!
SOB
THEY CAN DO WHATEVER THEY WANT AS MUCH AS THEY WANT!!
HURRAY THE BAN IS LIFTED WHOOP-DE-DOO!!!
B-DMP

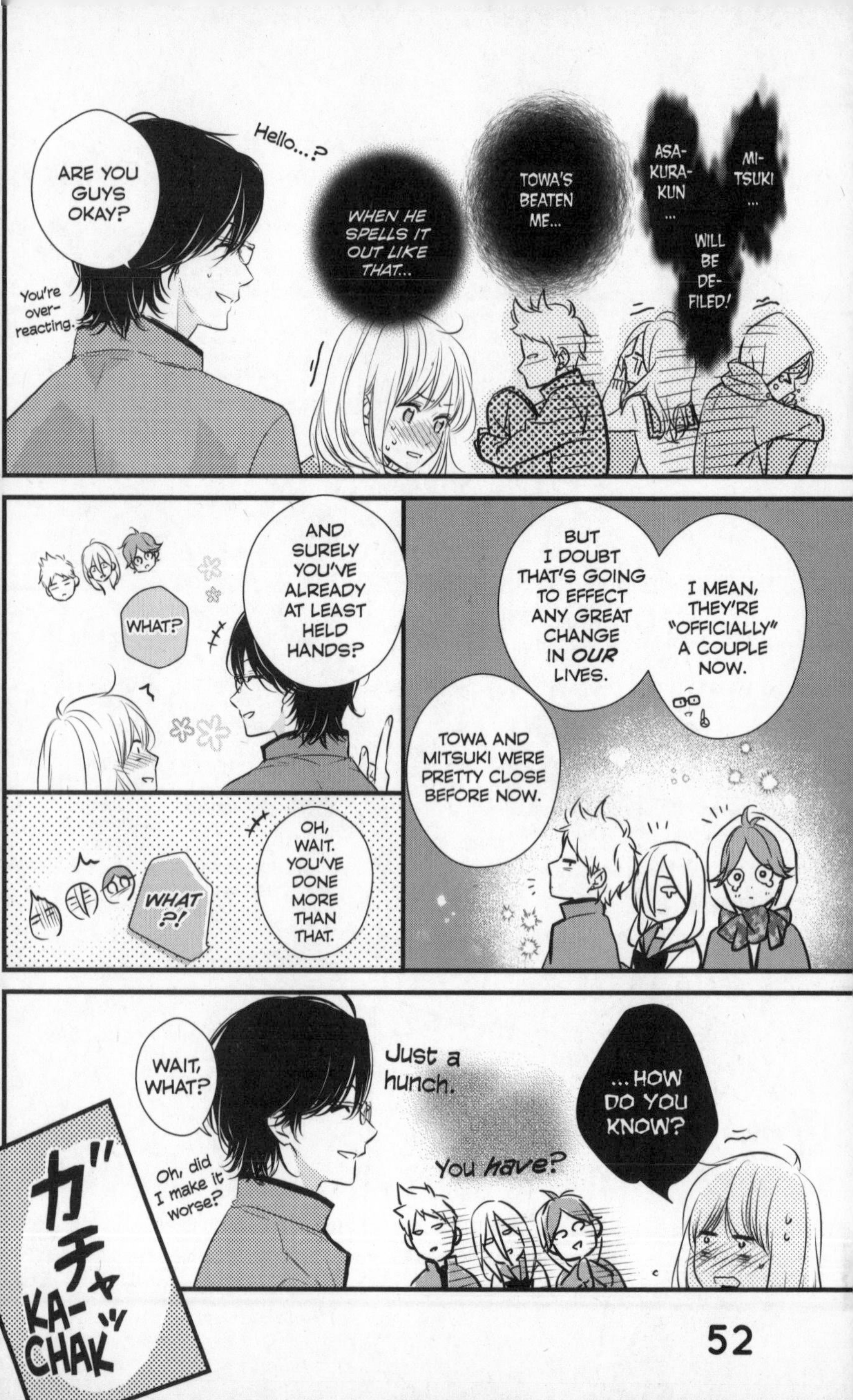
MI-TSUKI...
ASA-KURA-KUN...
WILL BE DE-FILED!
TOWA'S BEATEN ME...
WHEN HE SPELLS IT OUT LIKE THAT...
Hello...?
ARE YOU GUYS OKAY?
You're over-reacting.
I MEAN, THEY'RE "OFFICIALLY" A COUPLE NOW.
BUT I DOUBT THAT'S GOING TO EFFECT ANY GREAT CHANGE IN *OUR* LIVES.
TOWA AND MITSUKI WERE PRETTY CLOSE BEFORE NOW.
AND SURELY YOU'VE ALREADY AT LEAST HELD HANDS?
WHAT?
OH, WAIT. YOU'VE DONE MORE THAN THAT.
WHAT?!
...HOW DO YOU KNOW?
You *have*?
Just a hunch.
WAIT, WHAT?
Oh, did I make it worse?
ガチャッ
KA-CHAK

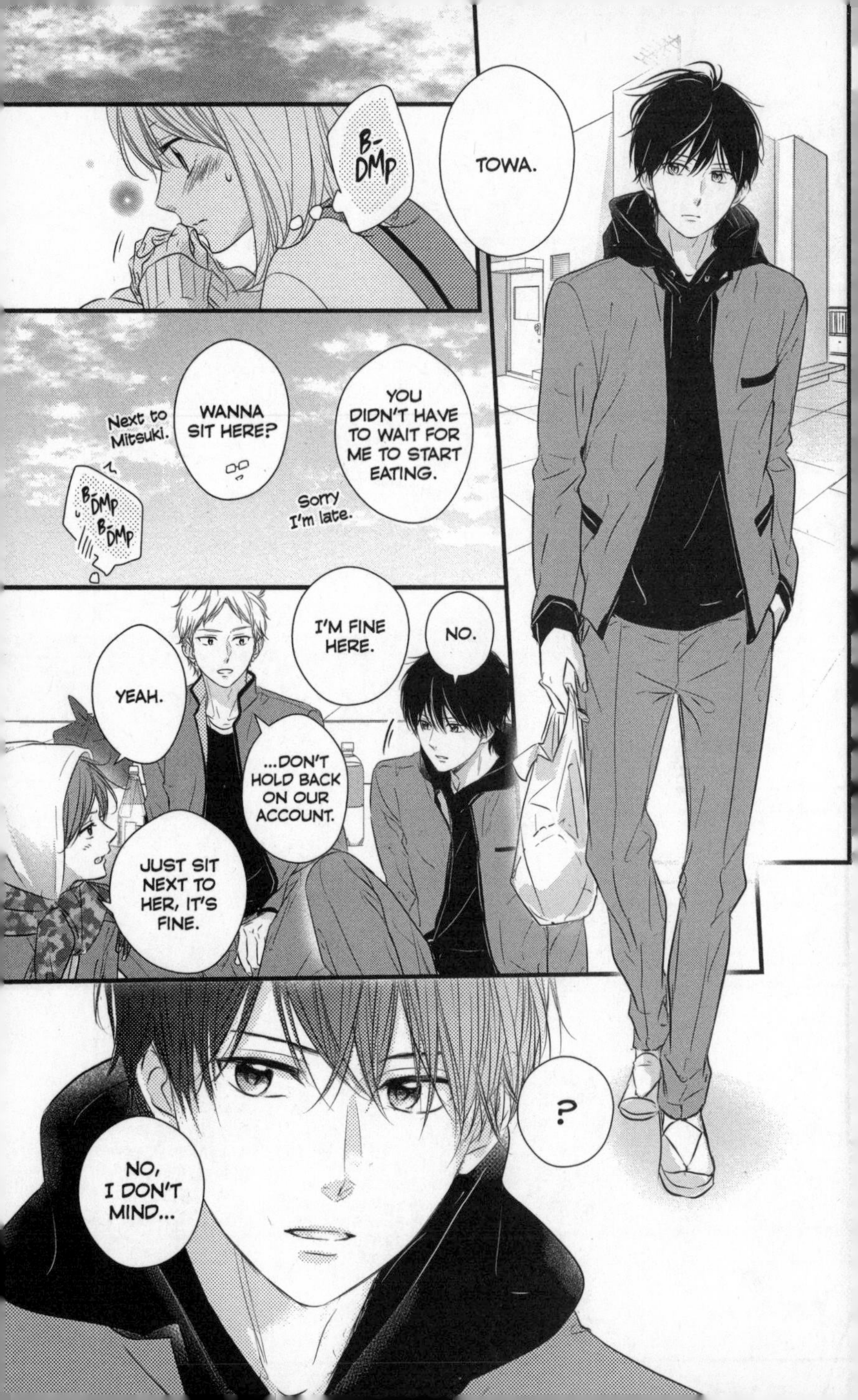

TOWA.
B-DMP
YOU DIDN'T HAVE TO WAIT FOR ME TO START EATING.
Sorry I'm late.
WANNA SIT HERE?
Next to Mitsuki.
B-DMP B-DMP
NO.
I'M FINE HERE.
...DON'T HOLD BACK ON OUR ACCOUNT.
YEAH.
JUST SIT NEXT TO HER, IT'S FINE.
?
NO, I DON'T MIND...

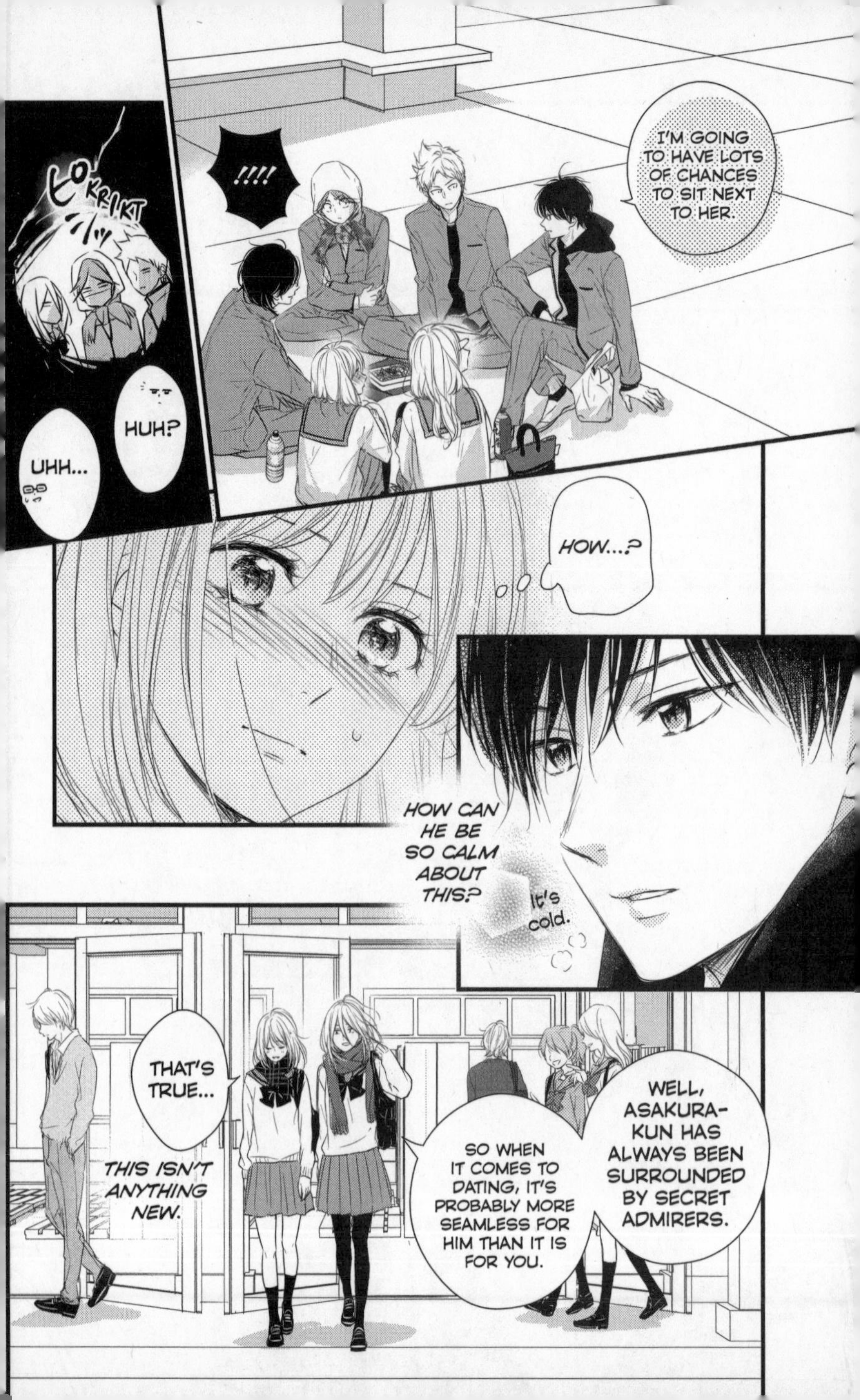
I'M GOING TO HAVE LOTS OF CHANCES TO SIT NEXT TO HER.
!!!!
KRIKT
HUH?
UHH...
HOW...?
HOW CAN HE BE SO CALM ABOUT THIS?
It's cold.
WELL, ASAKURA-KUN HAS ALWAYS BEEN SURROUNDED BY SECRET ADMIRERS.
SO WHEN IT COMES TO DATING, IT'S PROBABLY MORE SEAMLESS FOR HIM THAN IT IS FOR YOU.
THAT'S TRUE...
THIS ISN'T ANYTHING NEW.

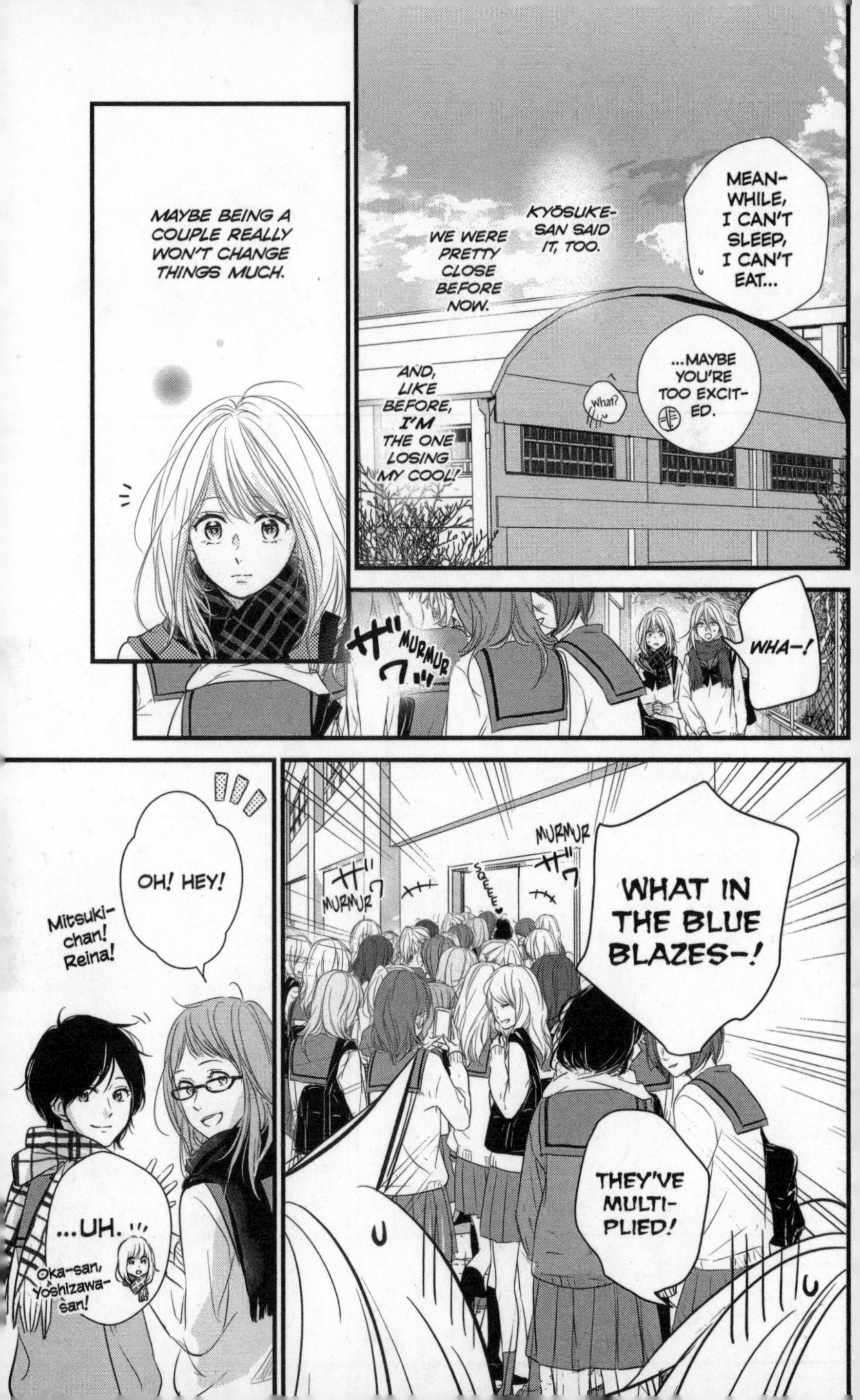

MEAN-WHILE, I CAN'T SLEEP, I CAN'T EAT...
KYŌSUKE-SAN SAID IT, TOO.
WE WERE PRETTY CLOSE BEFORE NOW.
...MAYBE YOU'RE TOO EXCIT-ED.
What?
AND, LIKE BEFORE, I'M THE ONE LOSING MY COOL!
WHA-!
MURMUR
MAYBE BEING A COUPLE REALLY WON'T CHANGE THINGS MUCH.
WHAT IN THE BLUE BLAZES-!
MURMUR
SQUEE
MURMUR
THEY'VE MULTI-PLIED!
OH! HEY!
Mitsuki-chan! Reina!
...UH.
Oka-san, Yoshizawa-san!

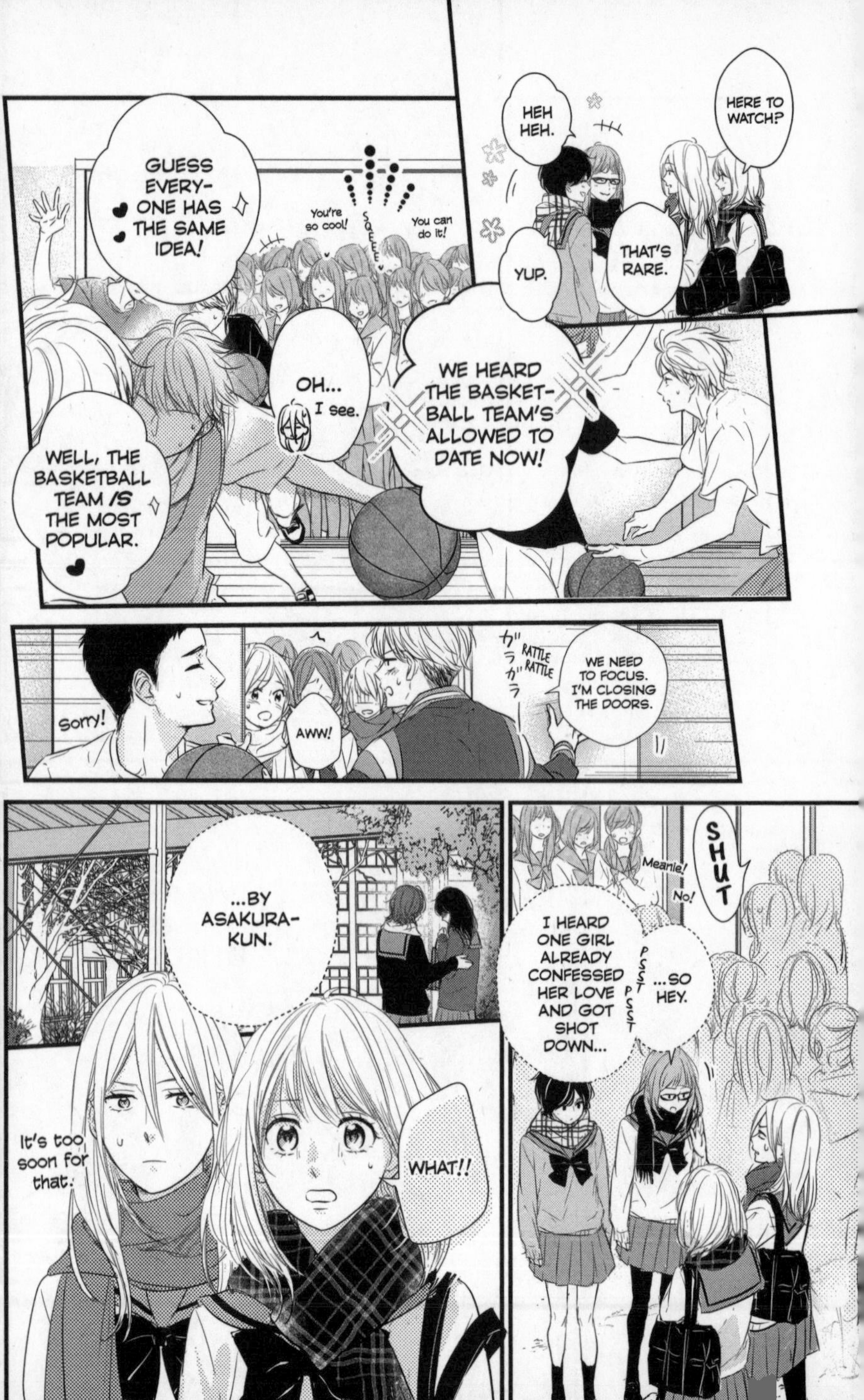
HERE TO WATCH?
HEH HEH.
THAT'S RARE.
YUP.
WE HEARD THE BASKET-BALL TEAM'S ALLOWED TO DATE NOW!
GUESS EVERY-ONE HAS THE SAME IDEA!
You can do it!
SQEEE
You're so cool!
OH... I see.
WELL, THE BASKETBALL TEAM IS THE MOST POPULAR.
ガラガラ RATTLE RATTLE
WE NEED TO FOCUS. I'M CLOSING THE DOORS.
AWW!
Sorry!
SHUT
Meanie!
No!
...SO HEY.
PSST PSST
I HEARD ONE GIRL ALREADY CONFESSED HER LOVE AND GOT SHOT DOWN...
...BY ASAKURA-KUN.
WHAT!!
It's too soon for that.

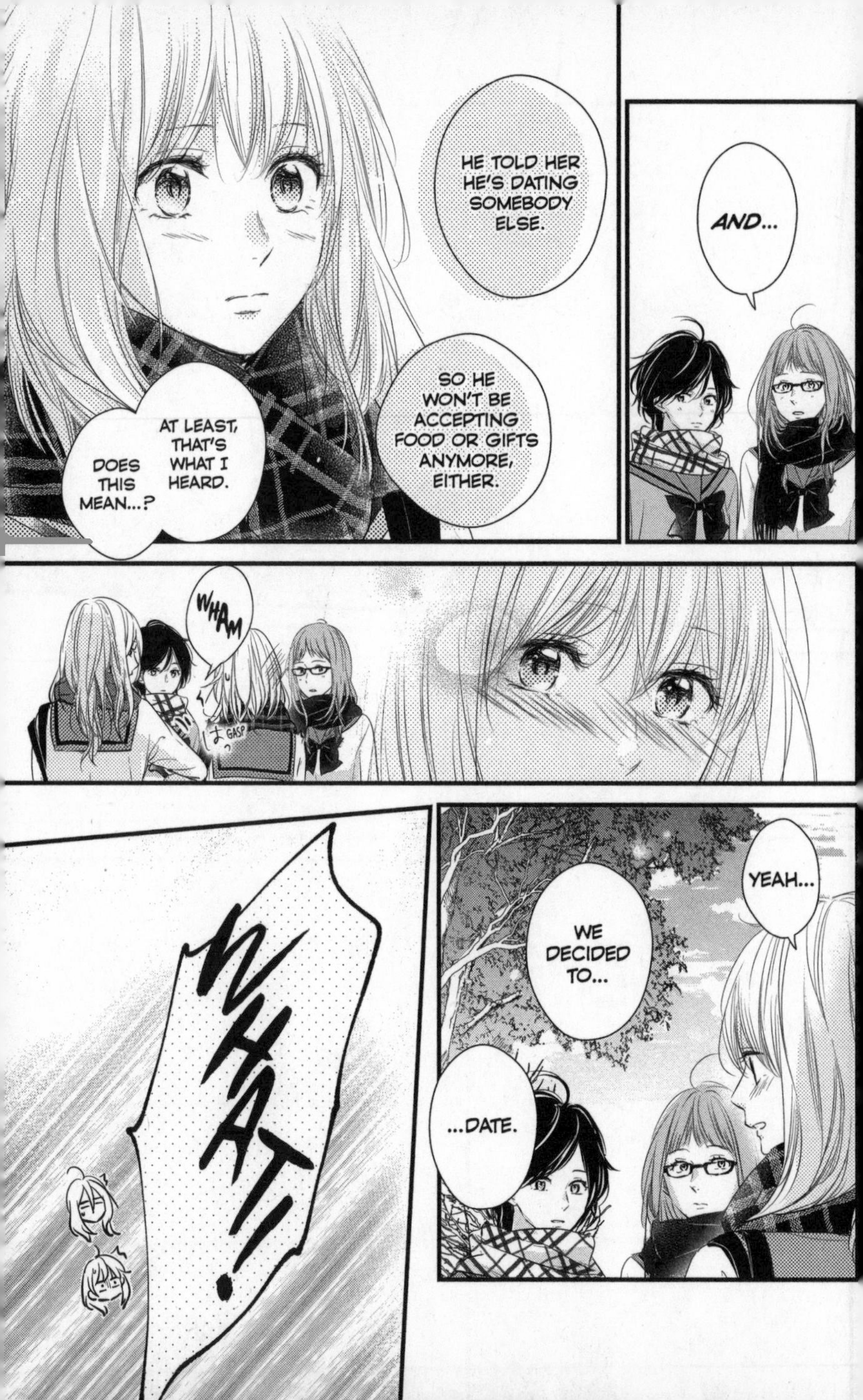
AND...
HE TOLD HER HE'S DATING SOMEBODY ELSE.
SO HE WON'T BE ACCEPTING FOOD OR GIFTS ANYMORE, EITHER.
AT LEAST, THAT'S WHAT I HEARD.
DOES THIS MEAN...?
WHAM
は GASP
YEAH...
WE DECIDED TO...
...DATE.
WHAT!!

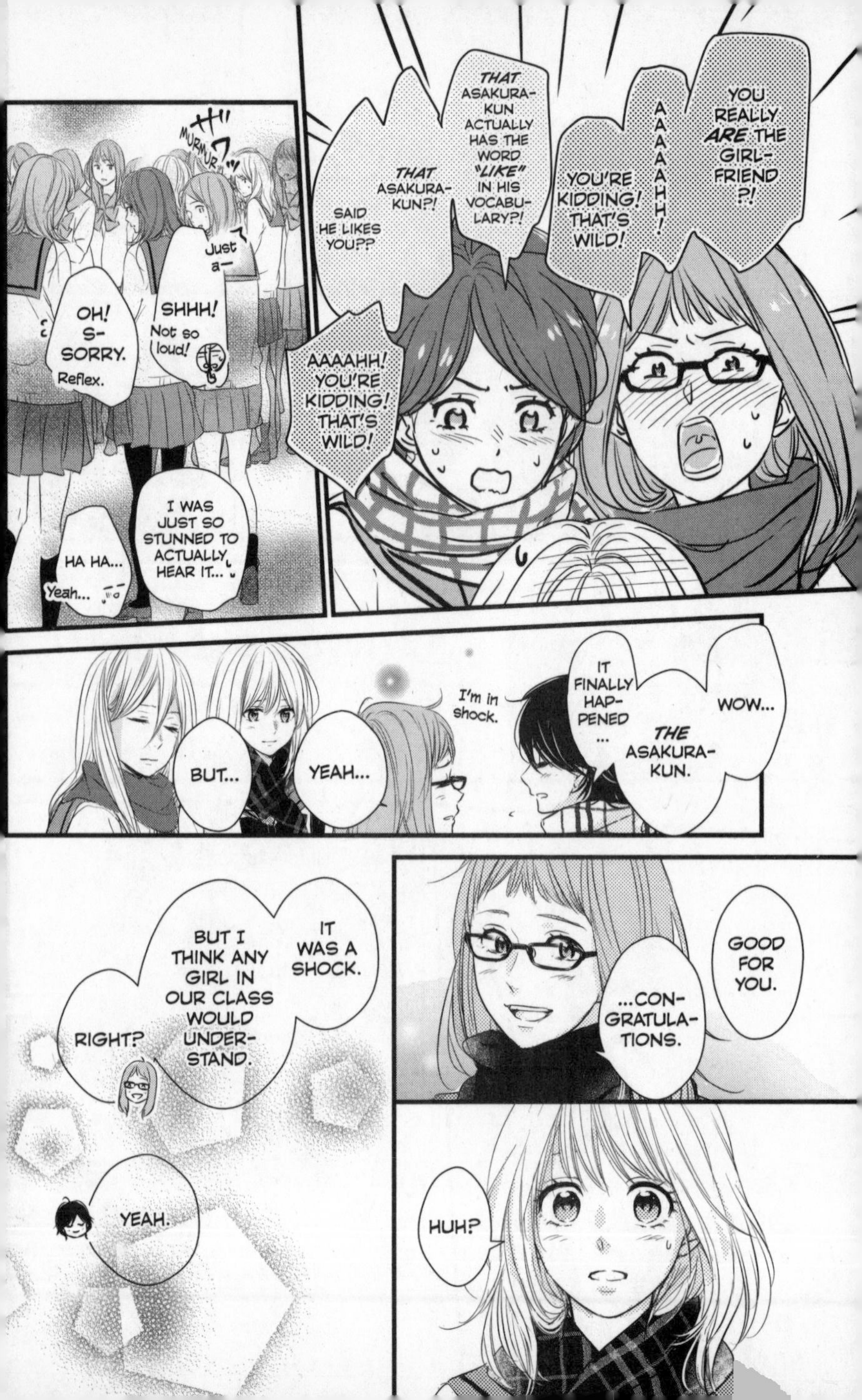
YOU REALLY ARE THE GIRL-FRIEND?!
AAAAAHH!
YOU'RE KIDDING! THAT'S WILD!
THAT ASAKURA-KUN ACTUALLY HAS THE WORD "LIKE" IN HIS VOCABULARY?!
THAT ASAKURA-KUN?!
SAID HE LIKES YOU??
AAAAHH! YOU'RE KIDDING! THAT'S WILD!
MURMUR
Just a—
SHHH! Not so loud!
OH! S-SORRY.
Reflex.
I WAS JUST SO STUNNED TO ACTUALLY HEAR IT...
HA HA...
Yeah...
WOW...
THE ASAKURA-KUN.
IT FINALLY HAPPENED...
I'm in shock.
YEAH...
BUT...
GOOD FOR YOU.
...CONGRATULATIONS.
HUH?
IT WAS A SHOCK.
BUT I THINK ANY GIRL IN OUR CLASS WOULD UNDERSTAND.
RIGHT?
YEAH.

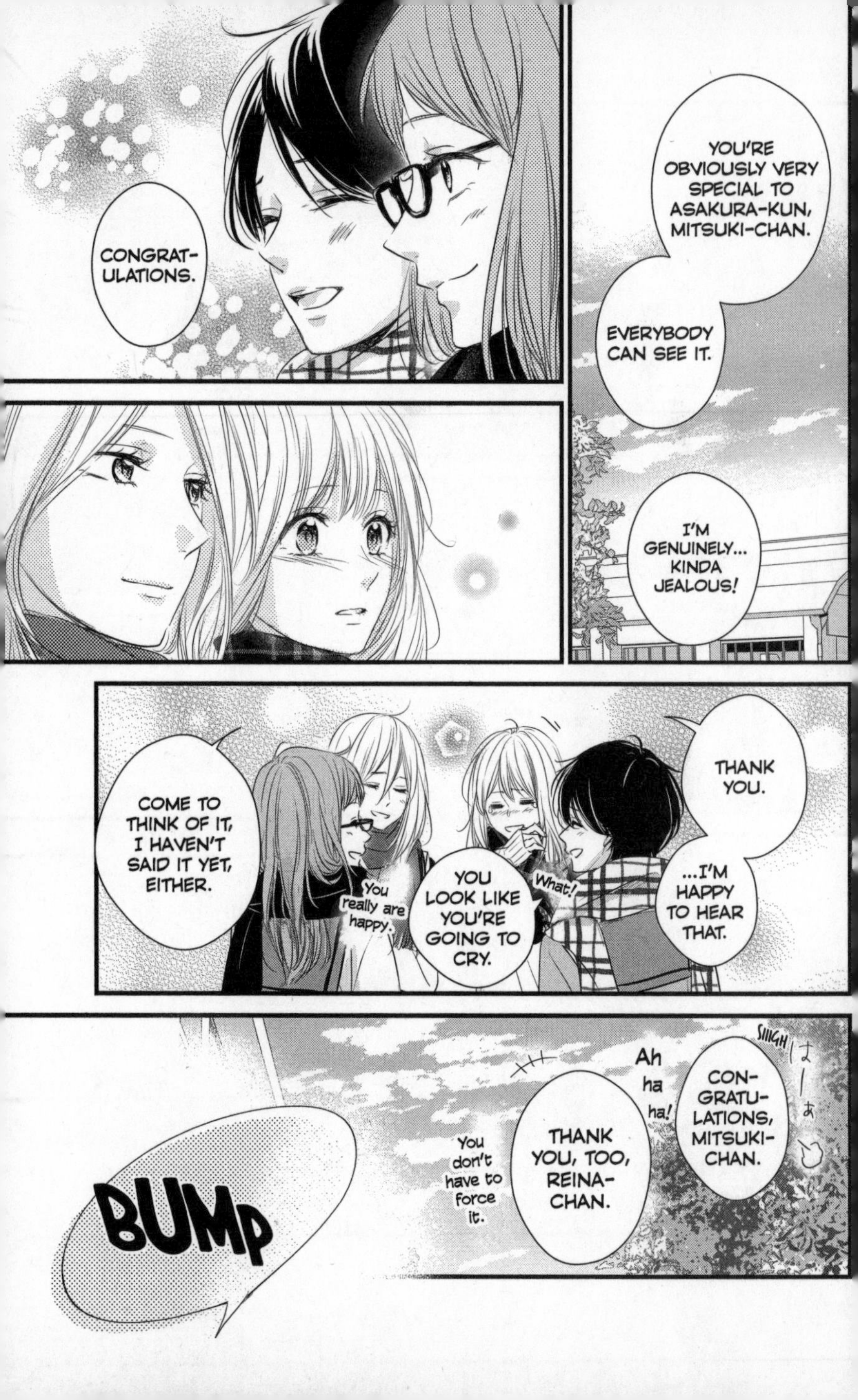

YOU'RE OBVIOUSLY VERY SPECIAL TO ASAKURA-KUN, MITSUKI-CHAN.
EVERYBODY CAN SEE IT.
I'M GENUINELY... KINDA JEALOUS!
CONGRAT-ULATIONS.
THANK YOU.
...I'M HAPPY TO HEAR THAT.
What!
YOU LOOK LIKE YOU'RE GOING TO CRY.
You really are happy.
COME TO THINK OF IT, I HAVEN'T SAID IT YET, EITHER.
SIIGH はーあ
CON-GRATU-LATIONS, MITSUKI-CHAN.
Ah ha ha!
THANK YOU, TOO, REINA-CHAN.
You don't have to force it.
BUMP

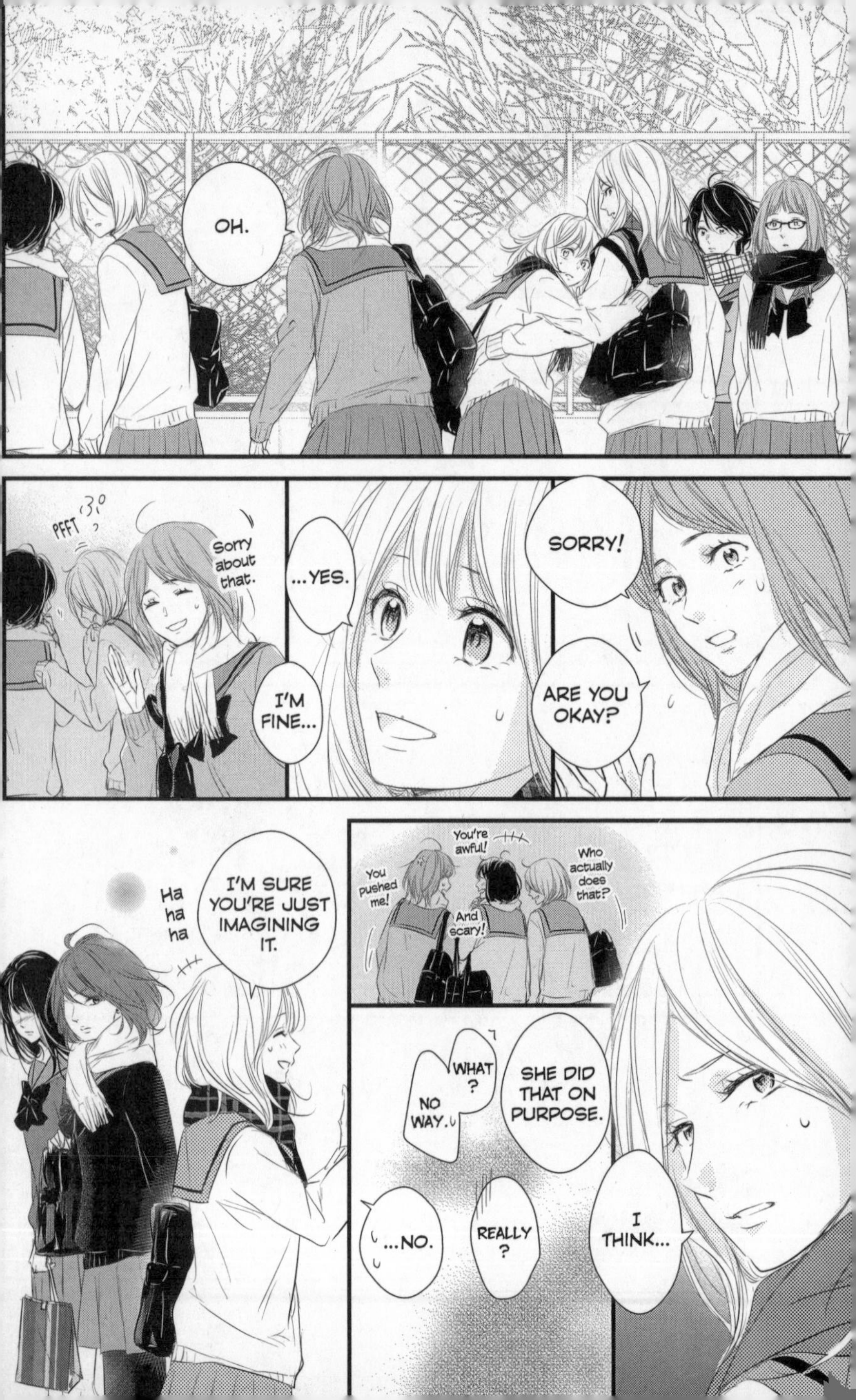
OH.
SORRY!
ARE YOU OKAY?
...YES.
I'M FINE...
PFFT
Sorry about that.
Who actually does that?
You're awful!
You pushed me!
And scary!
I THINK...
SHE DID THAT ON PURPOSE.
WHAT? NO WAY.
REALLY?
...NO.
I'M SURE YOU'RE JUST IMAGINING IT.
Ha ha ha

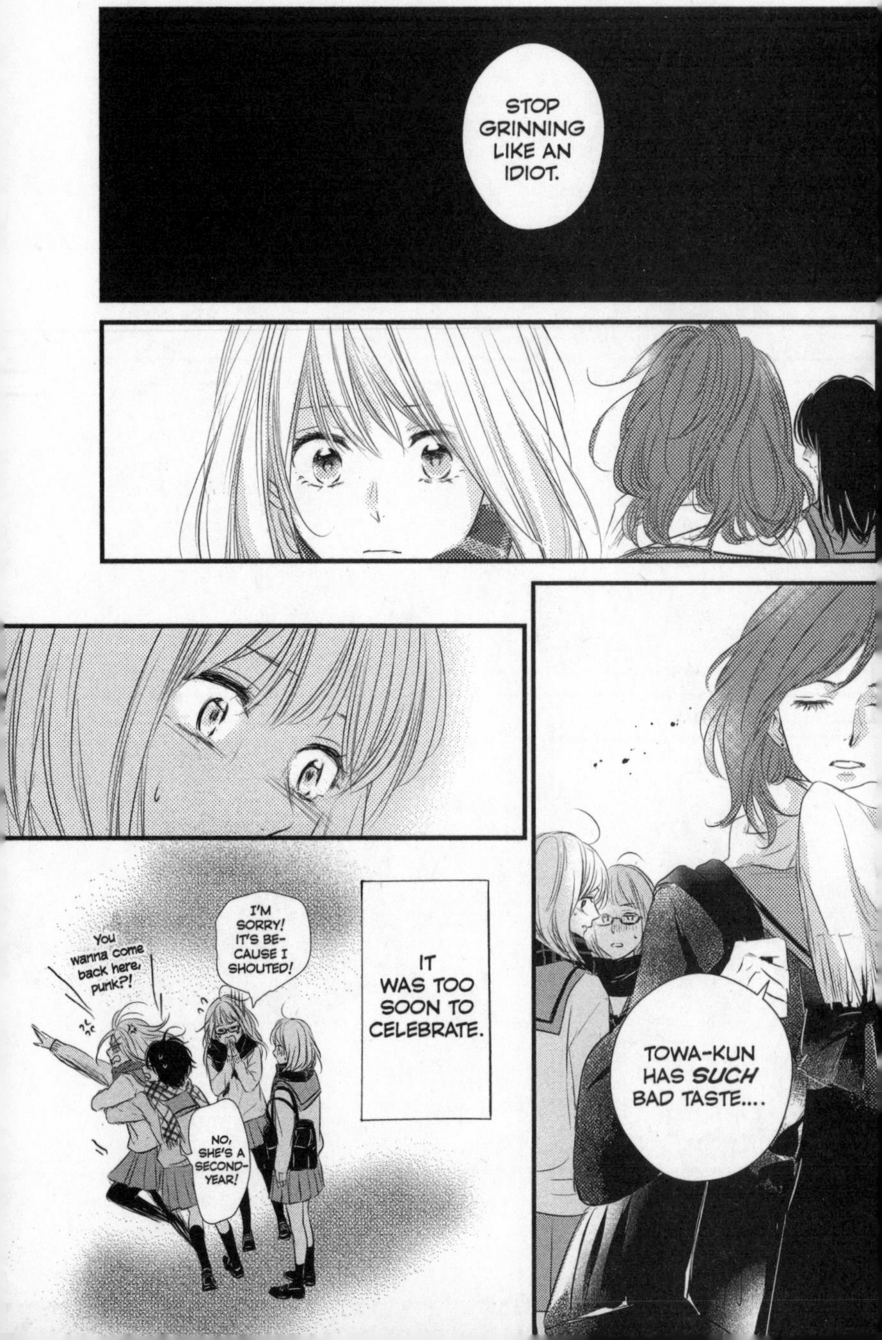
STOP GRINNING LIKE AN IDIOT.
TOWA-KUN HAS SUCH BAD TASTE....
IT WAS TOO SOON TO CELEBRATE.
I'M SORRY! IT'S BE-CAUSE I SHOUTED!
You wanna come back here, punk?!
NO, SHE'S A SECOND-YEAR!

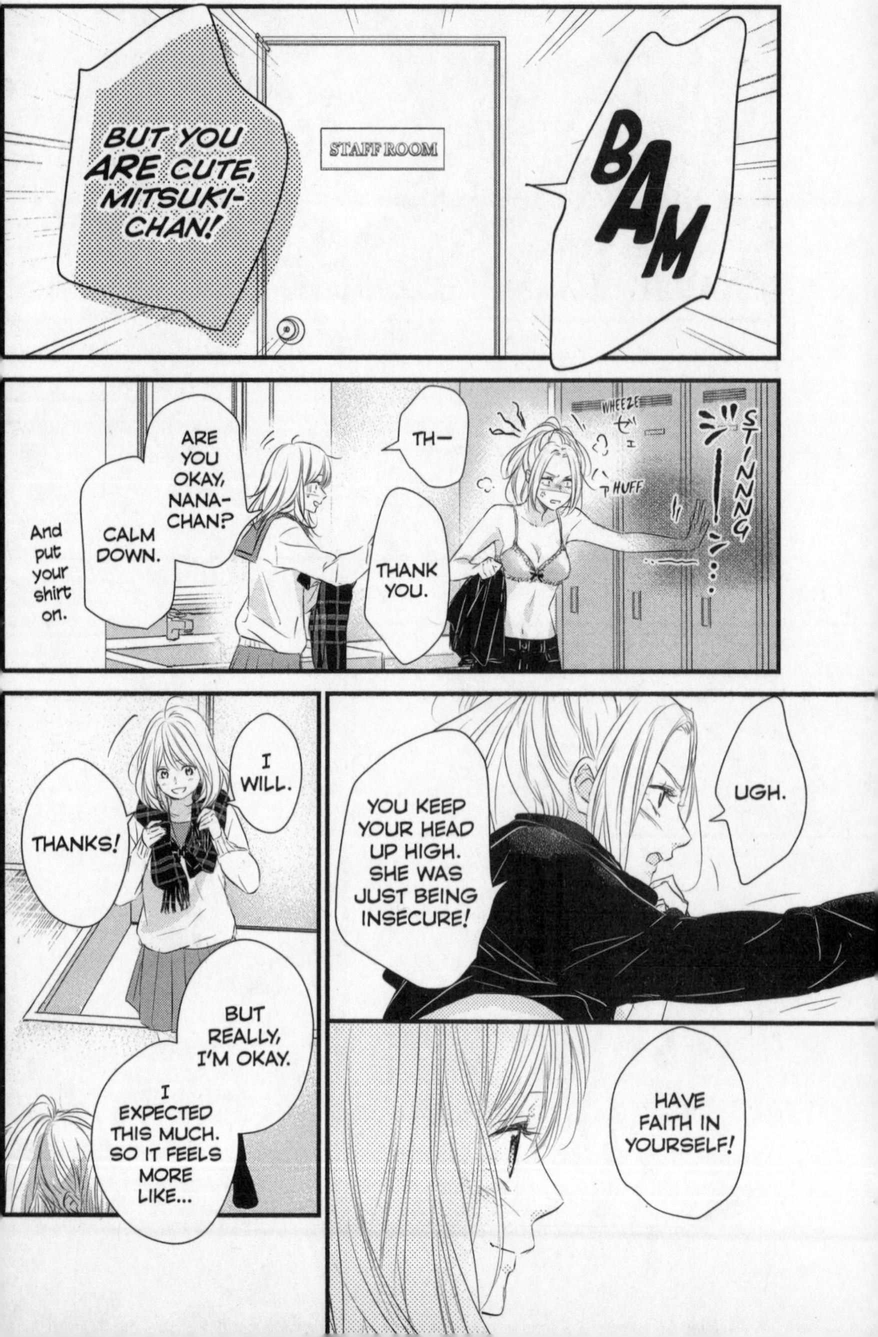
BAM
STAFF ROOM
BUT YOU ARE CUTE, MITSUKI-CHAN!
STINNNG
WHEEZE
HUFF
TH—
THANK YOU.
ARE YOU OKAY, NANA-CHAN?
CALM DOWN.
And put your shirt on.
UGH.
YOU KEEP YOUR HEAD UP HIGH. SHE WAS JUST BEING INSECURE!
HAVE FAITH IN YOURSELF!
I WILL.
THANKS!
BUT REALLY, I'M OKAY.
I EXPECTED THIS MUCH. SO IT FEELS MORE LIKE...

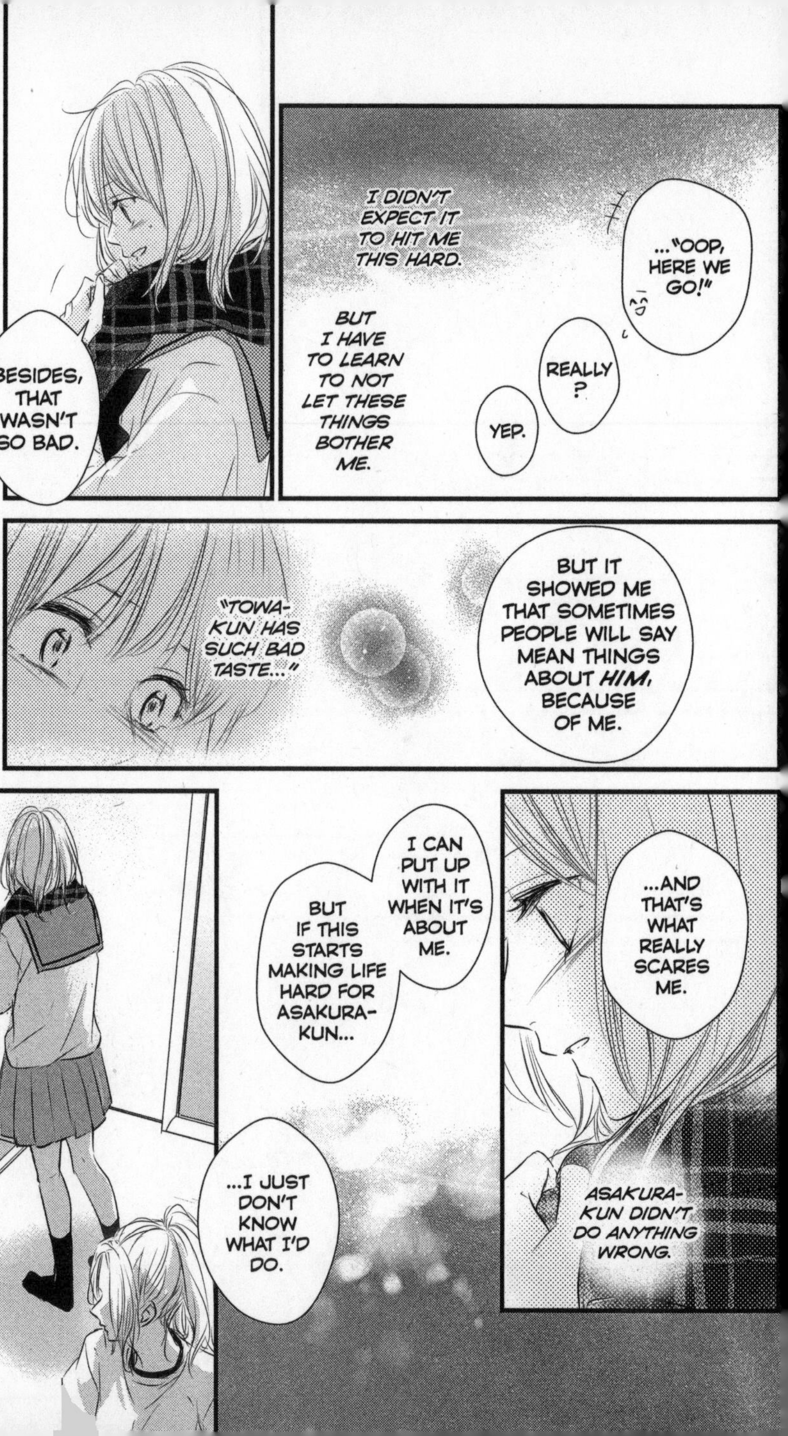
..."OOP, HERE WE GO!"
REALLY?
YEP.
I DIDN'T EXPECT IT TO HIT ME THIS HARD.
BUT I HAVE TO LEARN TO NOT LET THESE THINGS BOTHER ME.
BESIDES, THAT WASN'T SO BAD.
BUT IT SHOWED ME THAT SOMETIMES PEOPLE WILL SAY MEAN THINGS ABOUT *HIM*, BECAUSE OF ME.
"TOWA-KUN HAS SUCH BAD TASTE..."
...AND THAT'S WHAT REALLY SCARES ME.
ASAKURA-KUN DIDN'T DO ANYTHING WRONG.
I CAN PUT UP WITH IT WHEN IT'S ABOUT ME.
BUT IF THIS STARTS MAKING LIFE HARD FOR ASAKURA-KUN...
...I JUST DON'T KNOW WHAT I'D DO.

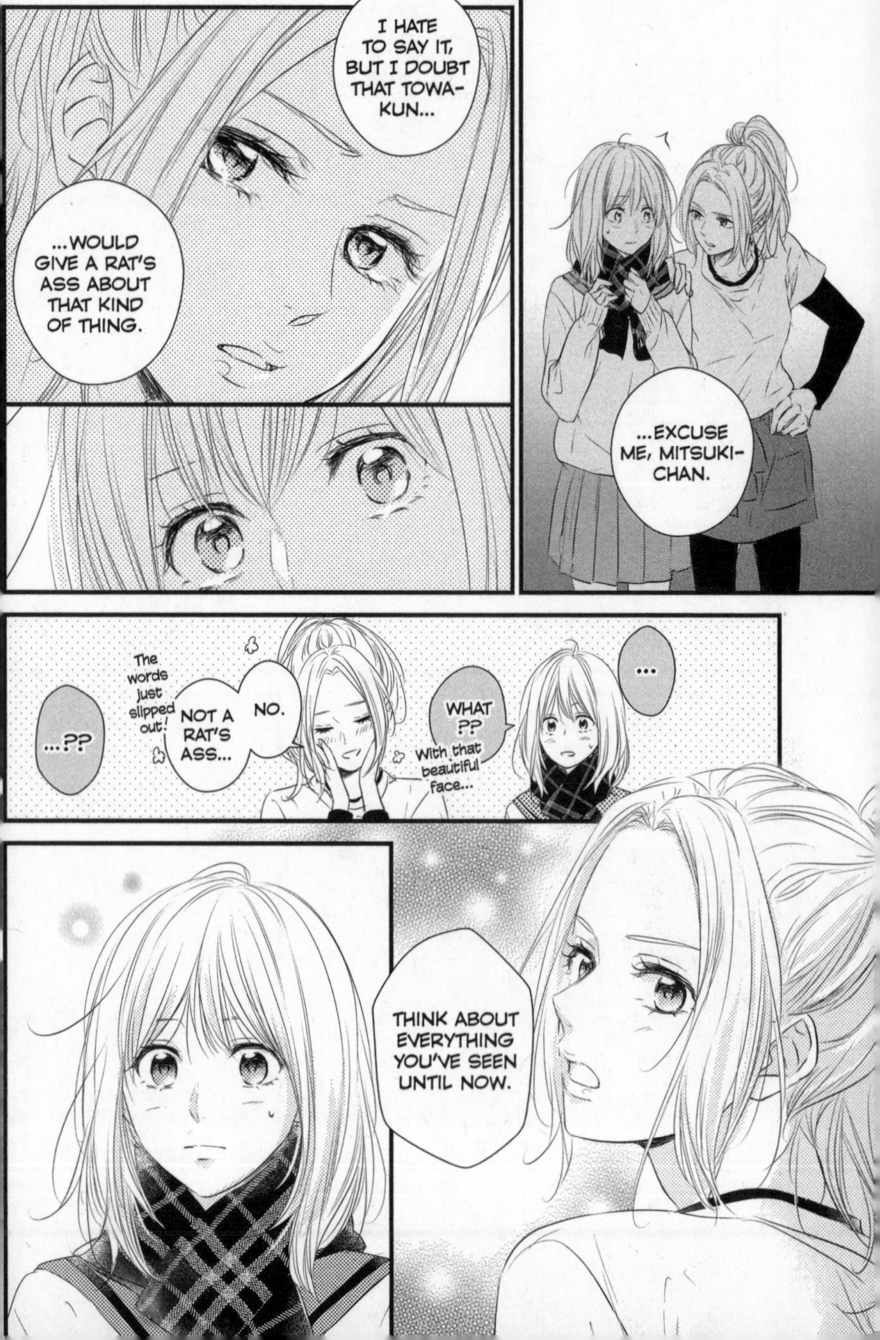
...EXCUSE ME, MITSUKI-CHAN.
I HATE TO SAY IT, BUT I DOUBT THAT TOWA-KUN...
...WOULD GIVE A RAT'S ASS ABOUT THAT KIND OF THING.
...
WHAT ??
With that beautiful face...
NO.
NOT A RAT'S ASS...
The words just slipped out!
...??
THINK ABOUT EVERYTHING YOU'VE SEEN UNTIL NOW.

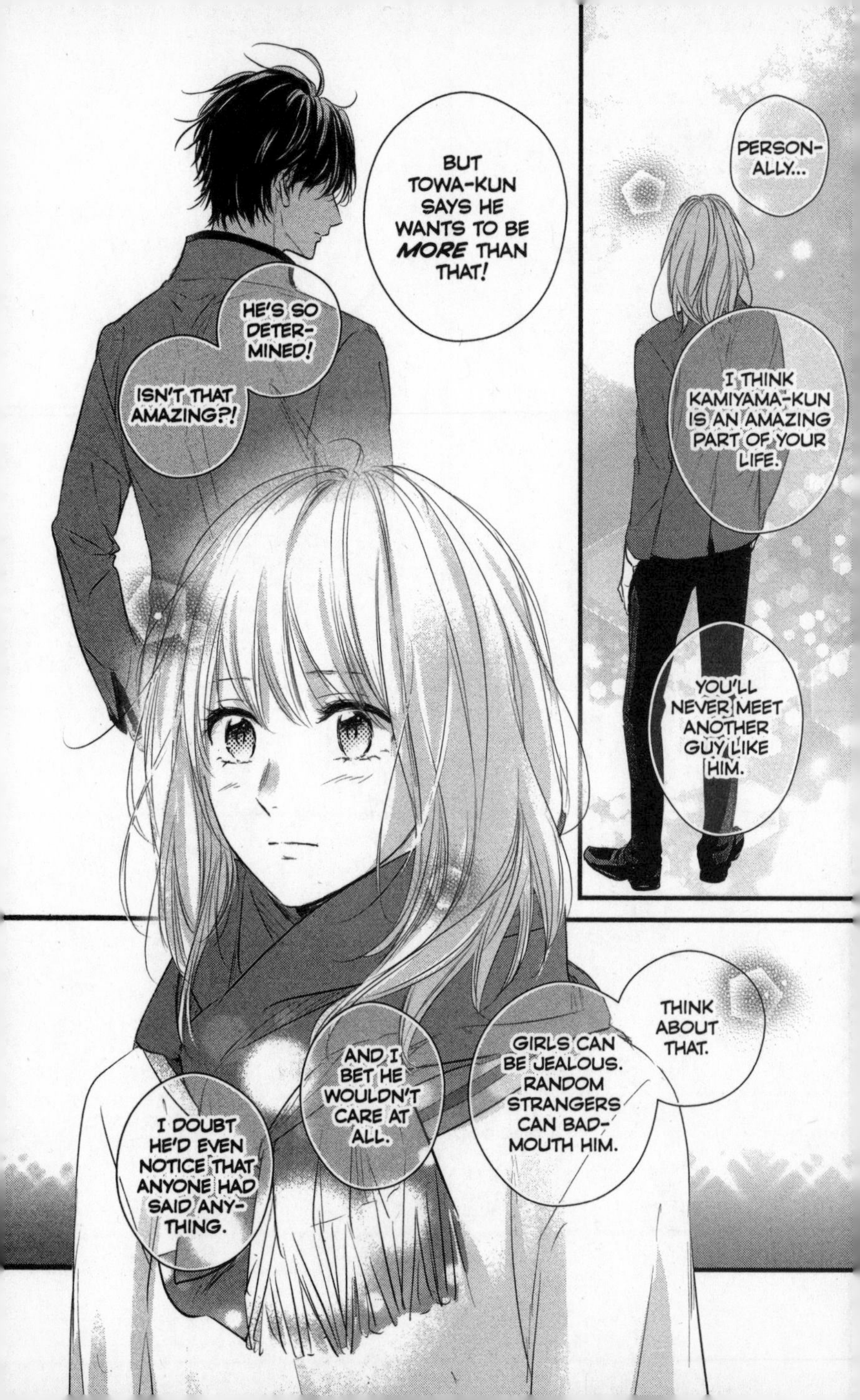
PERSON-ALLY...
I THINK KAMIYAMA-KUN IS AN AMAZING PART OF YOUR LIFE.
YOU'LL NEVER MEET ANOTHER GUY LIKE HIM.
BUT TOWA-KUN SAYS HE WANTS TO BE *MORE* THAN THAT!
HE'S SO DETER-MINED!
ISN'T THAT AMAZING?!
THINK ABOUT THAT.
GIRLS CAN BE JEALOUS. RANDOM STRANGERS CAN BAD-MOUTH HIM.
AND I BET HE WOULDN'T CARE AT ALL.
I DOUBT HE'D EVEN NOTICE THAT ANYONE HAD SAID ANY-THING.

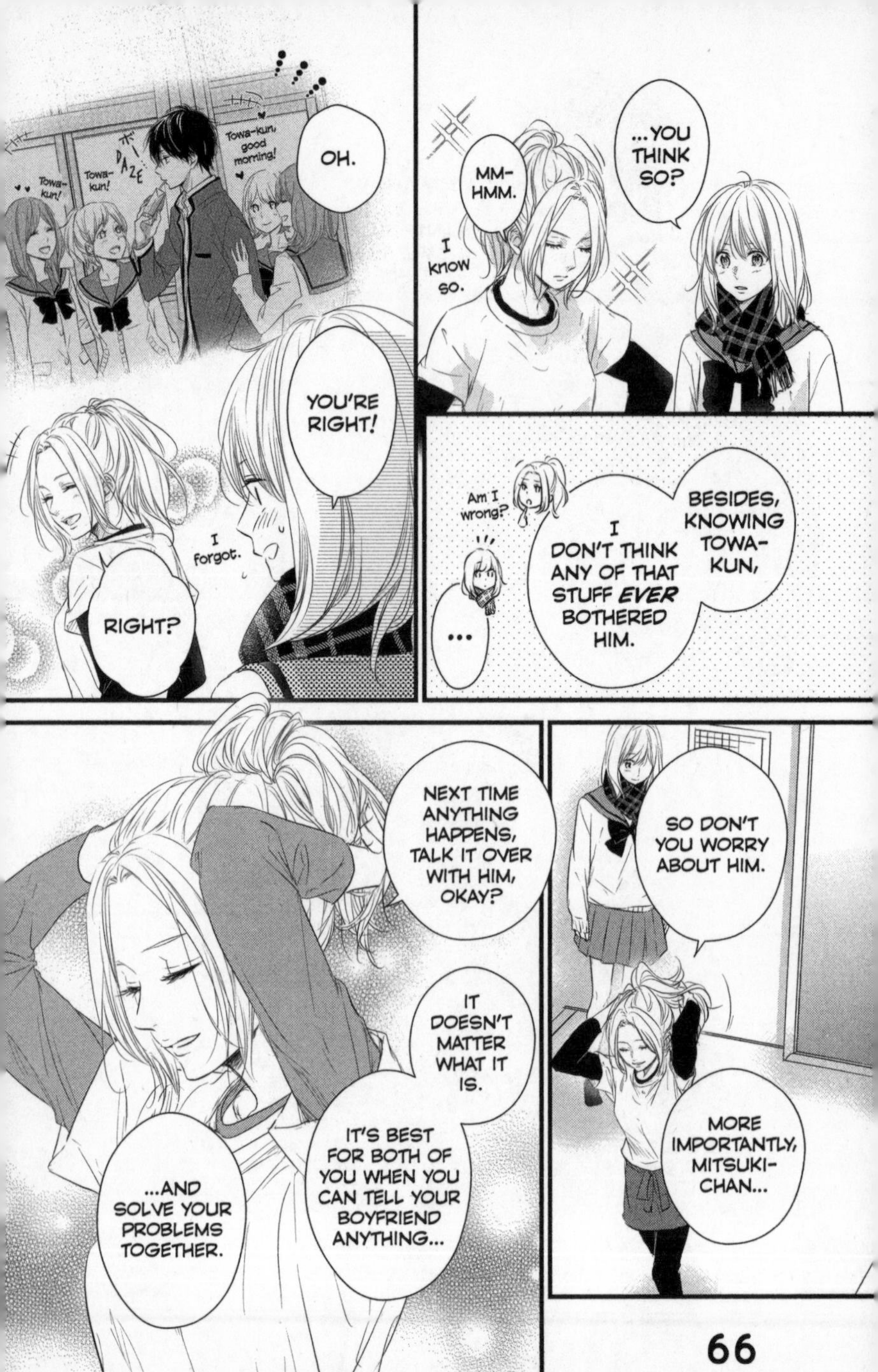
...YOU THINK SO?
MM-HMM.
I know so.
BESIDES, KNOWING TOWA-KUN,
I DON'T THINK ANY OF THAT STUFF *EVER* BOTHERED HIM.
Am I wrong?
...
OH.
Towa-kun, good morning!
DAZE
Towa-kun!
Towa-kun!
YOU'RE RIGHT!
I forgot.
RIGHT?
SO DON'T YOU WORRY ABOUT HIM.
MORE IMPORTANTLY, MITSUKI-CHAN...
NEXT TIME ANYTHING HAPPENS, TALK IT OVER WITH HIM, OKAY?
IT DOESN'T MATTER WHAT IT IS.
IT'S BEST FOR BOTH OF YOU WHEN YOU CAN TELL YOUR BOYFRIEND ANYTHING...
...AND SOLVE YOUR PROBLEMS TOGETHER.

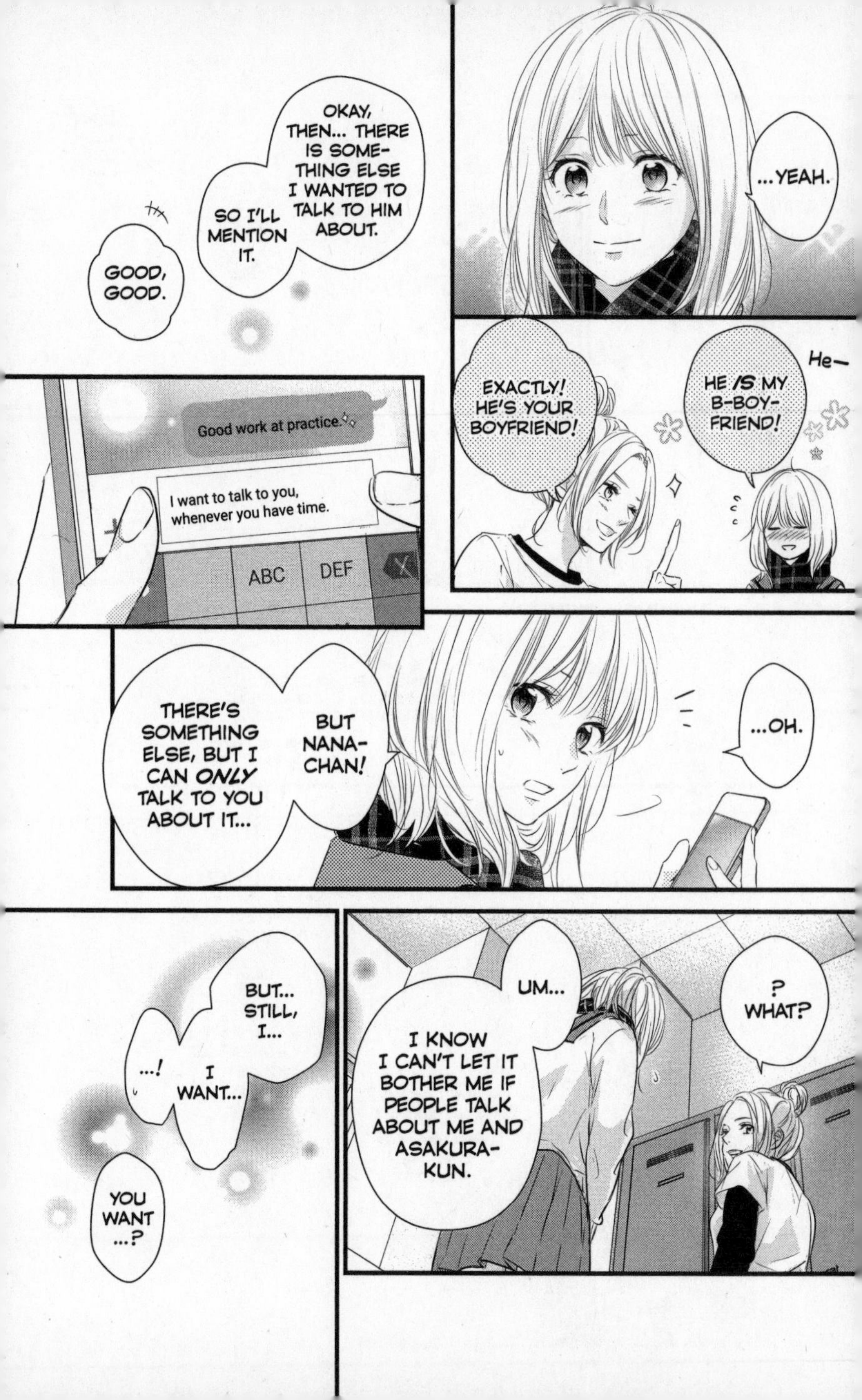
...YEAH.
OKAY, THEN... THERE IS SOME-THING ELSE I WANTED TO TALK TO HIM ABOUT.
SO I'LL MENTION IT.
GOOD, GOOD.
He—
HE *IS* MY B-BOY-FRIEND!
EXACTLY! HE'S YOUR BOYFRIEND!
Good work at practice.
I want to talk to you, whenever you have time.
ABC
DEF
...OH.
BUT NANA-CHAN!
THERE'S SOMETHING ELSE, BUT I CAN *ONLY* TALK TO YOU ABOUT IT...
? WHAT?
UM...
I KNOW I CAN'T LET IT BOTHER ME IF PEOPLE TALK ABOUT ME AND ASAKURA-KUN.
BUT... STILL, I...
I WANT...
...!
YOU WANT ...?

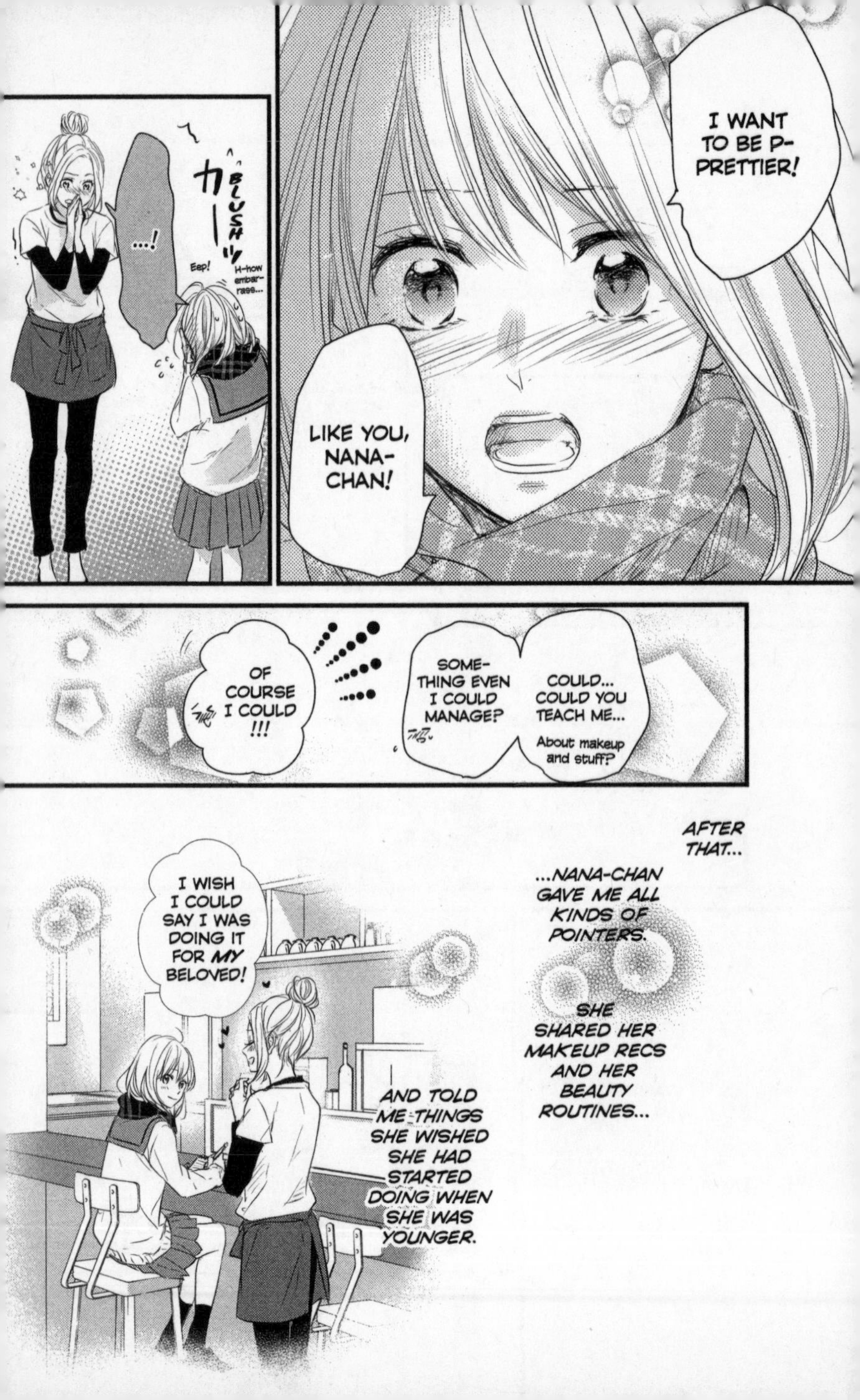
I WANT TO BE P-PRETTIER!
LIKE YOU, NANA-CHAN!
カー BLUSH ッ
...!
H-how embarrass...
Eep!
COULD... COULD YOU TEACH ME...
About makeup and stuff?
SOME-THING EVEN I COULD MANAGE?
OF COURSE I COULD!!!
AFTER THAT...
...NANA-CHAN GAVE ME ALL KINDS OF POINTERS.
SHE SHARED HER MAKEUP RECS AND HER BEAUTY ROUTINES...
AND TOLD ME THINGS SHE WISHED SHE HAD STARTED DOING WHEN SHE WAS YOUNGER.
I WISH I COULD SAY I WAS DOING IT FOR *MY* BELOVED!

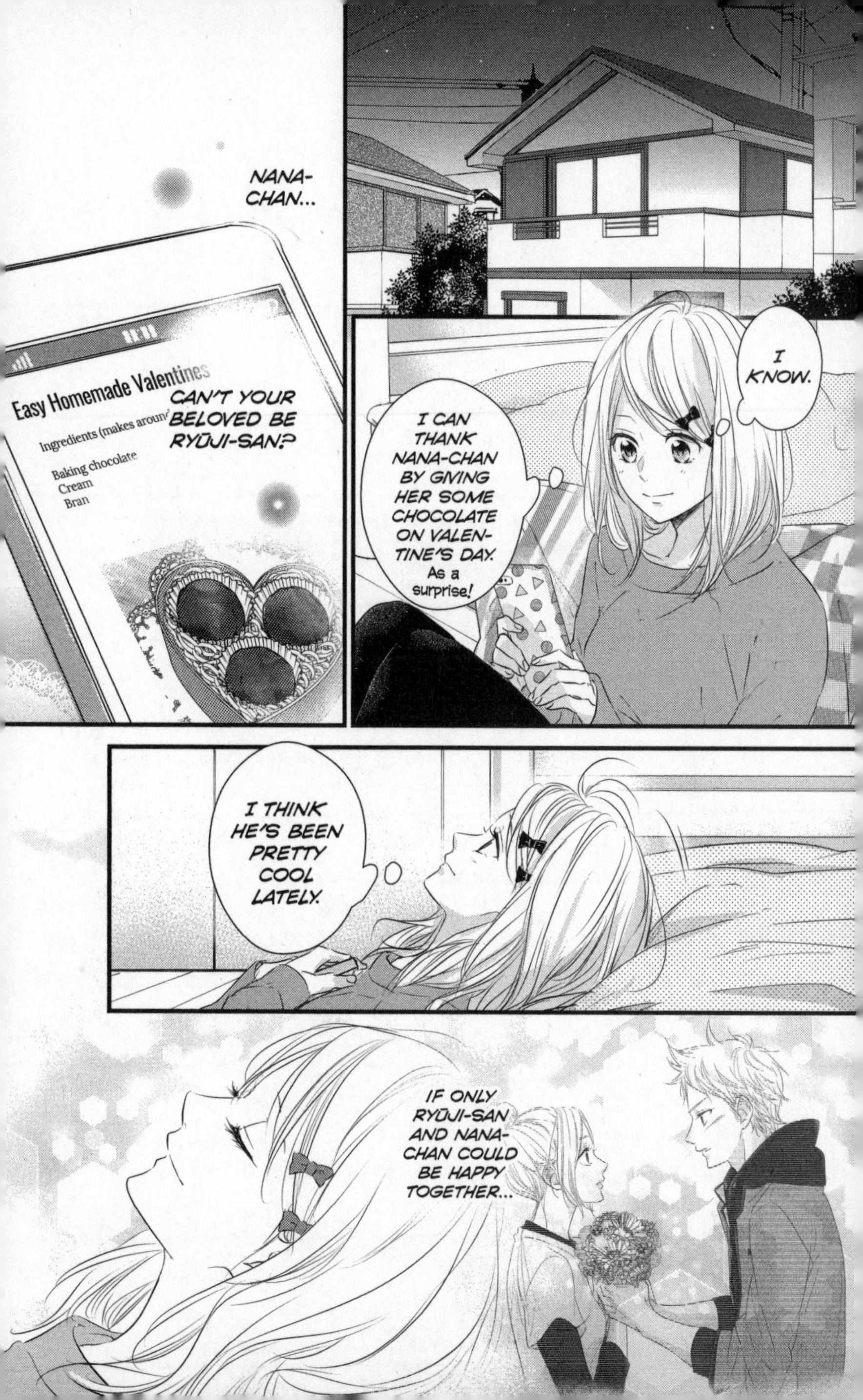
I KNOW.
I CAN THANK NANA-CHAN BY GIVING HER SOME CHOCOLATE ON VALEN-TINE'S DAY. As a surprise!
NANA-CHAN...
CAN'T YOUR BELOVED BE RYŪJI-SAN?
Easy Homemade Valentines
Ingredients (makes around
Baking chocolate
Cream
Bran
I THINK HE'S BEEN PRETTY COOL LATELY.
IF ONLY RYŪJI-SAN AND NANA-CHAN COULD BE HAPPY TOGETHER...

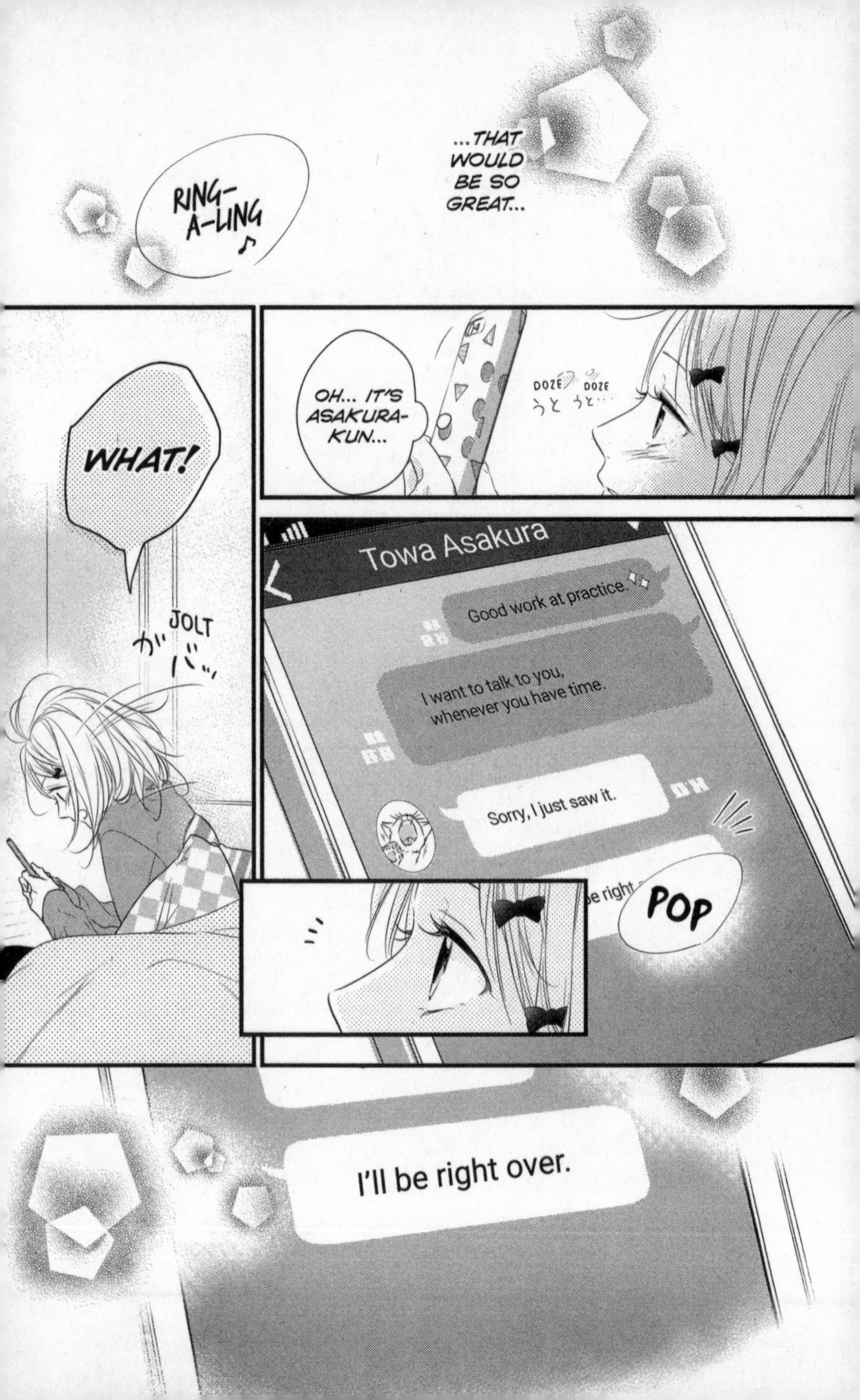
...THAT WOULD BE SO GREAT...
RING-A-LING ♪
DOZE DOZE
うと うと…
OH... IT'S ASAKURA-KUN...
Towa Asakura
Good work at practice.
I want to talk to you, whenever you have time.
Sorry, I just saw it.
POP
WHAT!
JOLT
ガバッ
I'll be right over.

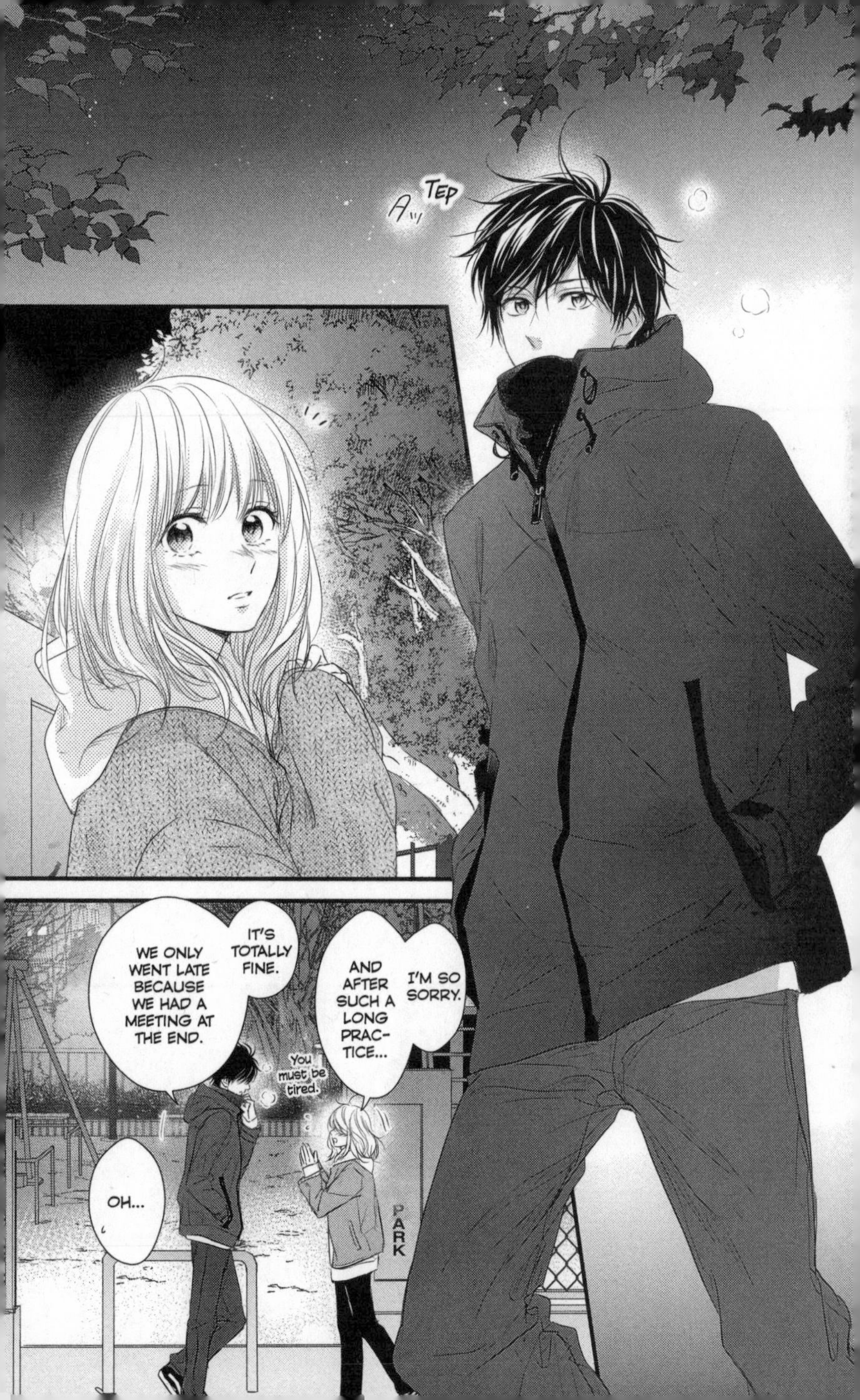
TEP
I'M SO SORRY.
AND AFTER SUCH A LONG PRACTICE...
You must be tired.
IT'S TOTALLY FINE.
WE ONLY WENT LATE BECAUSE WE HAD A MEETING AT THE END.
OH...
PARK

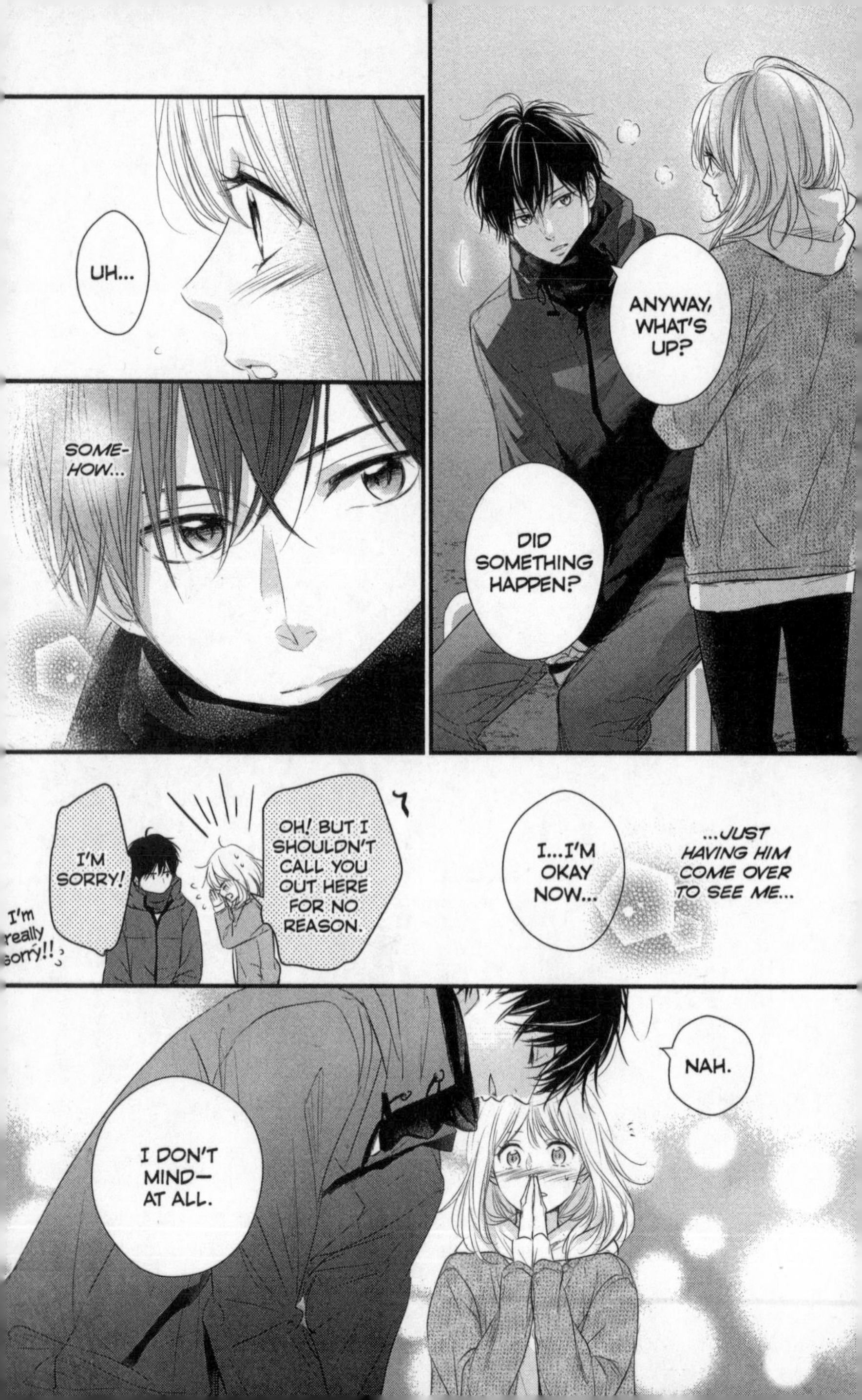
ANYWAY, WHAT'S UP?
DID SOMETHING HAPPEN?
UH...
SOME-HOW...
...JUST HAVING HIM COME OVER TO SEE ME...
I...I'M OKAY NOW...
OH! BUT I SHOULDN'T CALL YOU OUT HERE FOR NO REASON.
I'M SORRY!
I'm really sorry!!
NAH.
I DON'T MIND— AT ALL.

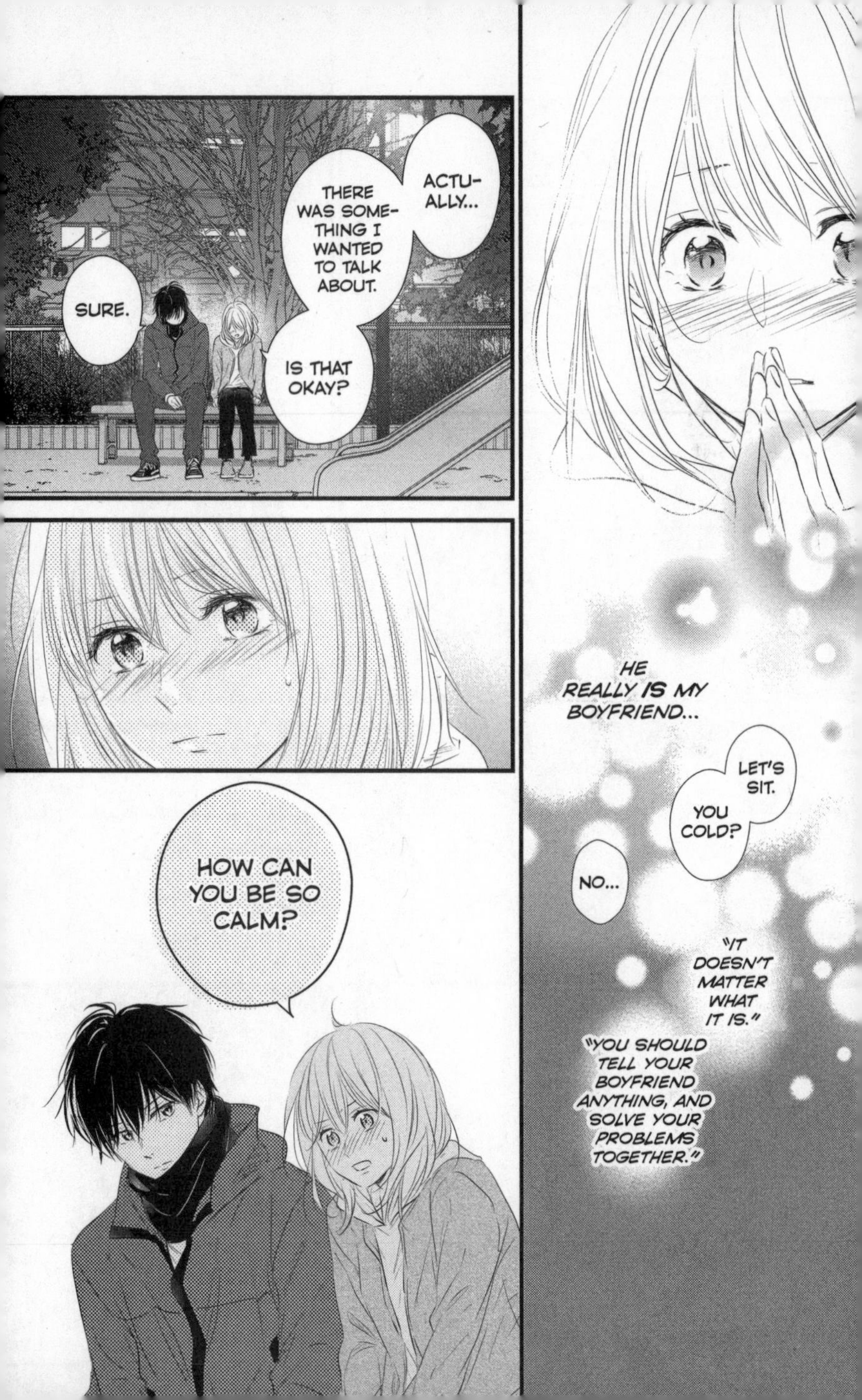
HE REALLY *IS* MY BOYFRIEND...
LET'S SIT.
YOU COLD?
NO...
"IT DOESN'T MATTER WHAT IT IS."
"YOU SHOULD TELL YOUR BOYFRIEND ANYTHING, AND SOLVE YOUR PROBLEMS TOGETHER."
ACTUALLY...
THERE WAS SOMETHING I WANTED TO TALK ABOUT.
IS THAT OKAY?
SURE.
HOW CAN YOU BE SO CALM?

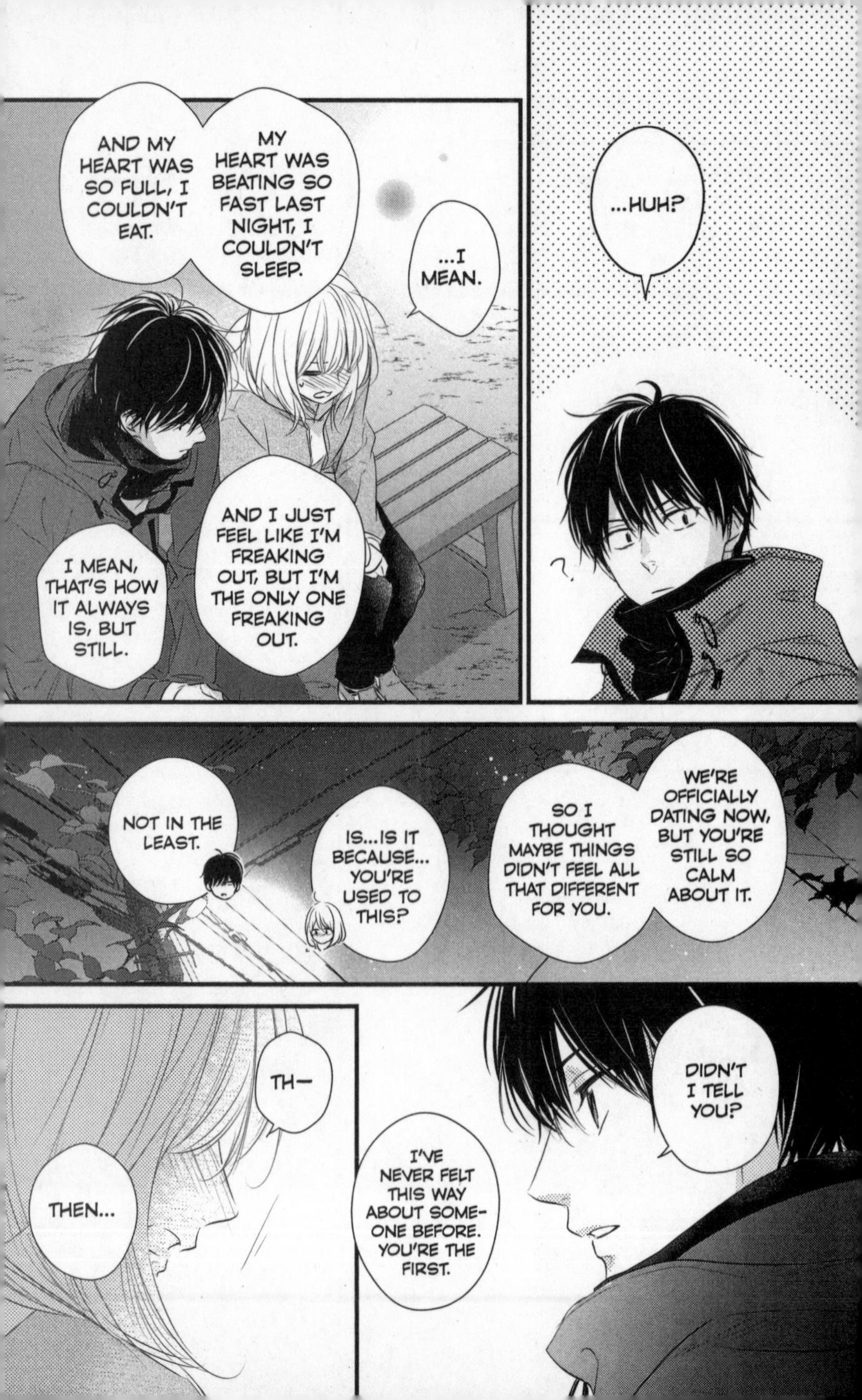

...HUH?
...I MEAN.
MY HEART WAS BEATING SO FAST LAST NIGHT, I COULDN'T SLEEP.
AND MY HEART WAS SO FULL, I COULDN'T EAT.
AND I JUST FEEL LIKE I'M FREAKING OUT, BUT I'M THE ONLY ONE FREAKING OUT.
I MEAN, THAT'S HOW IT ALWAYS IS, BUT STILL.
WE'RE OFFICIALLY DATING NOW, BUT YOU'RE STILL SO CALM ABOUT IT.
SO I THOUGHT MAYBE THINGS DIDN'T FEEL ALL THAT DIFFERENT FOR YOU.
IS...IS IT BECAUSE... YOU'RE USED TO THIS?
NOT IN THE LEAST.
DIDN'T I TELL YOU?
I'VE NEVER FELT THIS WAY ABOUT SOME-ONE BEFORE. YOU'RE THE FIRST.
TH—
THEN...

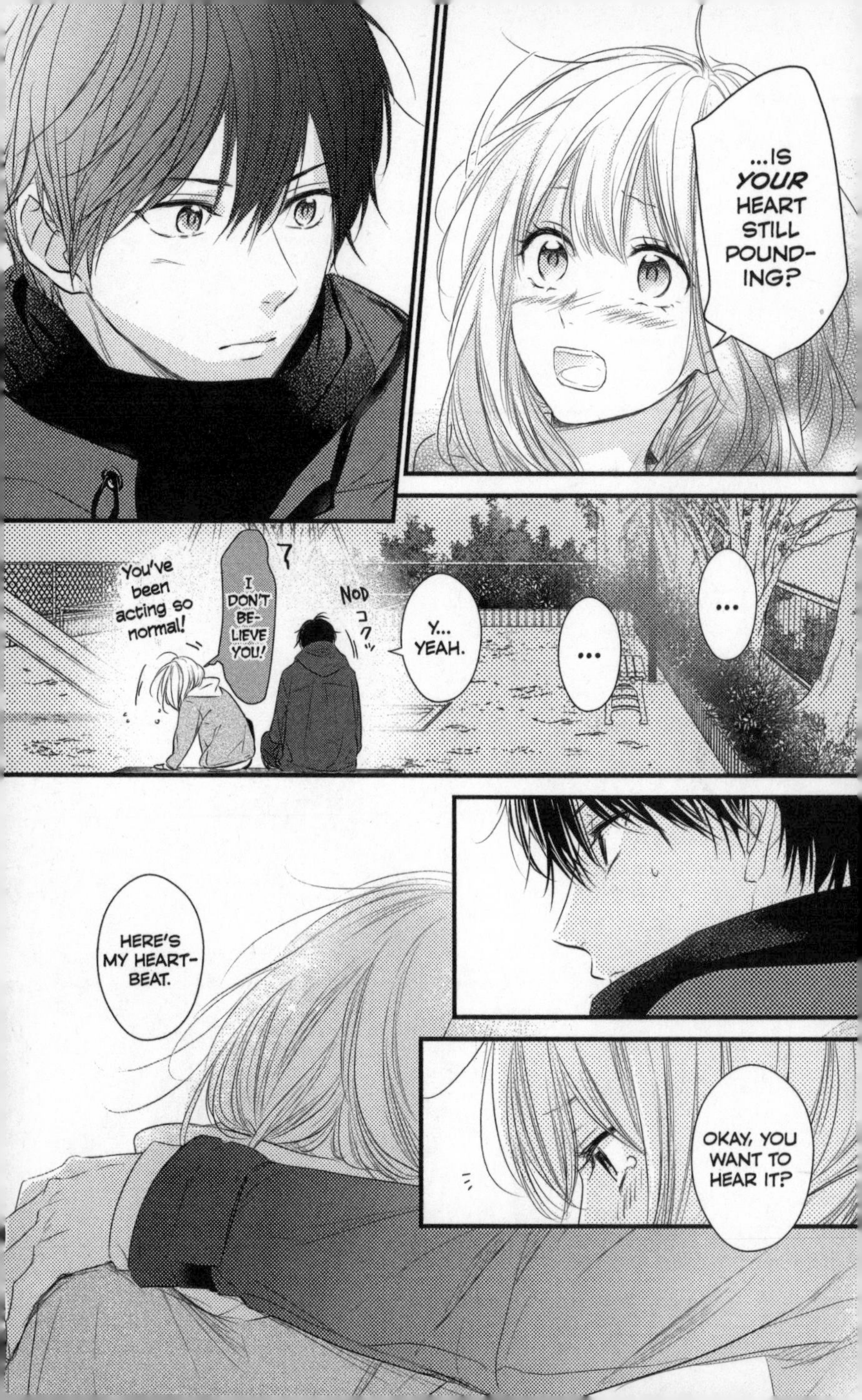
...IS YOUR HEART STILL POUNDING?
...
...
Y... YEAH.
NOD
コクッ
I DON'T BE-LIEVE YOU!
You've been acting so normal!
OKAY, YOU WANT TO HEAR IT?
HERE'S MY HEART-BEAT.

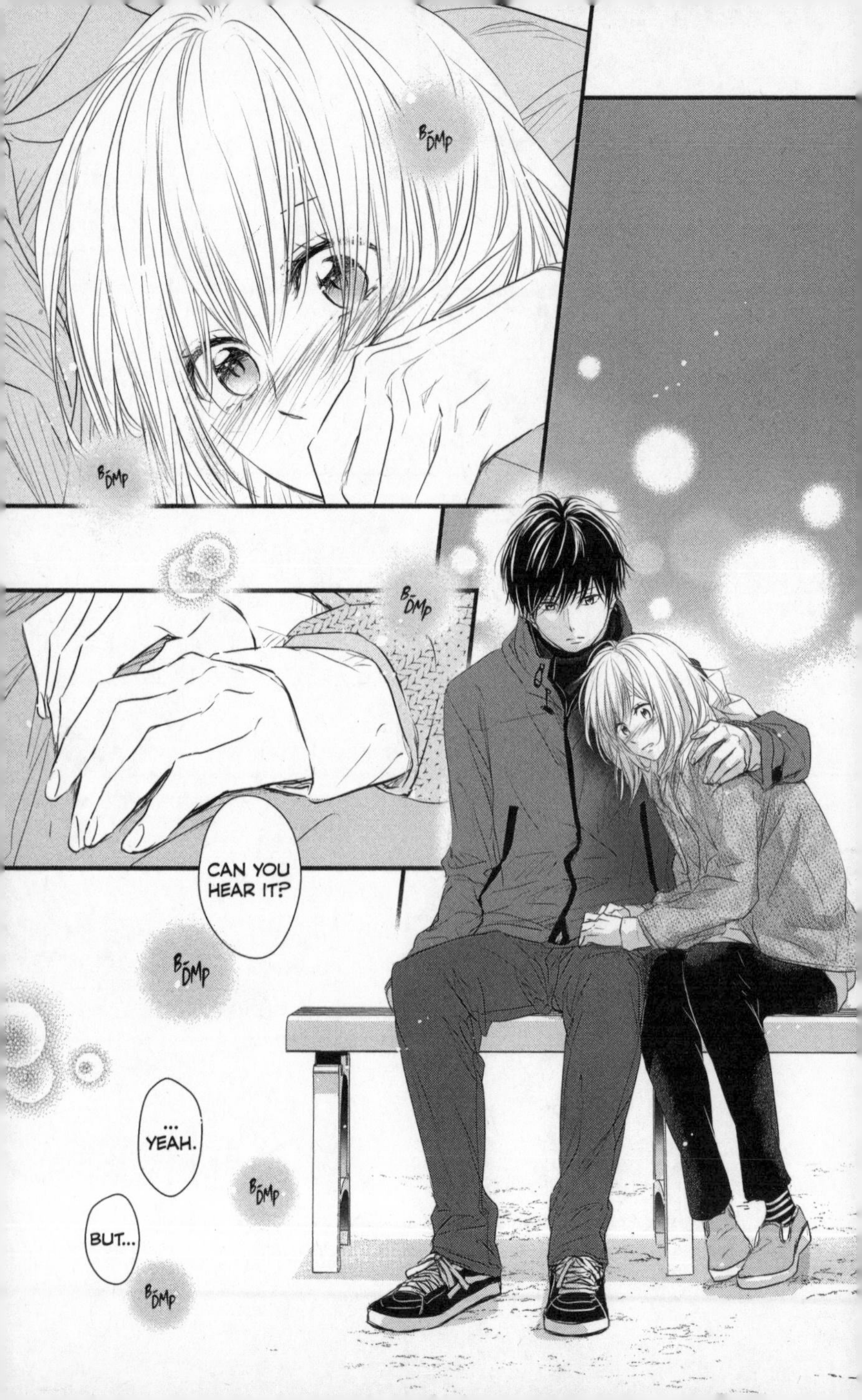
B-DMP
B-DMP
B-DMP
CAN YOU HEAR IT?
B-DMP
... YEAH.
B-DMP
BUT...
B-DMP

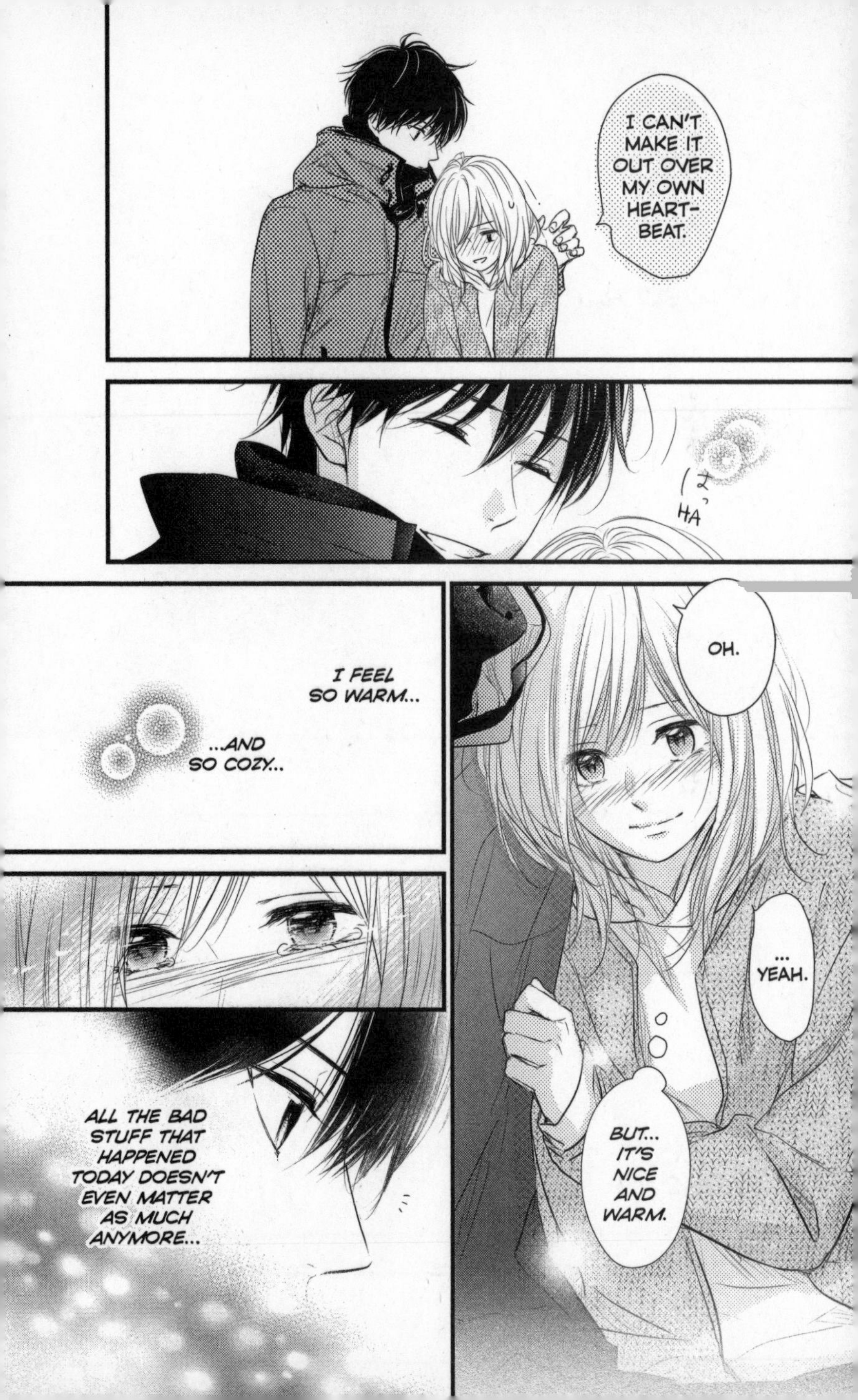
I CAN'T MAKE IT OUT OVER MY OWN HEART-BEAT.
は HA
OH.
...YEAH.
BUT... IT'S NICE AND WARM.
I FEEL SO WARM...
...AND SO COZY...
ALL THE BAD STUFF THAT HAPPENED TODAY DOESN'T EVEN MATTER AS MUCH ANYMORE...

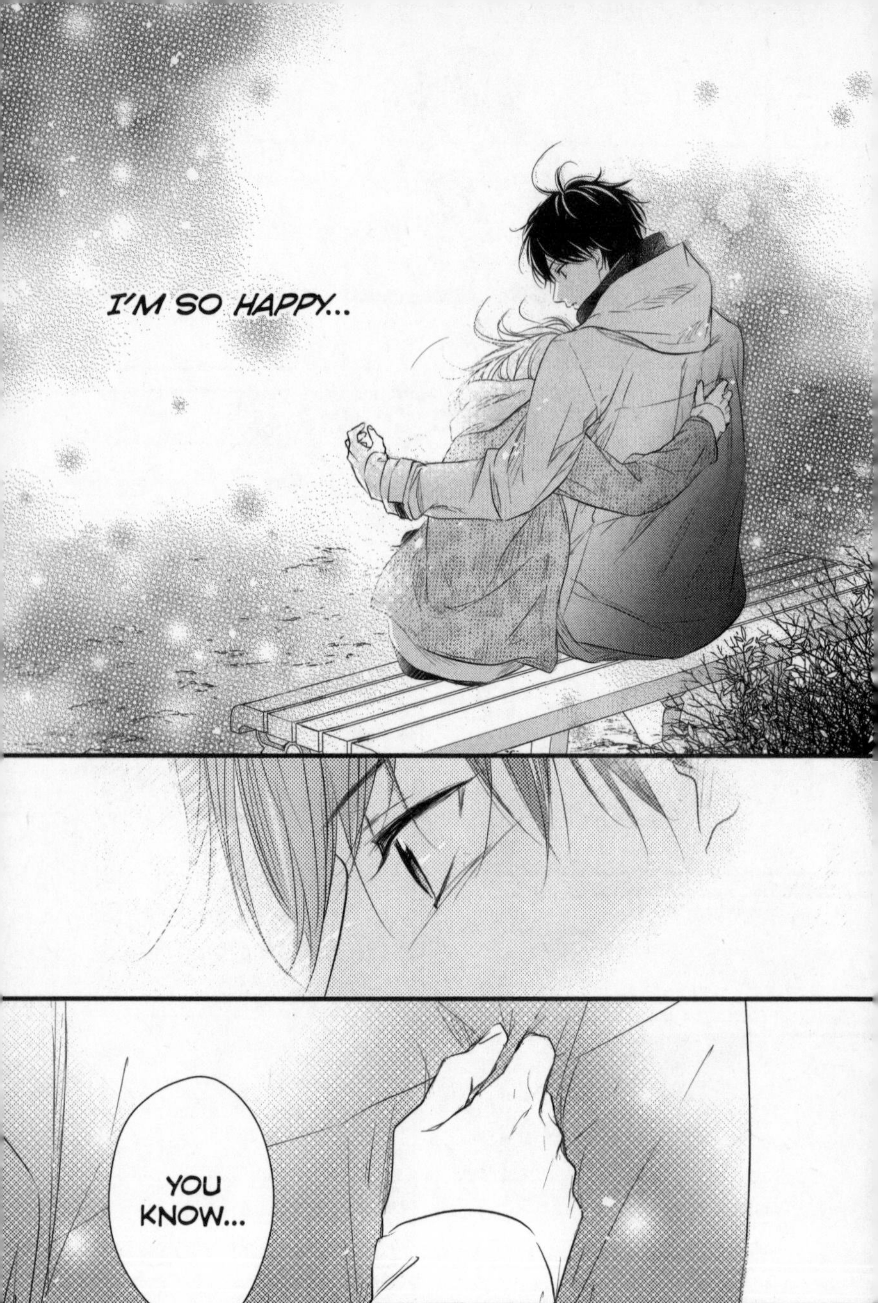
I'M SO HAPPY...
YOU KNOW...

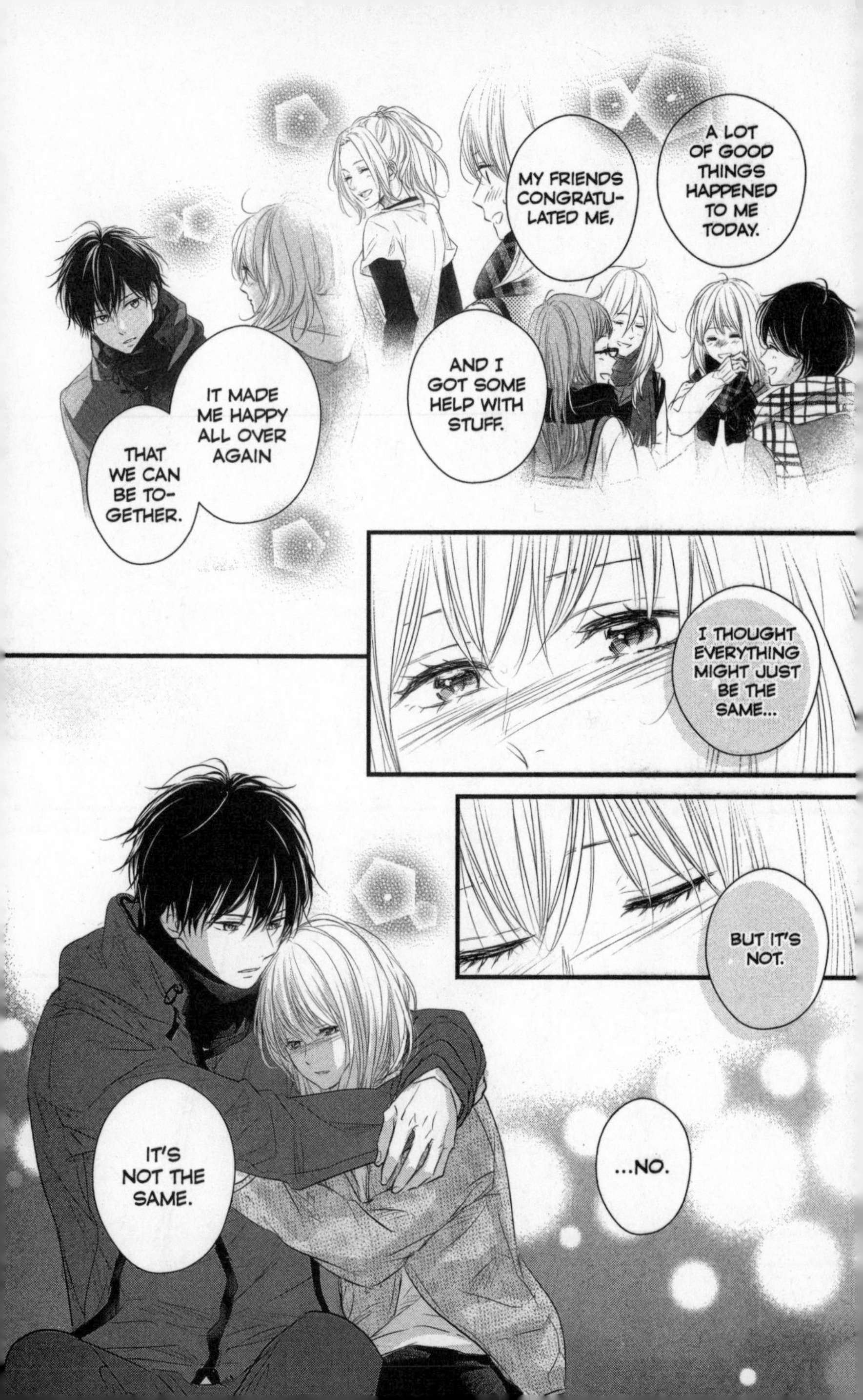
A LOT OF GOOD THINGS HAPPENED TO ME TODAY.
MY FRIENDS CONGRATULATED ME,
AND I GOT SOME HELP WITH STUFF.
IT MADE ME HAPPY ALL OVER AGAIN THAT WE CAN BE TOGETHER.
I THOUGHT EVERYTHING MIGHT JUST BE THE SAME...
BUT IT'S NOT.
...NO.
IT'S NOT THE SAME.

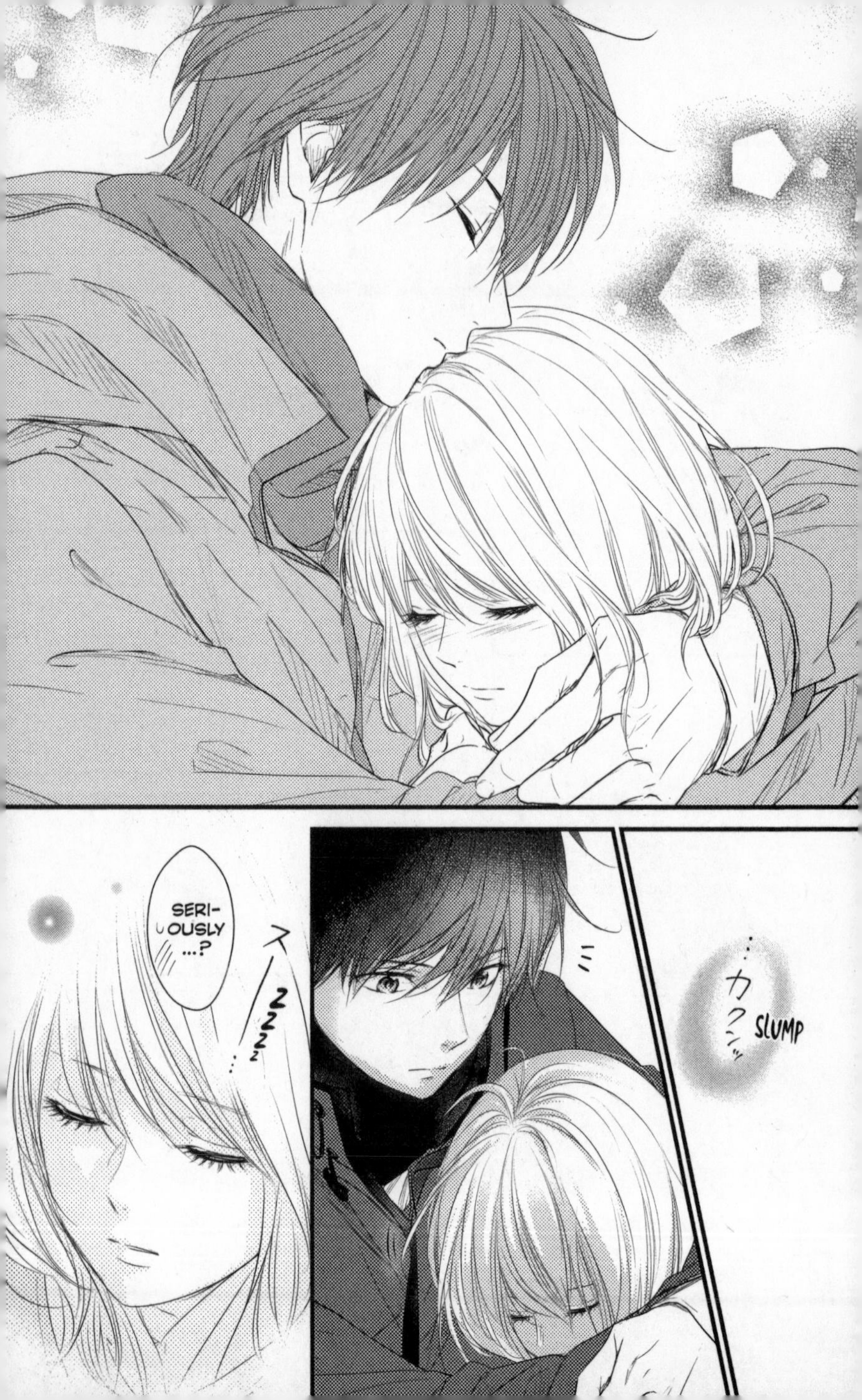
…カクンッ
SLUMP
ミ
ス—
ZZZZ
SERI-OUSLY …?

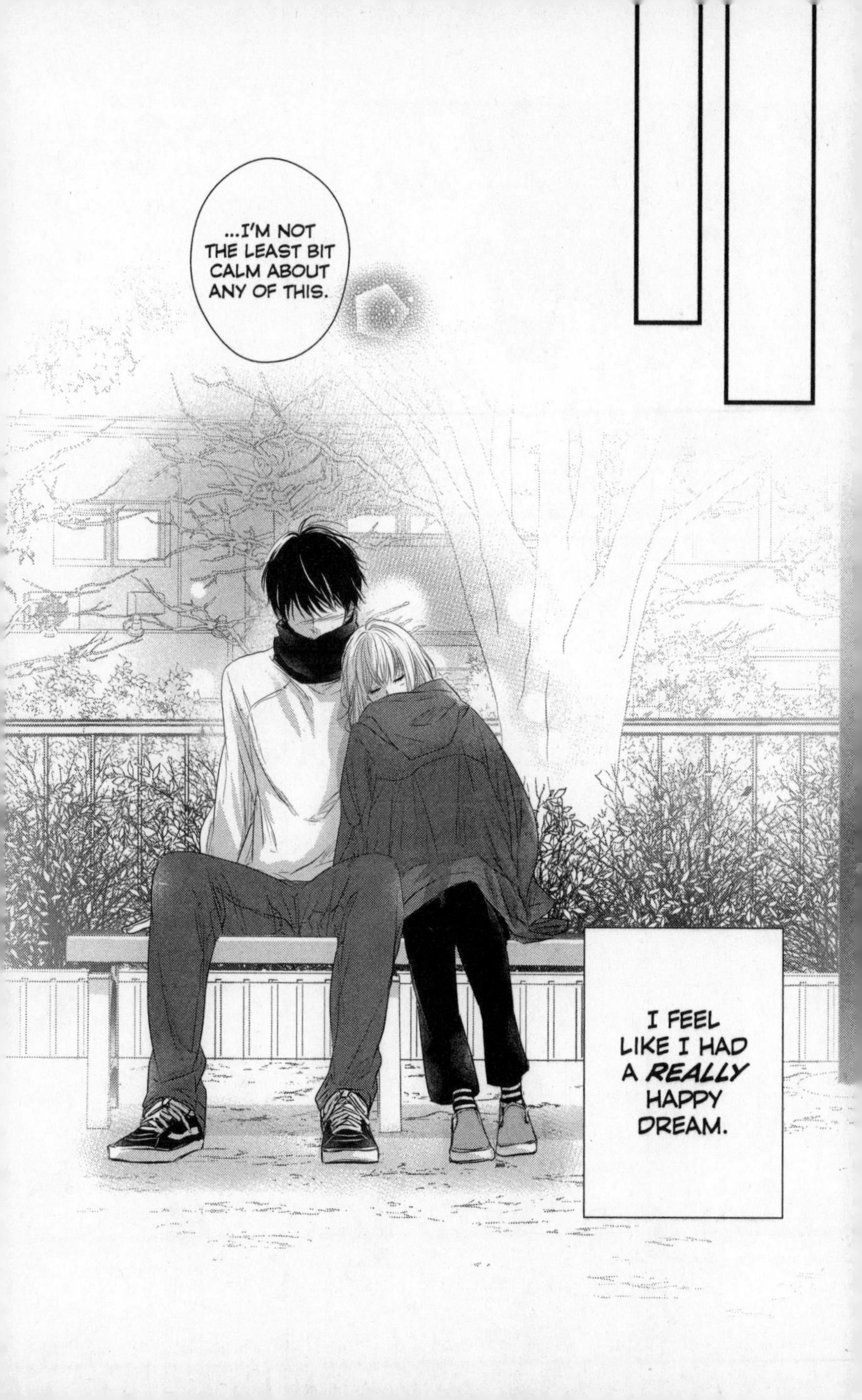
...I'M NOT THE LEAST BIT CALM ABOUT ANY OF THIS.
I FEEL LIKE I HAD A *REALLY* HAPPY DREAM.

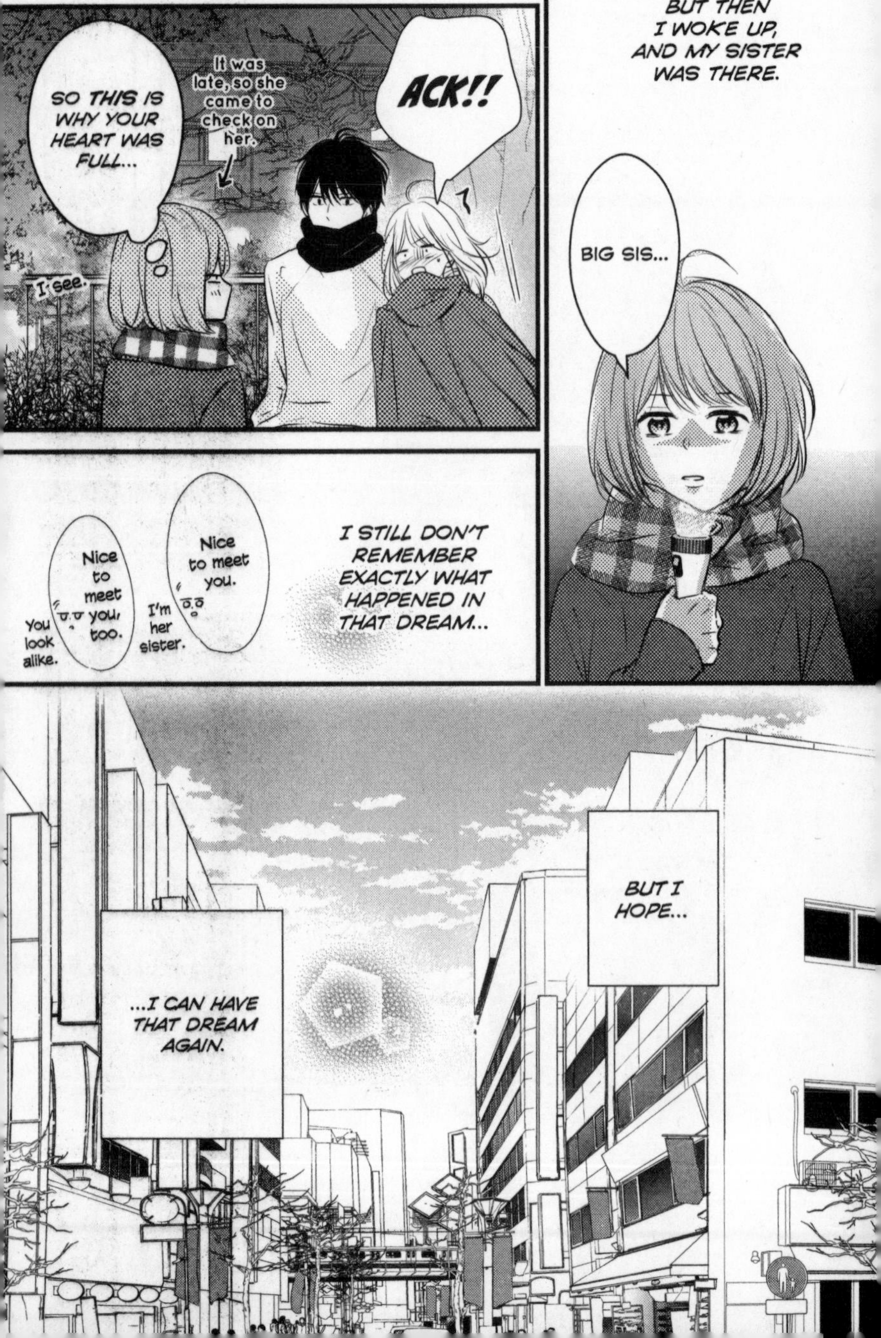
BUT THEN I WOKE UP, AND MY SISTER WAS THERE.
BIG SIS...
ACK!!
It was late, so she came to check on her.
SO THIS IS WHY YOUR HEART WAS FULL...
I see.
I STILL DON'T REMEMBER EXACTLY WHAT HAPPENED IN THAT DREAM...
Nice to meet you.
I'm her sister.
Nice to meet you, too.
You look alike.
BUT I HOPE...
...I CAN HAVE THAT DREAM AGAIN.

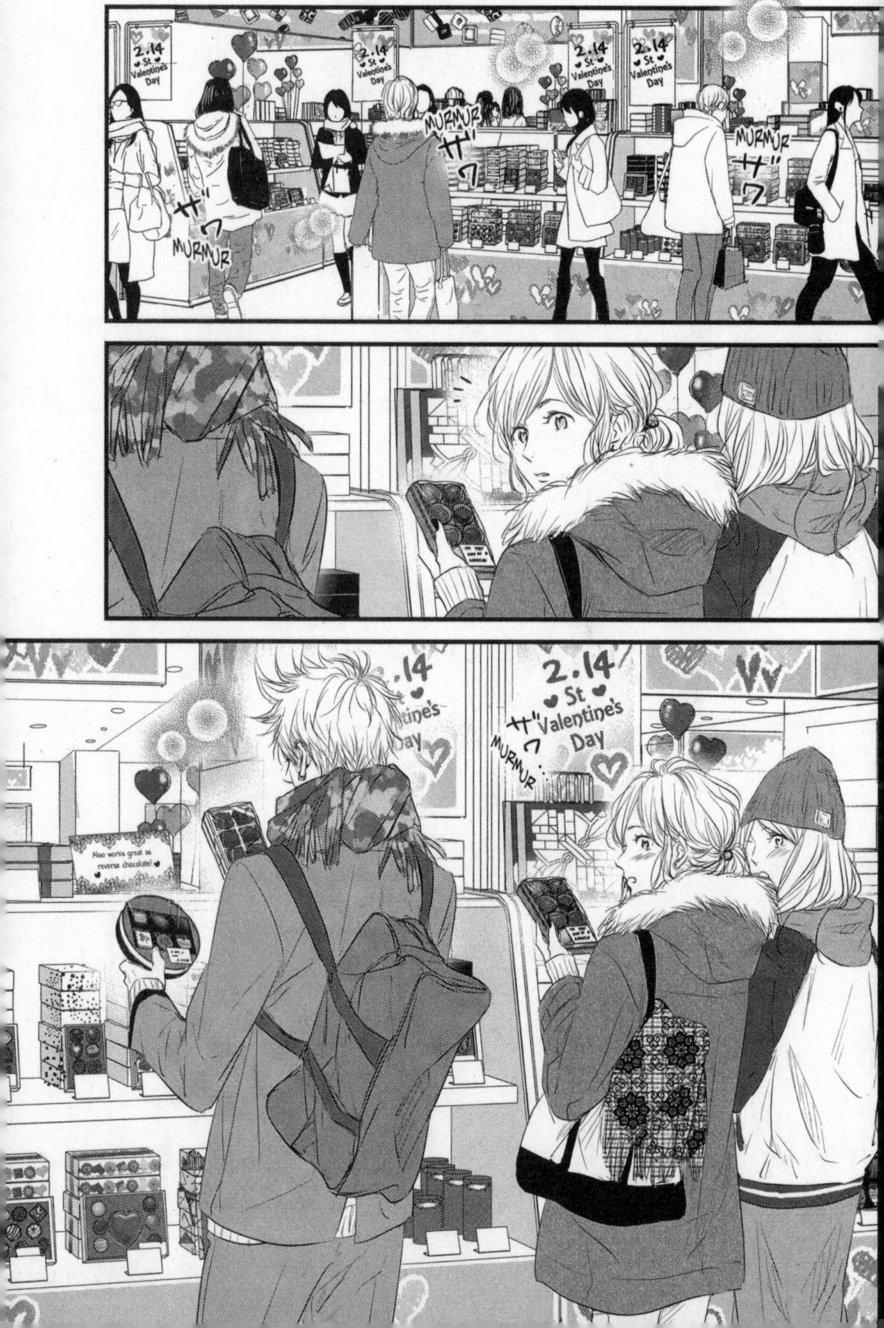

2.14 St Valentine's Day
MURMUR
ザワ
2.14 St Valentine's Day
2.14 St Valentine's Day
MURMUR
ザワ
2.14 St Valentine's Day
ザワ
MURMUR
2.14 St Valentine's Day
ザワ
MURMUR...
.14 Valentine's Day
Also works great as reverse chocolate!

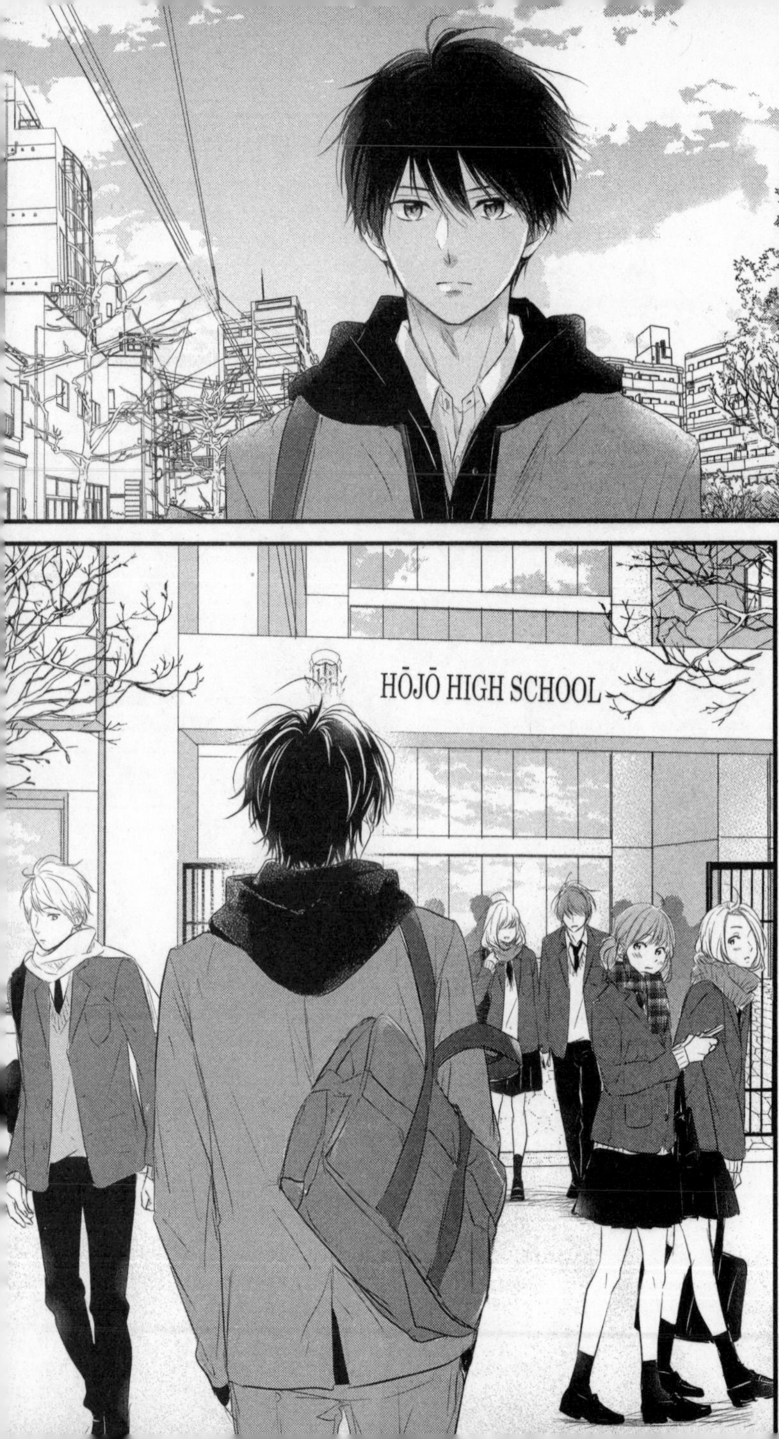
HŌJŌ HIGH SCHOOL

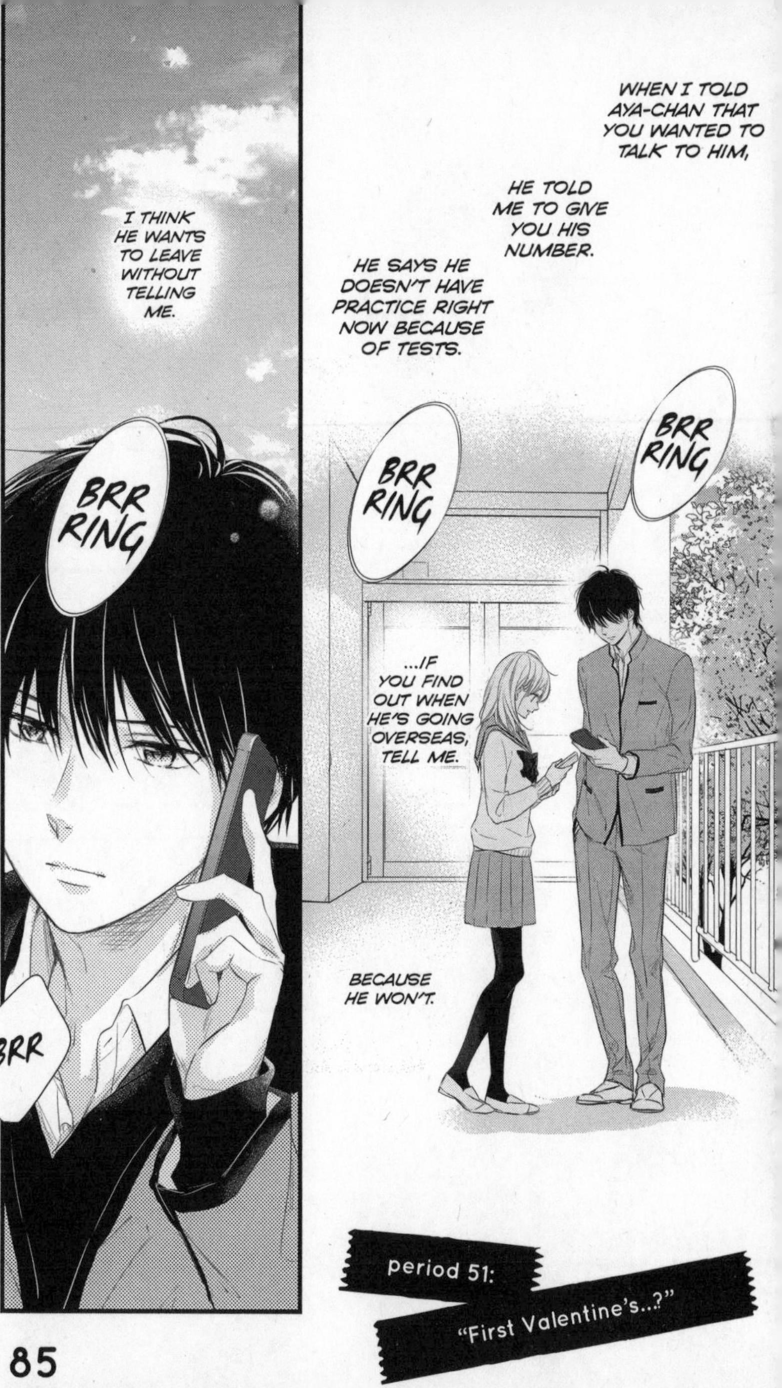
WHEN I TOLD AYA-CHAN THAT YOU WANTED TO TALK TO HIM,
HE TOLD ME TO GIVE YOU HIS NUMBER.
HE SAYS HE DOESN'T HAVE PRACTICE RIGHT NOW BECAUSE OF TESTS.
BRR RING
BRR RING
...IF YOU FIND OUT WHEN HE'S GOING OVERSEAS, TELL ME.
BECAUSE HE WON'T.
I THINK HE WANTS TO LEAVE WITHOUT TELLING ME.
BRR RING
BRR

period 51:
"First Valentine's..?"

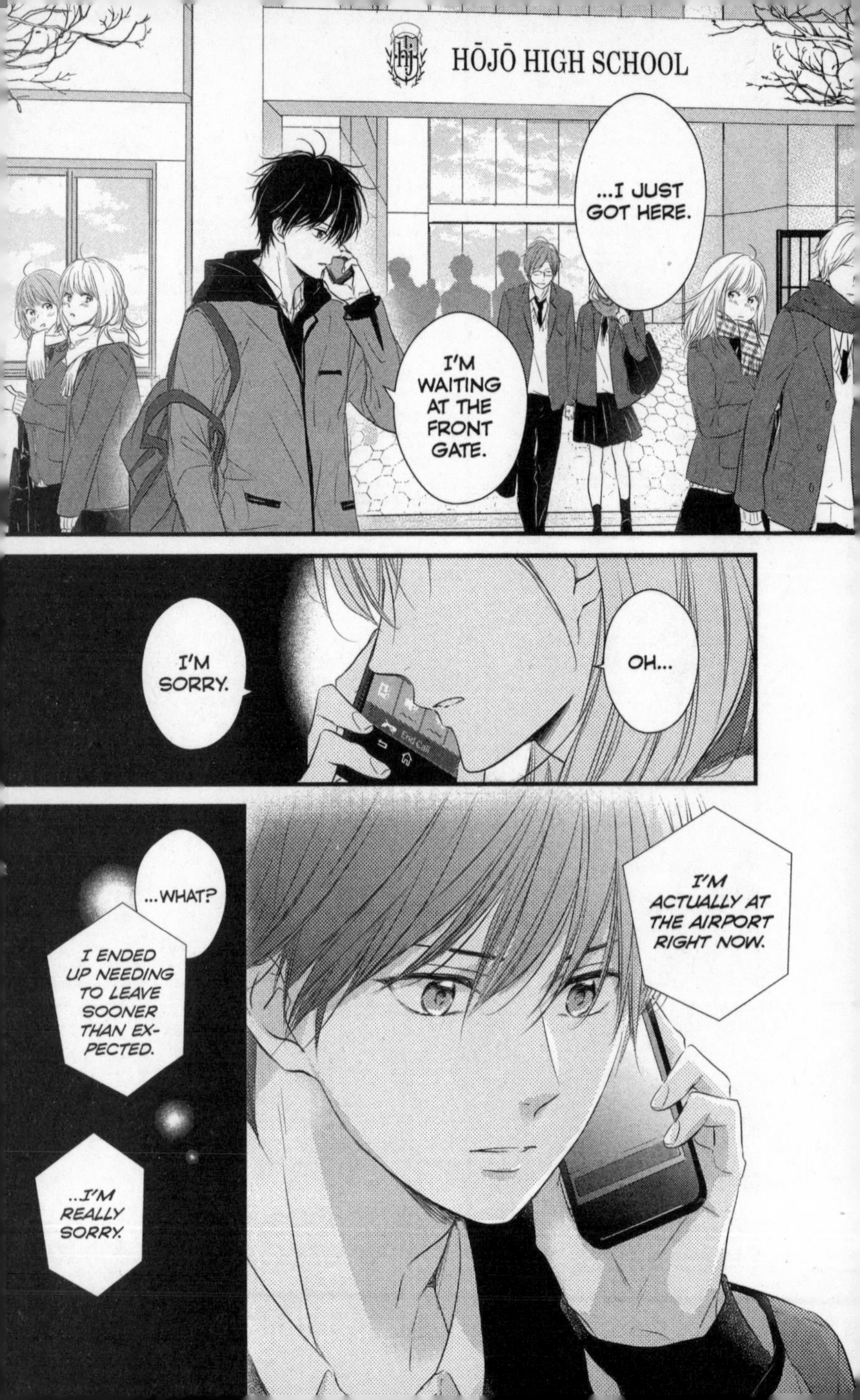
HŌJŌ HIGH SCHOOL
...I JUST GOT HERE.
I'M WAITING AT THE FRONT GATE.
OH...
I'M SORRY.
I'M ACTUALLY AT THE AIRPORT RIGHT NOW.
...WHAT?
I ENDED UP NEEDING TO LEAVE SOONER THAN EX-PECTED.
...I'M REALLY SORRY.

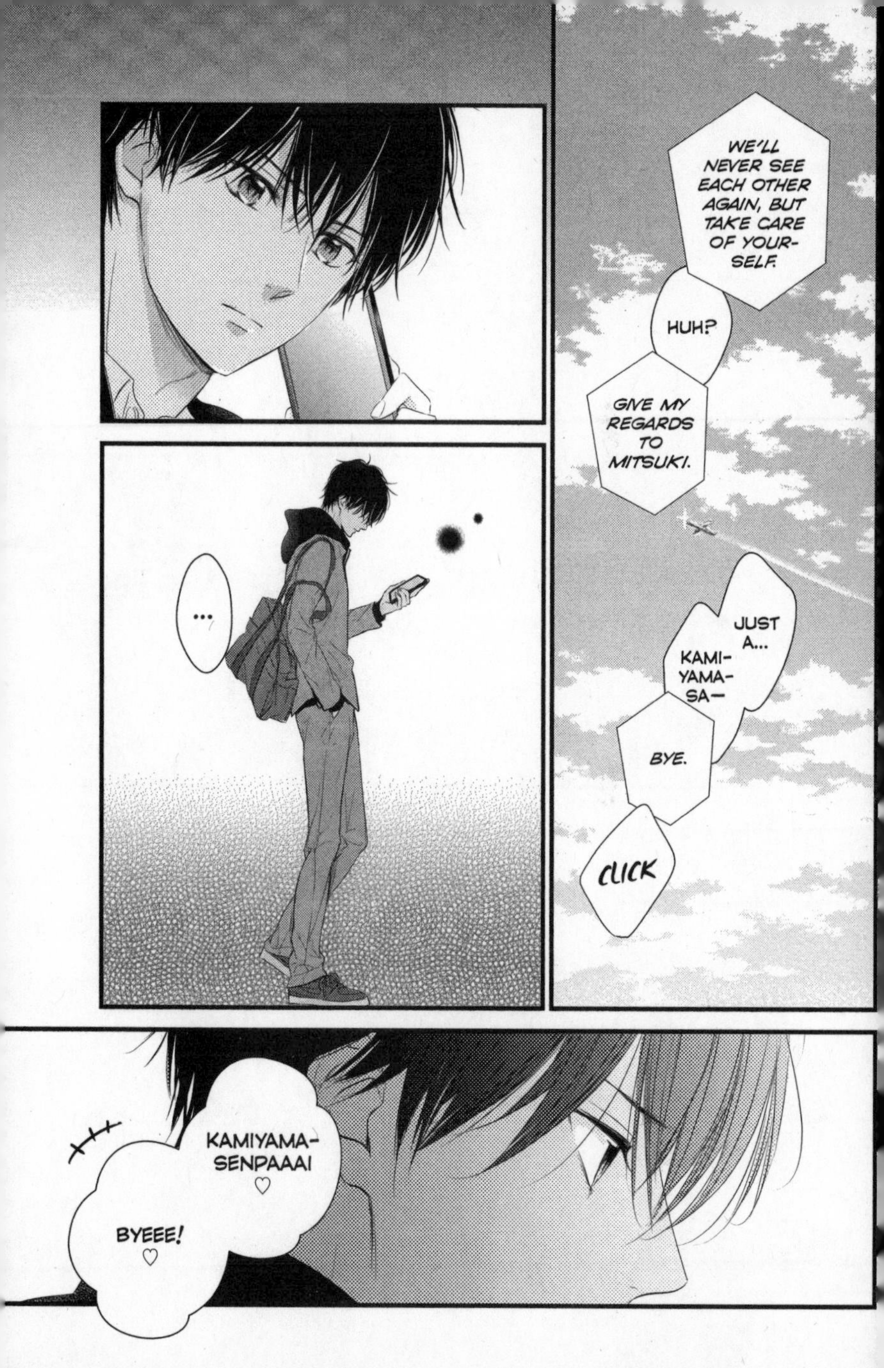
WE'LL NEVER SEE EACH OTHER AGAIN, BUT TAKE CARE OF YOUR-SELF.
HUH?
GIVE MY REGARDS TO MITSUKI.
JUST A...
KAMI-YAMA-SA—
BYE.
CLICK
...
KAMIYAMA-SENPAAAI ♡
BYEEE! ♡

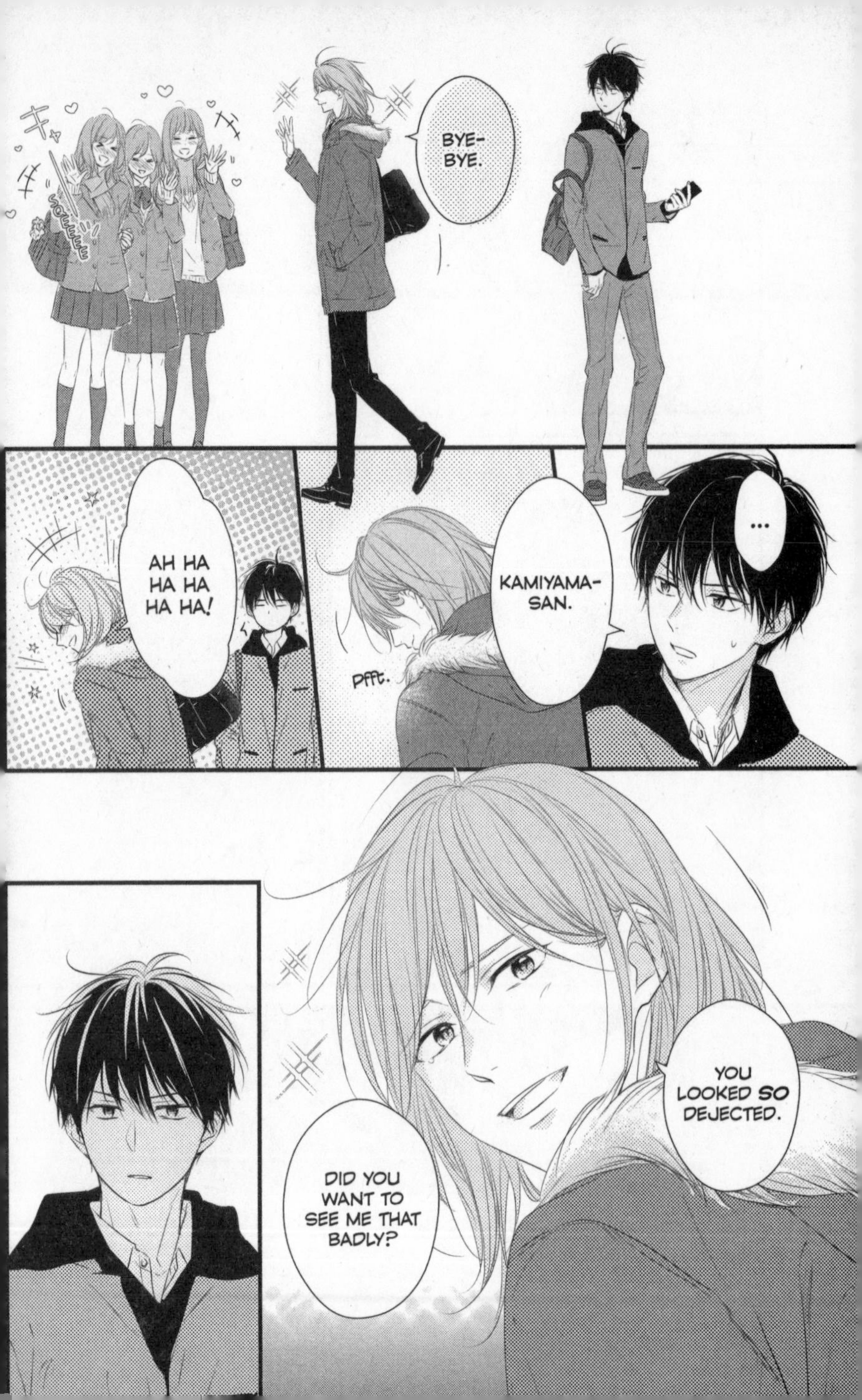

BYE-BYE.
キャ
...
KAMIYAMA-SAN.
Pfft.
AH HA HA HA HA HA!
YOU LOOKED SO DEJECTED.
DID YOU WANT TO SEE ME THAT BADLY?

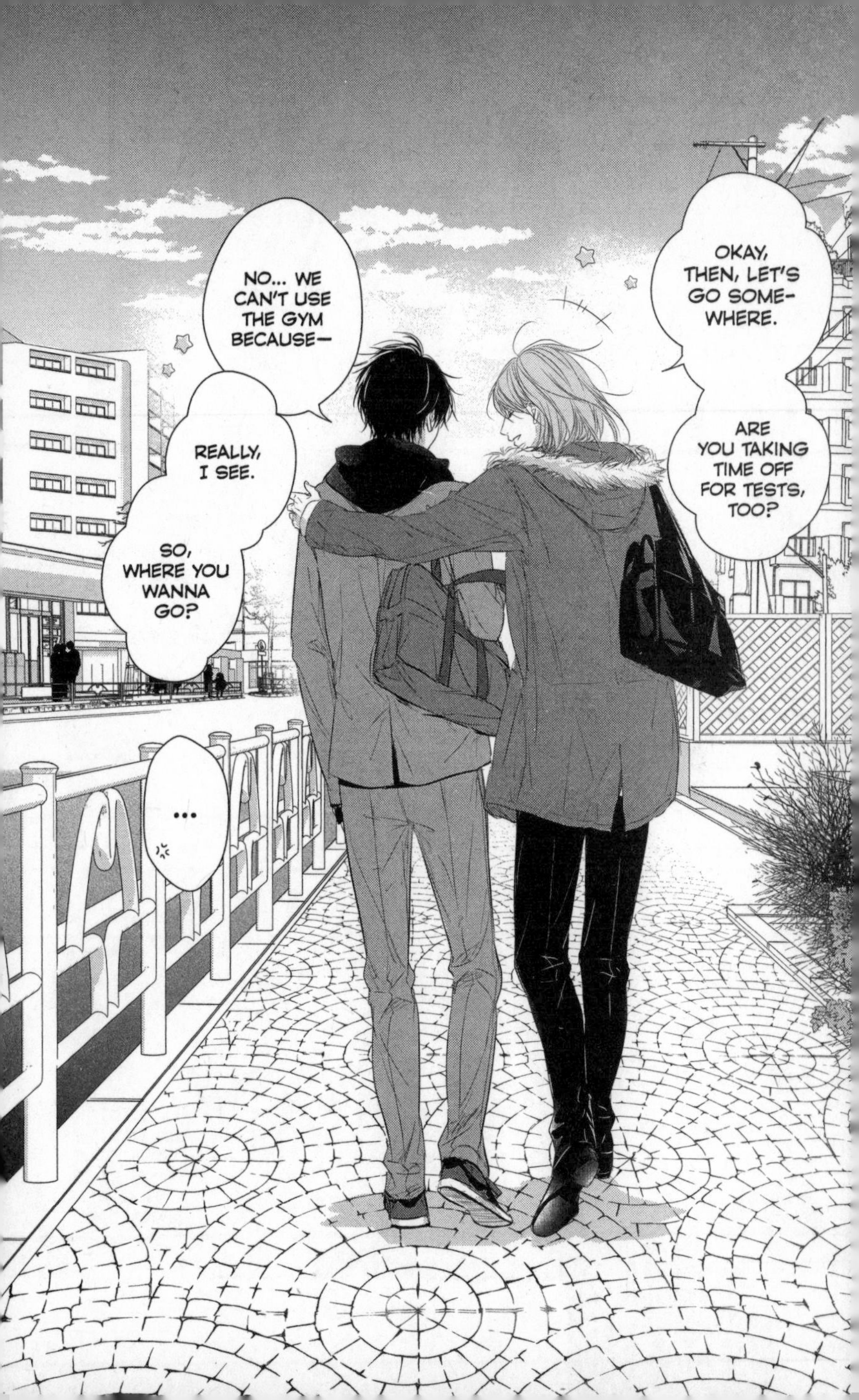
OKAY, THEN, LET'S GO SOME-WHERE.
ARE YOU TAKING TIME OFF FOR TESTS, TOO?
NO... WE CAN'T USE THE GYM BECAUSE—
REALLY, I SEE.
SO, WHERE YOU WANNA GO?
...

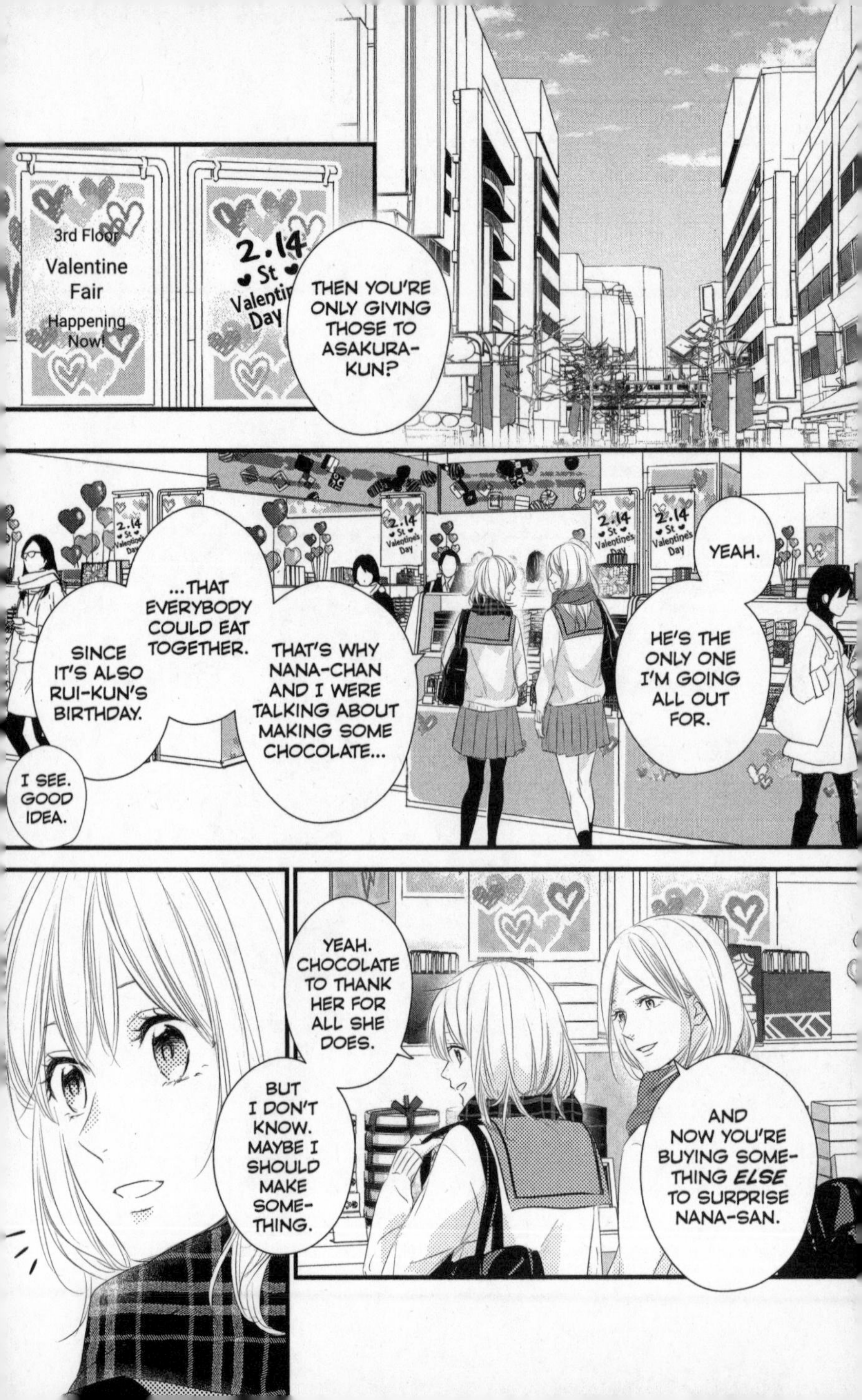
THEN YOU'RE ONLY GIVING THOSE TO ASAKURA-KUN?
2.14 St Valentine's Day
3rd Floor Valentine Fair Happening Now!
2.14 St Valentine's Day
YEAH.
HE'S THE ONLY ONE I'M GOING ALL OUT FOR.
THAT'S WHY NANA-CHAN AND I WERE TALKING ABOUT MAKING SOME CHOCOLATE...
...THAT EVERYBODY COULD EAT TOGETHER.
SINCE IT'S ALSO RUI-KUN'S BIRTHDAY.
I SEE. GOOD IDEA.
AND NOW YOU'RE BUYING SOMETHING *ELSE* TO SURPRISE NANA-SAN.
YEAH. CHOCOLATE TO THANK HER FOR ALL SHE DOES.
BUT I DON'T KNOW. MAYBE I SHOULD MAKE SOMETHING.

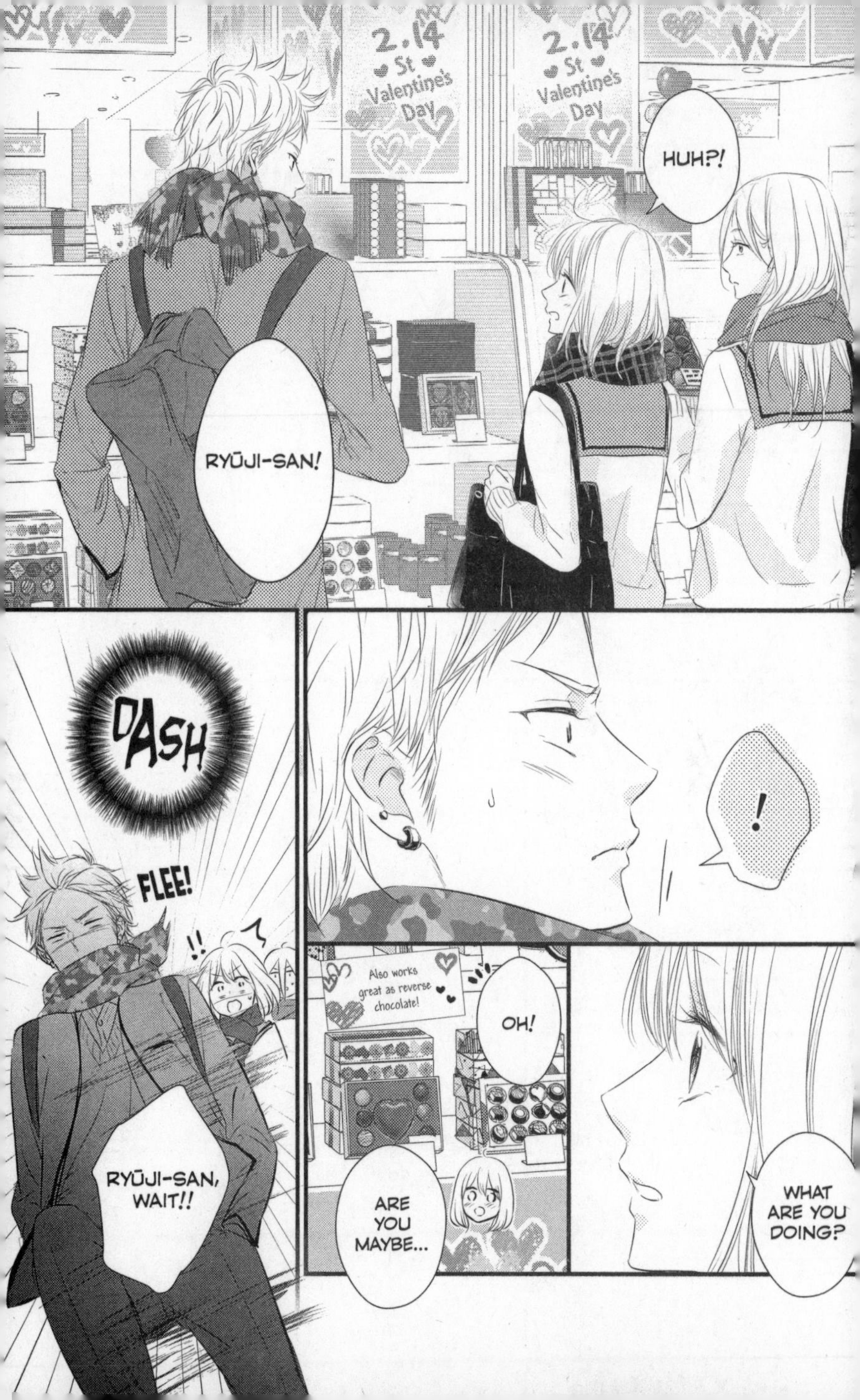
2.14 St Valentine's Day
2.14 St Valentine's Day
HUH?!
RYŪJI-SAN!
!
WHAT ARE YOU DOING?
OH!
Also works great as reverse chocolate!
ARE YOU MAYBE...
DASH
FLEE!
!!
RYŪJI-SAN, WAIT!!

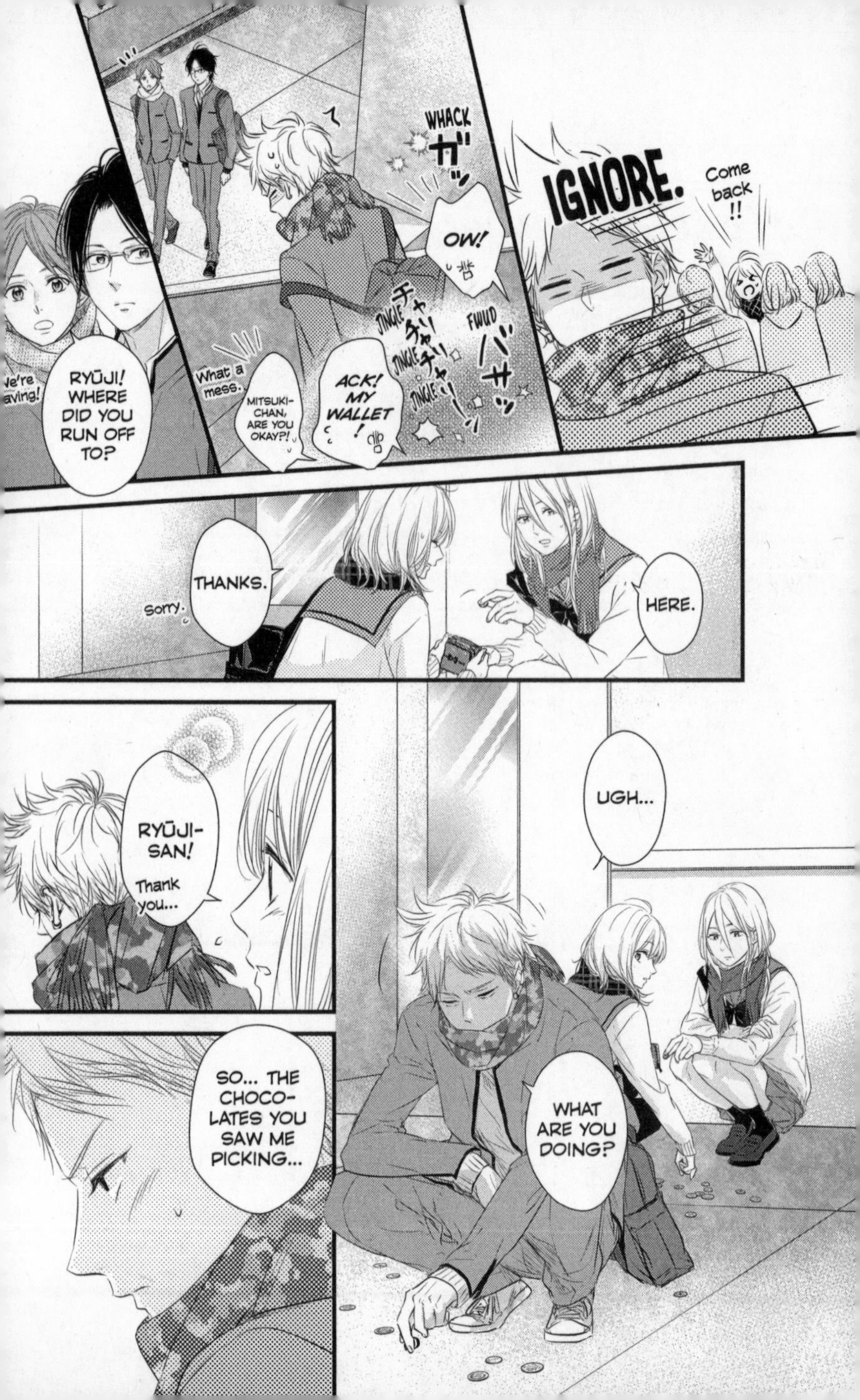
IGNORE.
Come back !!
WHACK
ガッ
OW!
JINGLE JINGLE JINGLE
チャリチャリチャリ
FWUD
バサッ
ACK! MY WALLET!
MITSUKI-CHAN, ARE YOU OKAY?!
What a mess.
RYŪJI! WHERE DID YOU RUN OFF TO?
We're aving!
HERE.
THANKS.
Sorry.
UGH...
WHAT ARE YOU DOING?
RYŪJI-SAN!
Thank you...
SO... THE CHOCOLATES YOU SAW ME PICKING...

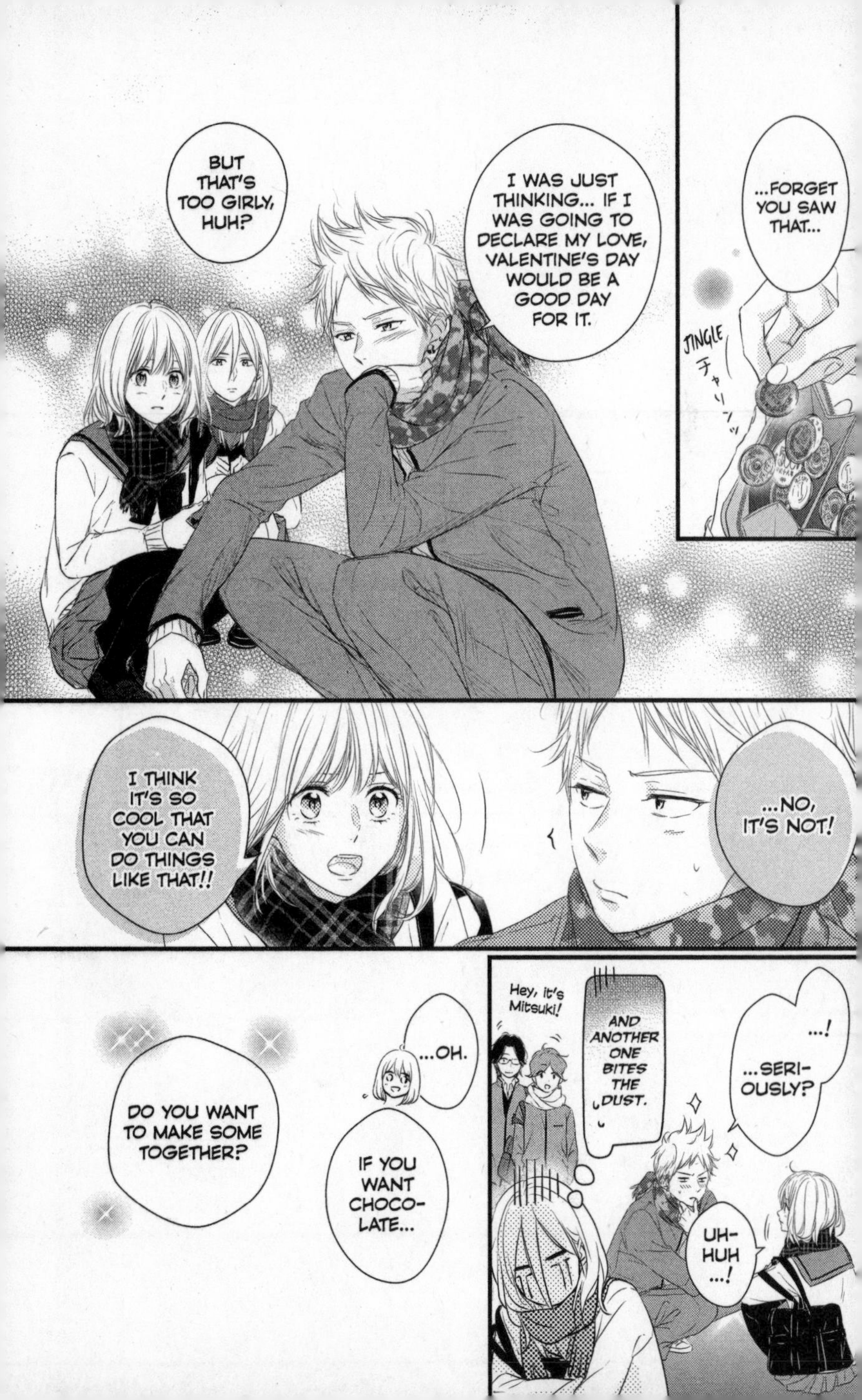
...FORGET YOU SAW THAT...
JINGLE
チャリッ
I WAS JUST THINKING... IF I WAS GOING TO DECLARE MY LOVE, VALENTINE'S DAY WOULD BE A GOOD DAY FOR IT.
BUT THAT'S TOO GIRLY, HUH?
I THINK IT'S SO COOL THAT YOU CAN DO THINGS LIKE THAT!!
...NO, IT'S NOT!
...!
...SERIOUSLY?
Hey, it's Mitsuki!
AND ANOTHER ONE BITES THE DUST.
UH-HUH...!
...OH.
IF YOU WANT CHOCOLATE...
DO YOU WANT TO MAKE SOME TOGETHER?

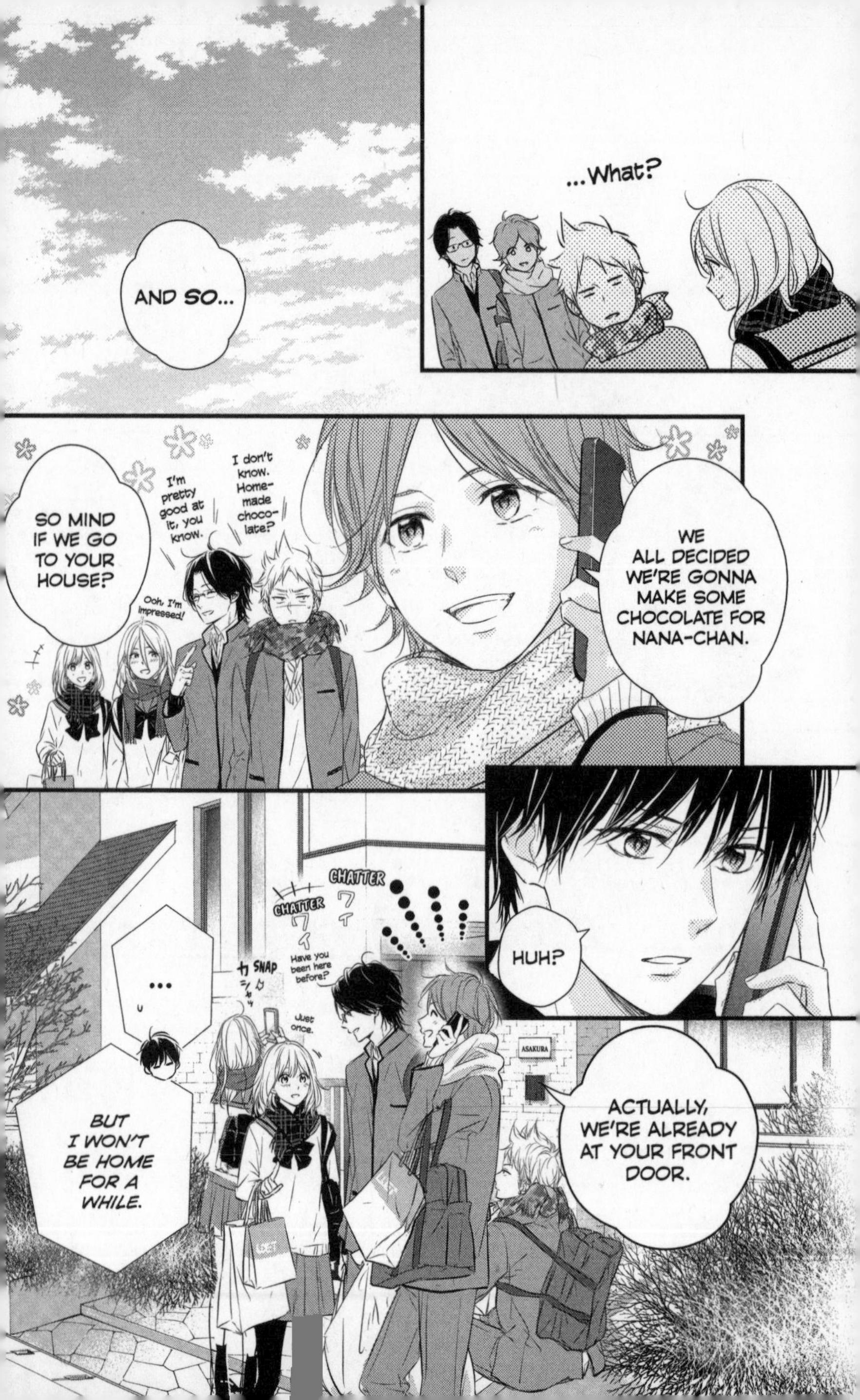
...What?
AND SO...
WE ALL DECIDED WE'RE GONNA MAKE SOME CHOCOLATE FOR NANA-CHAN.
I don't know. Home-made choco-late?
I'm pretty good at it, you know.
Ooh, I'm impressed!
SO MIND IF WE GO TO YOUR HOUSE?
HUH?
ACTUALLY, WE'RE ALREADY AT YOUR FRONT DOOR.
ASAKURA
CHATTER
CHATTER
Have you been here before?
Just once.
SNAP
...
BUT I WON'T BE HOME FOR A WHILE.

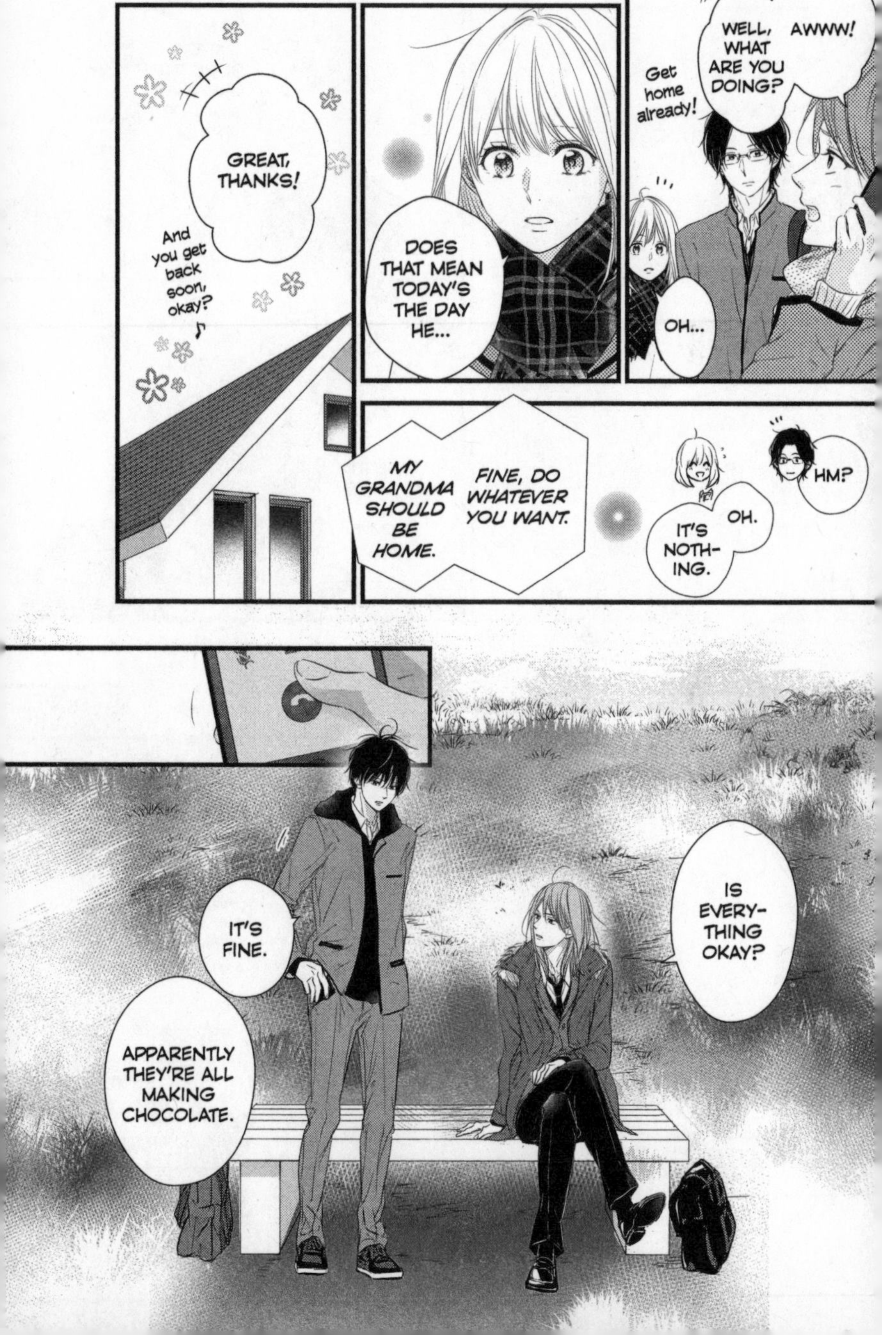
AWWW!
WELL, WHAT ARE YOU DOING?
Get home already!
OH...
DOES THAT MEAN TODAY'S THE DAY HE...
HM?
OH.
IT'S NOTHING.
FINE, DO WHATEVER YOU WANT.
MY GRANDMA SHOULD BE HOME.
GREAT, THANKS!
And you get back soon, okay? ♪
IS EVERYTHING OKAY?
IT'S FINE.
APPARENTLY THEY'RE ALL MAKING CHOCOLATE.

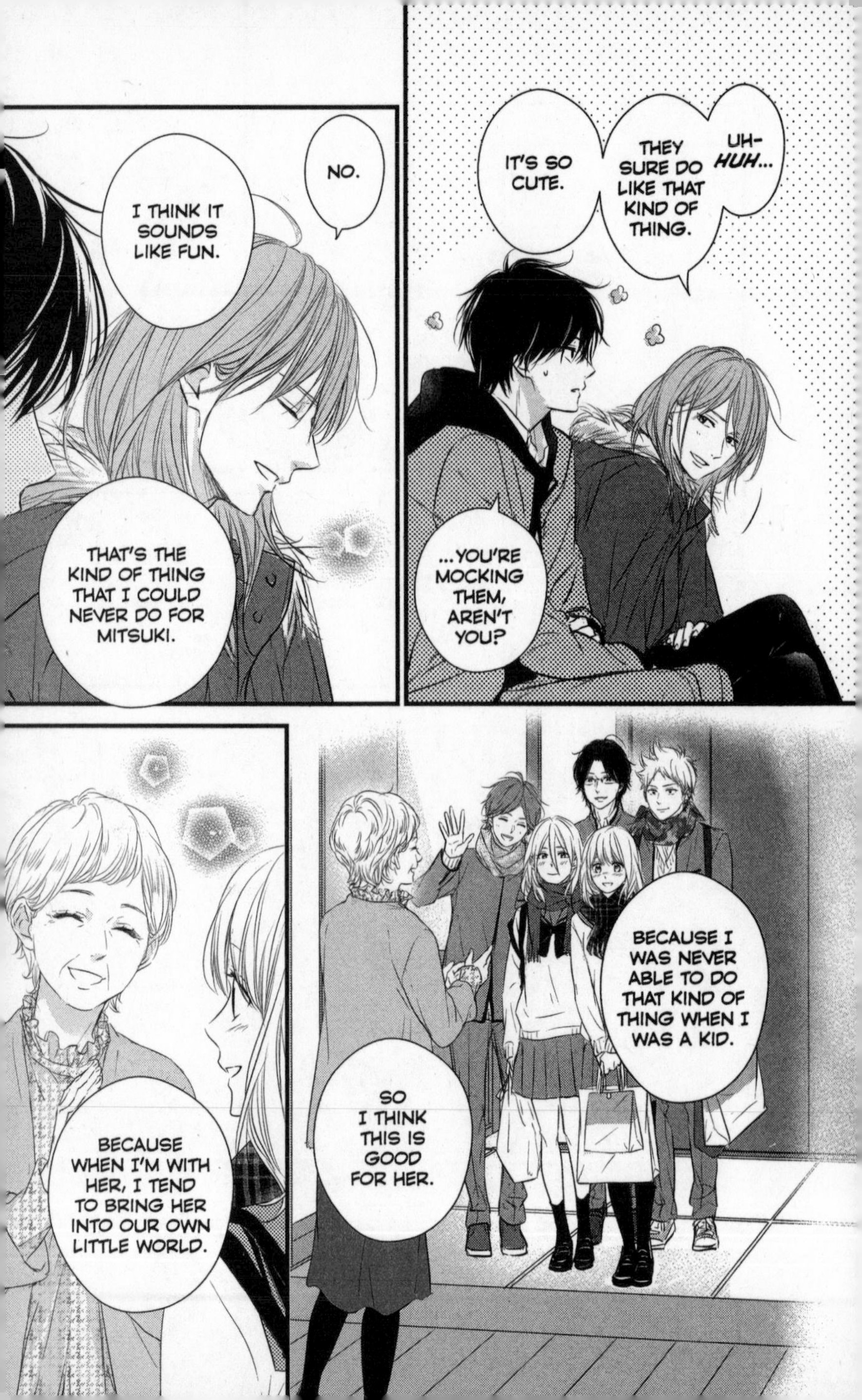
UH-HUH...
THEY SURE DO LIKE THAT KIND OF THING.
IT'S SO CUTE.
...YOU'RE MOCKING THEM, AREN'T YOU?
NO.
I THINK IT SOUNDS LIKE FUN.
THAT'S THE KIND OF THING THAT I COULD NEVER DO FOR MITSUKI.
BECAUSE I WAS NEVER ABLE TO DO THAT KIND OF THING WHEN I WAS A KID.
SO I THINK THIS IS GOOD FOR HER.
BECAUSE WHEN I'M WITH HER, I TEND TO BRING HER INTO OUR OWN LITTLE WORLD.

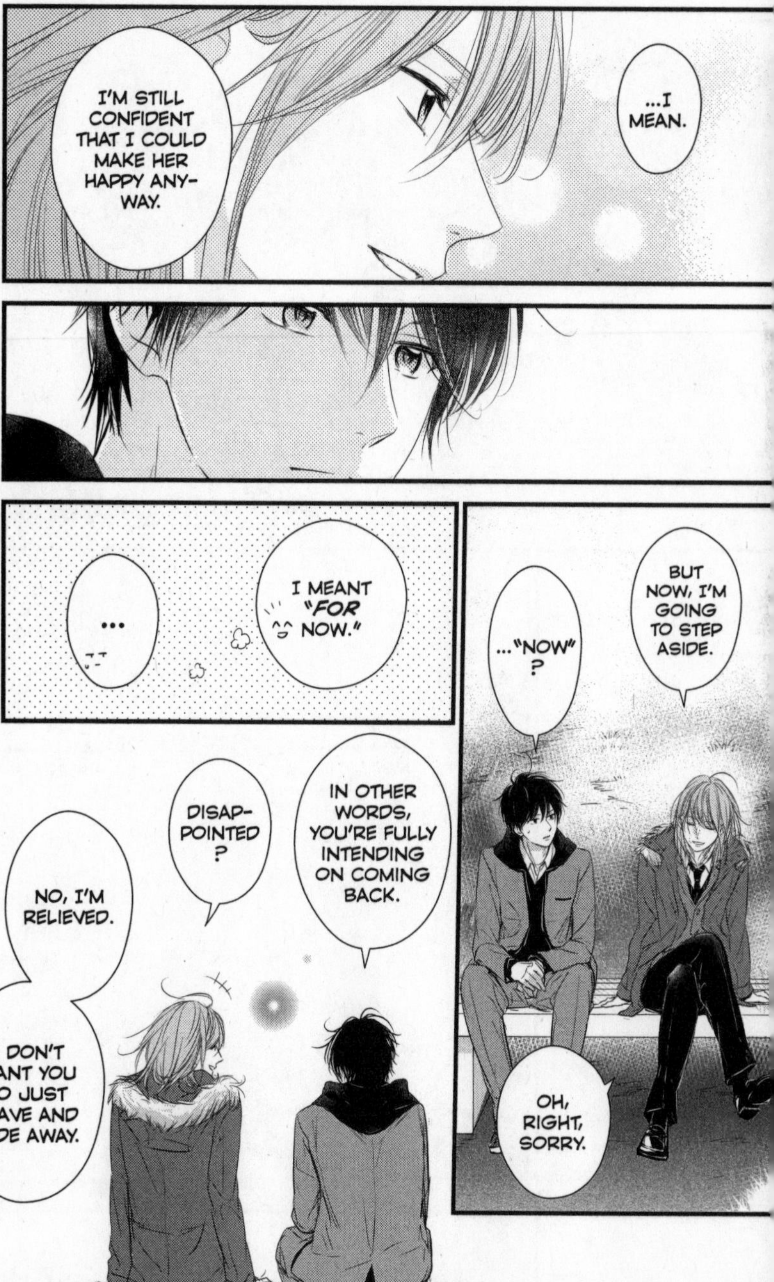
...I MEAN.
I'M STILL CONFIDENT THAT I COULD MAKE HER HAPPY ANY-WAY.
BUT NOW, I'M GOING TO STEP ASIDE.
..."NOW"?
OH, RIGHT, SORRY.
I MEANT "FOR NOW."
...
IN OTHER WORDS, YOU'RE FULLY INTENDING ON COMING BACK.
DISAP-POINTED?
NO, I'M RELIEVED.
I DON'T WANT YOU TO JUST LEAVE AND FADE AWAY.

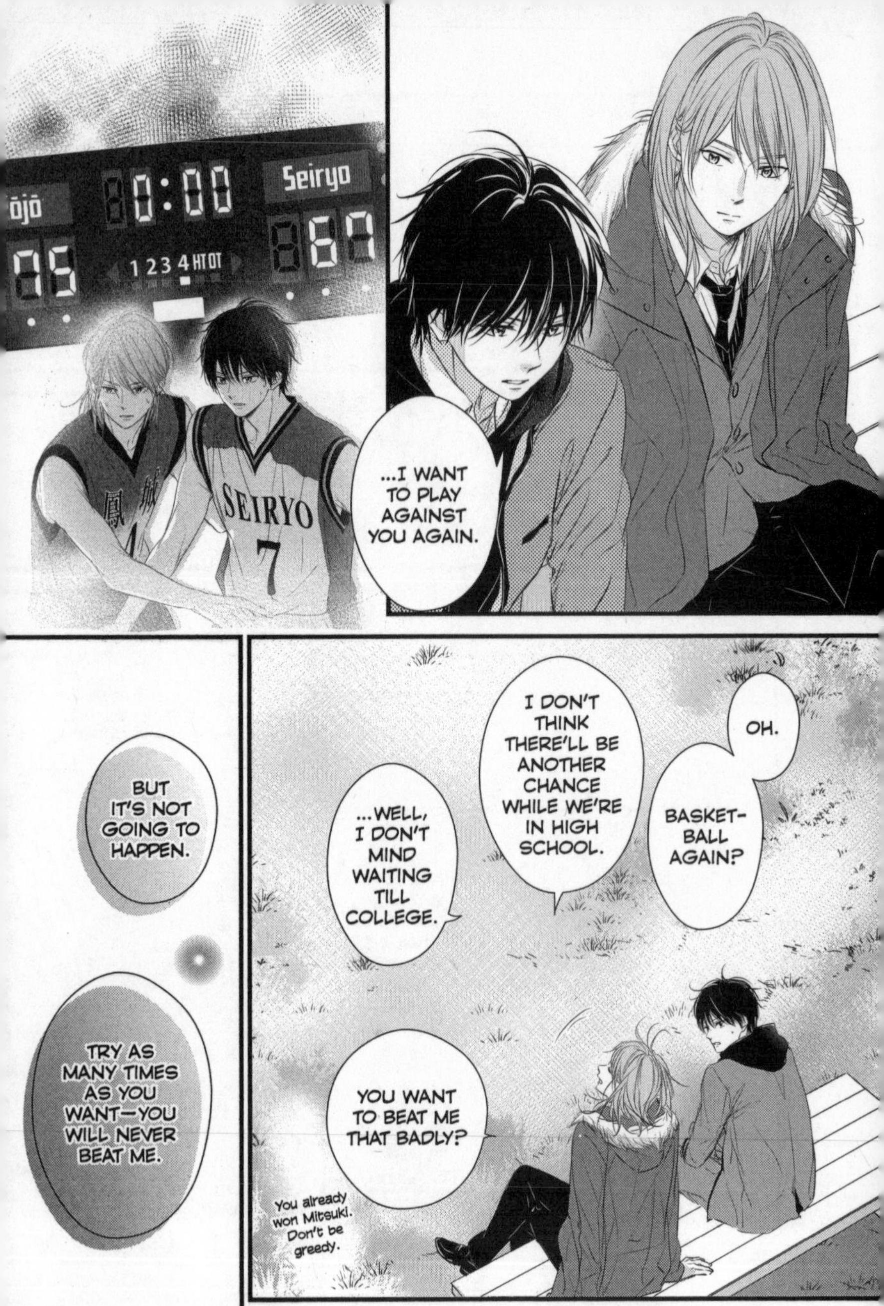
...I WANT TO PLAY AGAINST YOU AGAIN.
Seiryo
1 2 3 4 HT OT
SEIRYO
7
OH.
BASKET-BALL AGAIN?
I DON'T THINK THERE'LL BE ANOTHER CHANCE WHILE WE'RE IN HIGH SCHOOL.
...WELL, I DON'T MIND WAITING TILL COLLEGE.
YOU WANT TO BEAT ME THAT BADLY?
You already won Mitsuki. Don't be greedy.
BUT IT'S NOT GOING TO HAPPEN.
TRY AS MANY TIMES AS YOU WANT—YOU WILL NEVER BEAT ME.

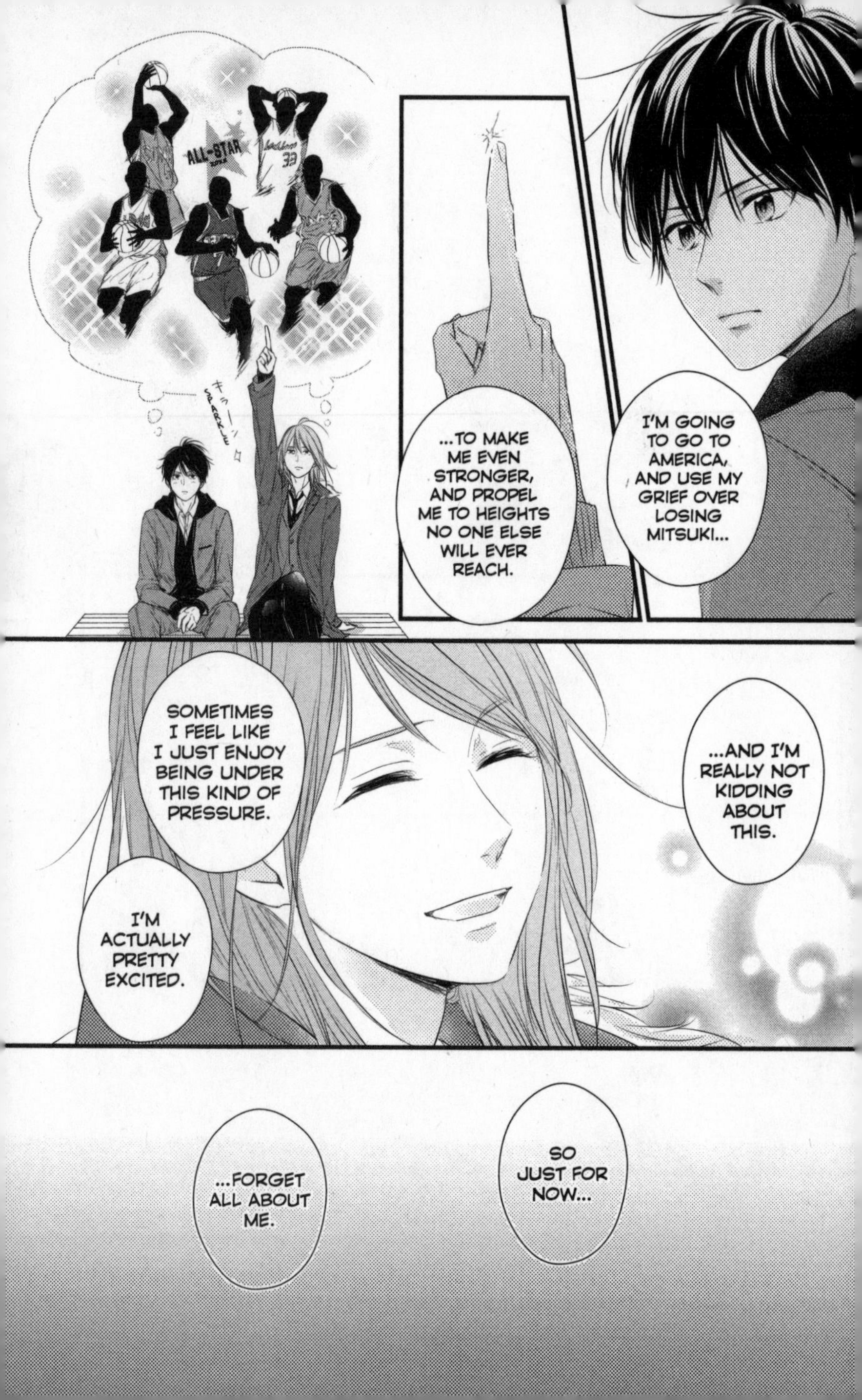
I'M GOING TO GO TO AMERICA, AND USE MY GRIEF OVER LOSING MITSUKI...
...TO MAKE ME EVEN STRONGER, AND PROPEL ME TO HEIGHTS NO ONE ELSE WILL EVER REACH.
ALL-STAR
SPARKLE
...AND I'M REALLY NOT KIDDING ABOUT THIS.
SOMETIMES I FEEL LIKE I JUST ENJOY BEING UNDER THIS KIND OF PRESSURE.
I'M ACTUALLY PRETTY EXCITED.
SO JUST FOR NOW...
...FORGET ALL ABOUT ME.

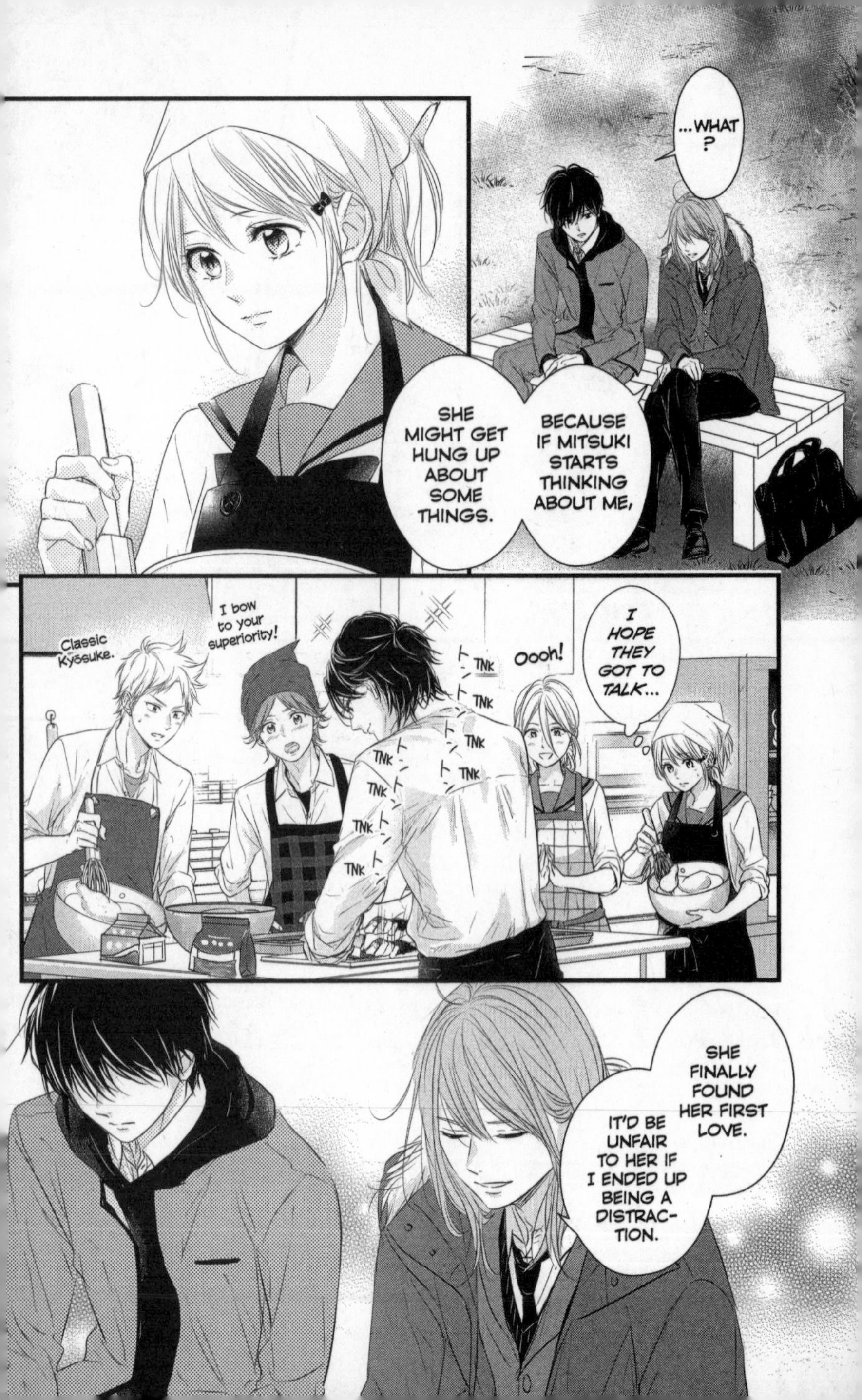
...WHAT?
BECAUSE IF MITSUKI STARTS THINKING ABOUT ME,
SHE MIGHT GET HUNG UP ABOUT SOME THINGS.
I HOPE THEY GOT TO TALK...
Oooh!
TNK TNK TNK TNK TNK TNK TNK TNK
I bow to your superiority!
Classic Kyōsuke.
SHE FINALLY FOUND HER FIRST LOVE.
IT'D BE UNFAIR TO HER IF I ENDED UP BEING A DISTRAC-TION.

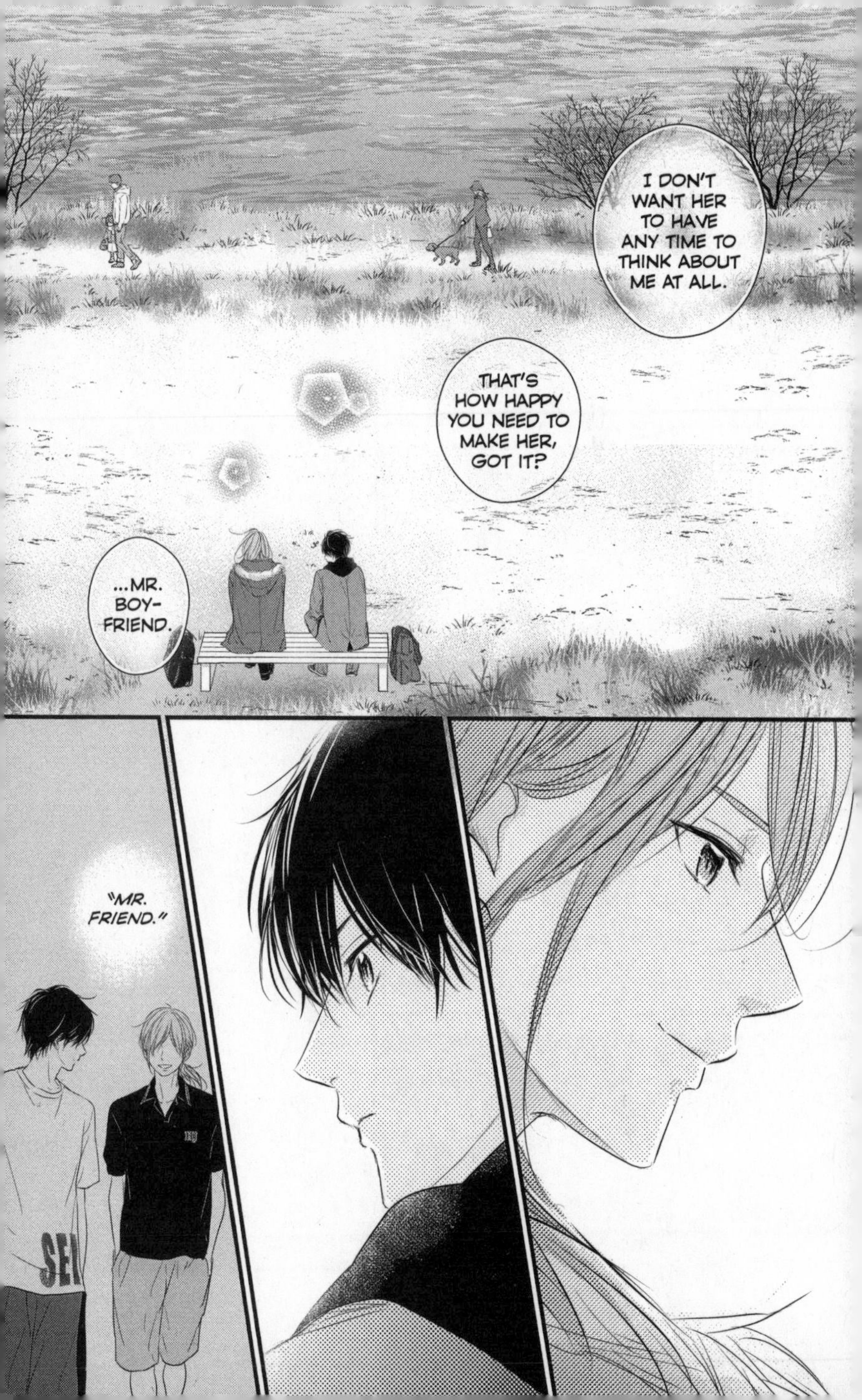
I DON'T WANT HER TO HAVE ANY TIME TO THINK ABOUT ME AT ALL.
THAT'S HOW HAPPY YOU NEED TO MAKE HER, GOT IT?
...MR. BOY-FRIEND.
"MR. FRIEND."

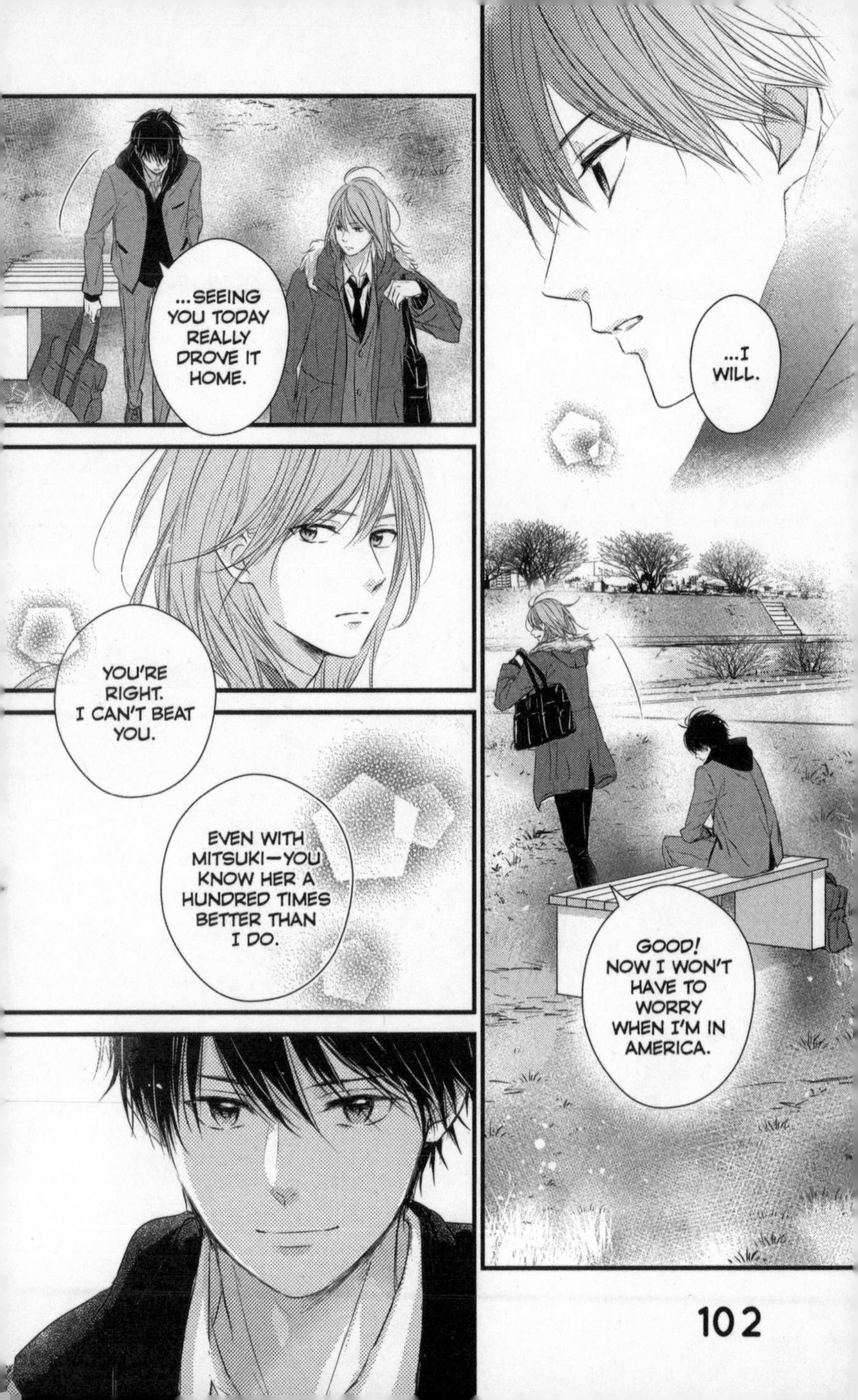
...I WILL.
GOOD! NOW I WON'T HAVE TO WORRY WHEN I'M IN AMERICA.
...SEEING YOU TODAY REALLY DROVE IT HOME.
YOU'RE RIGHT. I CAN'T BEAT YOU.
EVEN WITH MITSUKI—YOU KNOW HER A HUNDRED TIMES BETTER THAN I DO.

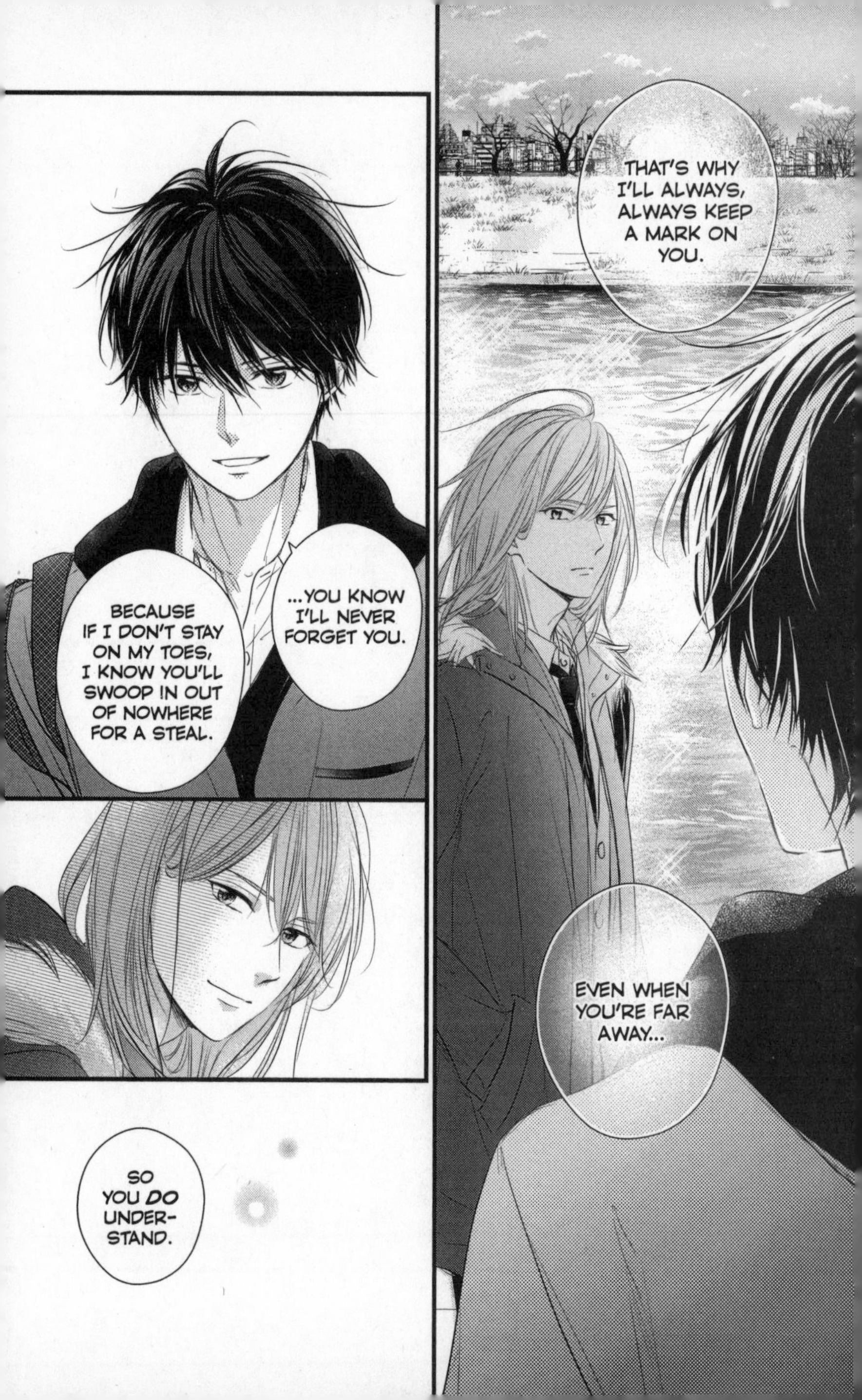
THAT'S WHY I'LL ALWAYS, ALWAYS KEEP A MARK ON YOU.
EVEN WHEN YOU'RE FAR AWAY...
...YOU KNOW I'LL NEVER FORGET YOU.
BECAUSE IF I DON'T STAY ON MY TOES, I KNOW YOU'LL SWOOP IN OUT OF NOWHERE FOR A STEAL.
SO YOU *DO* UNDER-STAND.

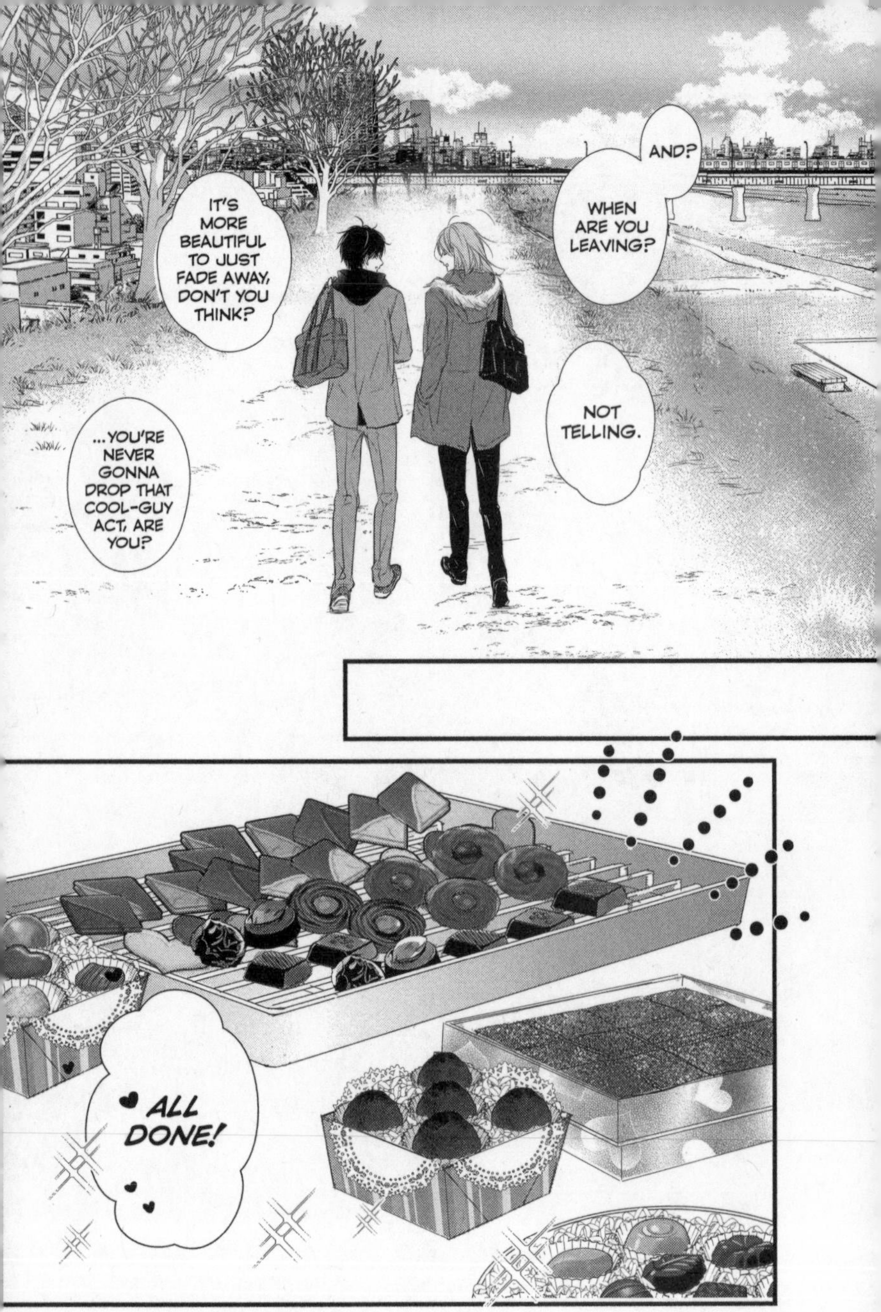
AND?
WHEN ARE YOU LEAVING?
IT'S MORE BEAUTIFUL TO JUST FADE AWAY, DON'T YOU THINK?
NOT TELLING.
...YOU'RE NEVER GONNA DROP THAT COOL-GUY ACT, ARE YOU?
ALL DONE!

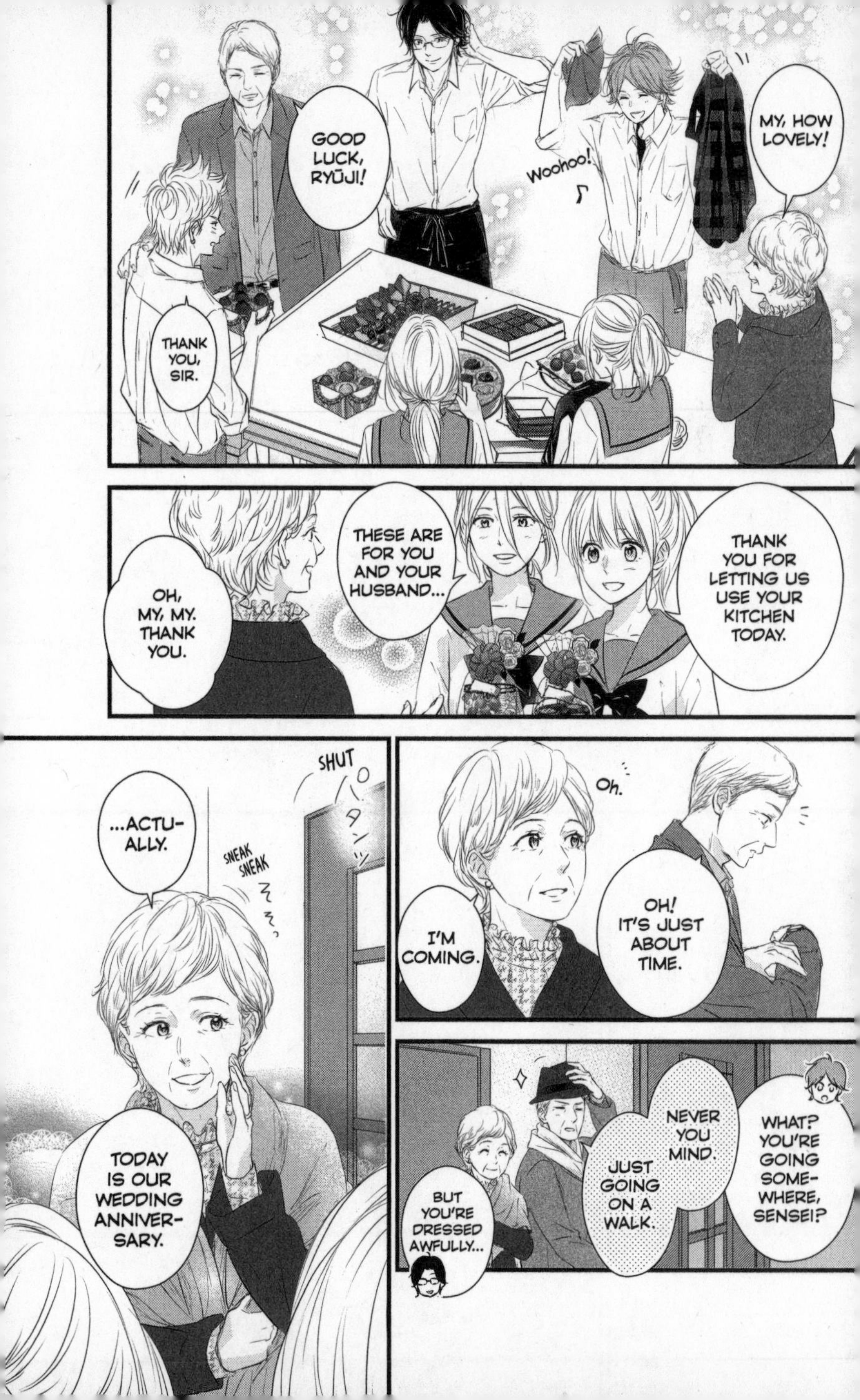
MY, HOW LOVELY!
Woohoo! ♪
GOOD LUCK, RYŪJI!
THANK YOU, SIR.
THANK YOU FOR LETTING US USE YOUR KITCHEN TODAY.
THESE ARE FOR YOU AND YOUR HUSBAND...
OH, MY, MY. THANK YOU.
Oh.
OH! IT'S JUST ABOUT TIME.
I'M COMING.
WHAT? YOU'RE GOING SOME-WHERE, SENSEI?
NEVER YOU MIND.
JUST GOING ON A WALK.
BUT YOU'RE DRESSED AWFULLY...
SHUT
SNEAK SNEAK
...ACTU-ALLY.
TODAY IS OUR WEDDING ANNIVER-SARY.

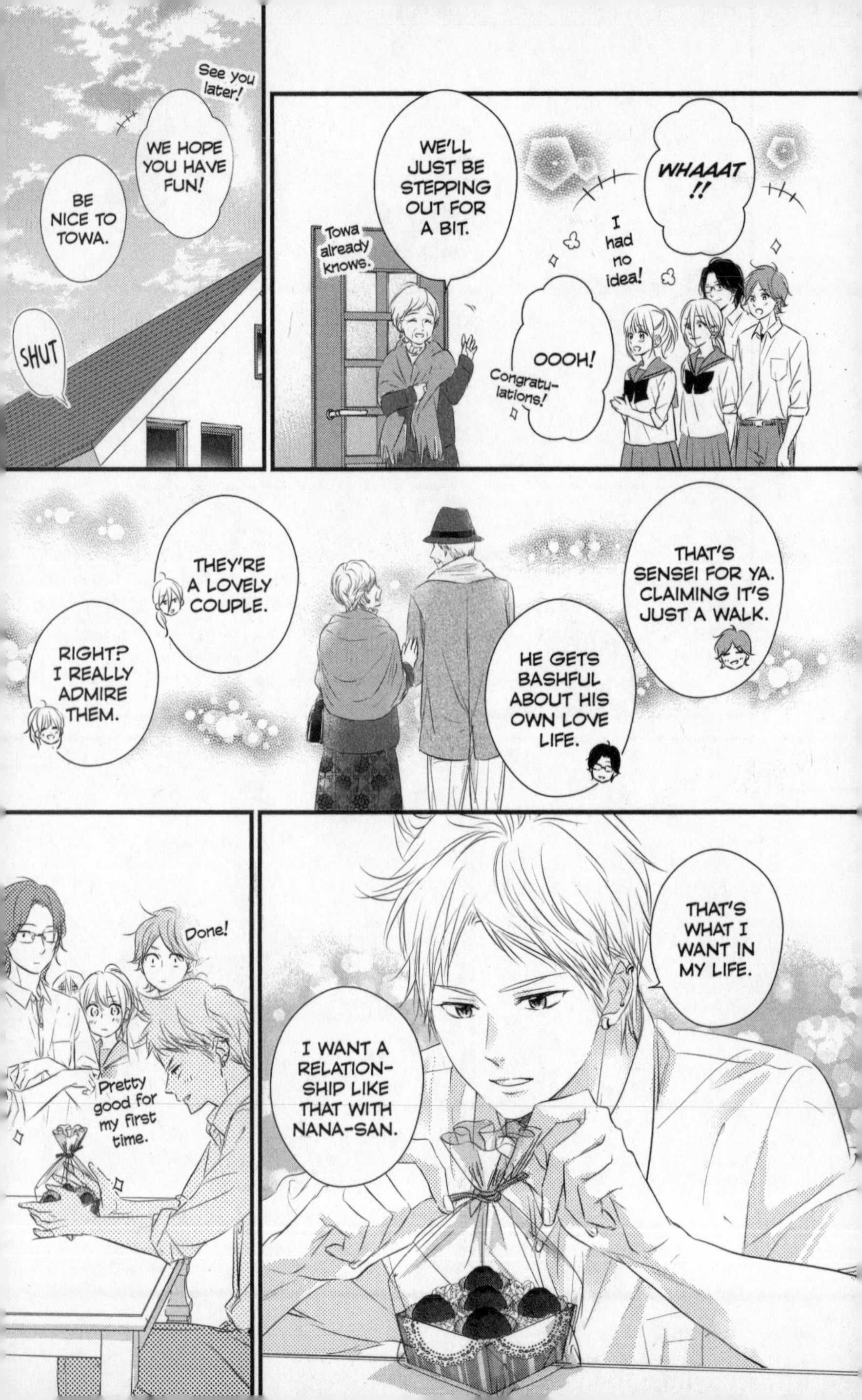
WE'LL JUST BE STEPPING OUT FOR A BIT.
Towa already knows.
WHAAAT!!
I had no idea!
OOOH!
Congratulations!
See you later!
WE HOPE YOU HAVE FUN!
BE NICE TO TOWA.
SHUT
THAT'S SENSEI FOR YA. CLAIMING IT'S JUST A WALK.
HE GETS BASHFUL ABOUT HIS OWN LOVE LIFE.
THEY'RE A LOVELY COUPLE.
RIGHT? I REALLY ADMIRE THEM.
THAT'S WHAT I WANT IN MY LIFE.
I WANT A RELATION-SHIP LIKE THAT WITH NANA-SAN.
Done!
Pretty good for my first time.

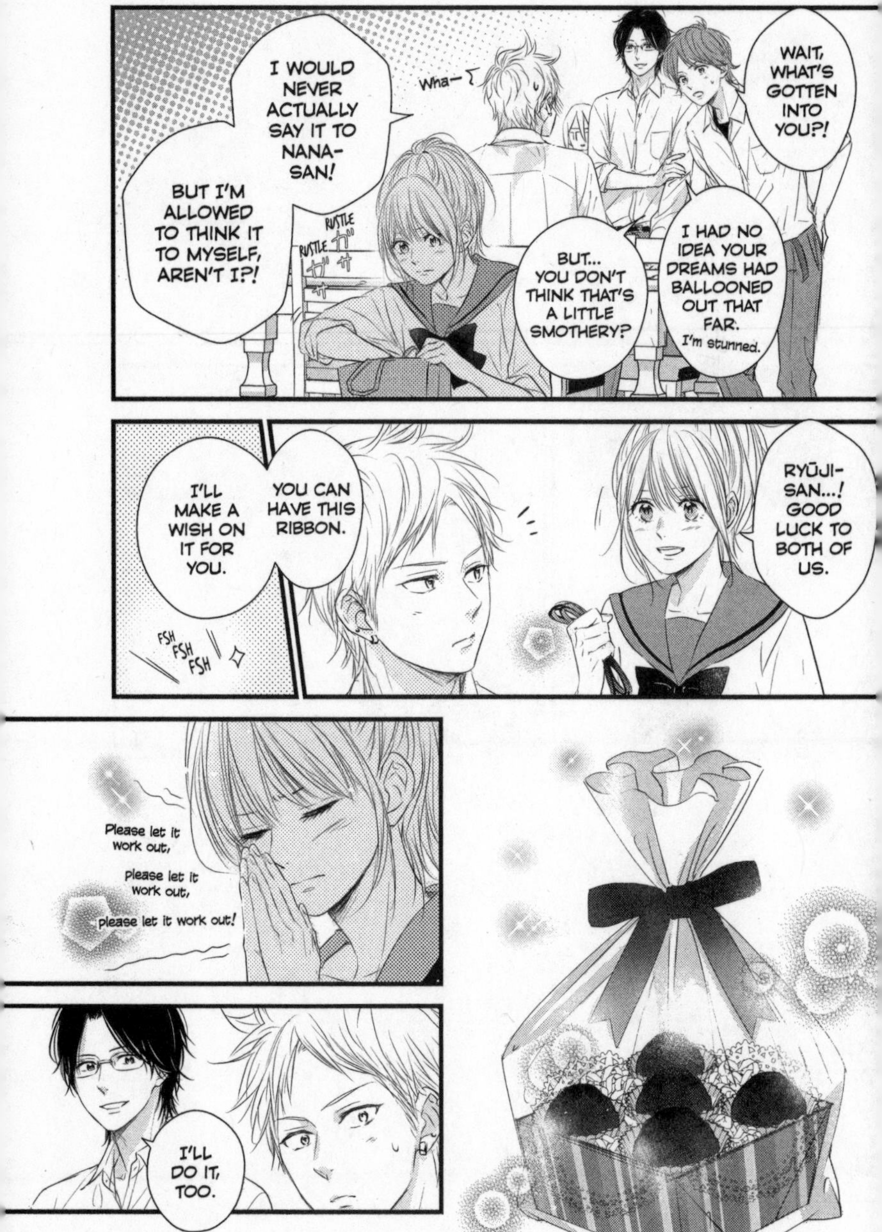
WAIT, WHAT'S GOTTEN INTO YOU?!
Wha—
I WOULD NEVER ACTUALLY SAY IT TO NANA-SAN!
I HAD NO IDEA YOUR DREAMS HAD BALLOONED OUT THAT FAR.
I'm stunned.
BUT... YOU DON'T THINK THAT'S A LITTLE SMOTHERY?
BUT I'M ALLOWED TO THINK IT TO MYSELF, AREN'T I?!
RUSTLE
RUSTLE
RYŪJI-SAN...! GOOD LUCK TO BOTH OF US.
YOU CAN HAVE THIS RIBBON.
I'LL MAKE A WISH ON IT FOR YOU.
FSH FSH FSH
Please let it work out,
please let it work out,
please let it work out!
I'LL DO IT, TOO.

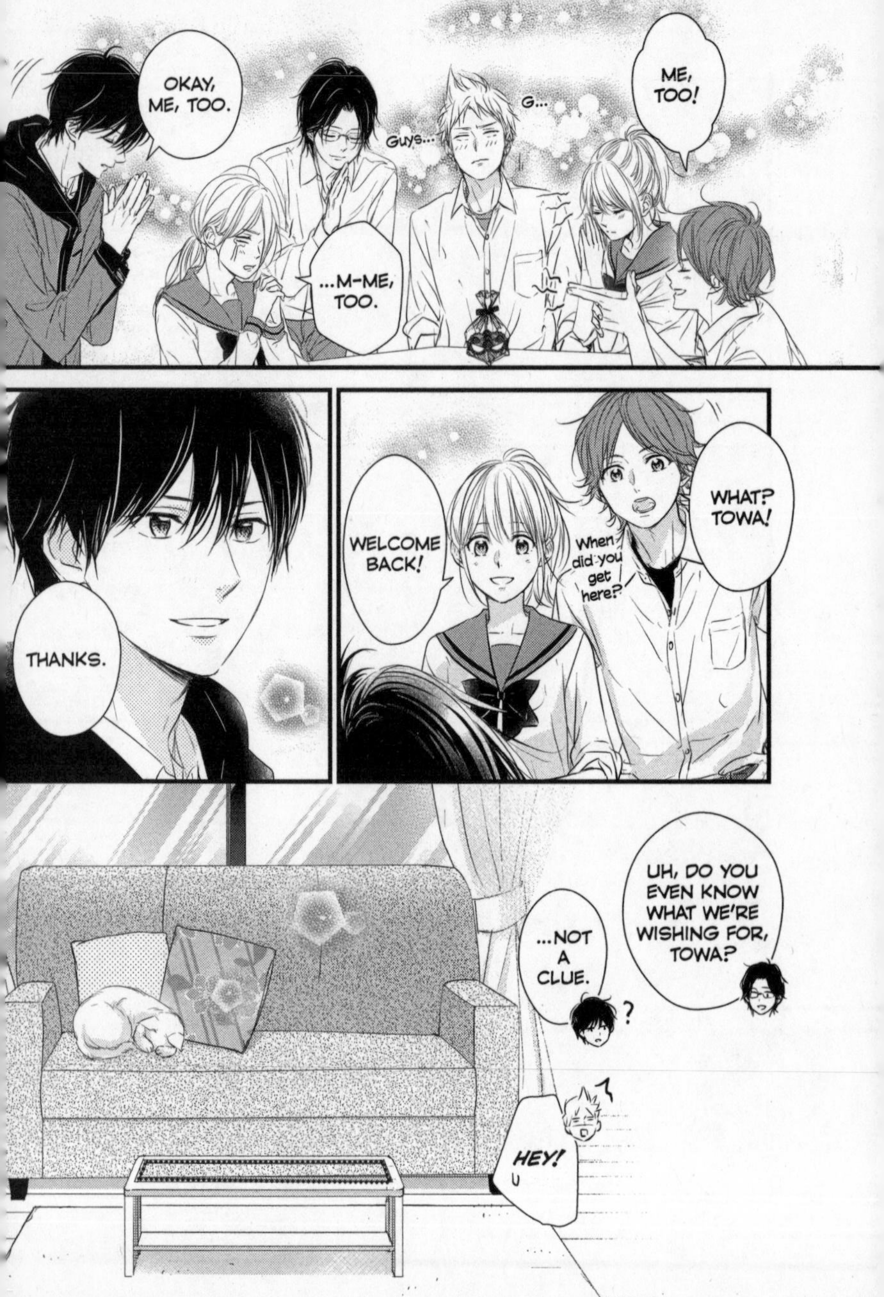
ME, TOO!
G...
Guys...
OKAY, ME, TOO.
...M-ME, TOO.
WHAT? TOWA!
When did you get here?
WELCOME BACK!
THANKS.
UH, DO YOU EVEN KNOW WHAT WE'RE WISHING FOR, TOWA?
...NOT A CLUE.
HEY!

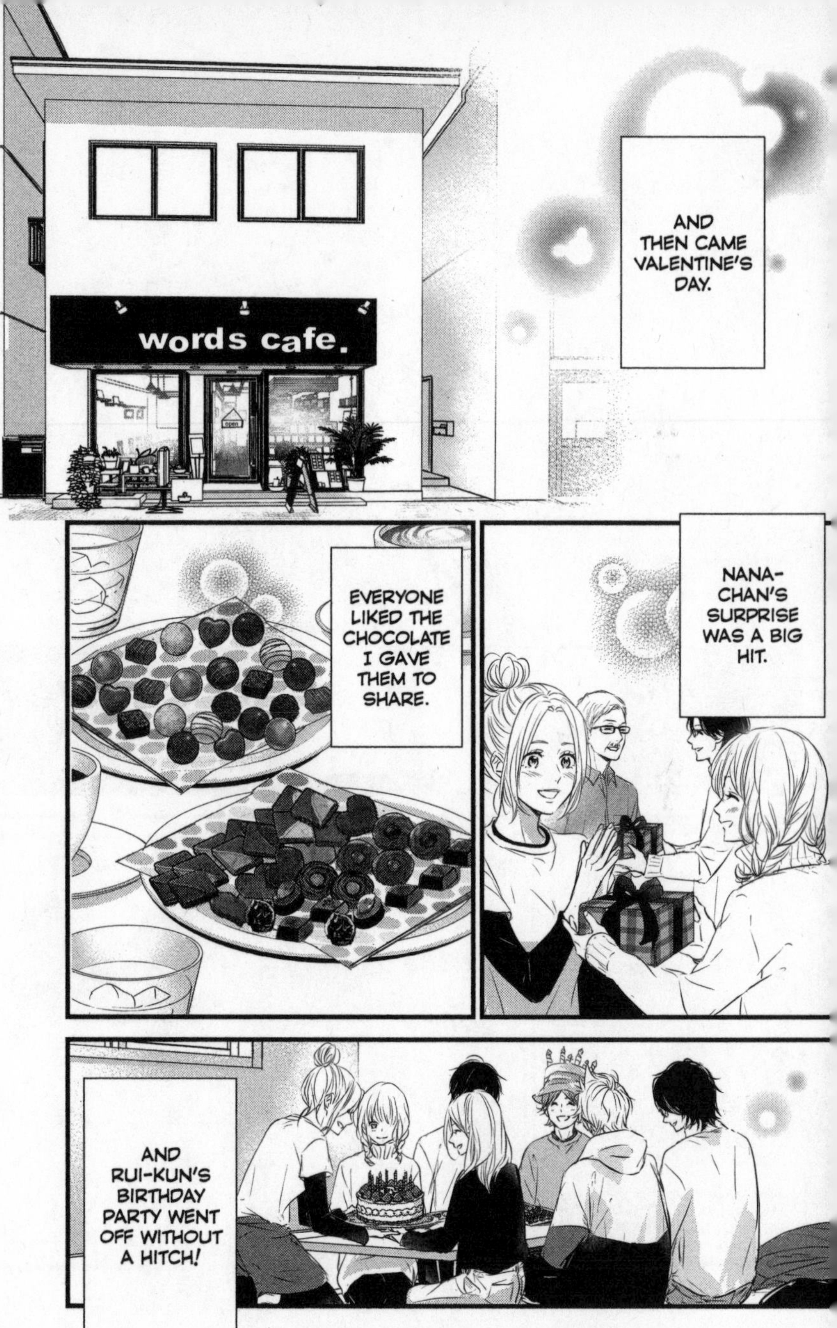
AND THEN CAME VALENTINE'S DAY.
words cafe.
NANA-CHAN'S SURPRISE WAS A BIG HIT.
EVERYONE LIKED THE CHOCOLATE I GAVE THEM TO SHARE.
AND RUI-KUN'S BIRTHDAY PARTY WENT OFF WITHOUT A HITCH!

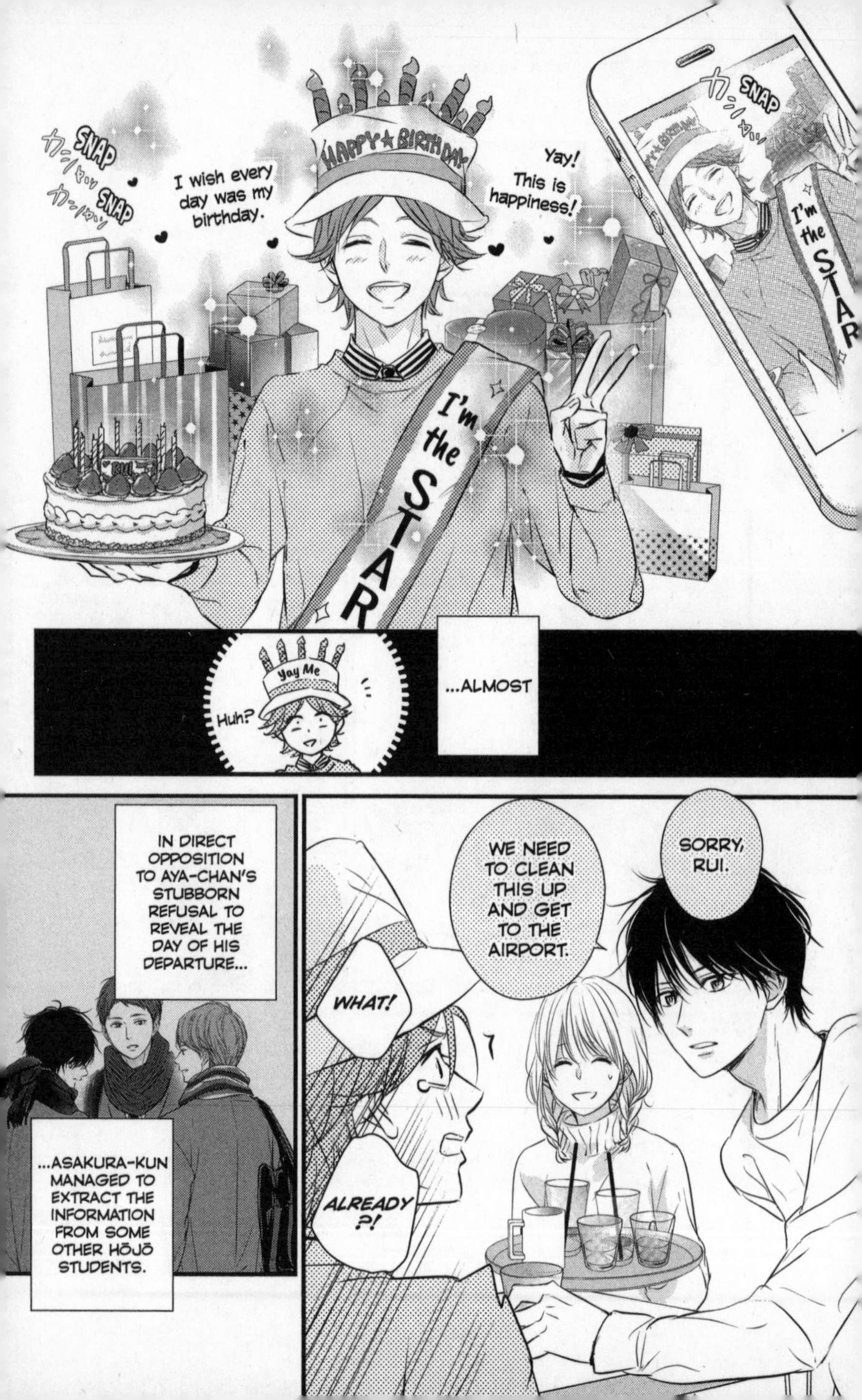
SNAP
I'm the STAR
Yay! This is happiness!
HAPPY★BIRTHDAY
I'm the STAR
I wish every day was my birthday.
SNAP
SNAP
...ALMOST
Yay Me
Huh?
SORRY, RUI.
WE NEED TO CLEAN THIS UP AND GET TO THE AIRPORT.
WHAT!
ALREADY ?!
IN DIRECT OPPOSITION TO AYA-CHAN'S STUBBORN REFUSAL TO REVEAL THE DAY OF HIS DEPARTURE...
...ASAKURA-KUN MANAGED TO EXTRACT THE INFORMATION FROM SOME OTHER HŌJŌ STUDENTS.

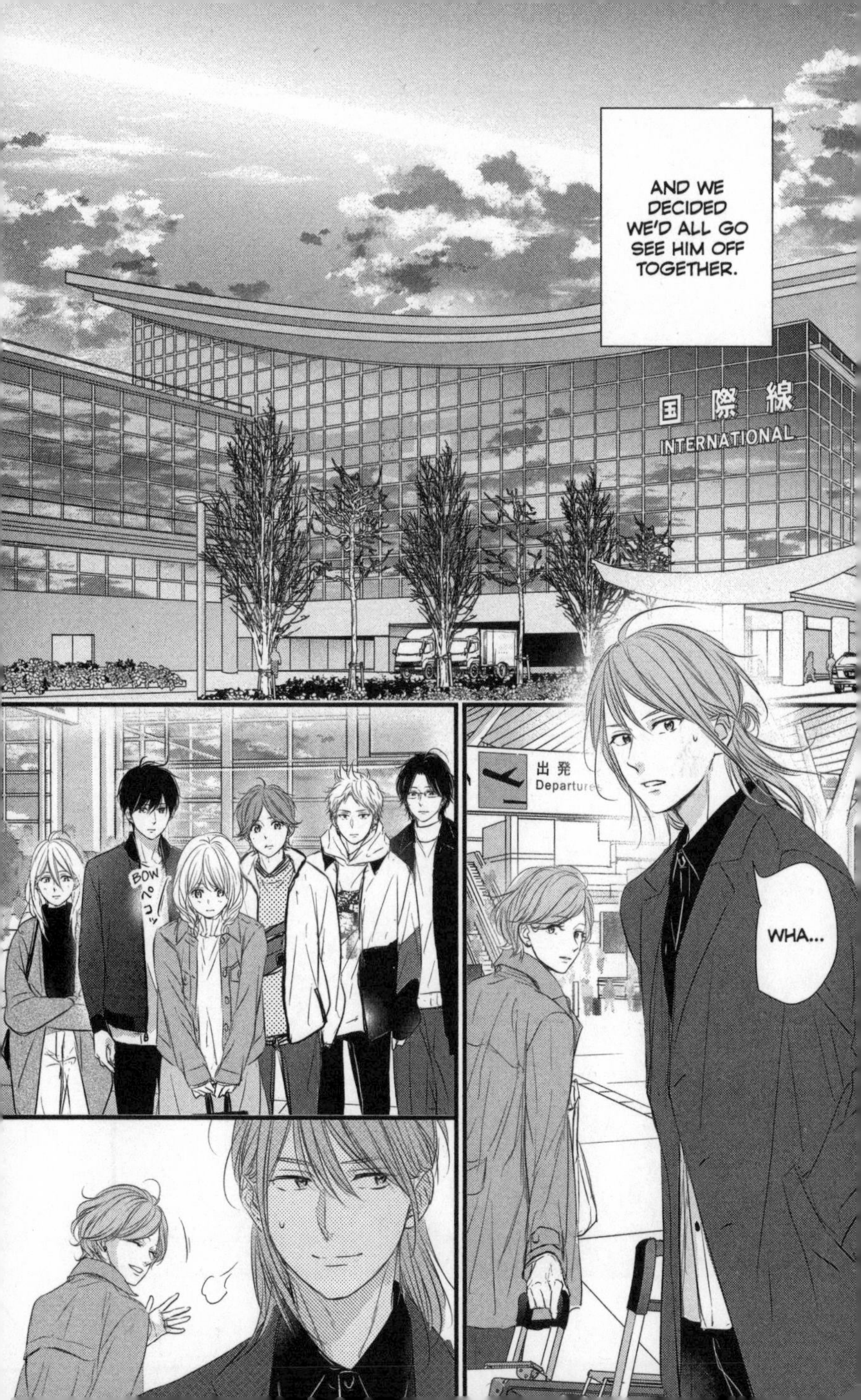
AND WE DECIDED WE'D ALL GO SEE HIM OFF TOGETHER.
国際線
INTERNATIONAL
出発
Departures
WHA...
BOW
ペコッ

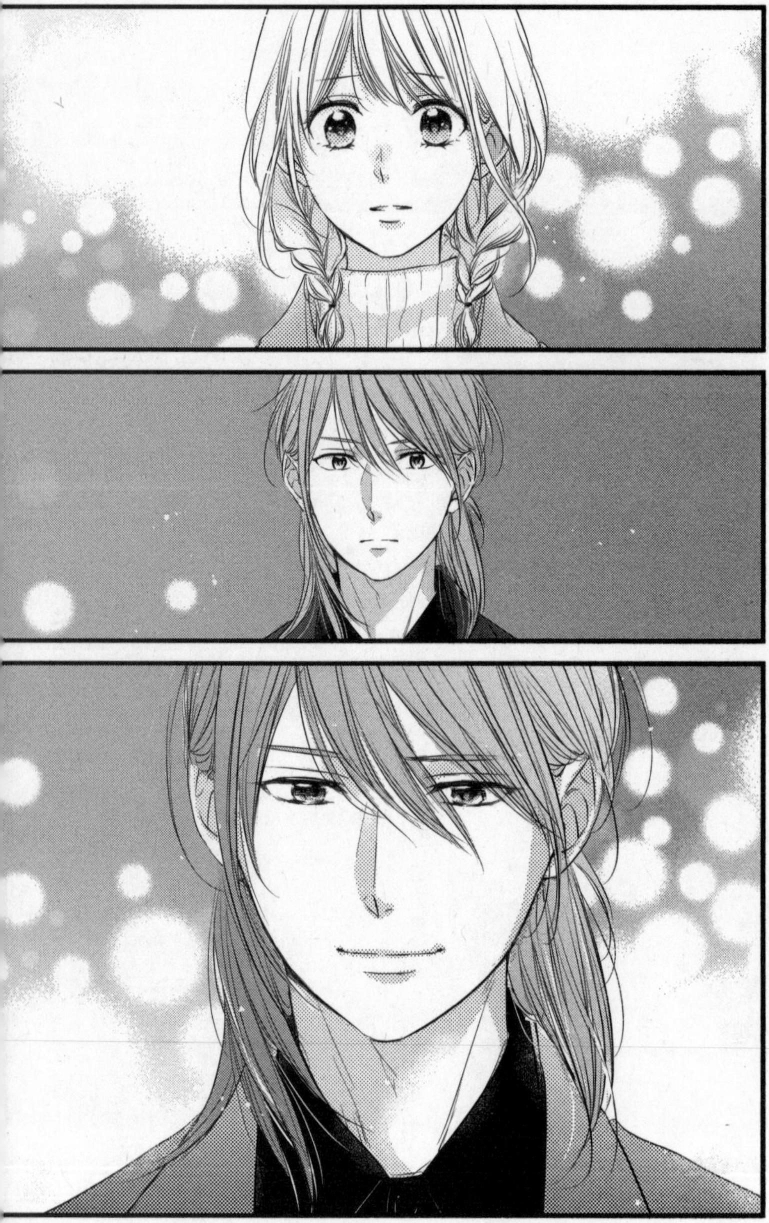

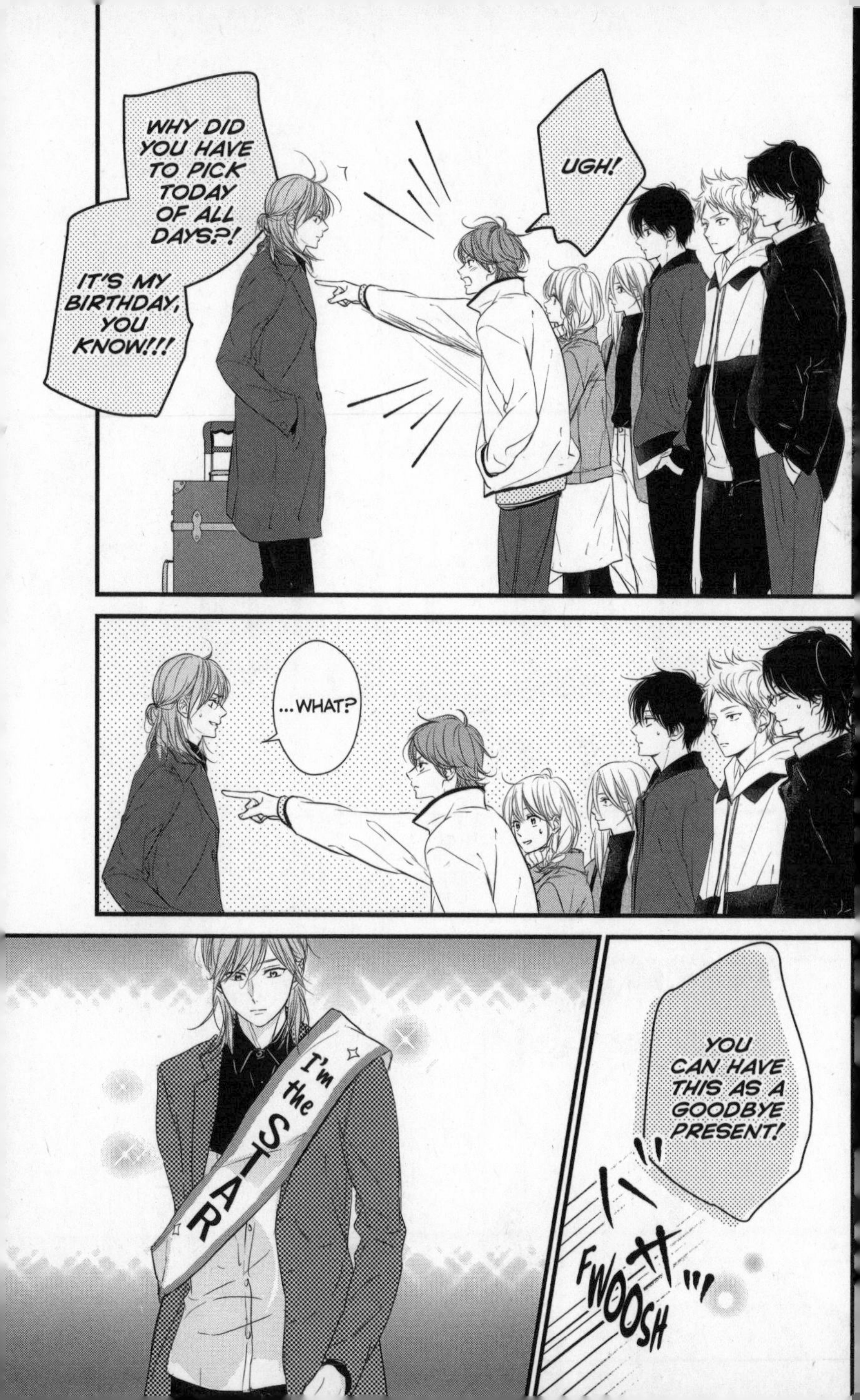
UGH!
WHY DID YOU HAVE TO PICK TODAY OF ALL DAYS?!
IT'S MY BIRTHDAY, YOU KNOW!!!
...WHAT?
YOU CAN HAVE THIS AS A GOODBYE PRESENT!
FWOOSH
I'm the STAR

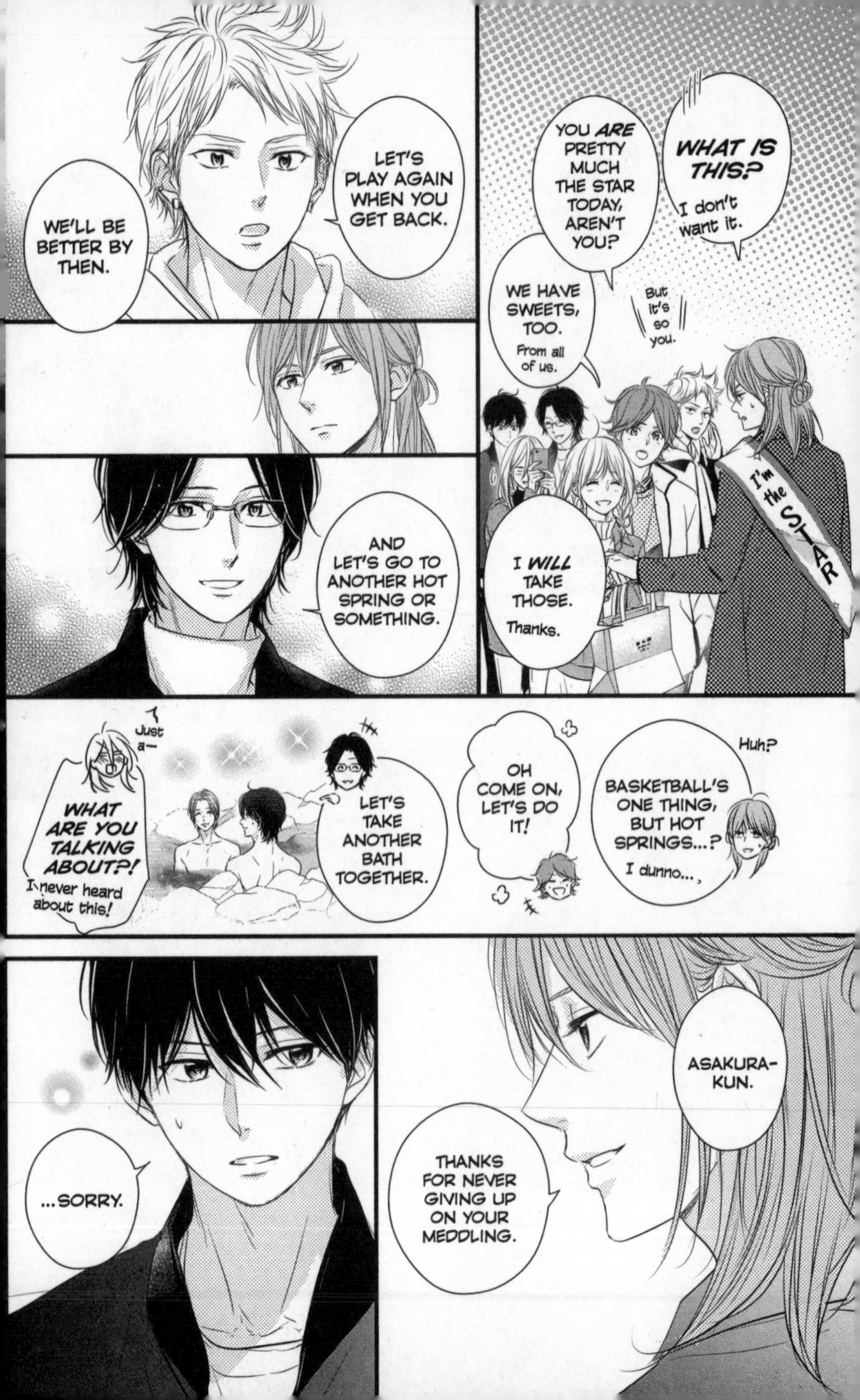
WHAT IS THIS? I don't want it.
YOU ARE PRETTY MUCH THE STAR TODAY, AREN'T YOU?
But it's so you.
WE HAVE SWEETS, TOO. From all of us.
I'm the STAR
I WILL TAKE THOSE. Thanks.
LET'S PLAY AGAIN WHEN YOU GET BACK.
WE'LL BE BETTER BY THEN.
AND LET'S GO TO ANOTHER HOT SPRING OR SOMETHING.
Huh?
BASKETBALL'S ONE THING, BUT HOT SPRINGS...? I dunno...
OH COME ON, LET'S DO IT!
LET'S TAKE ANOTHER BATH TOGETHER.
Just a—
WHAT ARE YOU TALKING ABOUT?! I never heard about this!
ASAKURA-KUN.
THANKS FOR NEVER GIVING UP ON YOUR MEDDLING.
...SORRY.

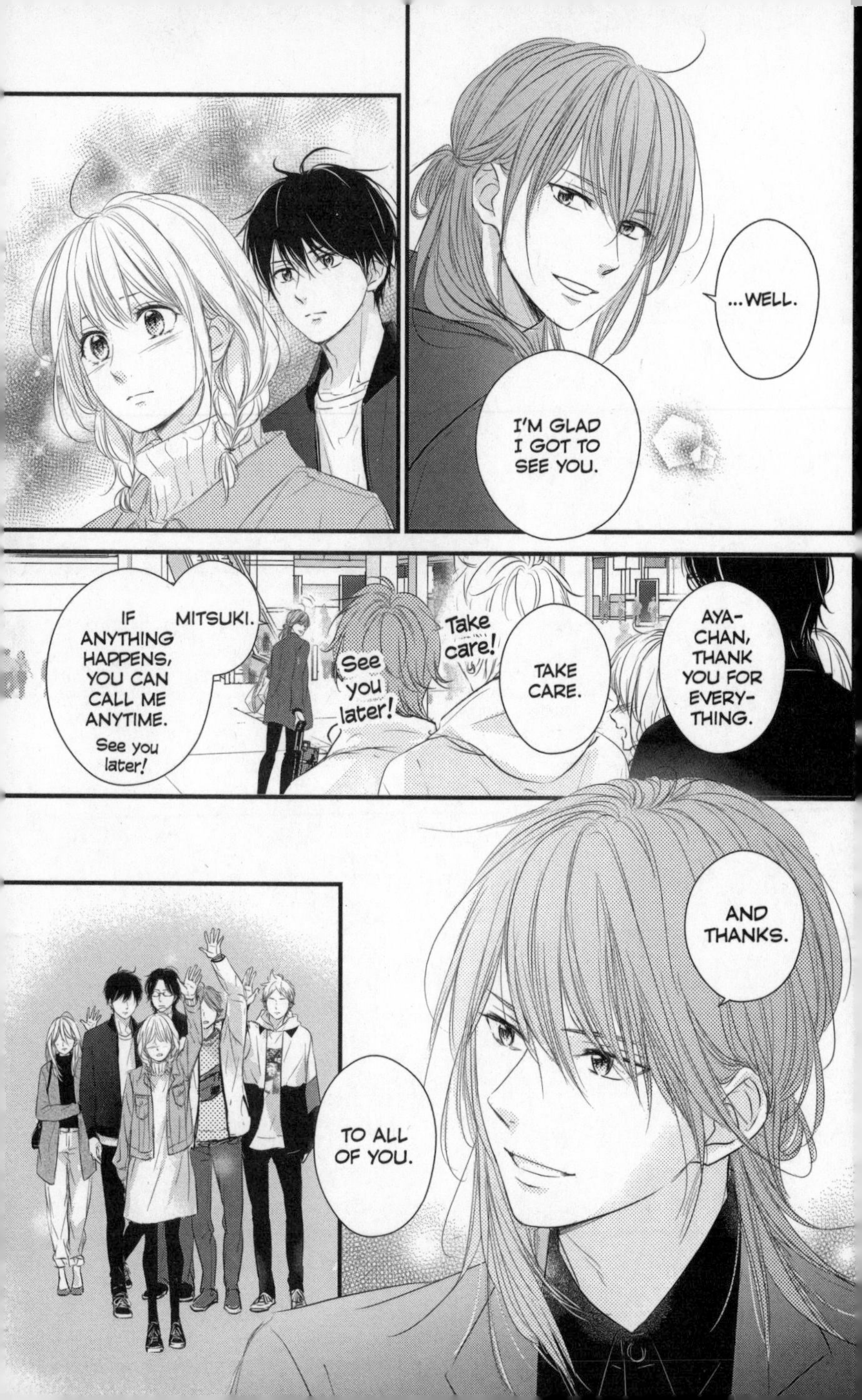

...WELL.
I'M GLAD I GOT TO SEE YOU.
AYA-CHAN, THANK YOU FOR EVERY-THING.
TAKE CARE.
Take care!
See you later!
MITSUKI. IF ANYTHING HAPPENS, YOU CAN CALL ME ANYTIME.
See you later!
AND THANKS.
TO ALL OF YOU.

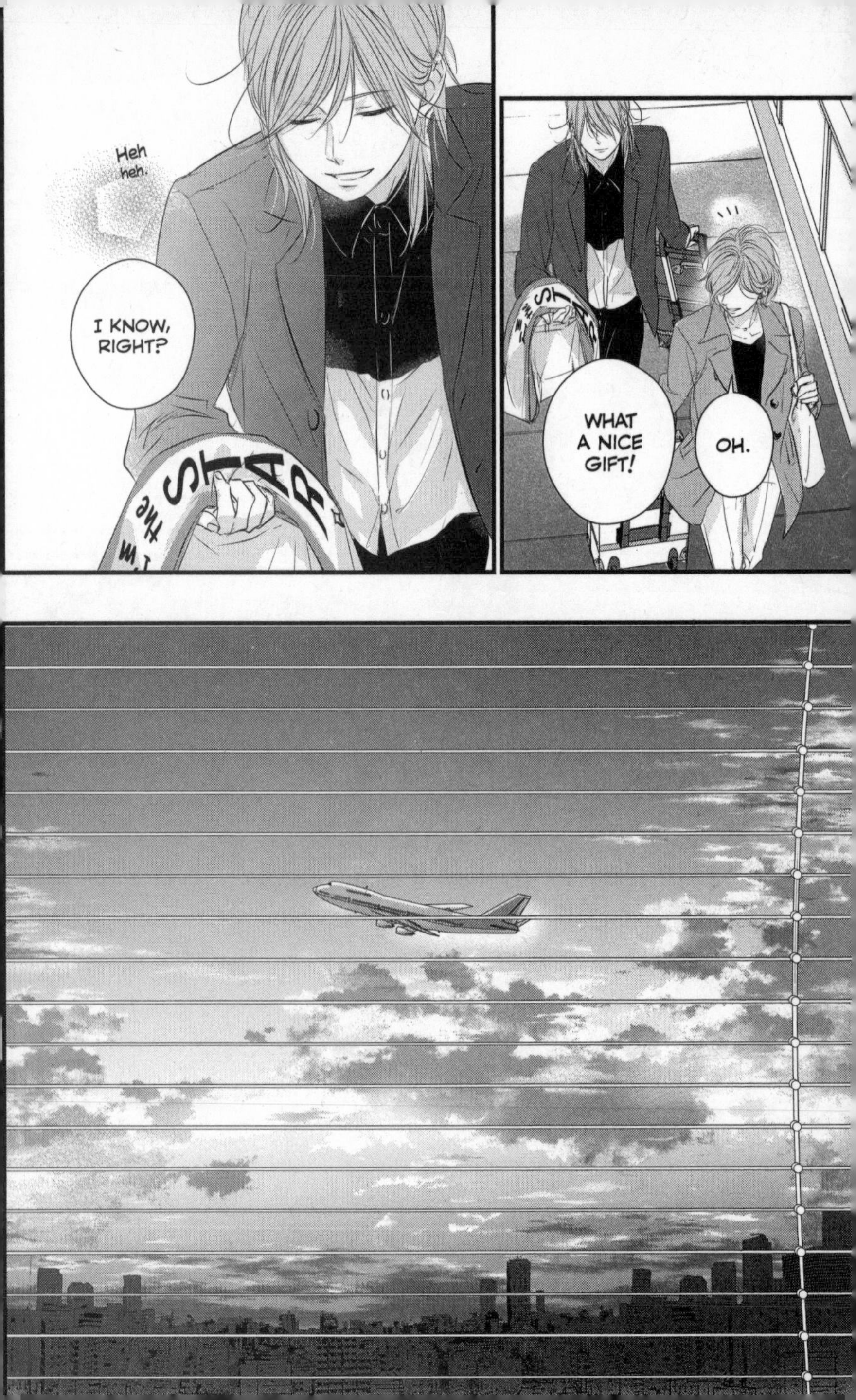
OH.
WHAT A NICE GIFT!
Heh heh.
I KNOW, RIGHT?

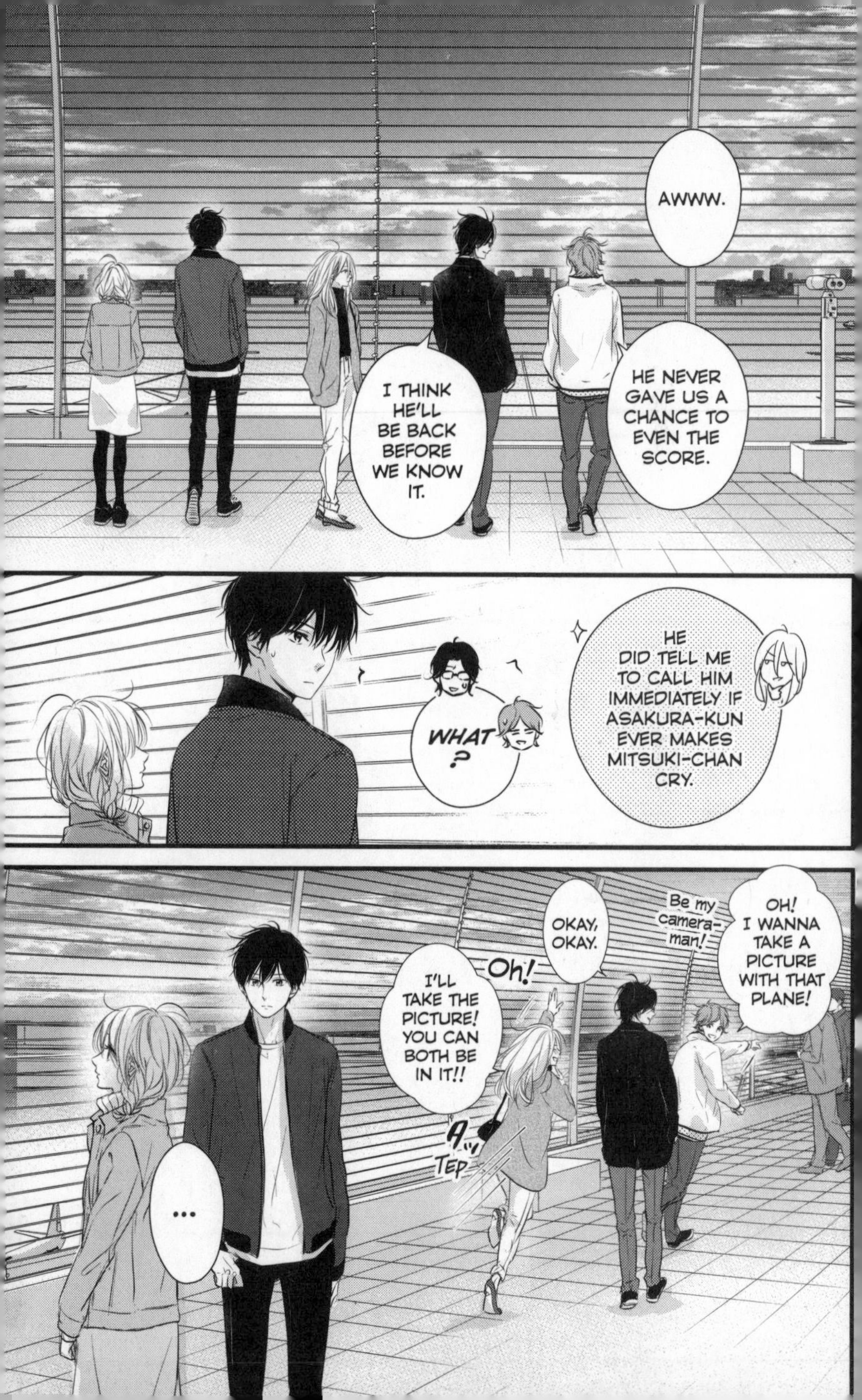
AWWW.
HE NEVER GAVE US A CHANCE TO EVEN THE SCORE.
I THINK HE'LL BE BACK BEFORE WE KNOW IT.
HE DID TELL ME TO CALL HIM IMMEDIATELY IF ASAKURA-KUN EVER MAKES MITSUKI-CHAN CRY.
WHAT?
OH! I WANNA TAKE A PICTURE WITH THAT PLANE!
Be my camera-man!
OKAY, OKAY.
Oh!
I'LL TAKE THE PICTURE! YOU CAN BOTH BE IN IT!!
TEP
...

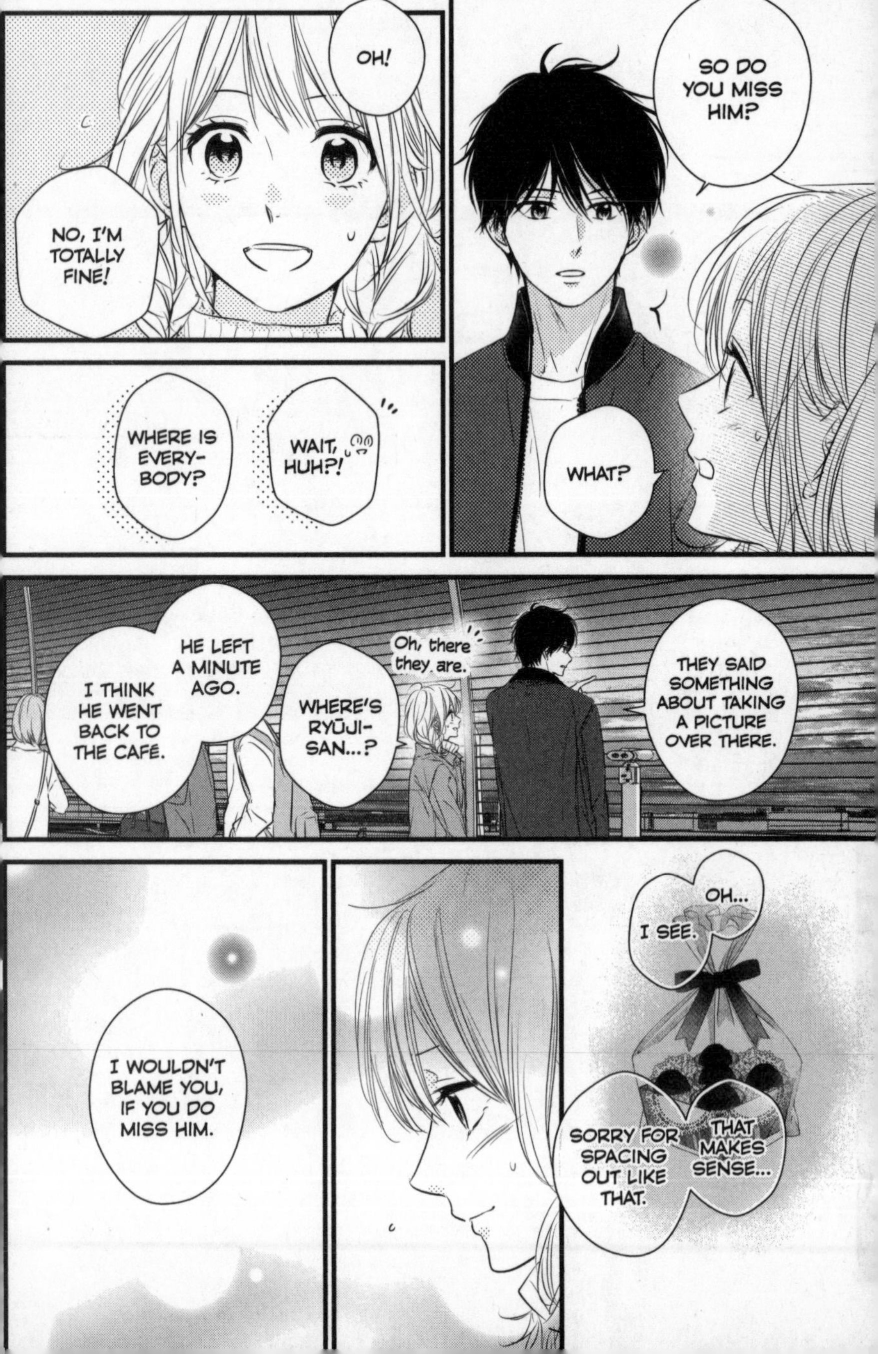
SO DO YOU MISS HIM?
WHAT?
OH!
NO, I'M TOTALLY FINE!
WAIT, HUH?!
WHERE IS EVERY-BODY?
THEY SAID SOMETHING ABOUT TAKING A PICTURE OVER THERE.
Oh, there they are.
WHERE'S RYŪJI-SAN...?
HE LEFT A MINUTE AGO.
I THINK HE WENT BACK TO THE CAFÉ.
OH... I SEE.
THAT MAKES SENSE...
SORRY FOR SPACING OUT LIKE THAT.
I WOULDN'T BLAME YOU, IF YOU DO MISS HIM.

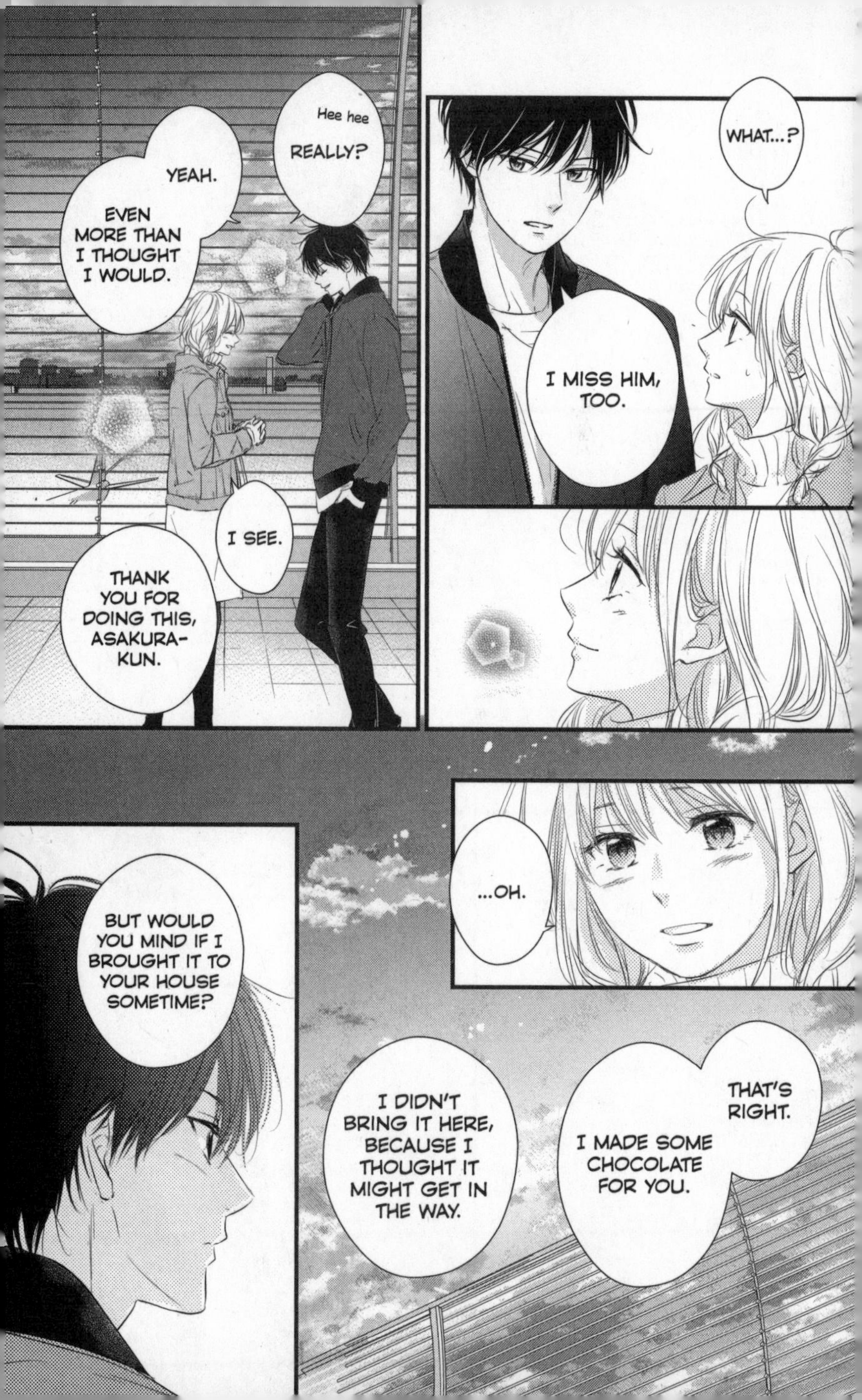
WHAT...?
I MISS HIM, TOO.
Hee hee
REALLY?
YEAH.
EVEN MORE THAN I THOUGHT I WOULD.
I SEE.
THANK YOU FOR DOING THIS, ASAKURA-KUN.
...OH.
THAT'S RIGHT.
I MADE SOME CHOCOLATE FOR YOU.
I DIDN'T BRING IT HERE, BECAUSE I THOUGHT IT MIGHT GET IN THE WAY.
BUT WOULD YOU MIND IF I BROUGHT IT TO YOUR HOUSE SOMETIME?

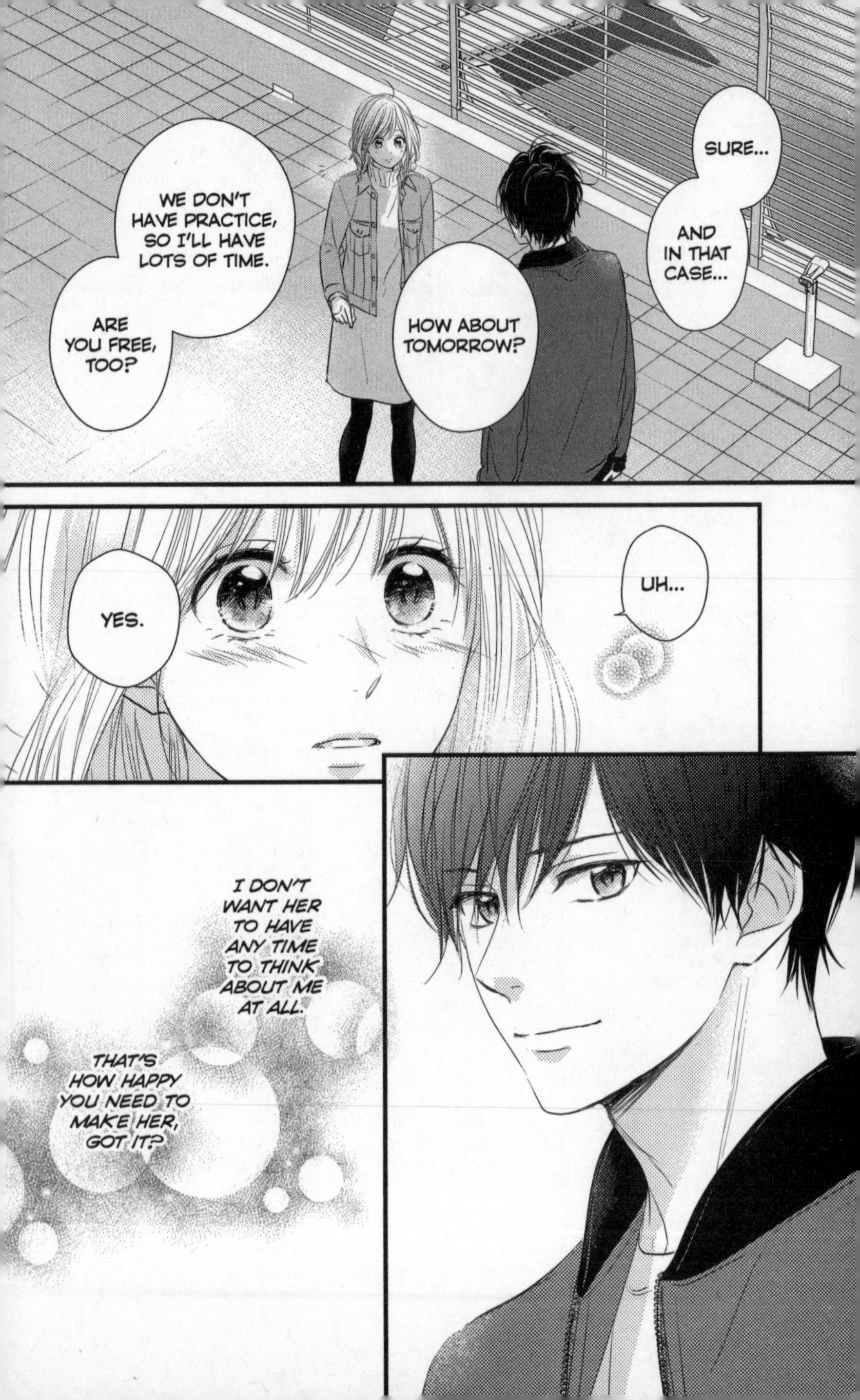
SURE...
AND IN THAT CASE...
HOW ABOUT TOMORROW?
WE DON'T HAVE PRACTICE, SO I'LL HAVE LOTS OF TIME.
ARE YOU FREE, TOO?
UH...
YES.
I DON'T WANT HER TO HAVE ANY TIME TO THINK ABOUT ME AT ALL.
THAT'S HOW HAPPY YOU NEED TO MAKE HER, GOT IT?

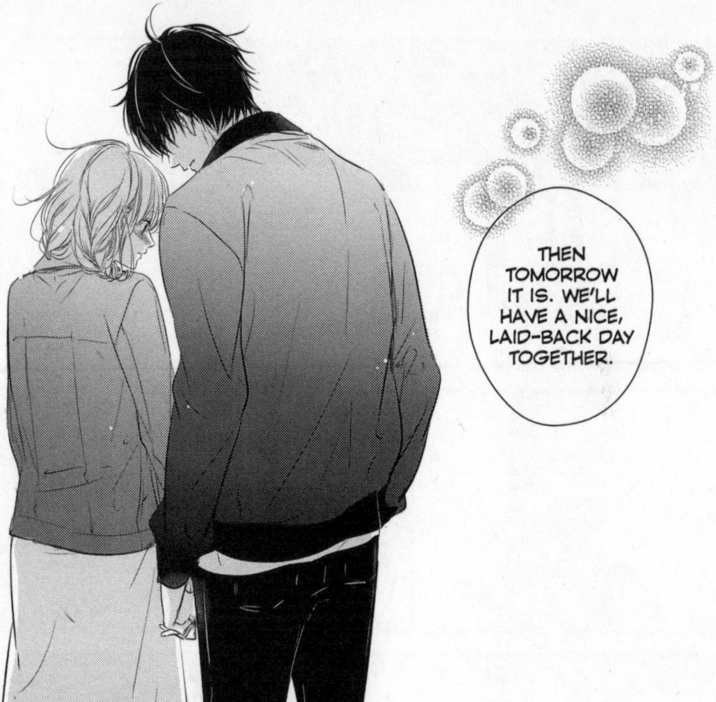
THEN TOMORROW IT IS. WE'LL HAVE A NICE, LAID-BACK DAY TOGETHER.
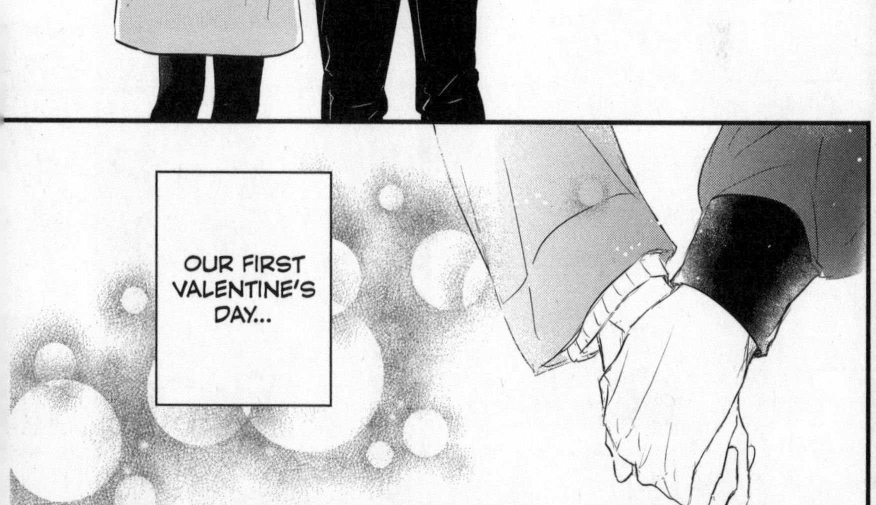
OUR FIRST VALENTINE'S DAY...

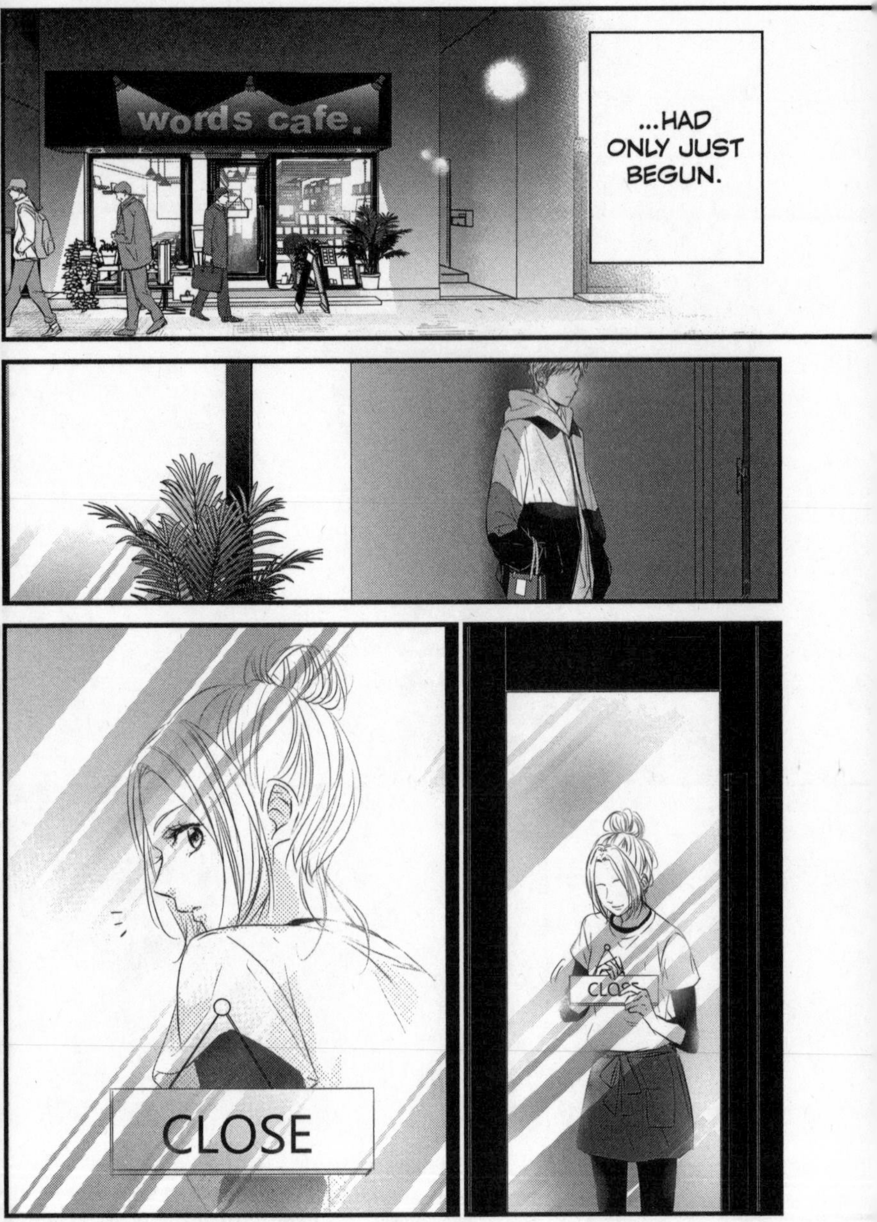
words cafe.
...HAD ONLY JUST BEGUN.
CLOSE
CLOSE

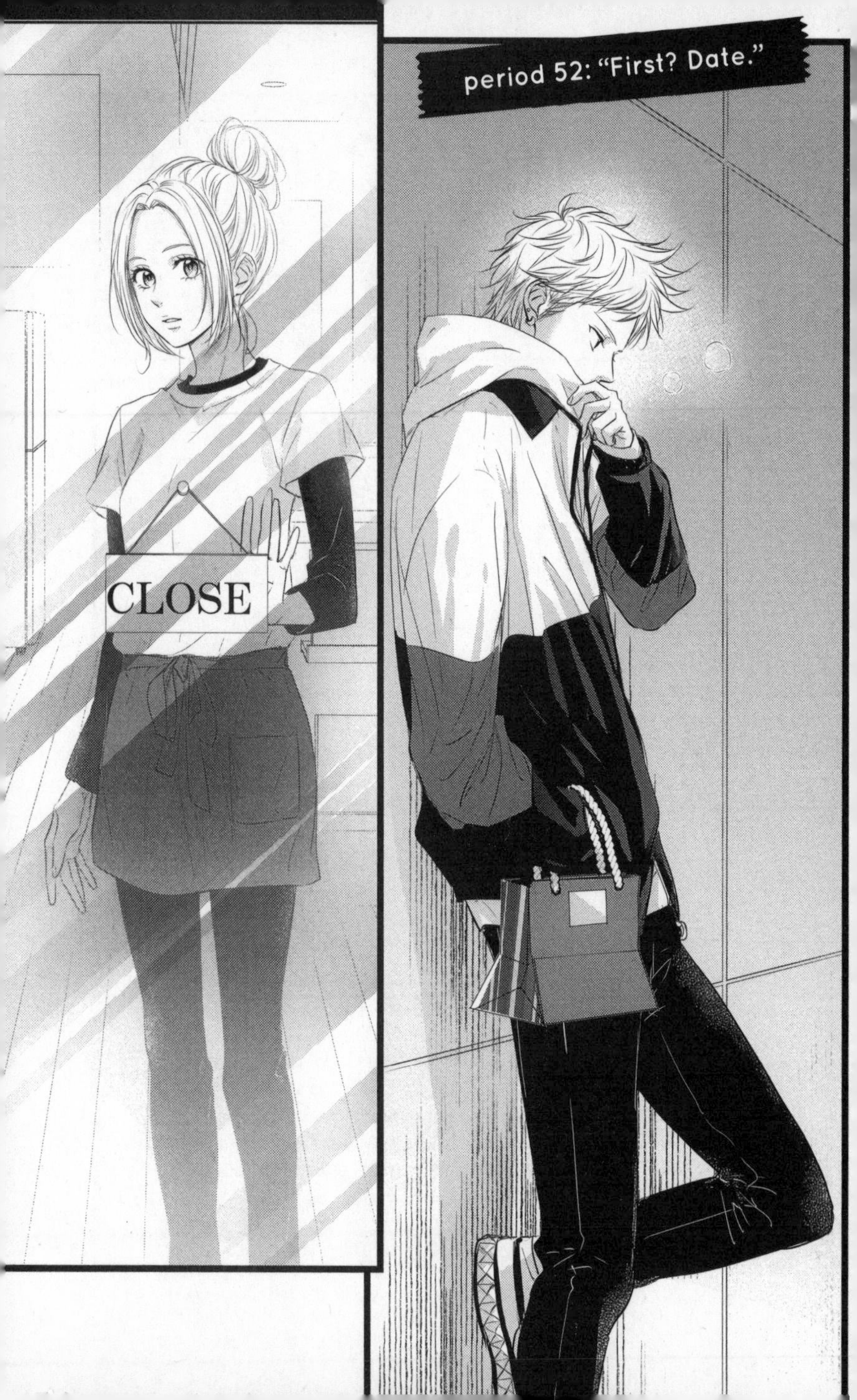
period 52: "First? Date."
CLOSE

HUH?!
WHAT
ARE YOU
DOING?

B-DMP

SPECIAL THANKS

To my editor-sama; the designer-sama; everyone on the Dessert editorial team; everyone who is involved in the creation of this work every month and every volume; everyone involved in the drama CDs, Words Cafe-sama, everyone in Owase, Shibayama-san, my assistants Masuda-san, Aki-chan, my family, And to all my readers.
I really appreciate all of you. Thank you with all my heart... ♡

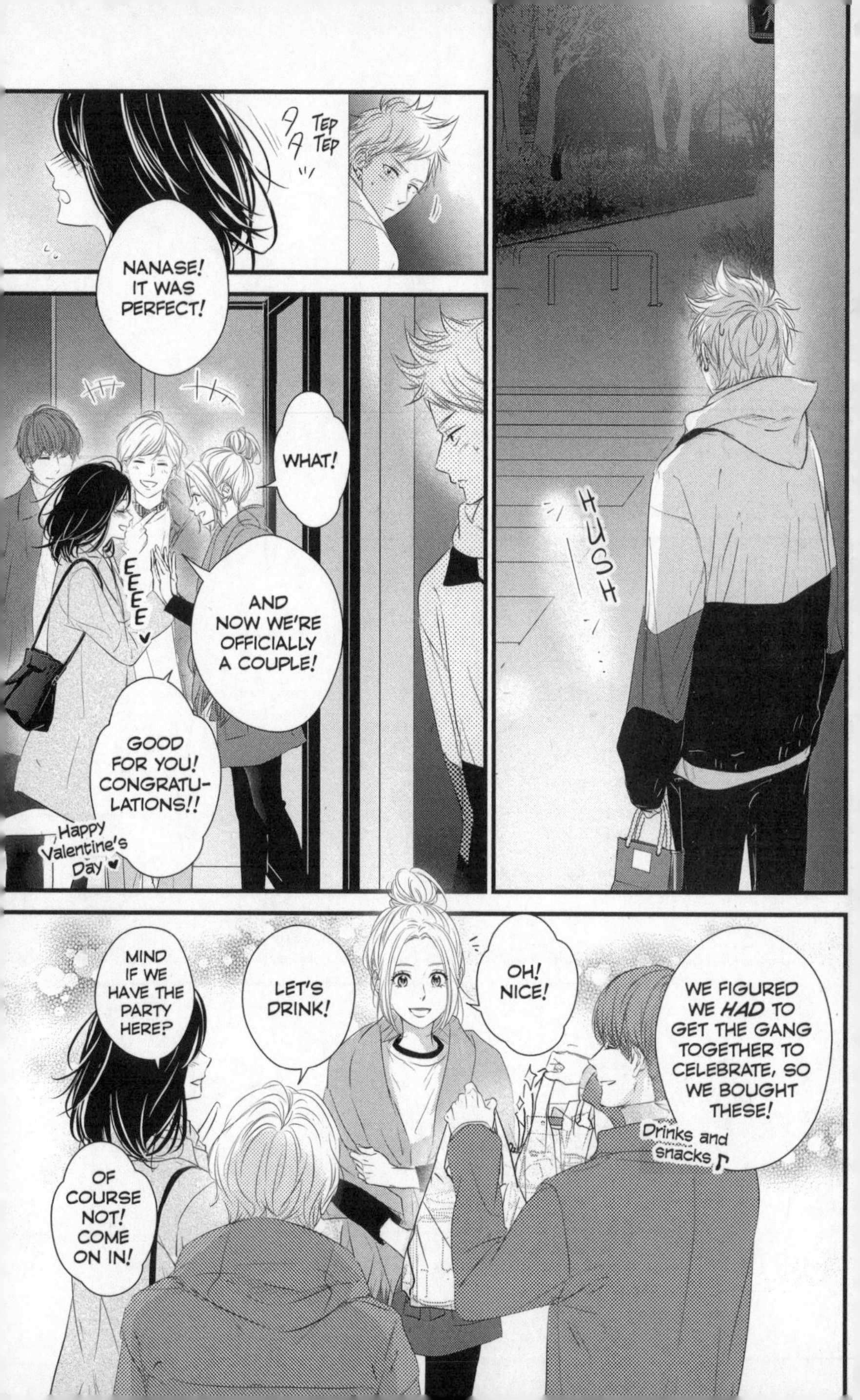
HUSH
TEP TEP
NANASE! IT WAS PERFECT!
WHAT!
AND NOW WE'RE OFFICIALLY A COUPLE!
EEEE♥
GOOD FOR YOU! CONGRATU-LATIONS!!
Happy Valentine's Day♥
WE FIGURED WE *HAD* TO GET THE GANG TOGETHER TO CELEBRATE, SO WE BOUGHT THESE!
Drinks and snacks♪
OH! NICE!
LET'S DRINK!
MIND IF WE HAVE THE PARTY HERE?
OF COURSE NOT! COME ON IN!

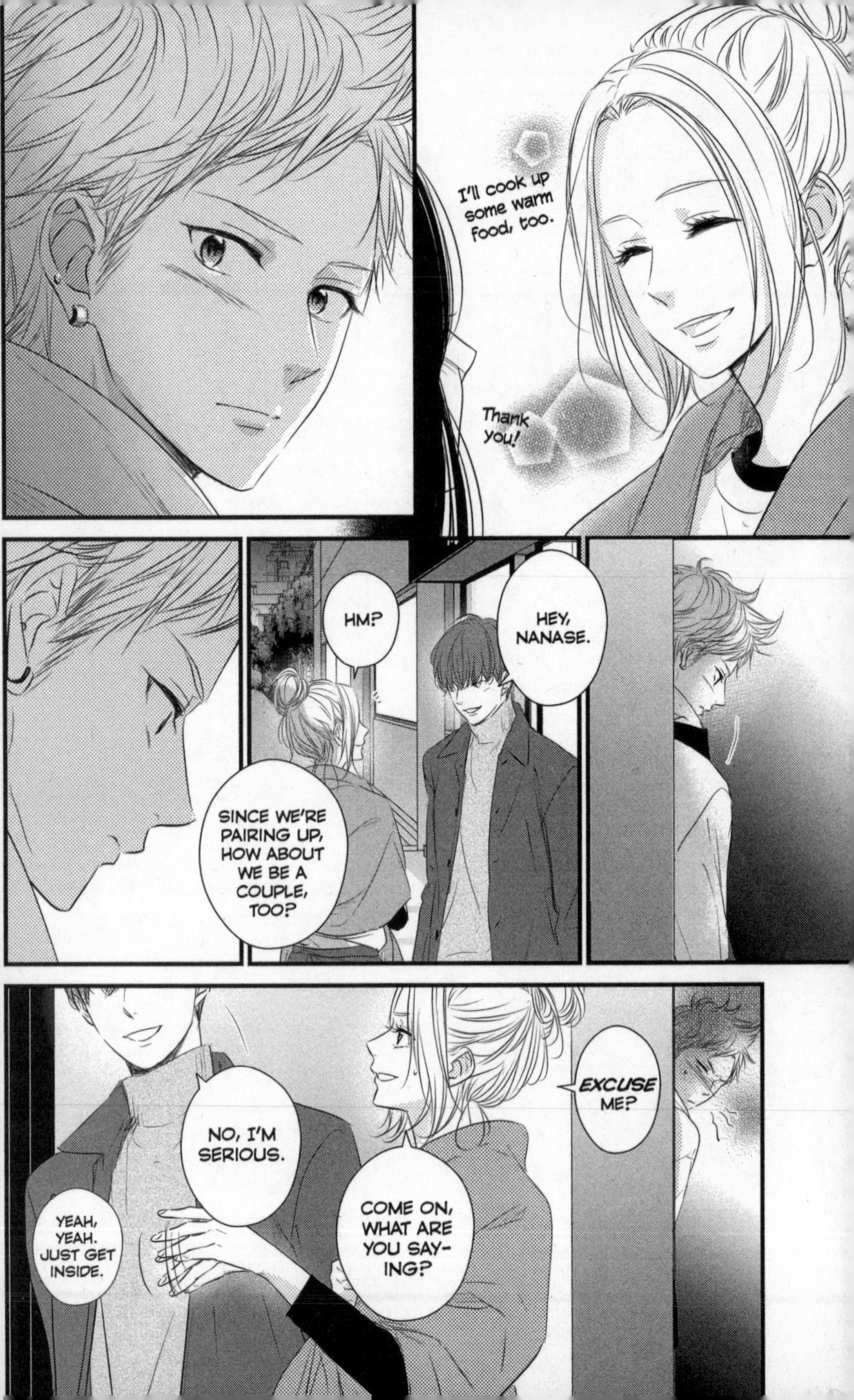
I'll cook up some warm food, too.
Thank you!
HEY, NANASE.
HM?
SINCE WE'RE PAIRING UP, HOW ABOUT WE BE A COUPLE, TOO?
EXCUSE ME?
COME ON, WHAT ARE YOU SAYING?
NO, I'M SERIOUS.
YEAH, YEAH. JUST GET INSIDE.

KA-CHAK

WE'RE GONNA PARTY HARD TONIGHT!

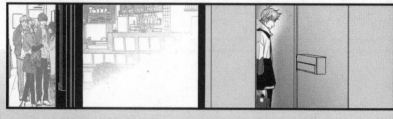

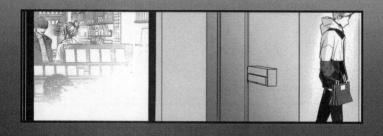

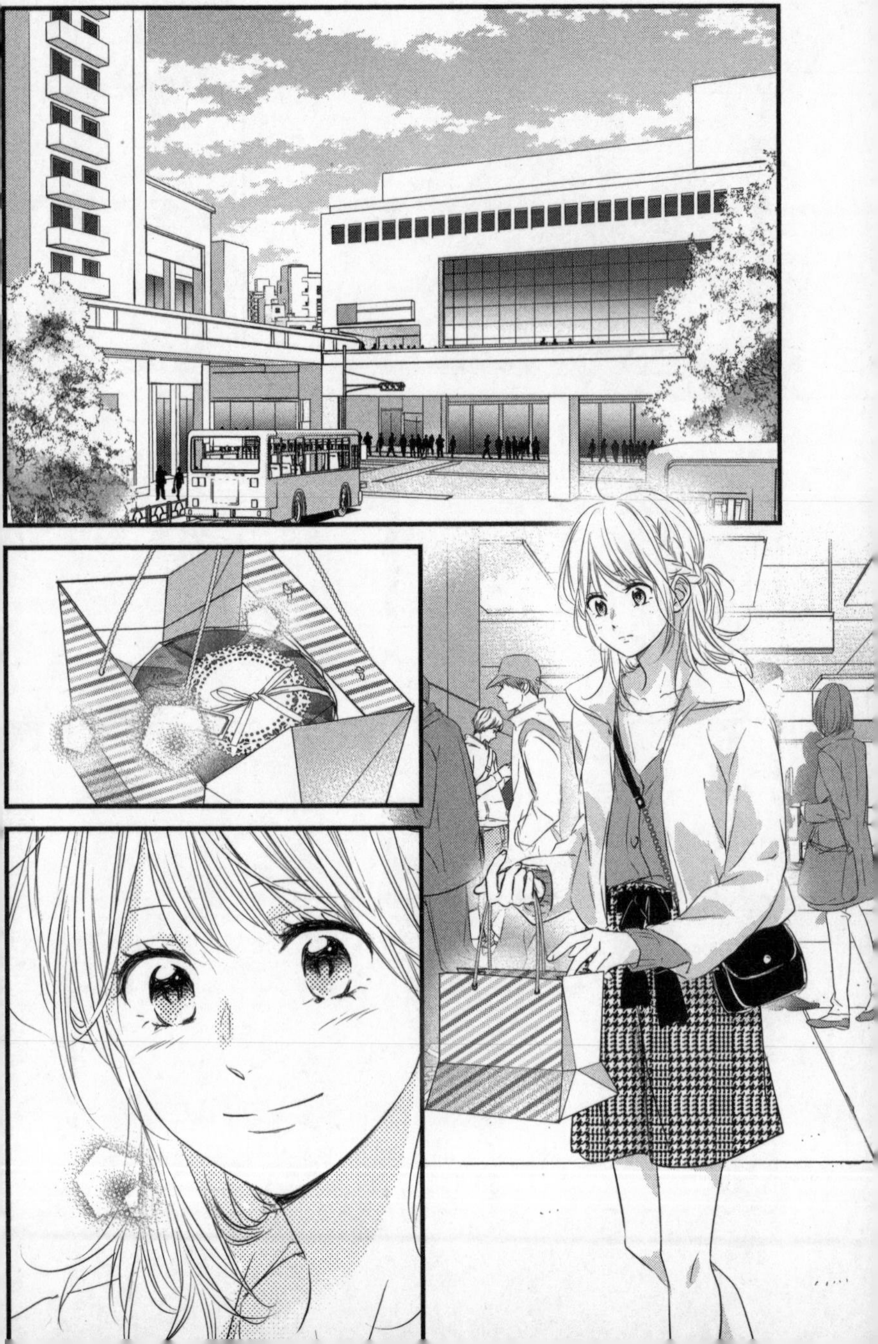

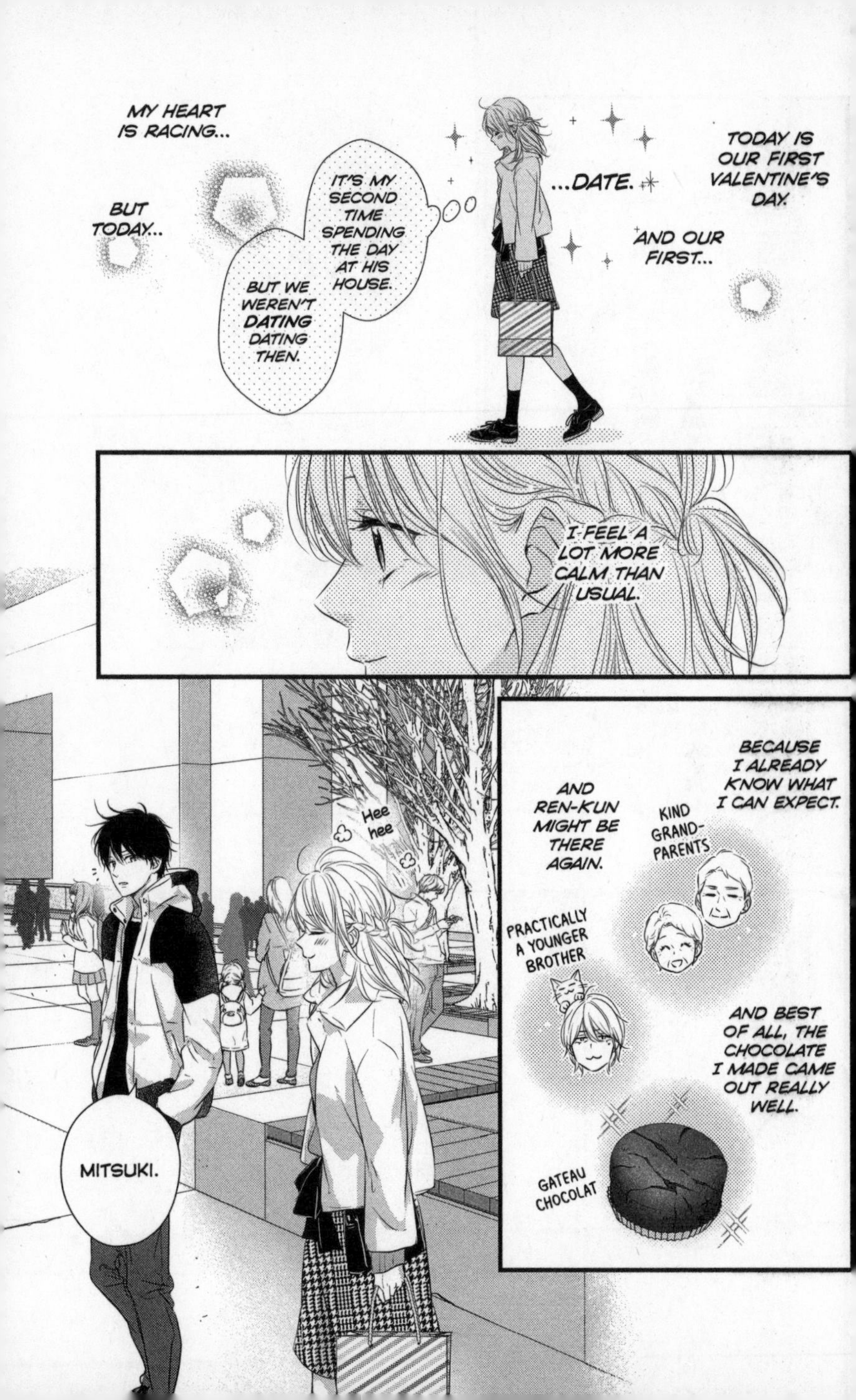
TODAY IS OUR FIRST VALENTINE'S DAY.
AND OUR FIRST...
...DATE.
IT'S MY SECOND TIME SPENDING THE DAY AT HIS HOUSE.
BUT WE WEREN'T DATING DATING THEN.
MY HEART IS RACING...
BUT TODAY...
I FEEL A LOT MORE CALM THAN USUAL.
BECAUSE I ALREADY KNOW WHAT I CAN EXPECT.
KIND GRAND-PARENTS
AND REN-KUN MIGHT BE THERE AGAIN.
PRACTICALLY A YOUNGER BROTHER
AND BEST OF ALL, THE CHOCOLATE I MADE CAME OUT REALLY WELL.
GATEAU CHOCOLAT
Hee hee
MITSUKI.

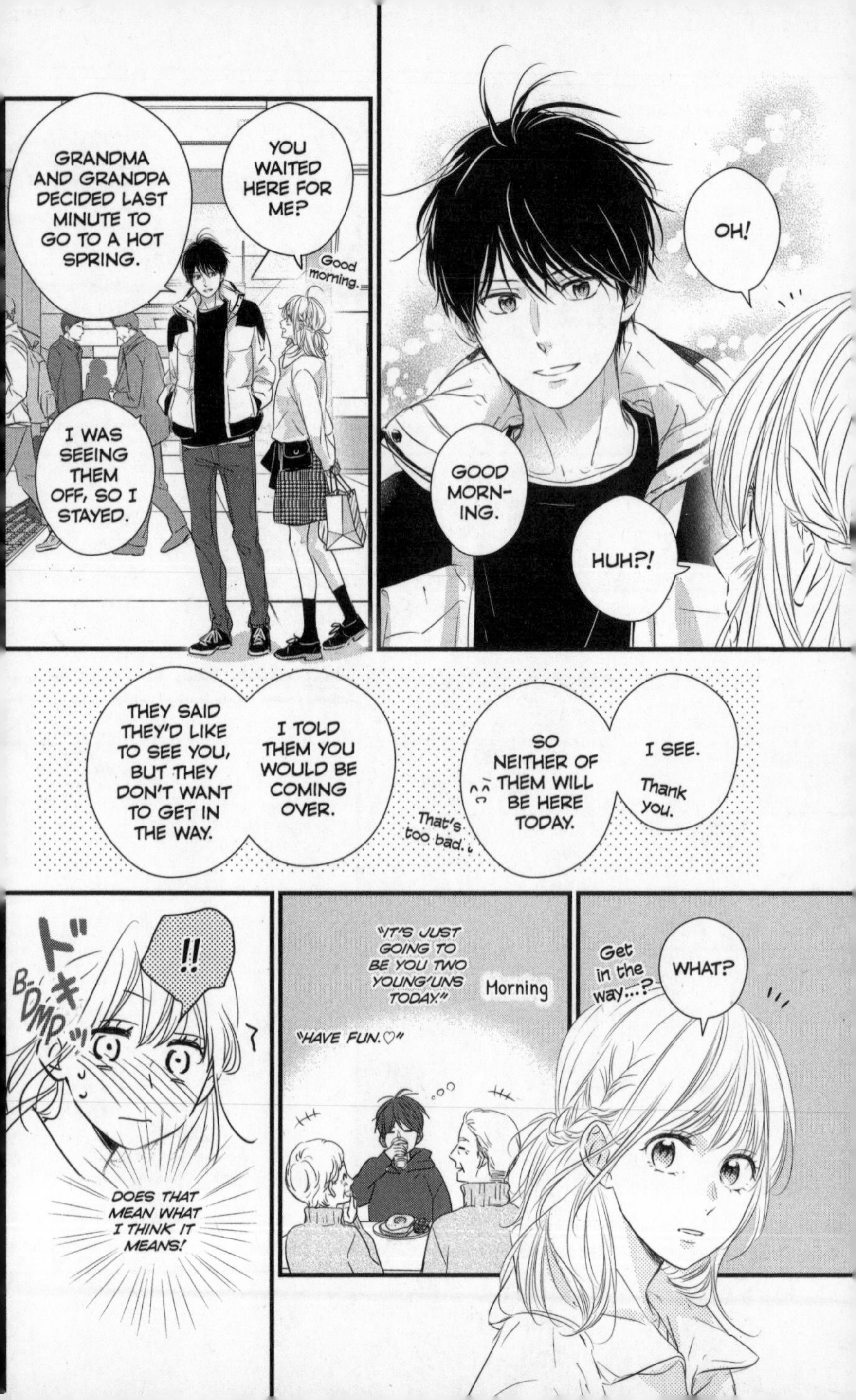
OH!
GOOD MORNING.
HUH?!
YOU WAITED HERE FOR ME?
Good morning.
GRANDMA AND GRANDPA DECIDED LAST MINUTE TO GO TO A HOT SPRING.
I WAS SEEING THEM OFF, SO I STAYED.
I SEE.
Thank you.
SO NEITHER OF THEM WILL BE HERE TODAY.
That's too bad.
I TOLD THEM YOU WOULD BE COMING OVER.
THEY SAID THEY'D LIKE TO SEE YOU, BUT THEY DON'T WANT TO GET IN THE WAY.
WHAT?
Get in the way...?
"IT'S JUST GOING TO BE YOU TWO YOUNG'UNS TODAY."
Morning
"HAVE FUN.♡"
!!
ドキ
B-DMP
DOES THAT MEAN WHAT I THINK IT MEANS!

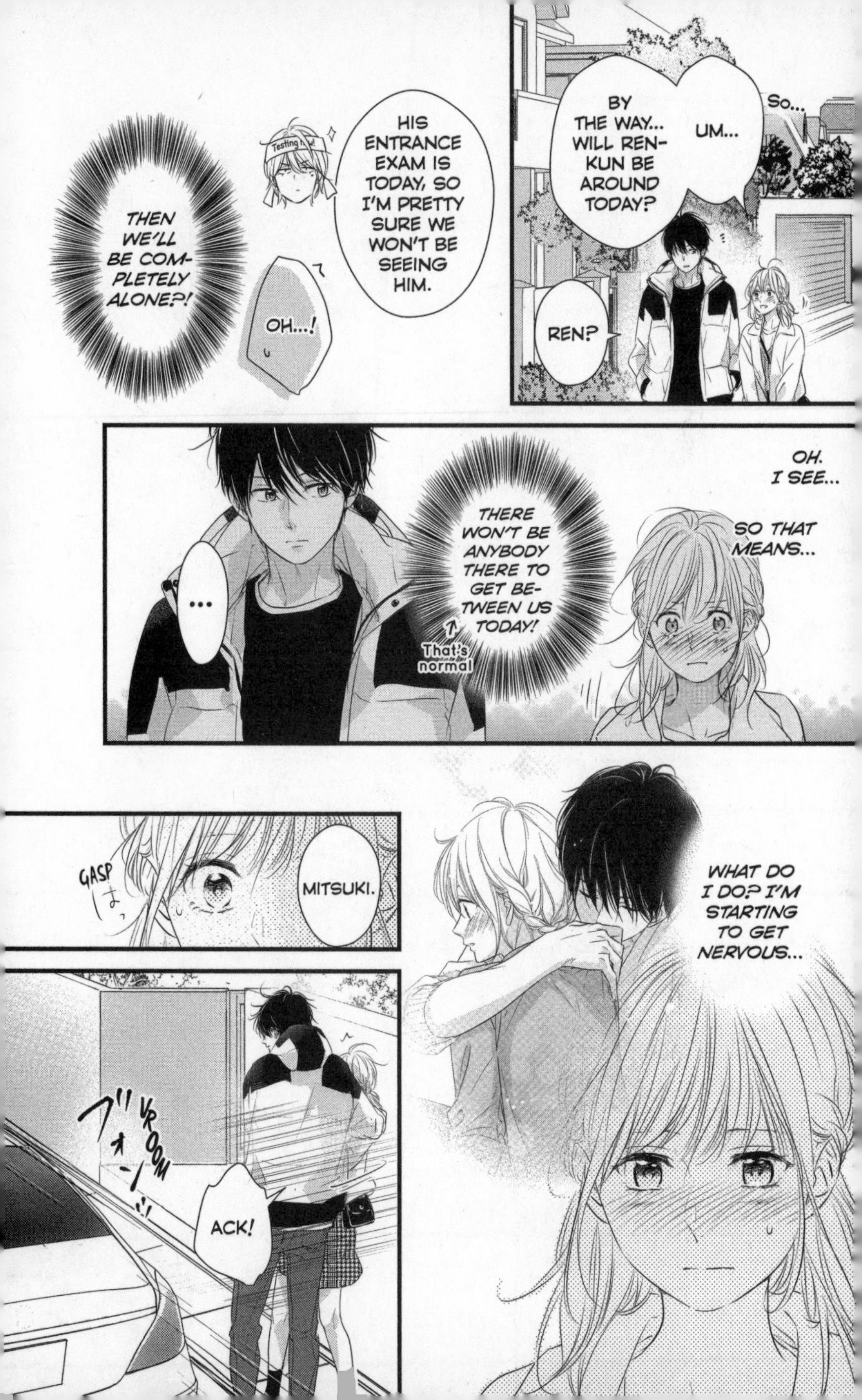
So...
UM...
BY THE WAY... WILL REN-KUN BE AROUND TODAY?
REN?
HIS ENTRANCE EXAM IS TODAY, SO I'M PRETTY SURE WE WON'T BE SEEING HIM.
OH...!
THEN WE'LL BE COMPLETELY ALONE?!
OH. I SEE...
SO THAT MEANS...
THERE WON'T BE ANYBODY THERE TO GET BETWEEN US TODAY!
That's normal
...
WHAT DO I DO? I'M STARTING TO GET NERVOUS...
MITSUKI.
GASP
VROOM
ACK!

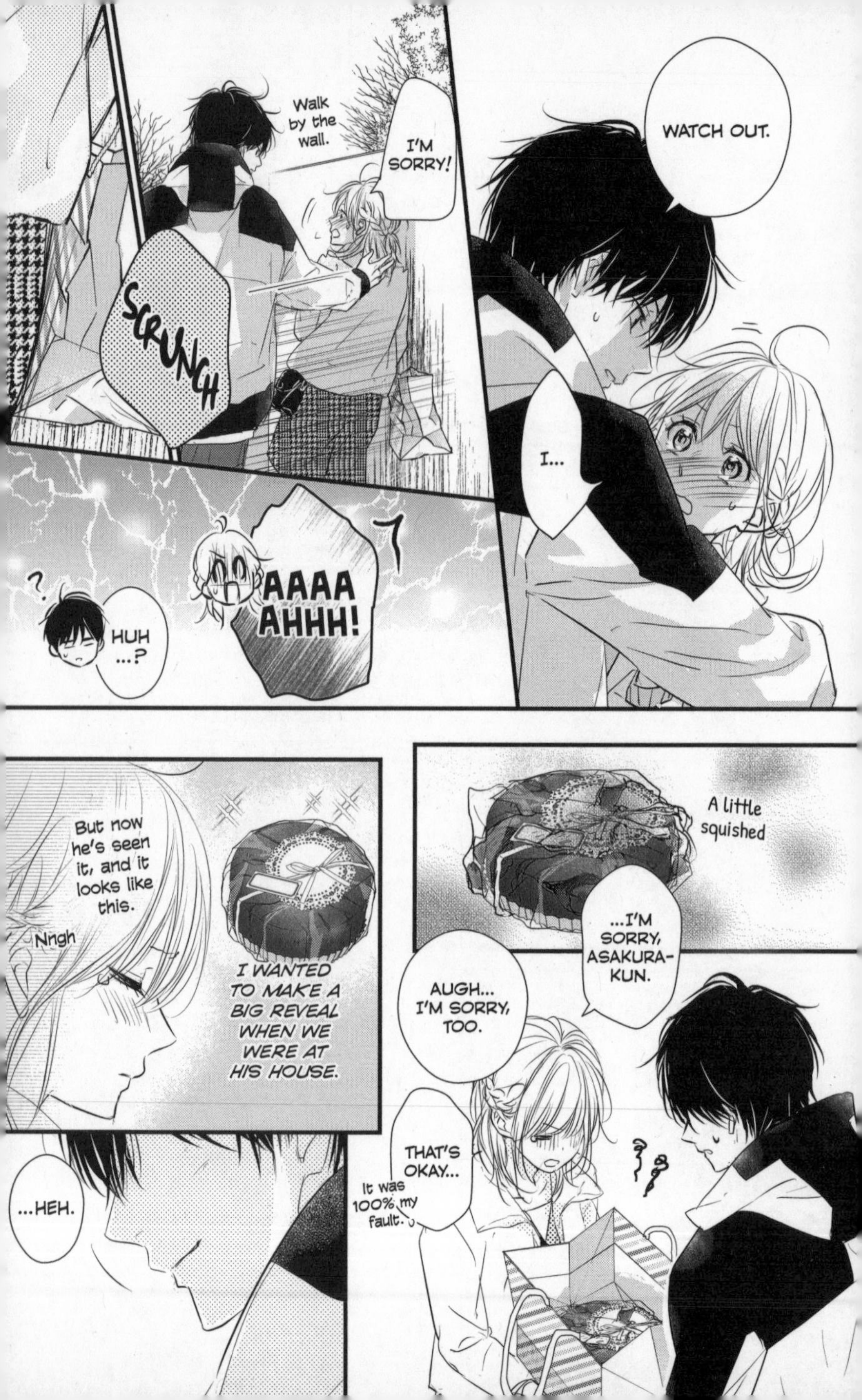
WATCH OUT.
I...
I'M SORRY!
Walk by the wall.
SCRUNCH
AAAA AHHH!
HUH ...?
A little squished
...I'M SORRY, ASAKURA-KUN.
But now he's seen it, and it looks like this.
I WANTED TO MAKE A BIG REVEAL WHEN WE WERE AT HIS HOUSE.
Nngh
AUGH... I'M SORRY, TOO.
THAT'S OKAY...
It was 100% my fault.
...HEH.

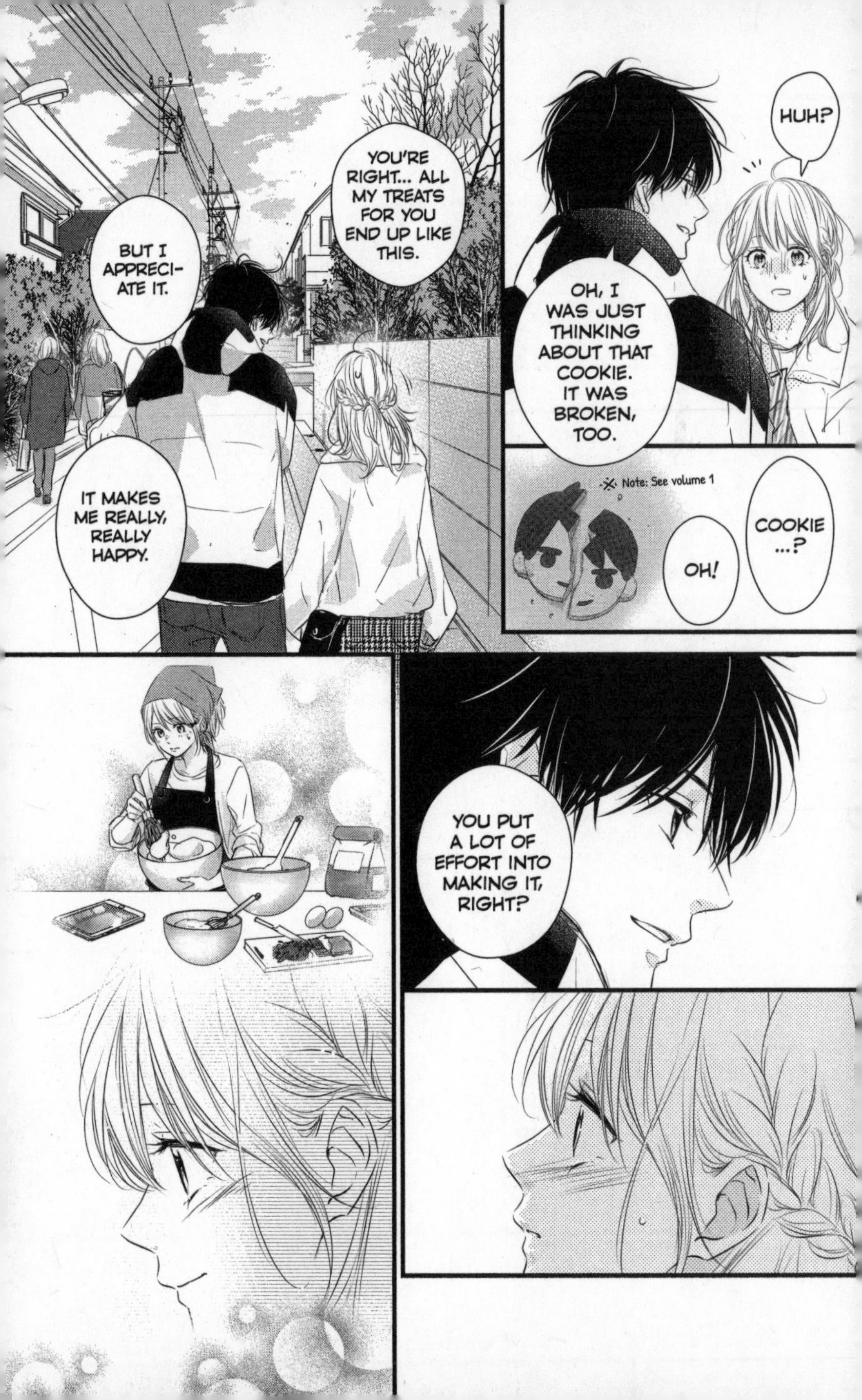
HUH?
OH, I WAS JUST THINKING ABOUT THAT COOKIE. IT WAS BROKEN, TOO.
COOKIE ...?
OH!
※ Note: See volume 1
YOU'RE RIGHT... ALL MY TREATS FOR YOU END UP LIKE THIS.
BUT I APPRECI-ATE IT.
IT MAKES ME REALLY, REALLY HAPPY.
YOU PUT A LOT OF EFFORT INTO MAKING IT, RIGHT?

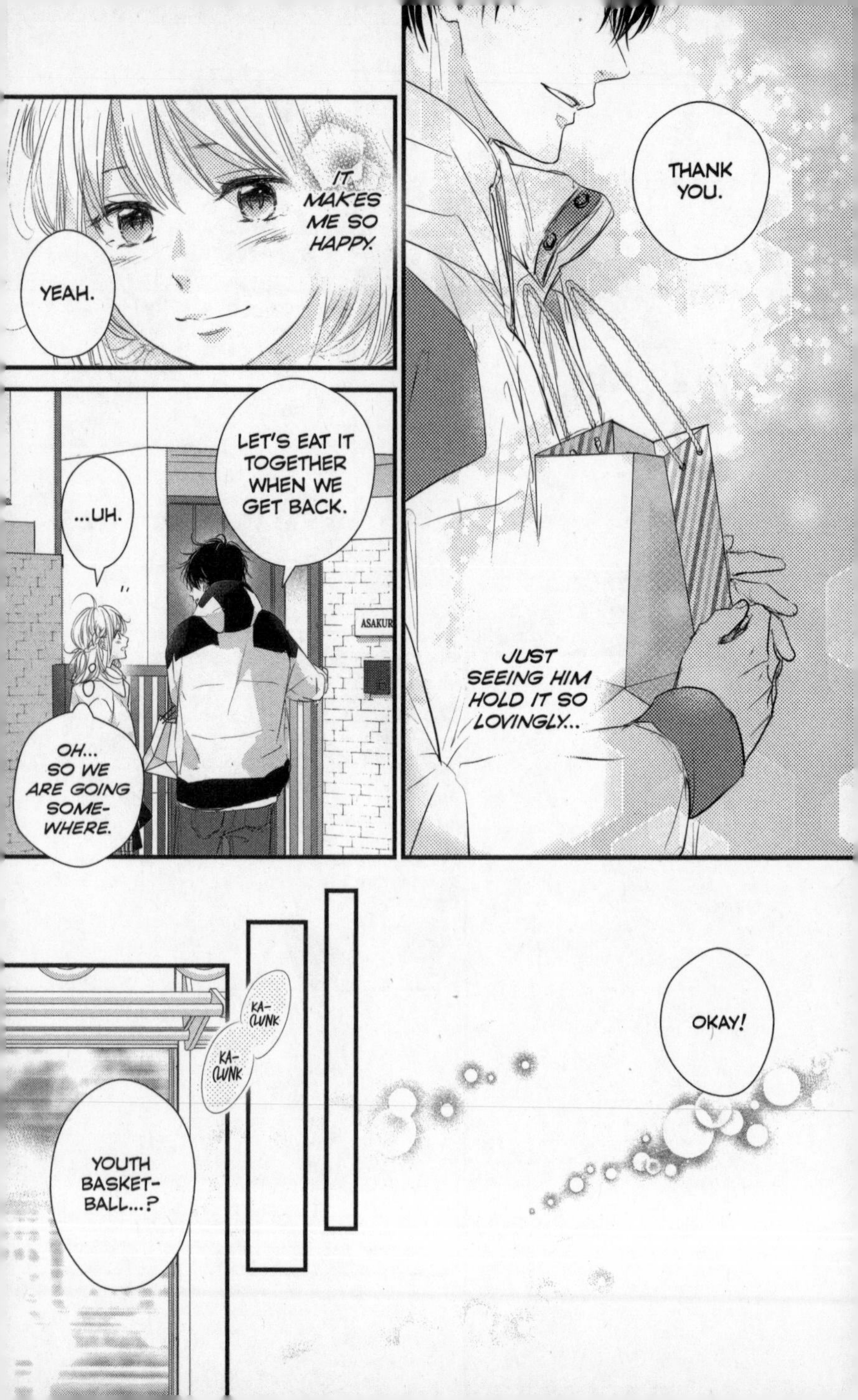
THANK YOU.
JUST SEEING HIM HOLD IT SO LOVINGLY...
IT MAKES ME SO HAPPY.
YEAH.
LET'S EAT IT TOGETHER WHEN WE GET BACK.
...UH.
OH... SO WE ARE GOING SOME-WHERE.
OKAY!
KA-CLUNK
KA-CLUNK
YOUTH BASKET-BALL...?

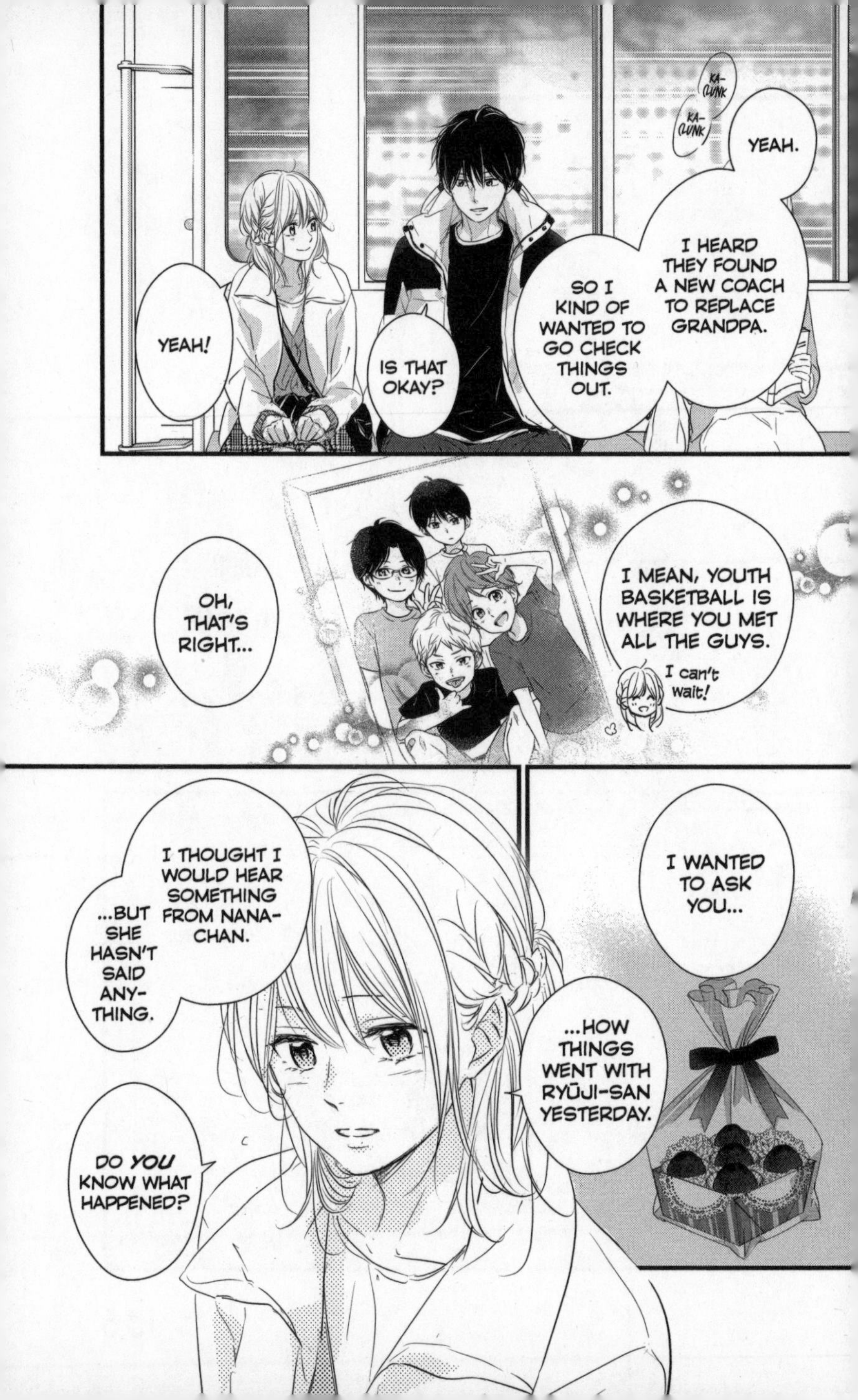
KA-CLUNK
KA-CLUNK
YEAH.
I HEARD THEY FOUND A NEW COACH TO REPLACE GRANDPA.
SO I KIND OF WANTED TO GO CHECK THINGS OUT.
IS THAT OKAY?
YEAH!
I MEAN, YOUTH BASKETBALL IS WHERE YOU MET ALL THE GUYS.
I can't wait!
OH, THAT'S RIGHT...
I WANTED TO ASK YOU...
...HOW THINGS WENT WITH RYŪJI-SAN YESTERDAY.
I THOUGHT I WOULD HEAR SOMETHING FROM NANA-CHAN.
...BUT SHE HASN'T SAID ANYTHING.
DO *YOU* KNOW WHAT HAPPENED?

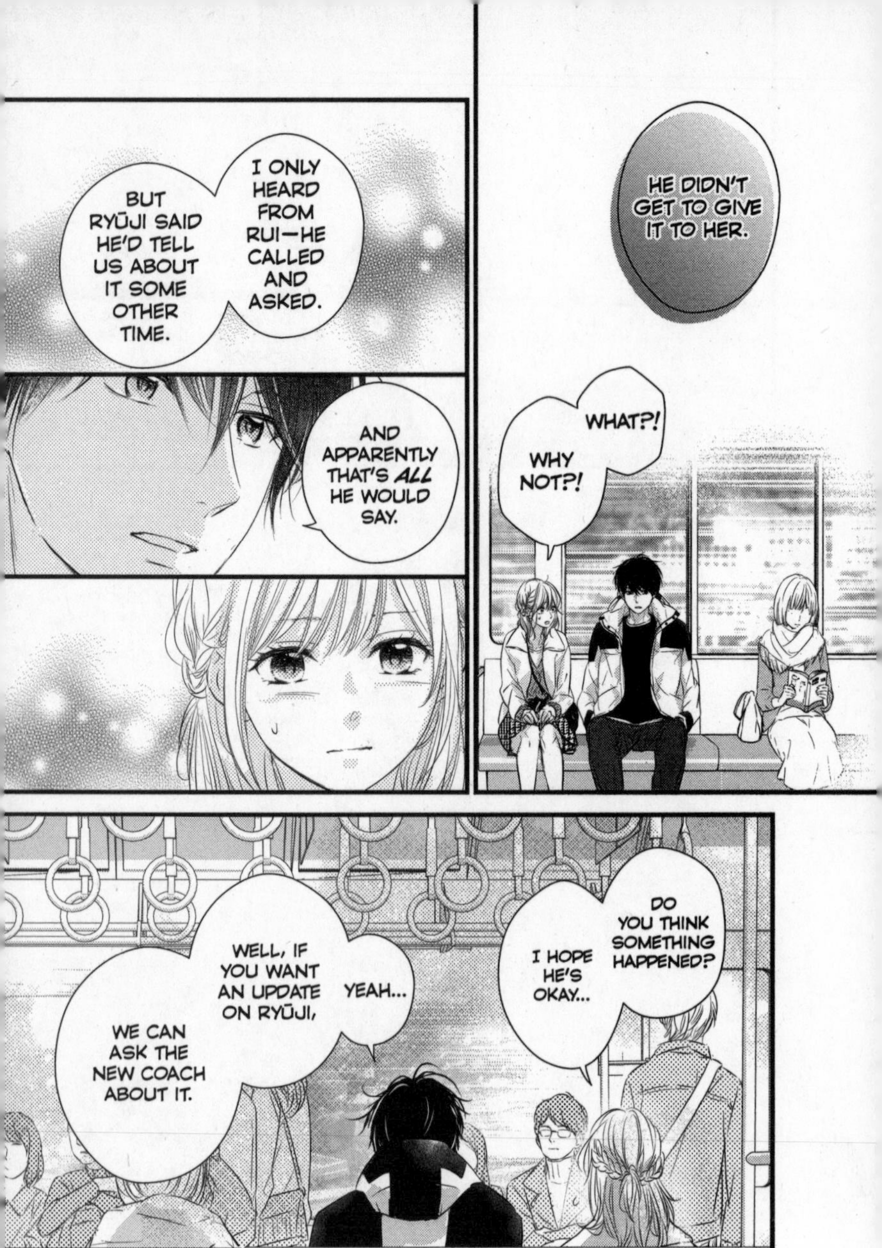
HE DIDN'T GET TO GIVE IT TO HER.
WHAT?!
WHY NOT?!
I ONLY HEARD FROM RUI—HE CALLED AND ASKED.
BUT RYŪJI SAID HE'D TELL US ABOUT IT SOME OTHER TIME.
AND APPARENTLY THAT'S *ALL* HE WOULD SAY.
DO YOU THINK SOMETHING HAPPENED?
I HOPE HE'S OKAY...
YEAH...
WELL, IF YOU WANT AN UPDATE ON RYŪJI,
WE CAN ASK THE NEW COACH ABOUT IT.

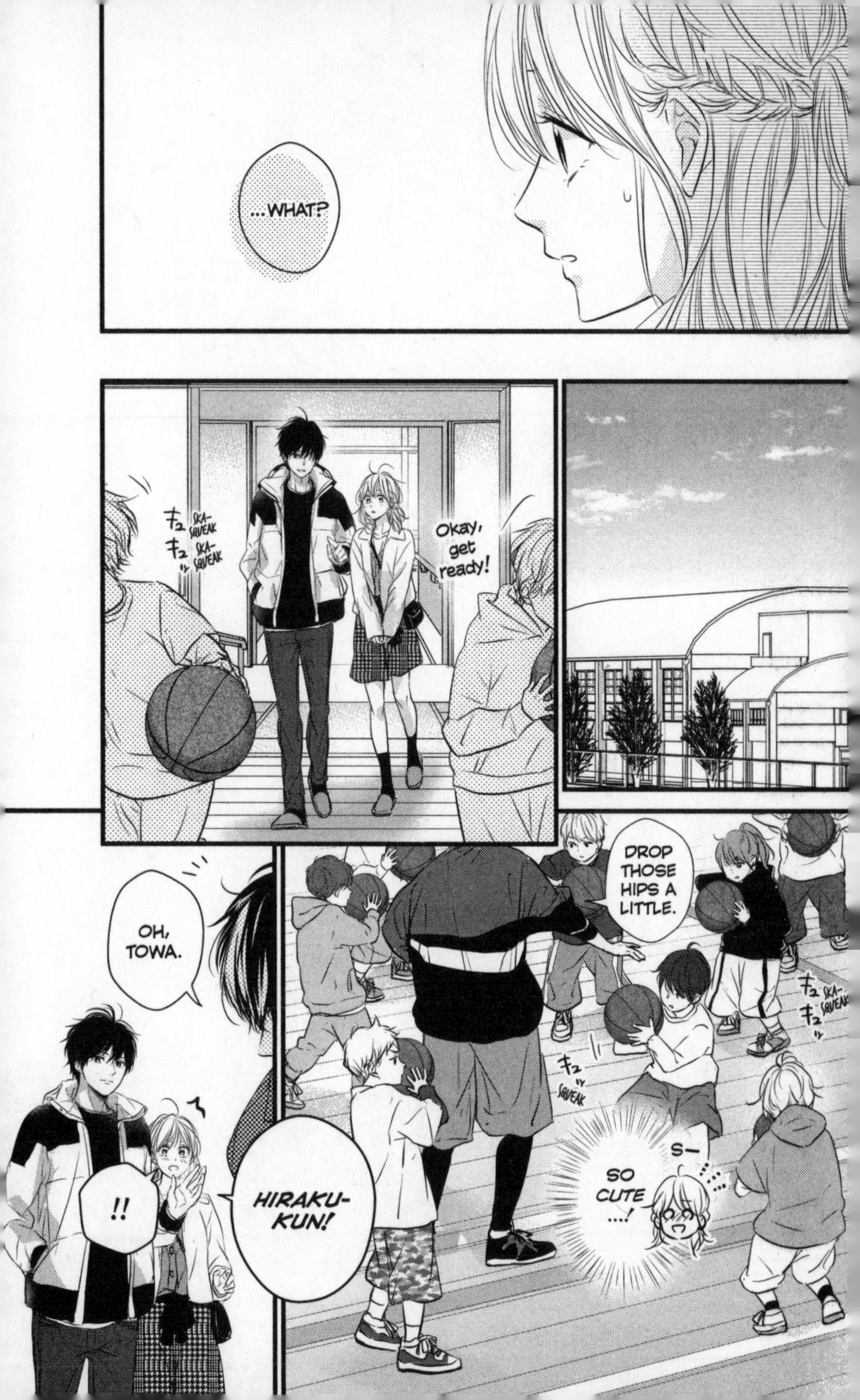
...WHAT?
Okay, get ready!
キュ SKA-SQUEAK
キュ SKA-SQUEAK
ッ
DROP THOSE HIPS A LITTLE.
キュ SKA-SQUEAK
キュ
ッ
キュ
ッ
SQUEAK
S—
SO CUTE ....!
OH, TOWA.
HIRAKU-KUN!
!!

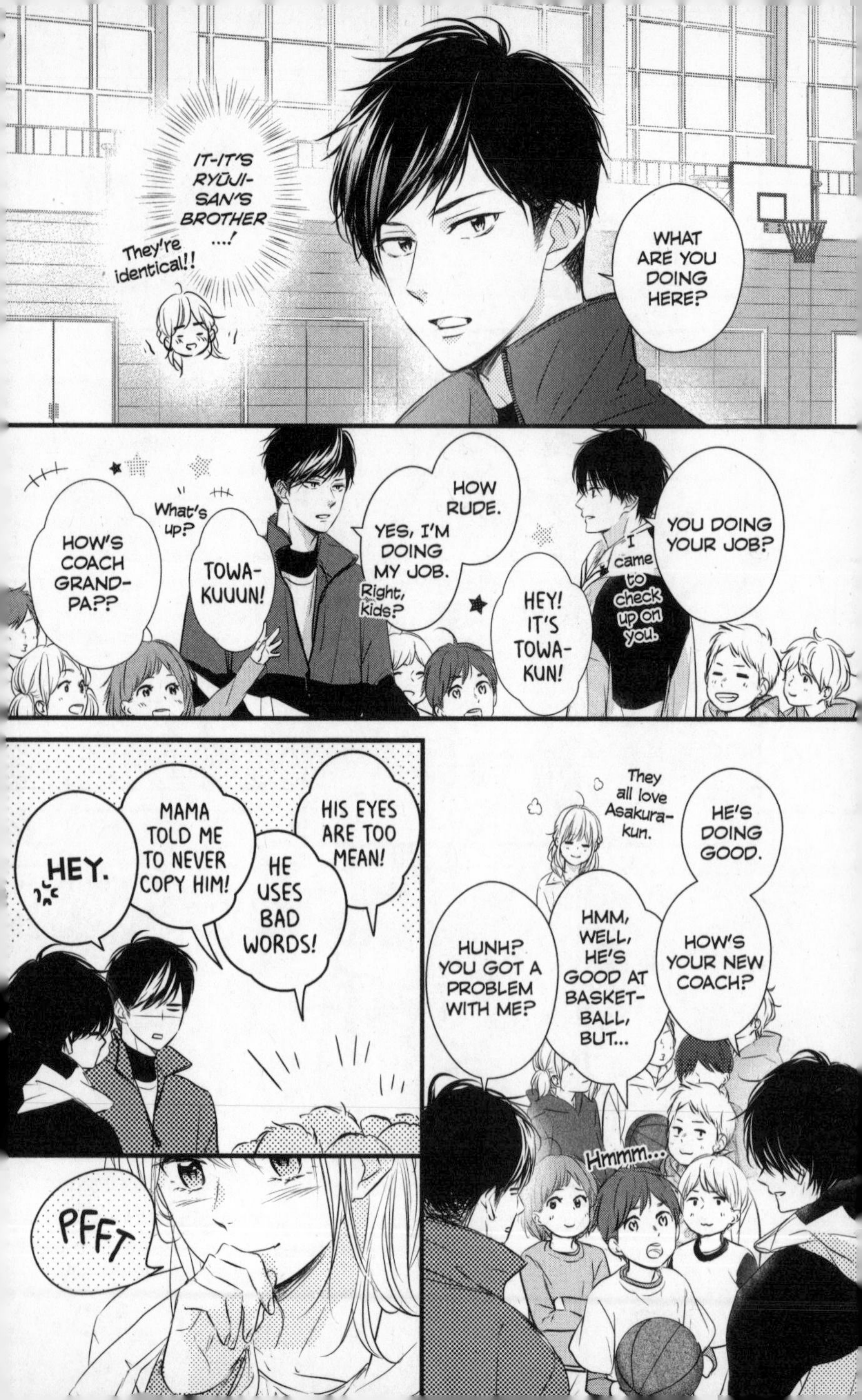
WHAT ARE YOU DOING HERE?
IT-IT'S RYŪJI-SAN'S BROTHER ...!
They're identical!!
YOU DOING YOUR JOB?
I came to check up on you.
HEY! IT'S TOWA-KUN!
HOW RUDE. YES, I'M DOING MY JOB.
Right, kids?
TOWA-KUUUN!
What's up?
HOW'S COACH GRANDPA??
They all love Asakura-kun.
HE'S DOING GOOD.
HOW'S YOUR NEW COACH?
HMM, WELL, HE'S GOOD AT BASKETBALL, BUT...
HUNH? YOU GOT A PROBLEM WITH ME?
Hmmm...
HIS EYES ARE TOO MEAN!
HE USES BAD WORDS!
MAMA TOLD ME TO NEVER COPY HIM!
HEY.
PFFT

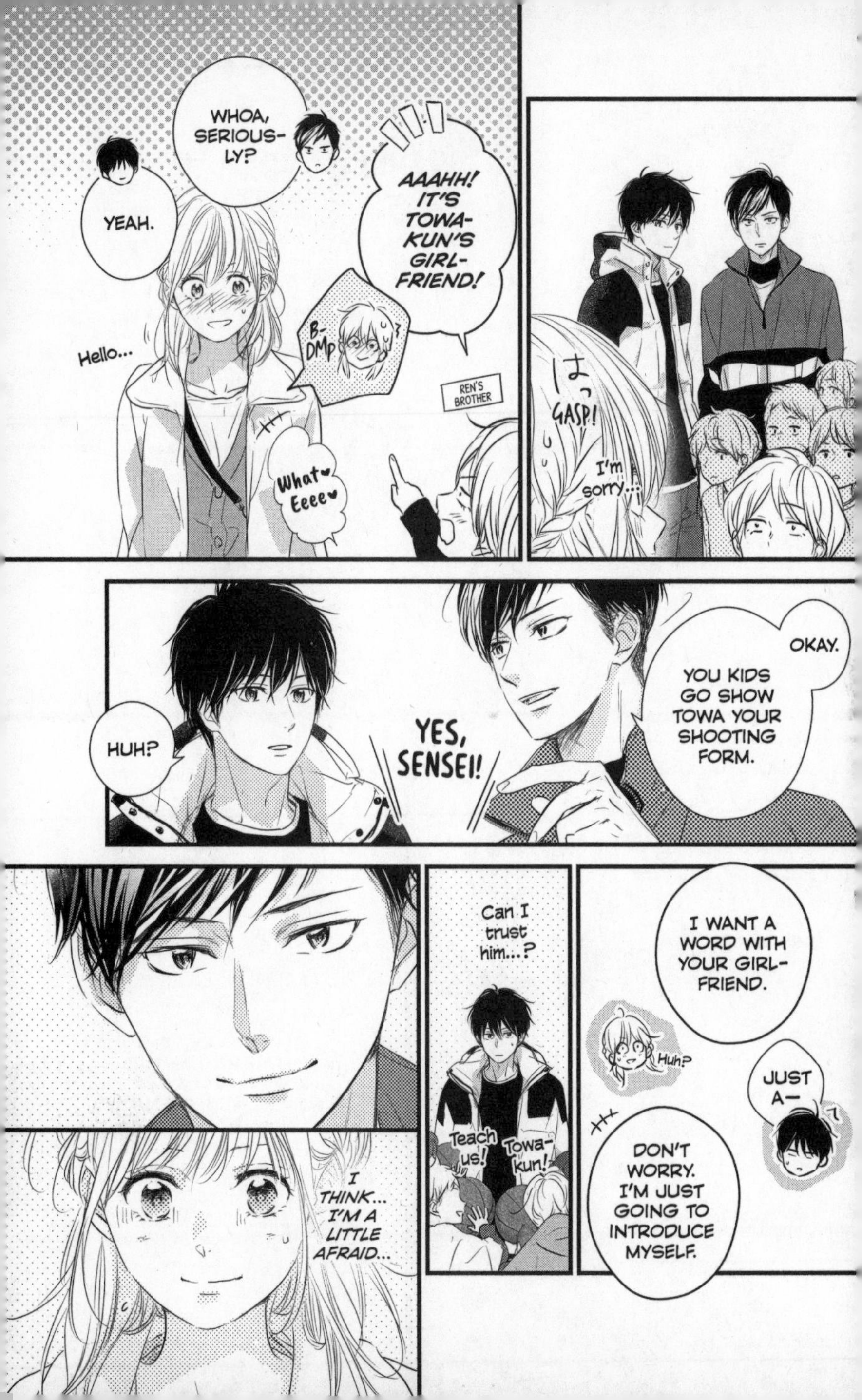
は っ
GASP!
I'm sorry...
AAAHH! IT'S TOWA-KUN'S GIRLFRIEND!
WHOA, SERIOUSLY?
YEAH.
B-DMP
REN'S BROTHER
Hello...
What♥ Eeee♥
OKAY.
YOU KIDS GO SHOW TOWA YOUR SHOOTING FORM.
YES, SENSEI!
HUH?
I WANT A WORD WITH YOUR GIRLFRIEND.
Huh?
JUST A—
DON'T WORRY. I'M JUST GOING TO INTRODUCE MYSELF.
Can I trust him...?
Towa-kun!
Teach us!
I THINK... I'M A LITTLE AFRAID...

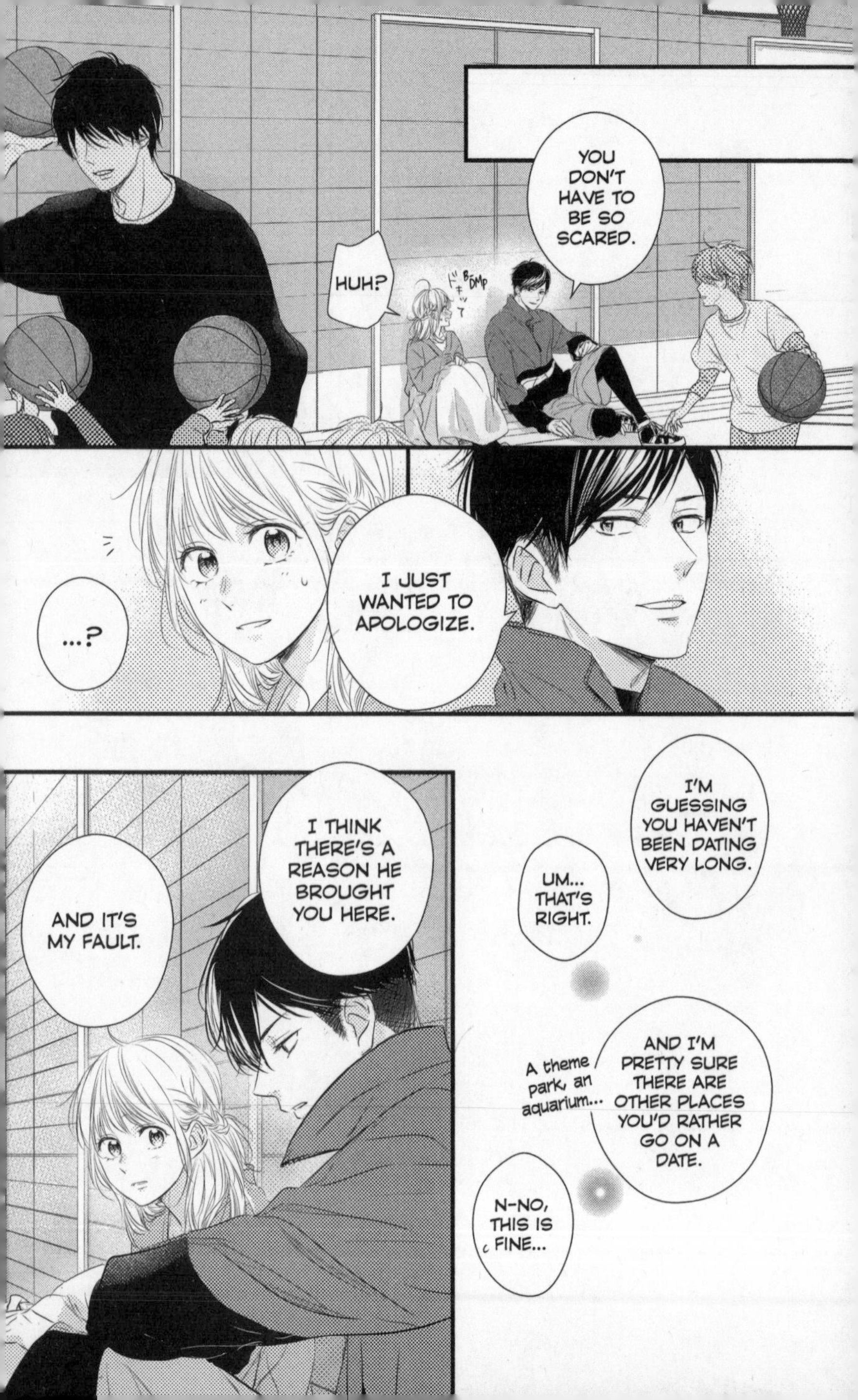
YOU DON'T HAVE TO BE SO SCARED.
B-DMP
HUH?
I JUST WANTED TO APOLOGIZE.
...?
I'M GUESSING YOU HAVEN'T BEEN DATING VERY LONG.
UM... THAT'S RIGHT.
AND I'M PRETTY SURE THERE ARE OTHER PLACES YOU'D RATHER GO ON A DATE.
A theme park, an aquarium...
N-NO, THIS IS FINE...
I THINK THERE'S A REASON HE BROUGHT YOU HERE.
AND IT'S MY FAULT.

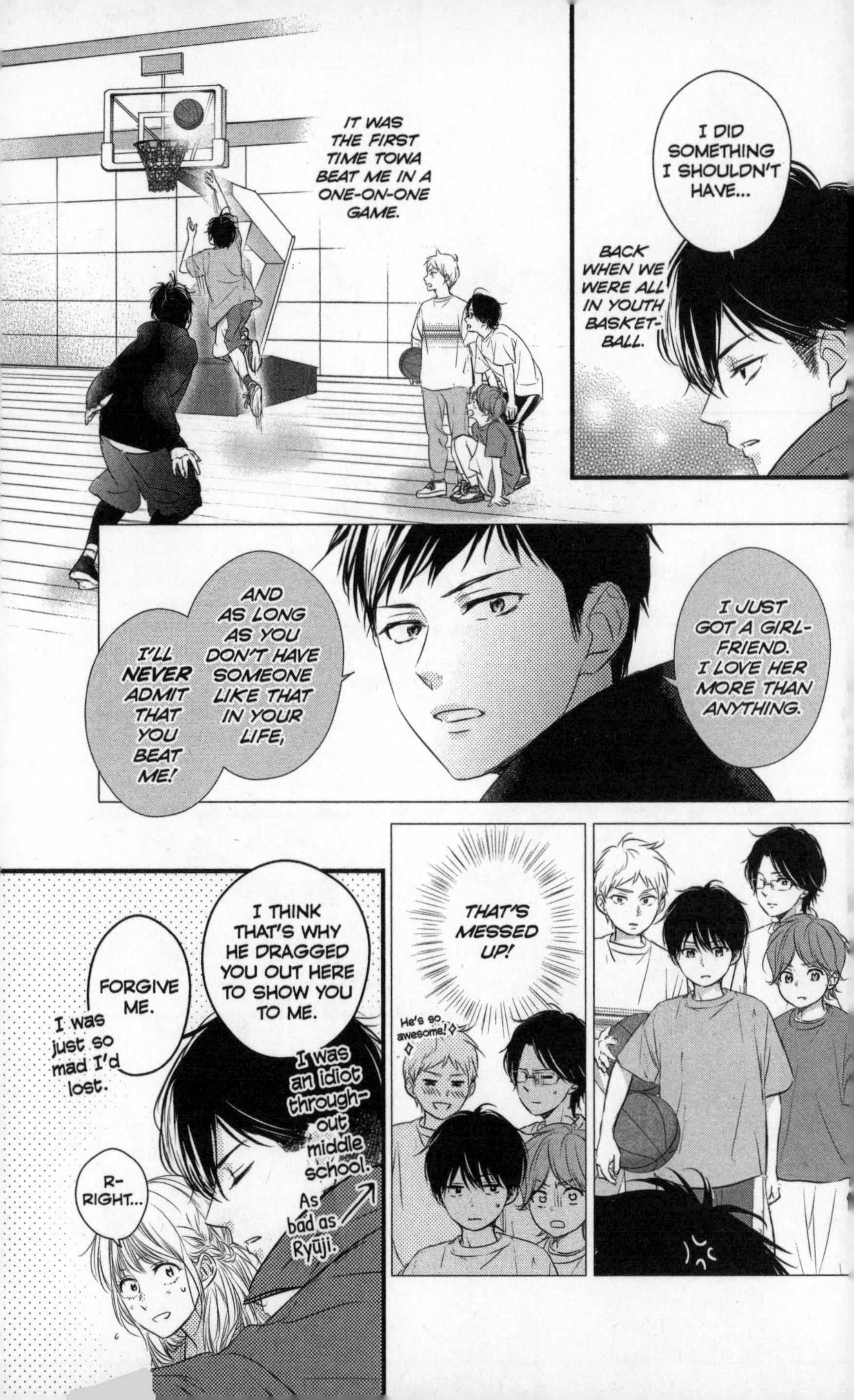
I DID SOMETHING I SHOULDN'T HAVE...
BACK WHEN WE WERE ALL IN YOUTH BASKET-BALL.
IT WAS THE FIRST TIME TOWA BEAT ME IN A ONE-ON-ONE GAME.
I JUST GOT A GIRL-FRIEND. I LOVE HER MORE THAN ANYTHING.
AND AS LONG AS YOU DON'T HAVE SOMEONE LIKE THAT IN YOUR LIFE,
I'LL **NEVER** ADMIT THAT YOU BEAT ME!
THAT'S MESSED UP!
He's so awesome!
I THINK THAT'S WHY HE DRAGGED YOU OUT HERE TO SHOW YOU TO ME.
I was an idiot through-out middle school.
As bad as Ryūji.
FORGIVE ME.
I was just so mad I'd lost.
R-RIGHT...

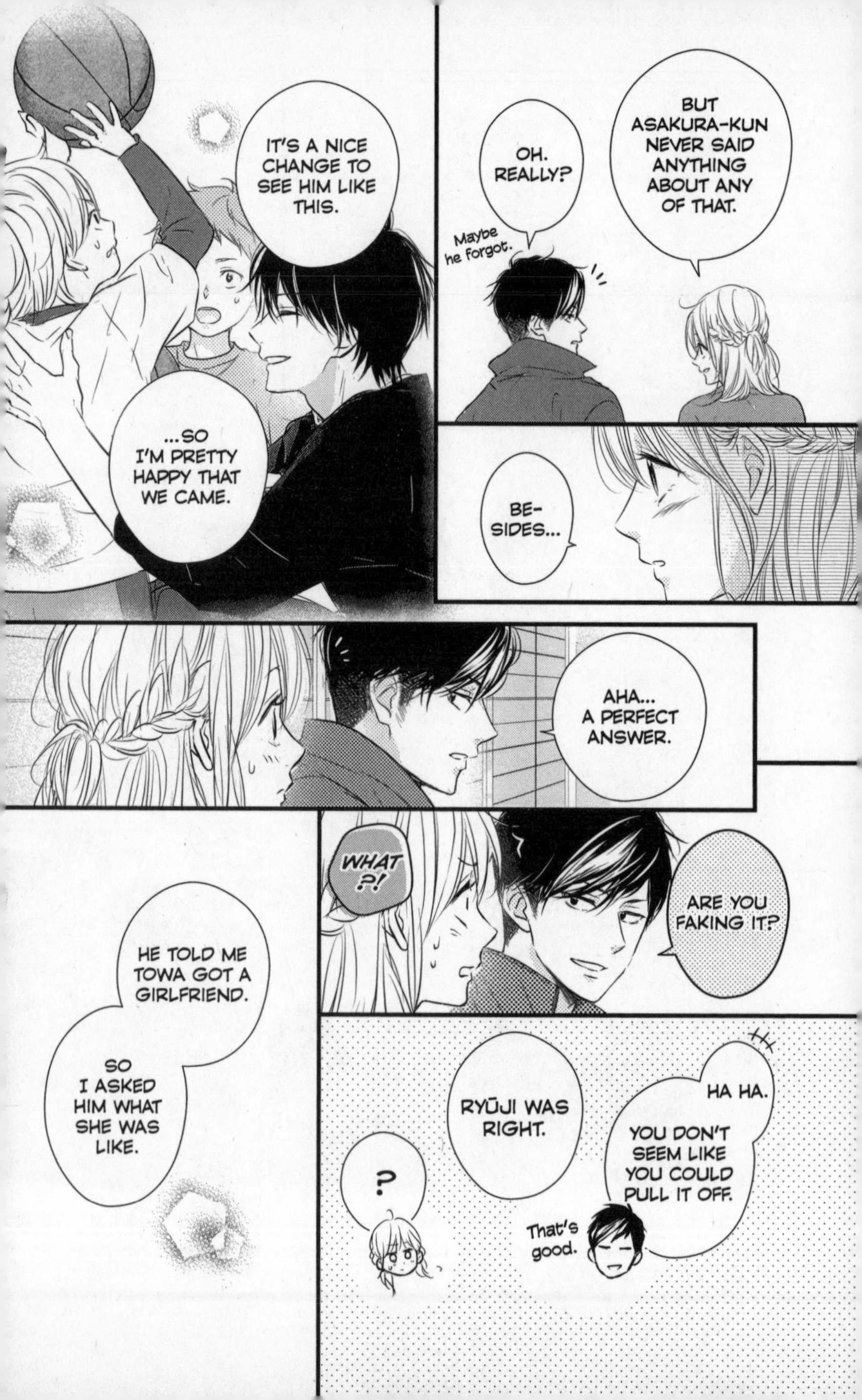
BUT ASAKURA-KUN NEVER SAID ANYTHING ABOUT ANY OF THAT.
OH. REALLY?
Maybe he forgot.
BE-SIDES...
IT'S A NICE CHANGE TO SEE HIM LIKE THIS.
...SO I'M PRETTY HAPPY THAT WE CAME.
AHA... A PERFECT ANSWER.
ARE YOU FAKING IT?
WHAT?!
HA HA.
YOU DON'T SEEM LIKE YOU COULD PULL IT OFF.
That's good.
RYŪJI WAS RIGHT.
?
HE TOLD ME TOWA GOT A GIRLFRIEND.
SO I ASKED HIM WHAT SHE WAS LIKE.

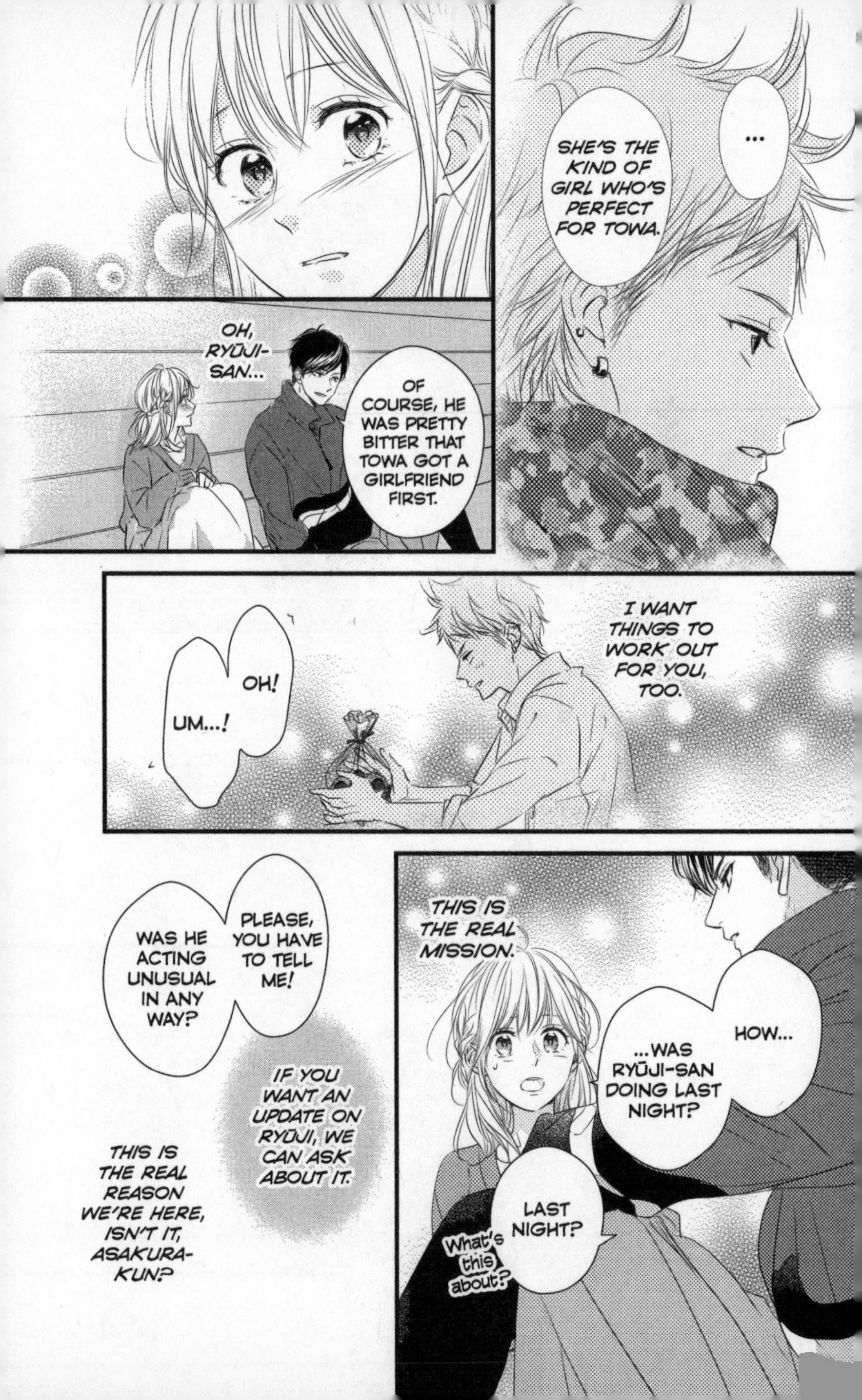
...
SHE'S THE KIND OF GIRL WHO'S PERFECT FOR TOWA.
OF COURSE, HE WAS PRETTY BITTER THAT TOWA GOT A GIRLFRIEND FIRST.
OH, RYŪJI-SAN...
I WANT THINGS TO WORK OUT FOR YOU, TOO.
OH!
UM...!
HOW...
...WAS RYŪJI-SAN DOING LAST NIGHT?
THIS IS THE REAL MISSION.
LAST NIGHT?
What's this about?
PLEASE, YOU HAVE TO TELL ME!
WAS HE ACTING UNUSUAL IN ANY WAY?
IF YOU WANT AN UPDATE ON RYŪJI, WE CAN ASK ABOUT IT.
THIS IS THE REAL REASON WE'RE HERE, ISN'T IT, ASAKURA-KUN?

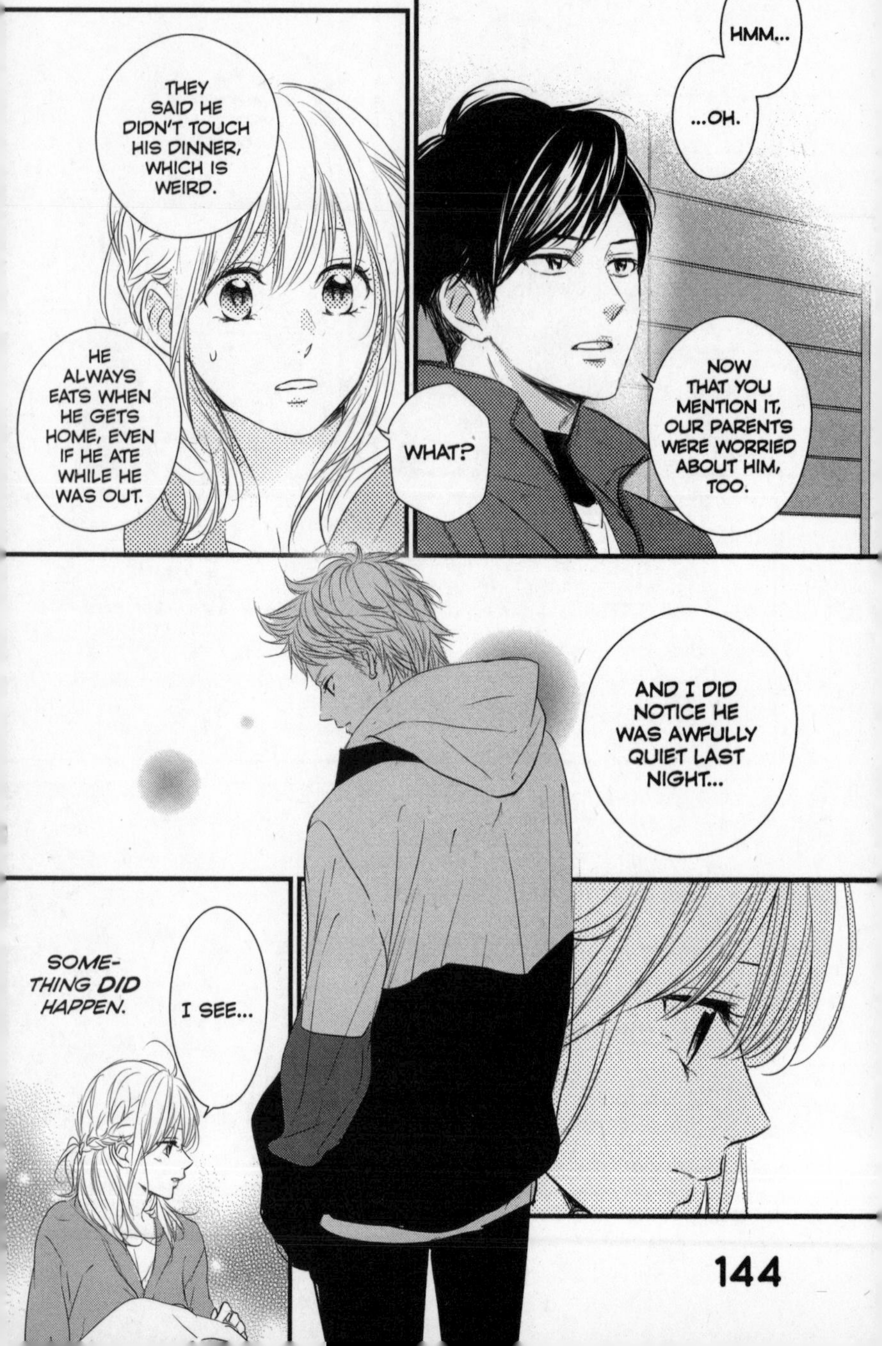
HMM...
...OH.
NOW THAT YOU MENTION IT, OUR PARENTS WERE WORRIED ABOUT HIM, TOO.
WHAT?
THEY SAID HE DIDN'T TOUCH HIS DINNER, WHICH IS WEIRD.
HE ALWAYS EATS WHEN HE GETS HOME, EVEN IF HE ATE WHILE HE WAS OUT.
AND I DID NOTICE HE WAS AWFULLY QUIET LAST NIGHT...
I SEE...
SOME-THING **DID** HAPPEN.

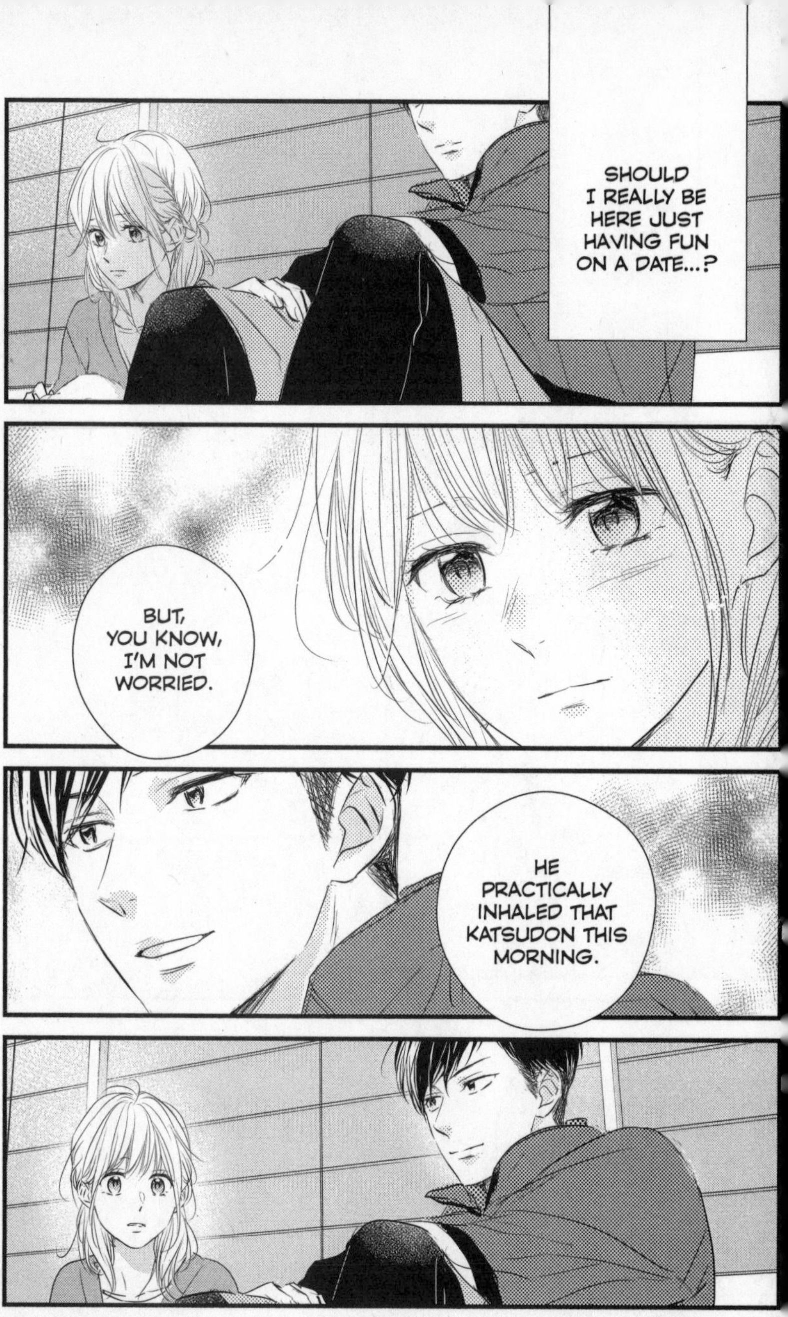
SHOULD I REALLY BE HERE JUST HAVING FUN ON A DATE...?
BUT, YOU KNOW, I'M NOT WORRIED.
HE PRACTICALLY INHALED THAT KATSUDON THIS MORNING.

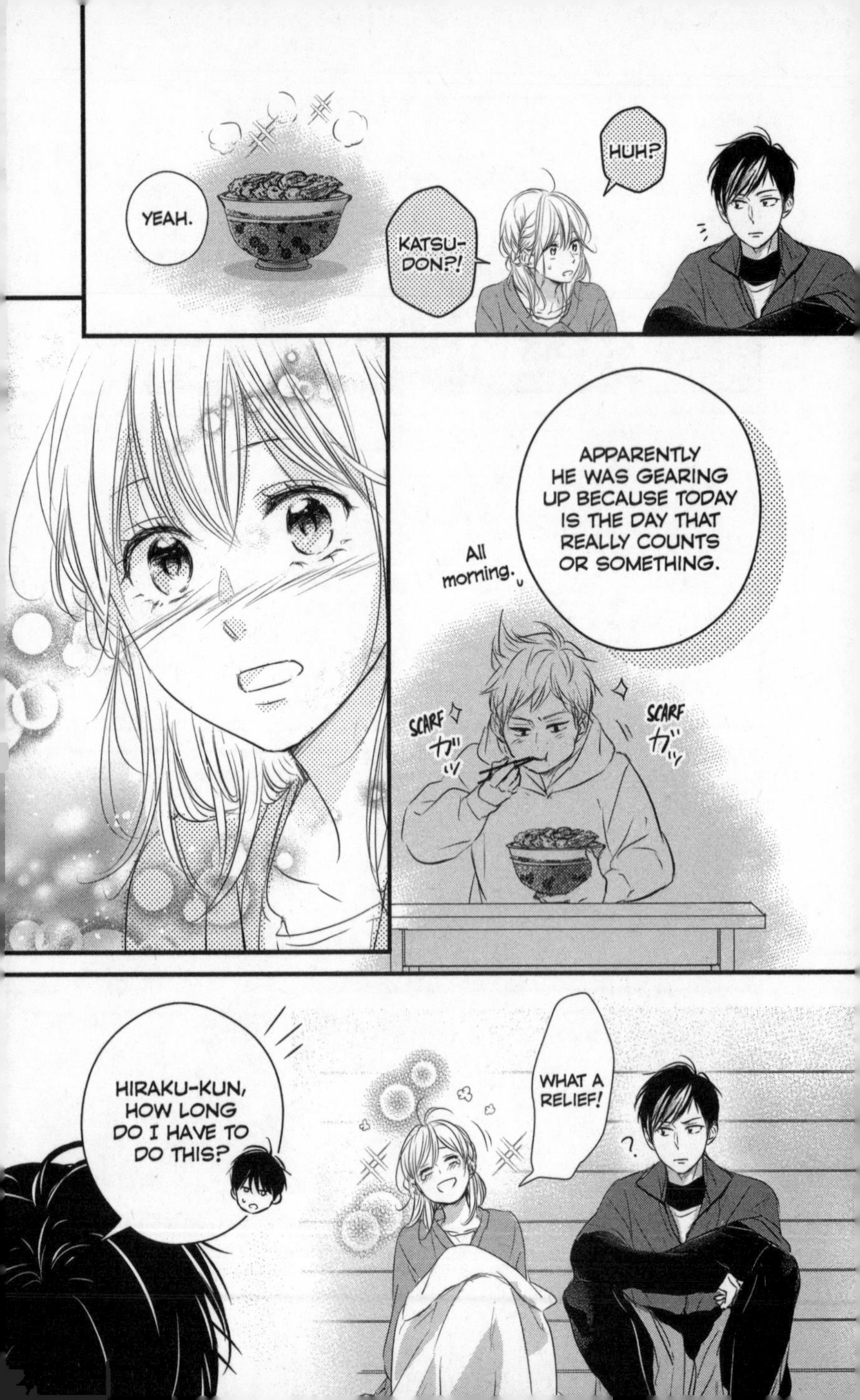
HUH?
KATSU-DON?!
YEAH.
APPARENTLY HE WAS GEARING UP BECAUSE TODAY IS THE DAY THAT REALLY COUNTS OR SOMETHING.
All morning.
SCARF ガッ
SCARF ガッ
WHAT A RELIEF!
HIRAKU-KUN, HOW LONG DO I HAVE TO DO THIS?

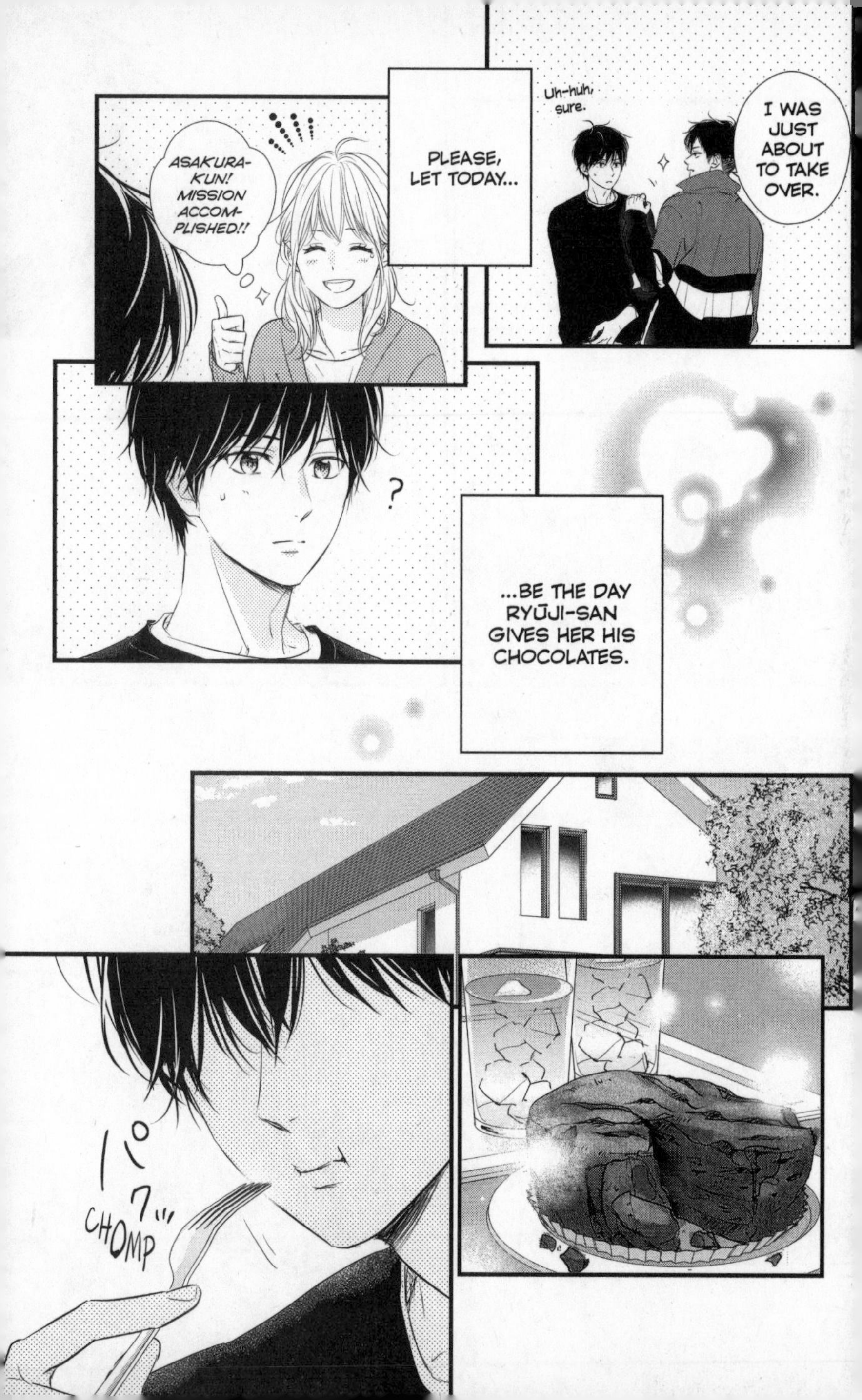
I WAS JUST ABOUT TO TAKE OVER.
Uh-huh, sure.
PLEASE, LET TODAY...
ASAKURA-KUN! MISSION ACCOM-PLISHED!!
...BE THE DAY RYŪJI-SAN GIVES HER HIS CHOCOLATES.
?
パクッ
CHOMP

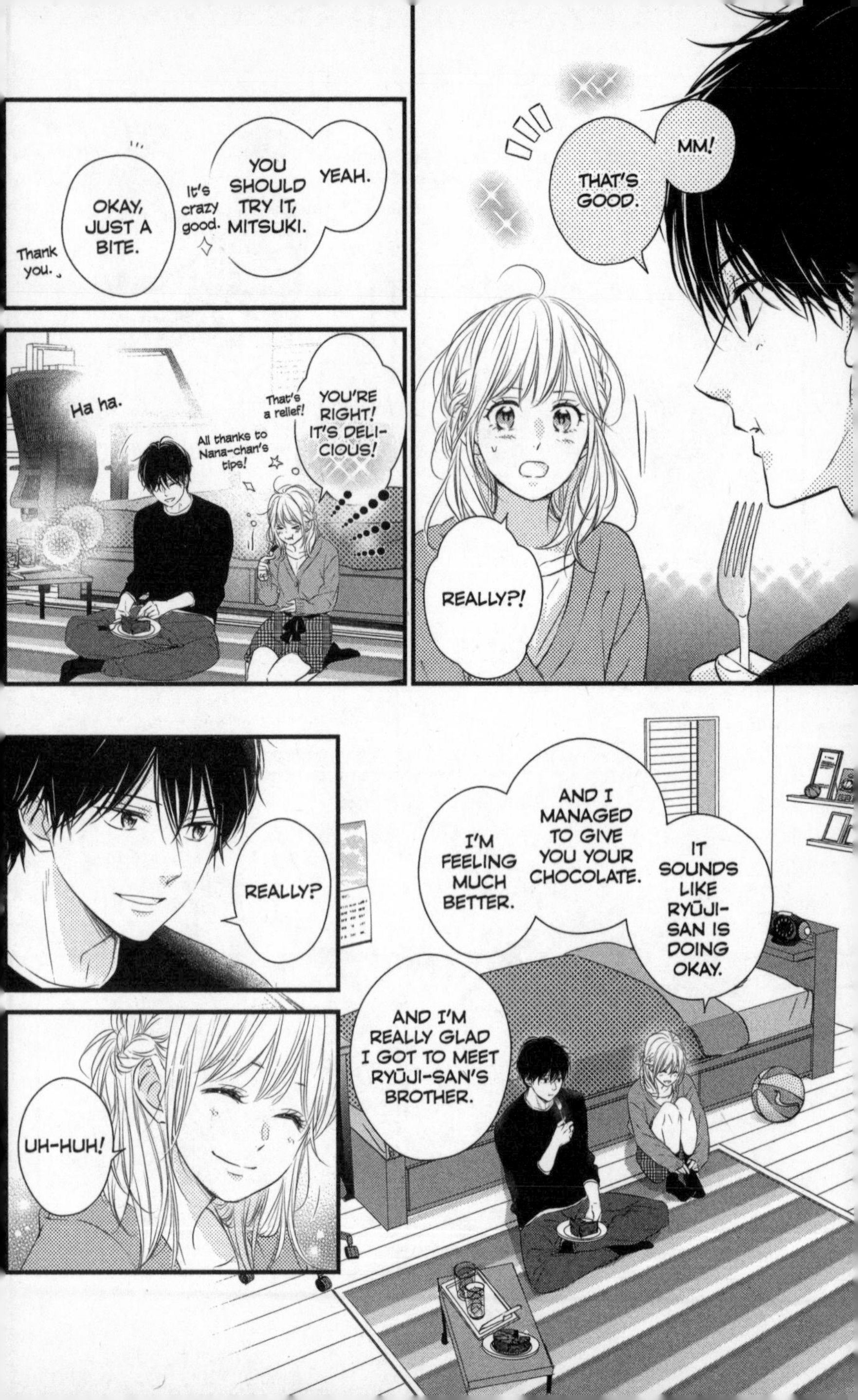
MM!
THAT'S GOOD.
REALLY?!
YEAH.
YOU SHOULD TRY IT, MITSUKI.
It's crazy good.
OKAY, JUST A BITE.
Thank you.
YOU'RE RIGHT! IT'S DELICIOUS!
That's a relief!
All thanks to Nana-chan's tips!
Ha ha.
IT SOUNDS LIKE RYŪJI-SAN IS DOING OKAY.
AND I MANAGED TO GIVE YOU YOUR CHOCOLATE.
I'M FEELING MUCH BETTER.
AND I'M REALLY GLAD I GOT TO MEET RYŪJI-SAN'S BROTHER.
REALLY?
UH-HUH!

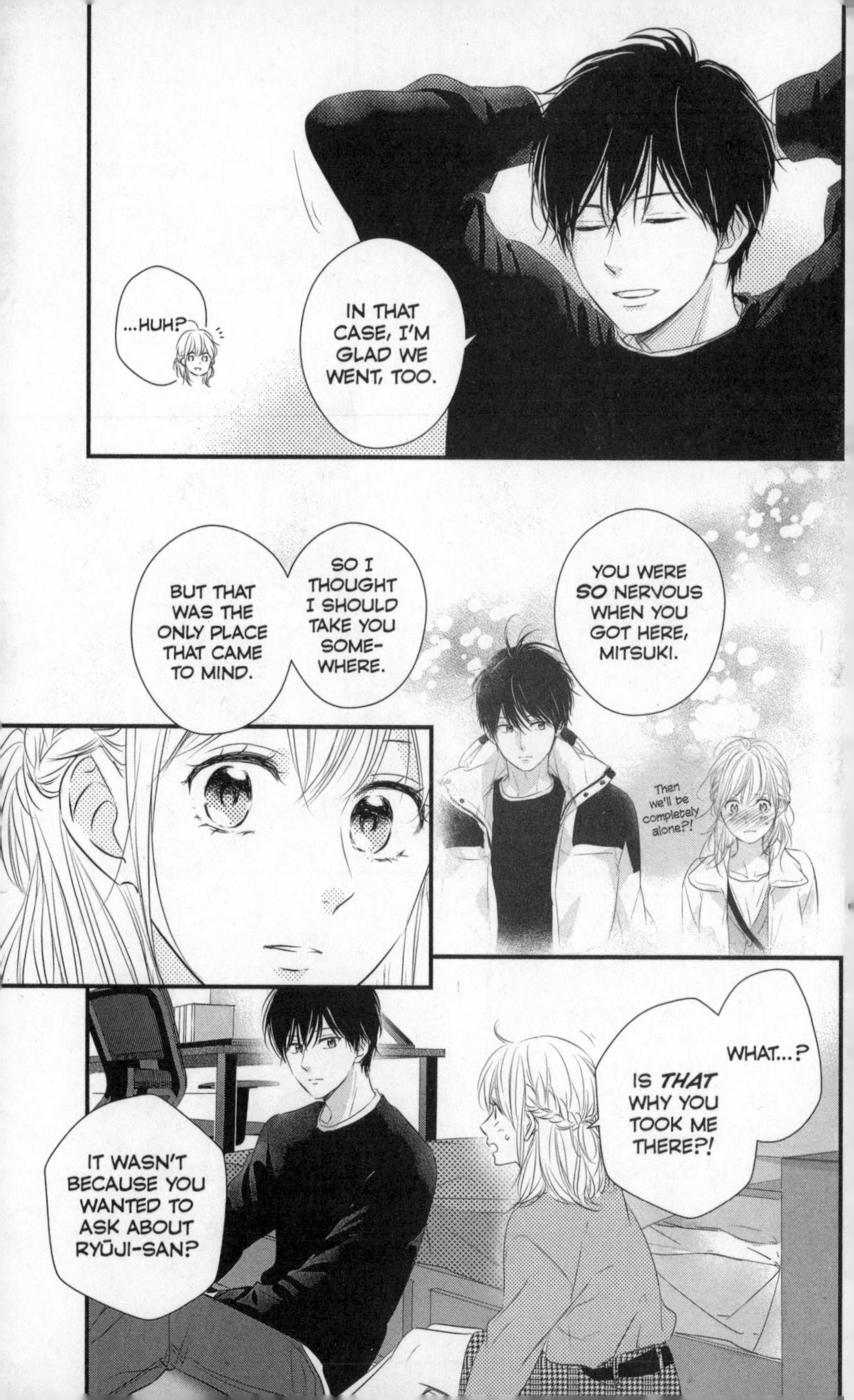
IN THAT CASE, I'M GLAD WE WENT, TOO.
...HUH?
YOU WERE SO NERVOUS WHEN YOU GOT HERE, MITSUKI.
Then we'll be completely alone?!
SO I THOUGHT I SHOULD TAKE YOU SOME-WHERE.
BUT THAT WAS THE ONLY PLACE THAT CAME TO MIND.
WHAT...?
IS *THAT* WHY YOU TOOK ME THERE?!
IT WASN'T BECAUSE YOU WANTED TO ASK ABOUT RYŪJI-SAN?

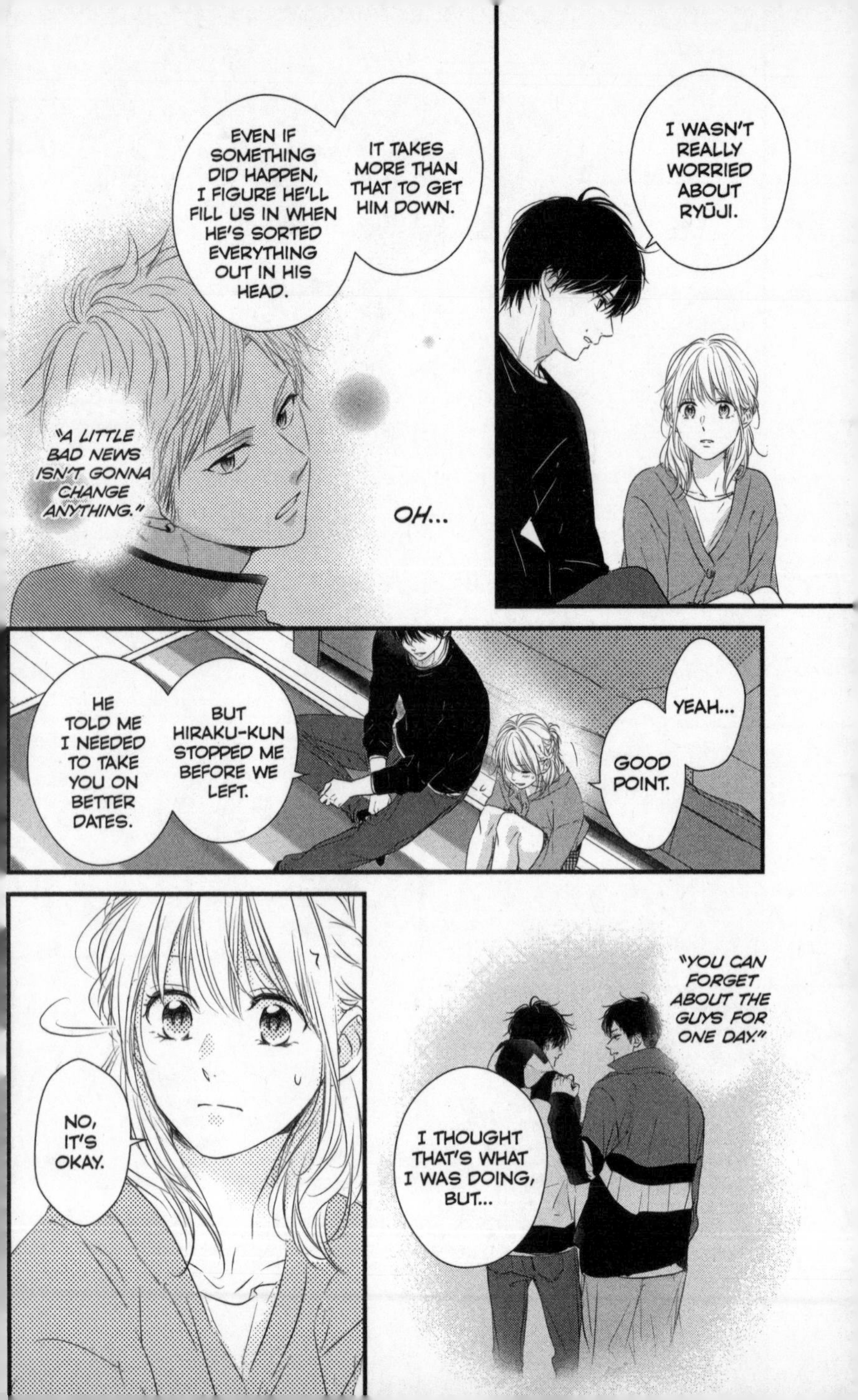
I WASN'T REALLY WORRIED ABOUT RYŪJI.
IT TAKES MORE THAN THAT TO GET HIM DOWN.
EVEN IF SOMETHING DID HAPPEN, I FIGURE HE'LL FILL US IN WHEN HE'S SORTED EVERYTHING OUT IN HIS HEAD.
OH...
"A LITTLE BAD NEWS ISN'T GONNA CHANGE ANYTHING."
YEAH...
GOOD POINT.
BUT HIRAKU-KUN STOPPED ME BEFORE WE LEFT.
HE TOLD ME I NEEDED TO TAKE YOU ON BETTER DATES.
"YOU CAN FORGET ABOUT THE GUYS FOR ONE DAY."
I THOUGHT THAT'S WHAT I WAS DOING, BUT...
NO, IT'S OKAY.

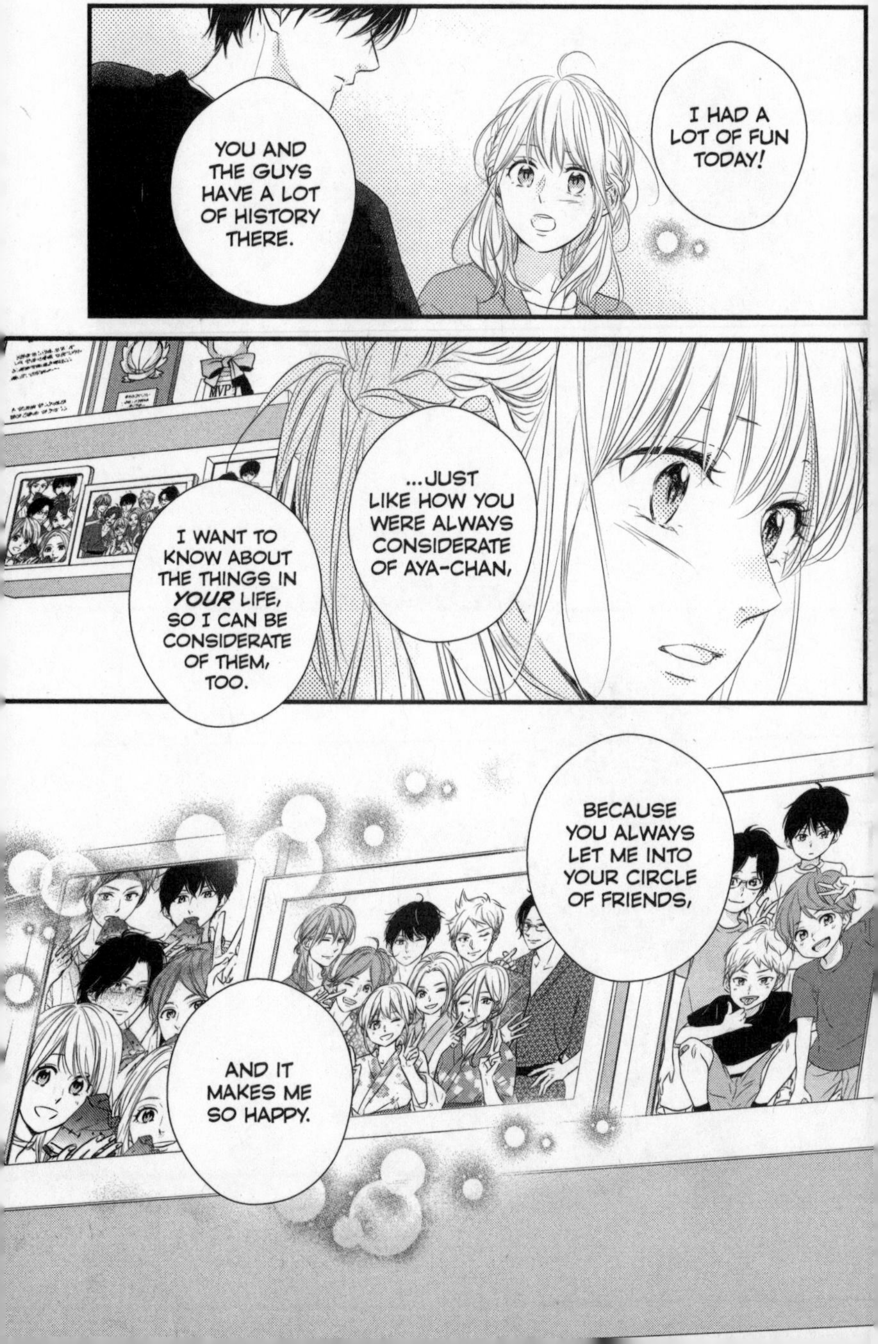
I HAD A LOT OF FUN TODAY!
YOU AND THE GUYS HAVE A LOT OF HISTORY THERE.
...JUST LIKE HOW YOU WERE ALWAYS CONSIDERATE OF AYA-CHAN,
I WANT TO KNOW ABOUT THE THINGS IN *YOUR* LIFE, SO I CAN BE CONSIDERATE OF THEM, TOO.
BECAUSE YOU ALWAYS LET ME INTO YOUR CIRCLE OF FRIENDS,
AND IT MAKES ME SO HAPPY.

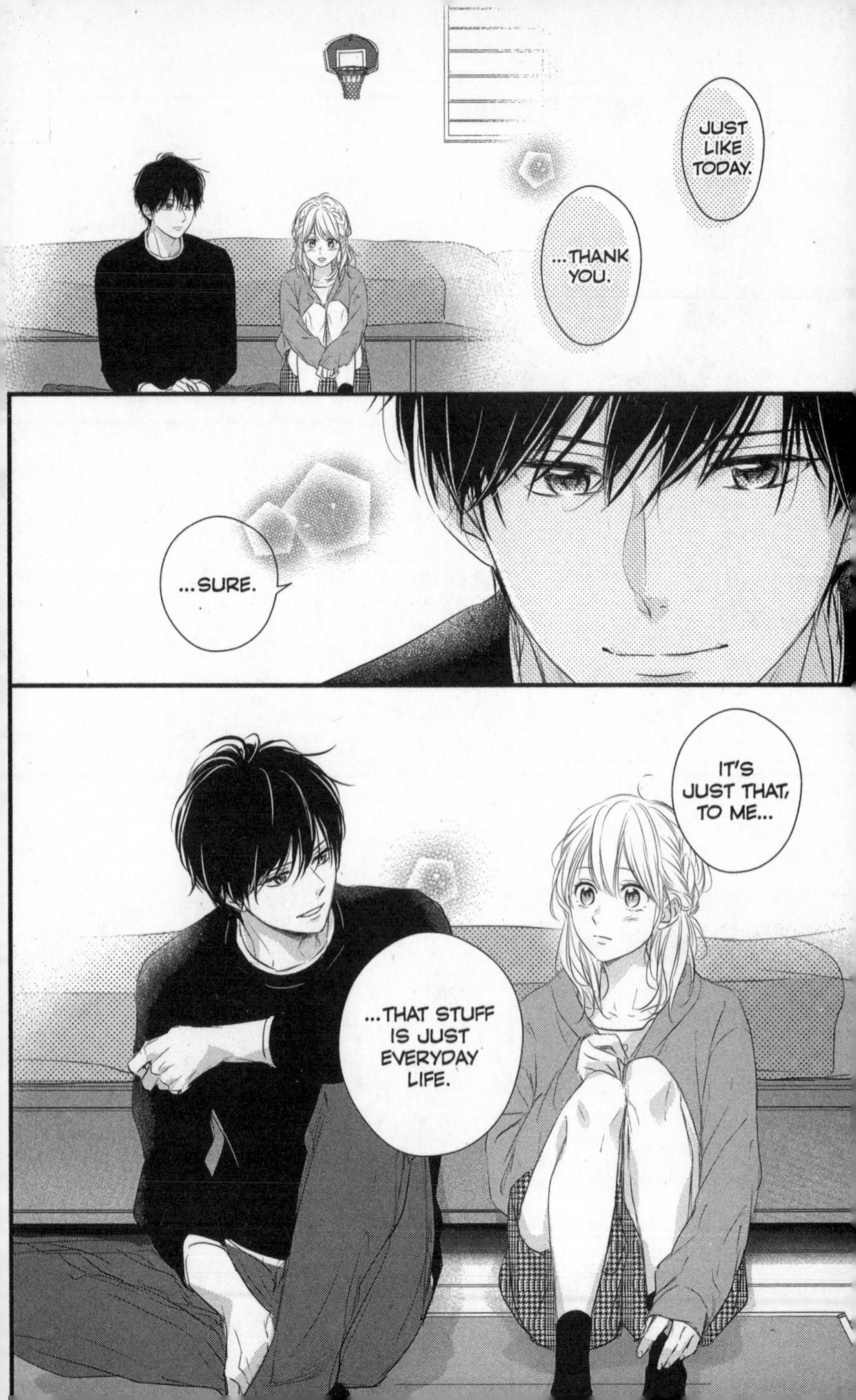
JUST LIKE TODAY.
...THANK YOU.
...SURE.
IT'S JUST THAT, TO ME...
...THAT STUFF IS JUST EVERYDAY LIFE.

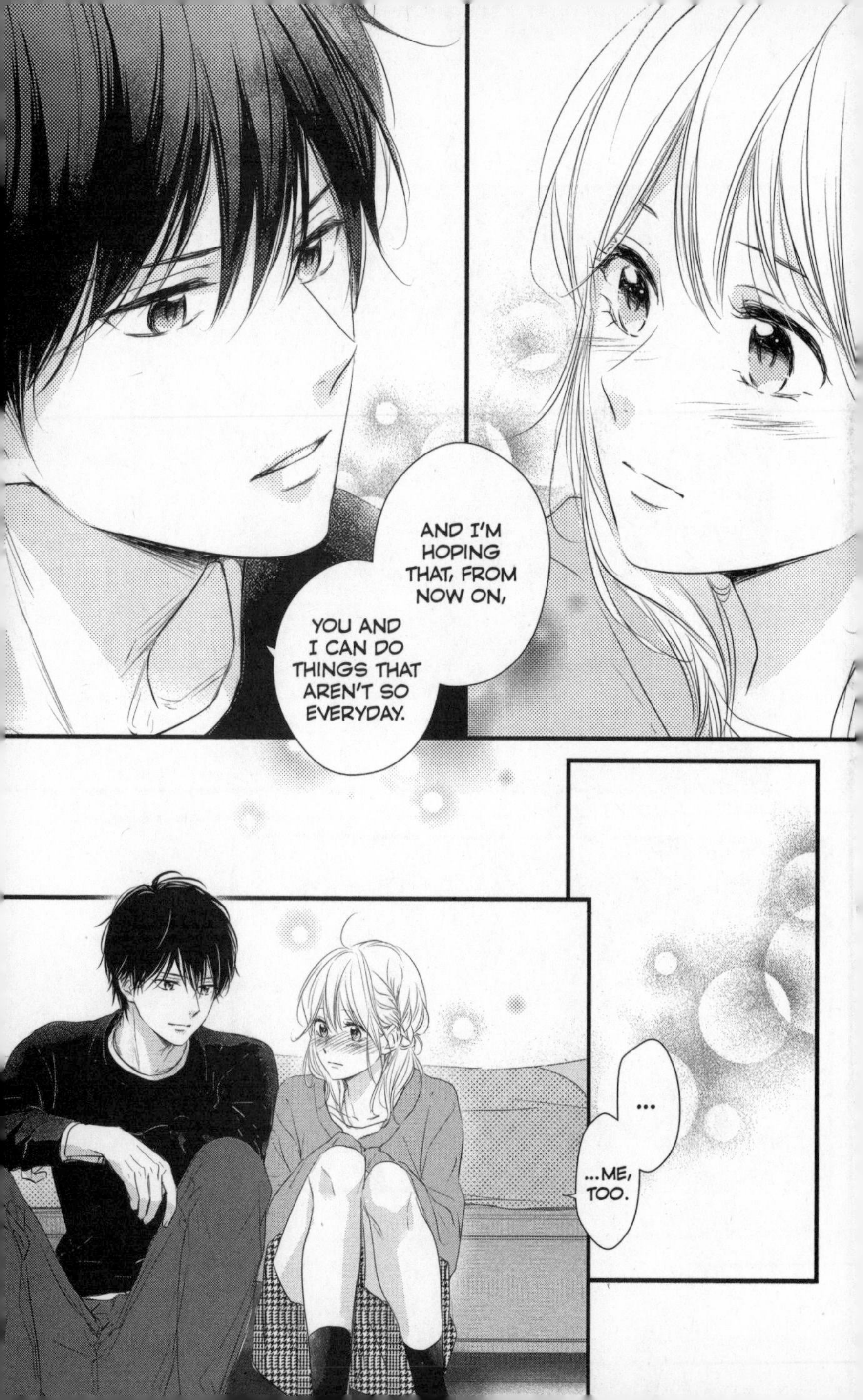
AND I'M HOPING THAT, FROM NOW ON,
YOU AND I CAN DO THINGS THAT AREN'T SO EVERYDAY.
...
...ME, TOO.

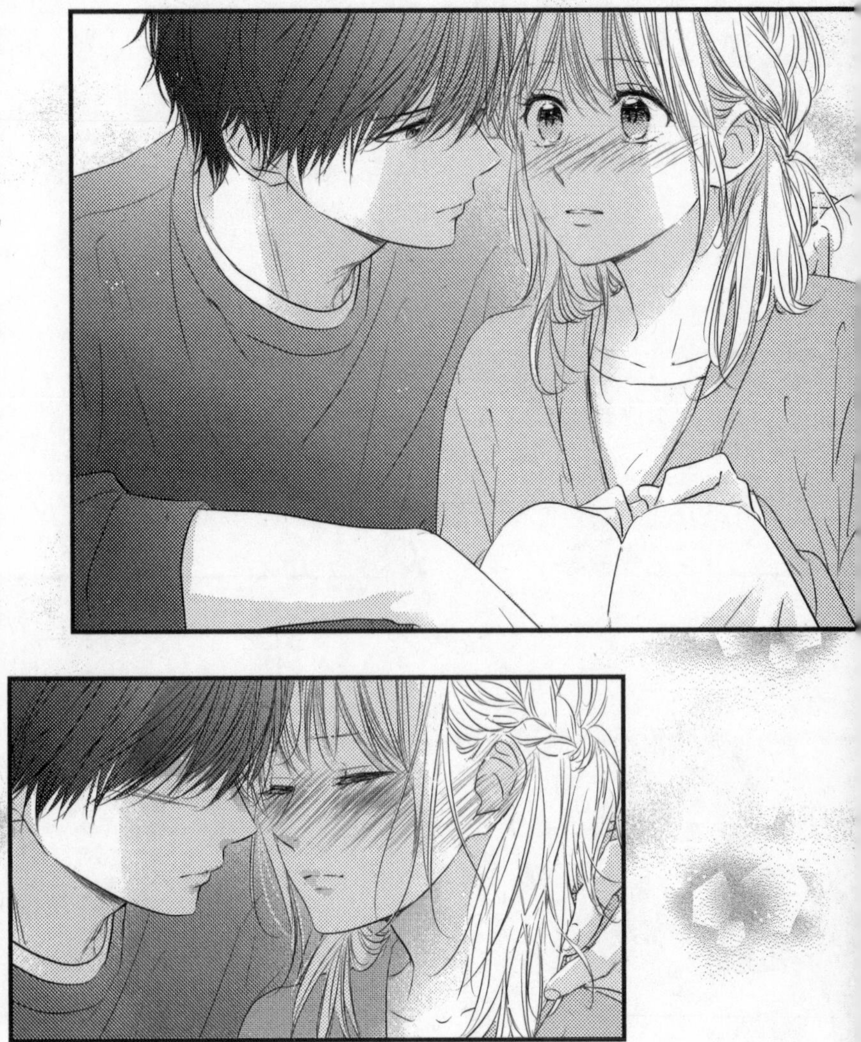

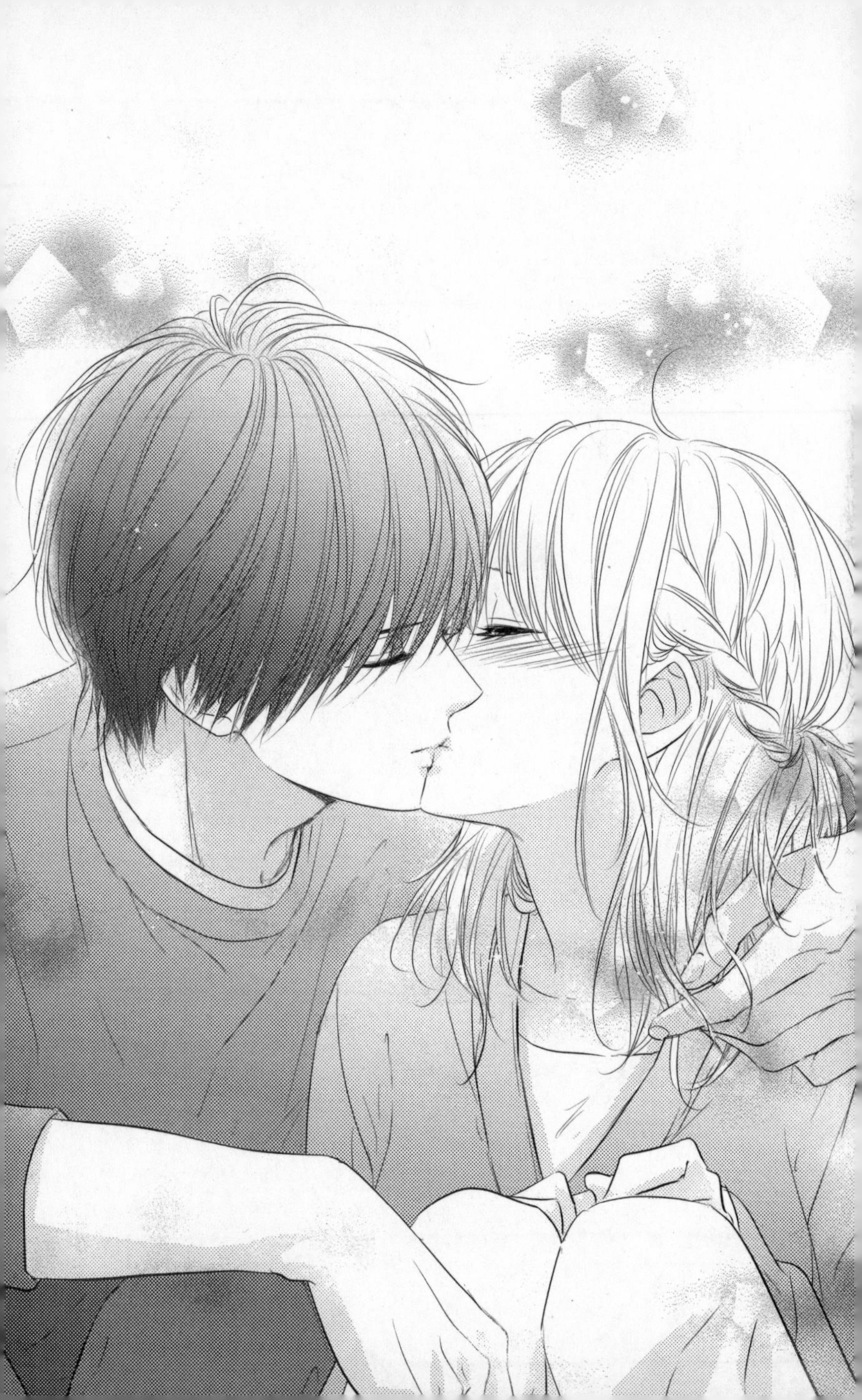

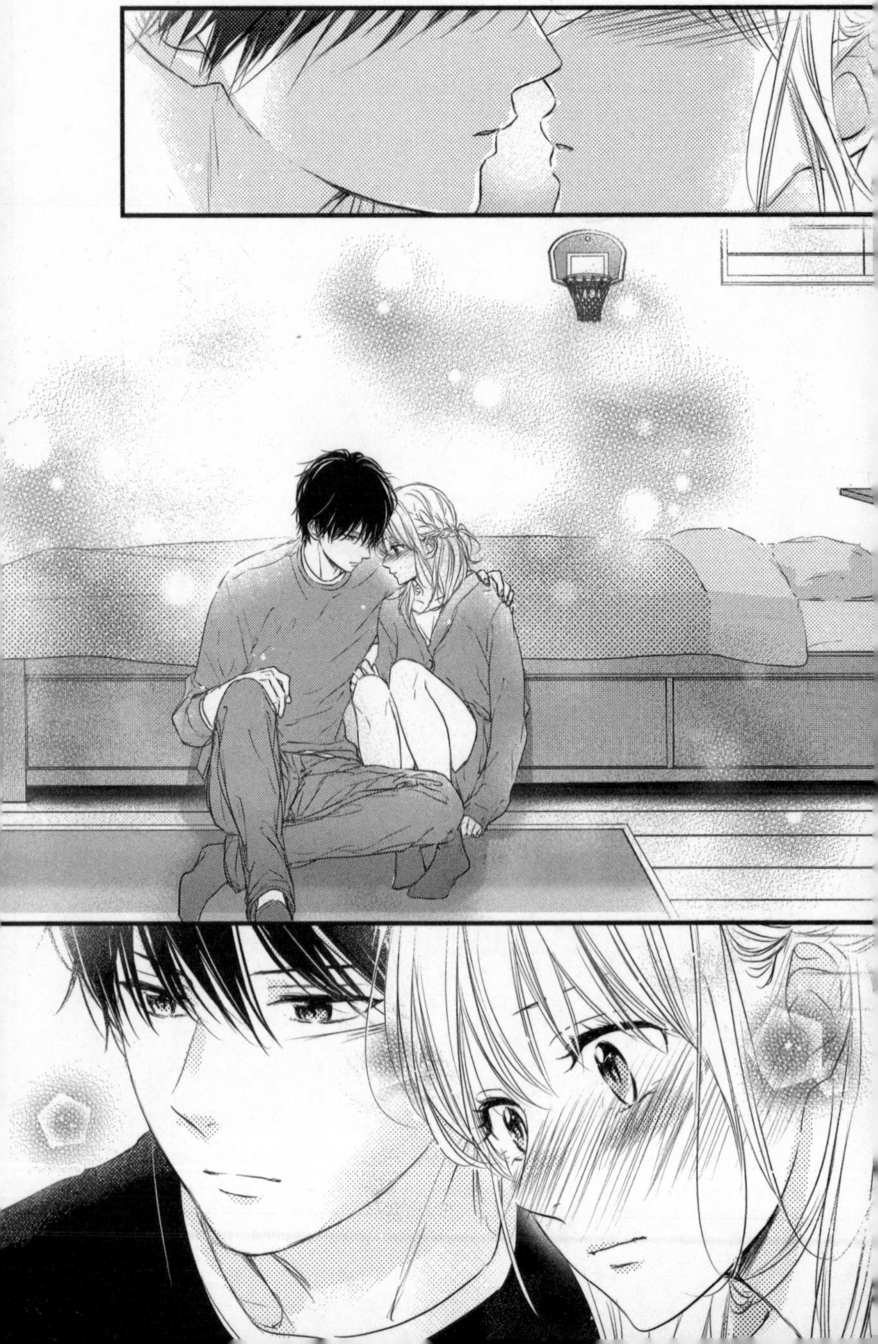

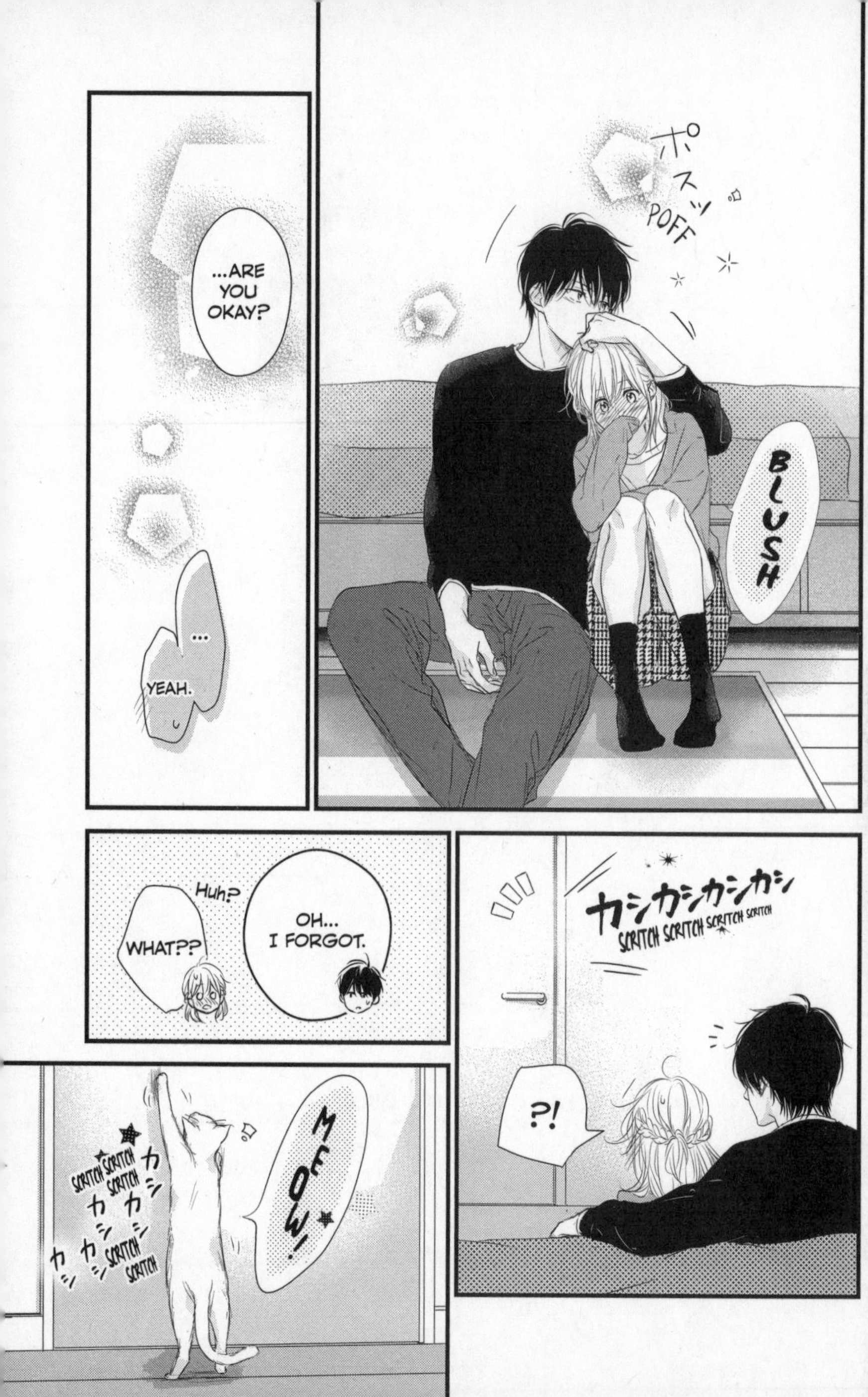
ポスッ
POFF
BLUSH
...ARE YOU OKAY?
...
YEAH.
カシカシカシカシ
SCRITCH SCRITCH SCRITCH SCRITCH
?!
OH... I FORGOT.
Huh?
WHAT??
カシカシカシカシ
SCRITCH SCRITCH SCRITCH SCRITCH
MEOW!

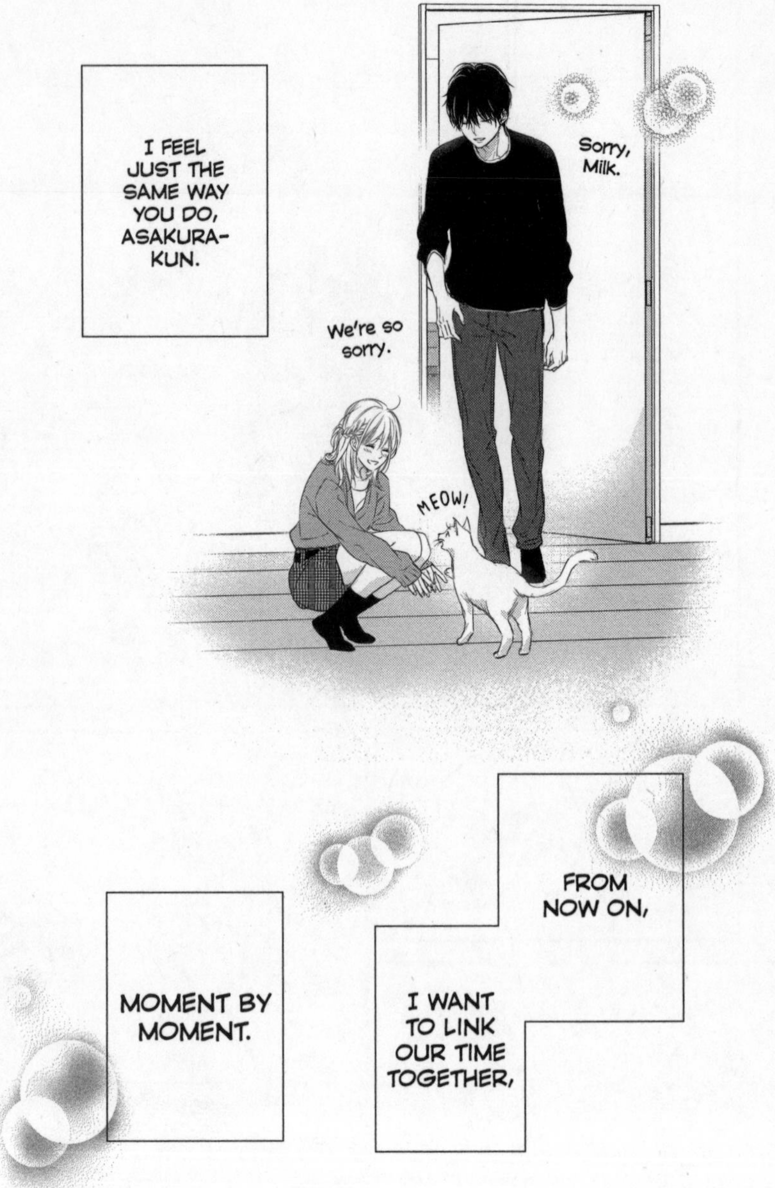
Sorry, Milk.
We're so sorry.
MEOW!
I FEEL JUST THE SAME WAY YOU DO, ASAKURA-KUN.
FROM NOW ON,
I WANT TO LINK OUR TIME TOGETHER,
MOMENT BY MOMENT.

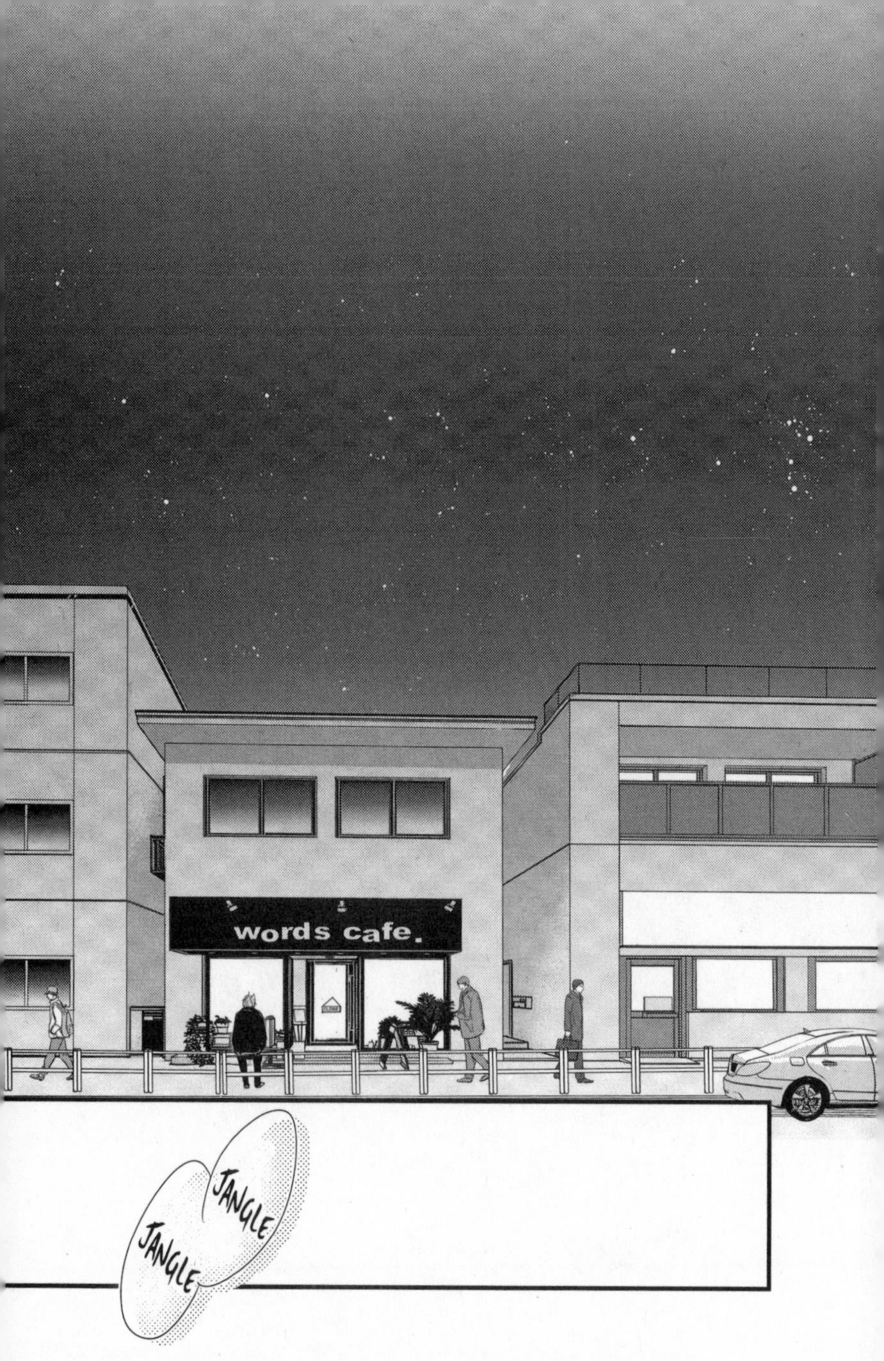
words cafe.
JANGLE
JANGLE

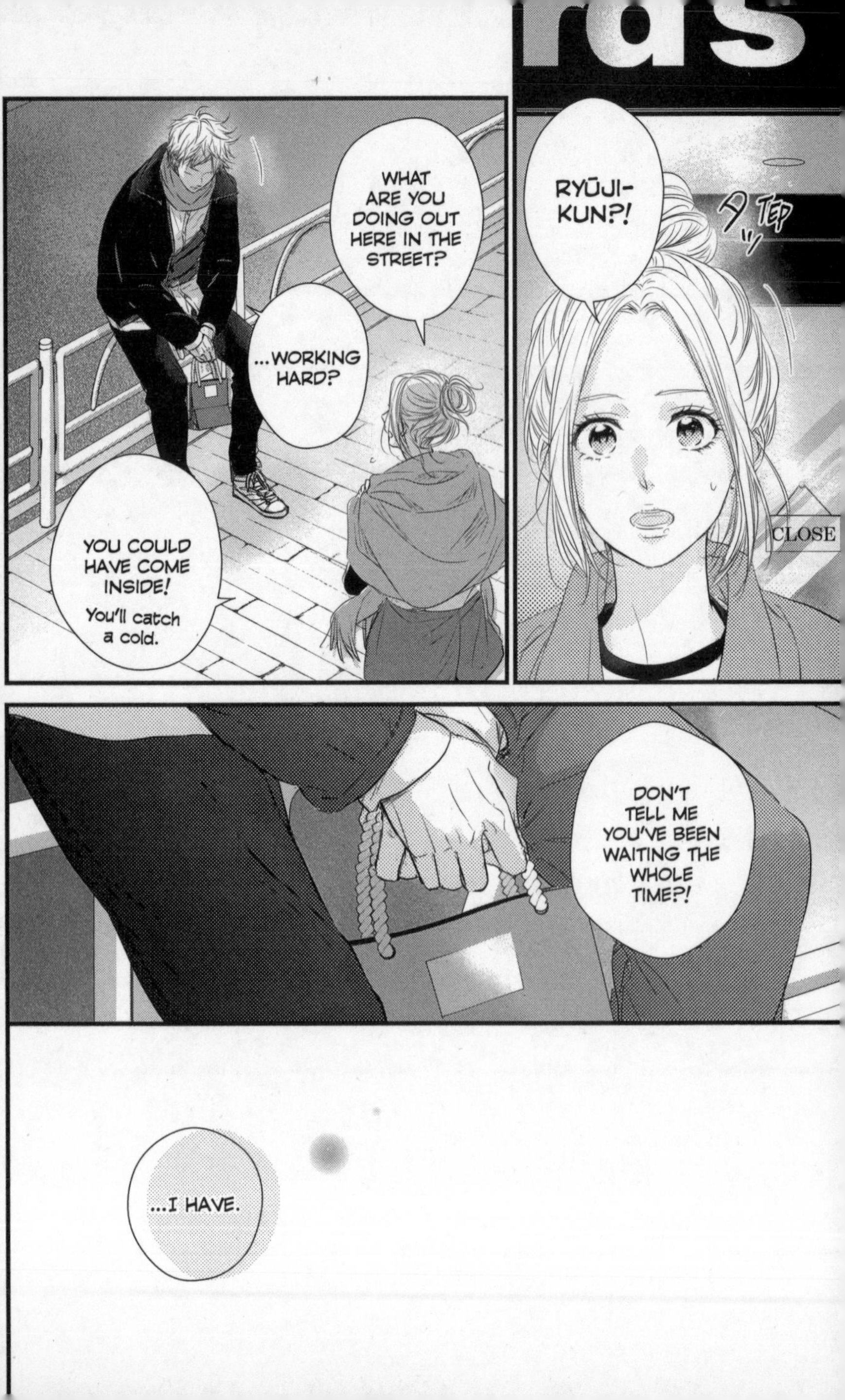
RYŪJI-KUN?!
TEP
CLOSE
WHAT ARE YOU DOING OUT HERE IN THE STREET?
...WORKING HARD?
YOU COULD HAVE COME INSIDE! You'll catch a cold.
DON'T TELL ME YOU'VE BEEN WAITING THE WHOLE TIME?!
...I HAVE.

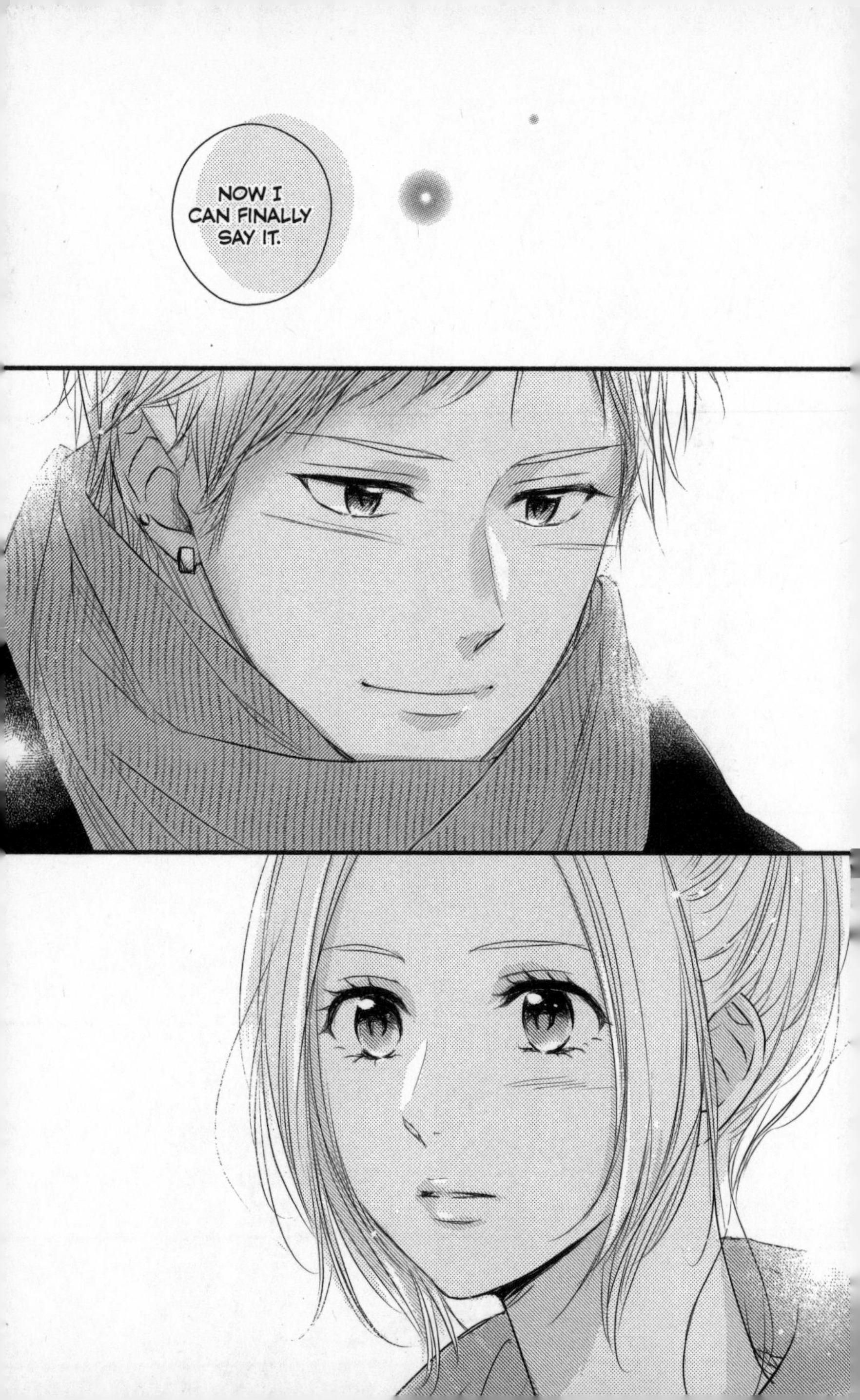
NOW I CAN FINALLY SAY IT.

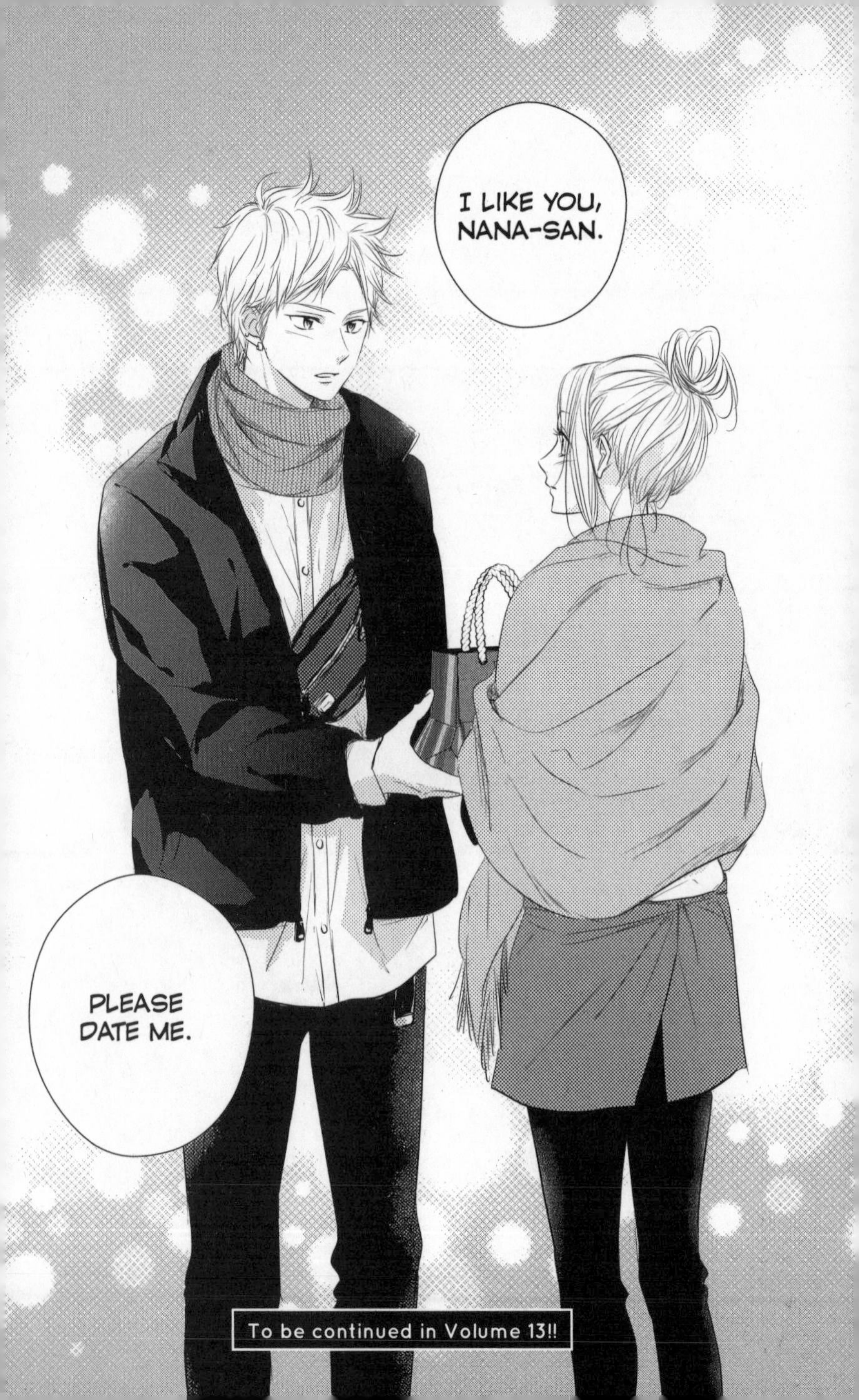
I LIKE YOU, NANA-SAN.
PLEASE DATE ME.
To be continued in Volume 13!!

Bonus Extra Manga

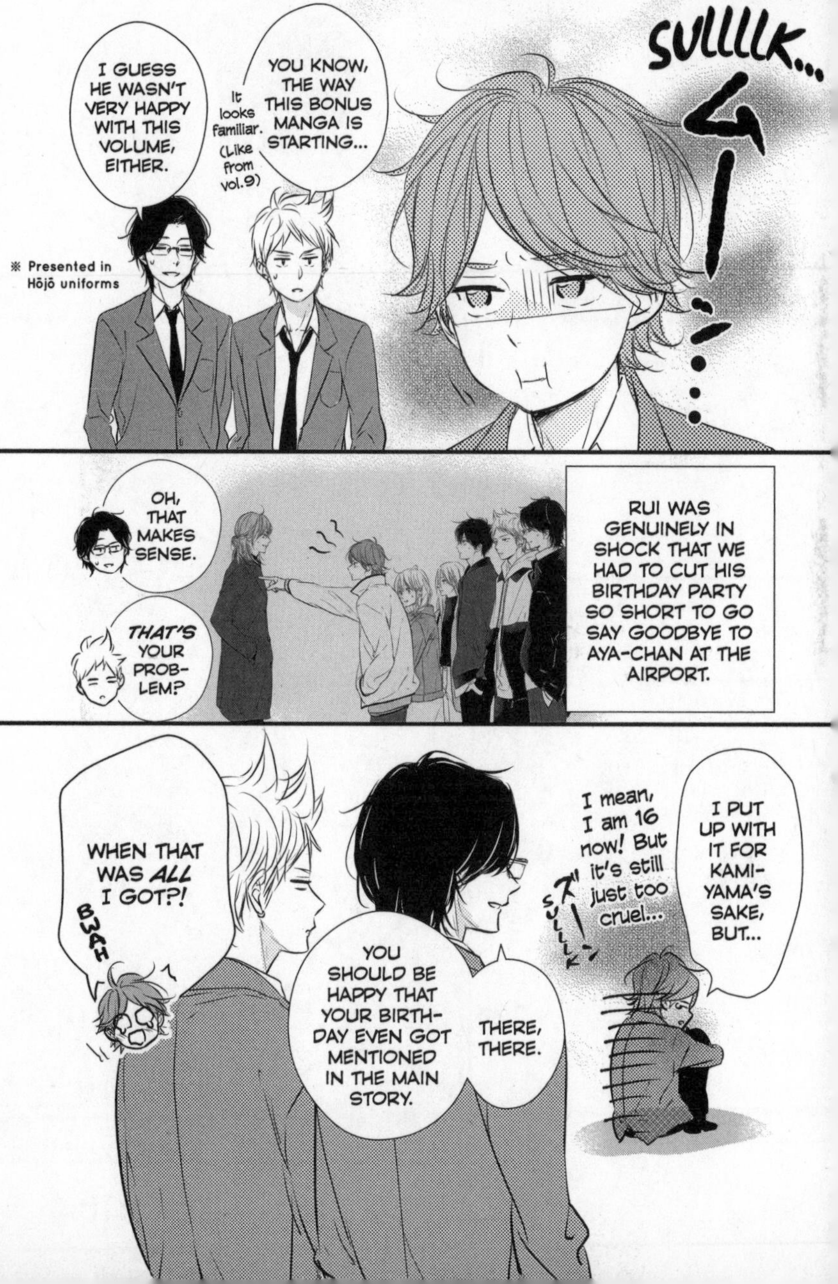
SULLLLK...
YOU KNOW, THE WAY THIS BONUS MANGA IS STARTING...
It looks familiar. (Like from vol.9)
I GUESS HE WASN'T VERY HAPPY WITH THIS VOLUME, EITHER.
※ Presented in Hōjō uniforms
RUI WAS GENUINELY IN SHOCK THAT WE HAD TO CUT HIS BIRTHDAY PARTY SO SHORT TO GO SAY GOODBYE TO AYA-CHAN AT THE AIRPORT.
OH, THAT MAKES SENSE.
THAT'S YOUR PROBLEM?
I PUT UP WITH IT FOR KAMI-YAMA'S SAKE, BUT...
I mean, I am 16 now! But it's still just too cruel...
SULLLLK
THERE, THERE.
YOU SHOULD BE HAPPY THAT YOUR BIRTHDAY EVEN GOT MENTIONED IN THE MAIN STORY.
WHEN THAT WAS ALL I GOT?!
BWAH

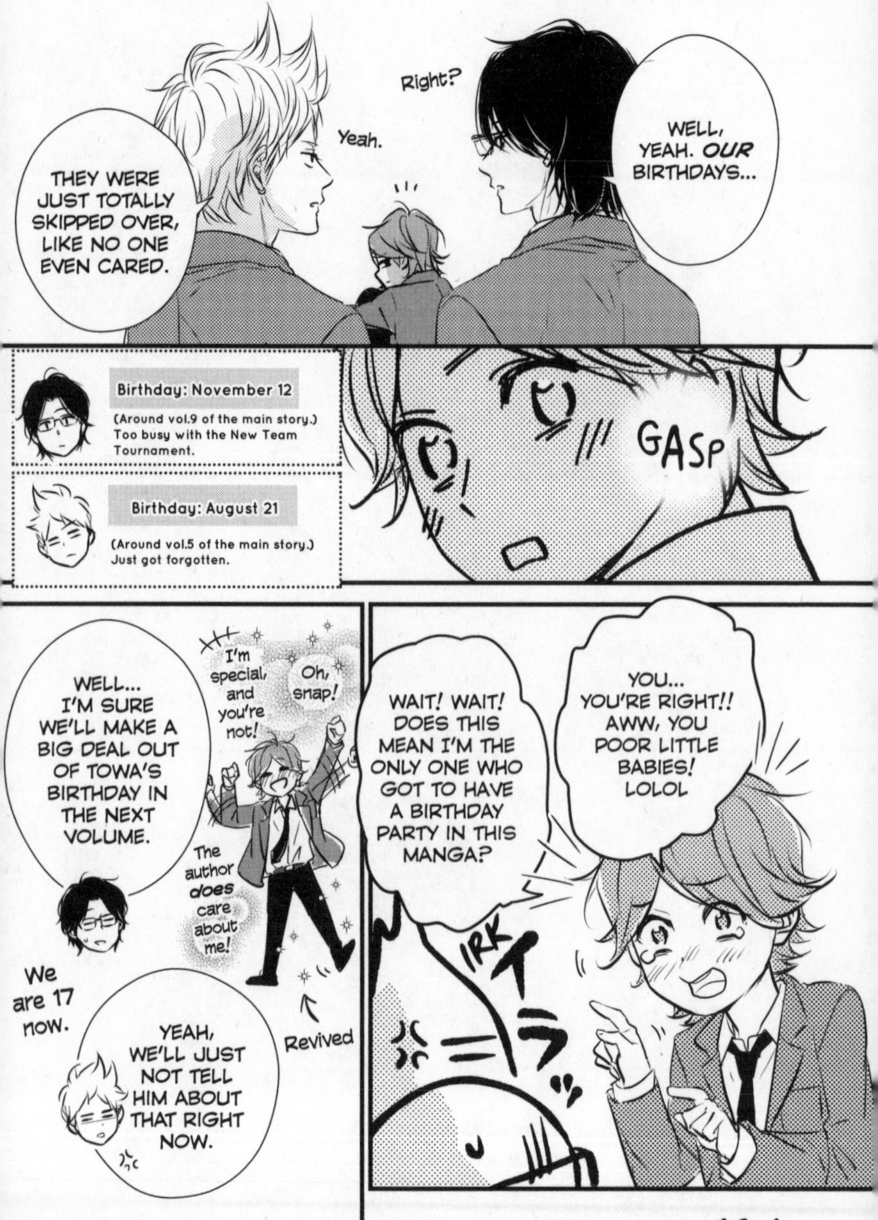
WELL, YEAH. *OUR* BIRTHDAYS...
Right?
Yeah.
THEY WERE JUST TOTALLY SKIPPED OVER, LIKE NO ONE EVEN CARED.
GASP
Birthday: November 12
(Around vol.9 of the main story.) Too busy with the New Team Tournament.
Birthday: August 21
(Around vol.5 of the main story.) Just got forgotten.
YOU... YOU'RE RIGHT!! AWW, YOU POOR LITTLE BABIES! LOLOL
WAIT! WAIT! DOES THIS MEAN I'M THE ONLY ONE WHO GOT TO HAVE A BIRTHDAY PARTY IN THIS MANGA?
IRK
Oh, snap!
I'm special, and you're not!
The author *does* care about me!
Revived
WELL... I'M SURE WE'LL MAKE A BIG DEAL OUT OF TOWA'S BIRTHDAY IN THE NEXT VOLUME.
We are 17 now.
YEAH, WE'LL JUST NOT TELL HIM ABOUT THAT RIGHT NOW.

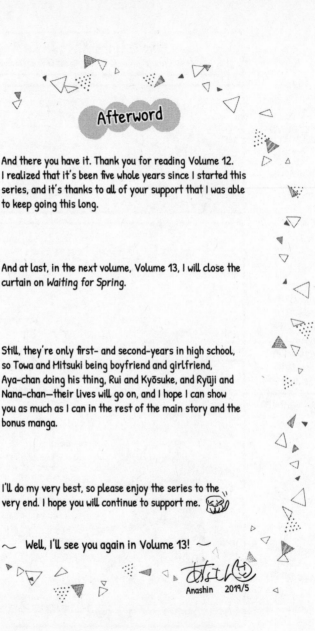

Afterword

And there you have it. Thank you for reading Volume 12. I realized that it's been five whole years since I started this series, and it's thanks to all of your support that I was able to keep going this long.

And at last, in the next volume, Volume 13, I will close the curtain on *Waiting for Spring*.

Still, they're only first- and second-years in high school, so Towa and Mitsuki being boyfriend and girlfriend, Aya-chan doing his thing, Rui and Kyōsuke, and Ryūji and Nana-chan—their lives will go on, and I hope I can show you as much as I can in the rest of the main story and the bonus manga.

I'll do my very best, so please enjoy the series to the very end. I hope you will continue to support me.

~ Well, I'll see you again in Volume 13! ~

Anashin   2019/5

Who Is Hardest to Draw?!

~ In Which I Give My Honest Opinion About Each of the Characters ~

Easy to draw, personality included

★ Aya-chan ★

(Reason)

I get excited drawing him because of his long hair.

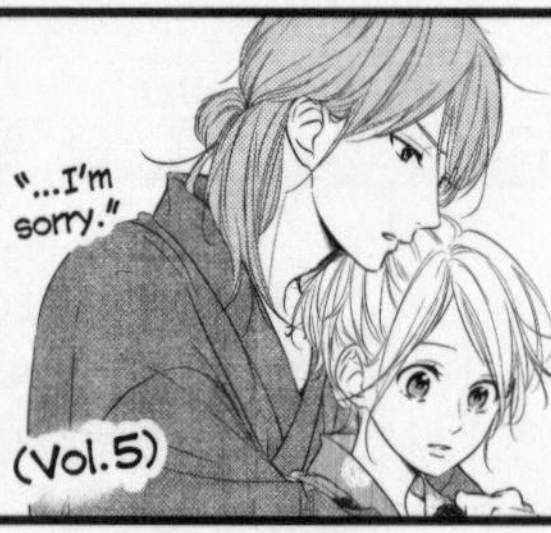
"...I'm sorry."
(Vol.5)

Pain in the neck, but still easy to draw

★ Kyōsuke ★

(Reason)

As long as I put glasses on him, it will be fine.

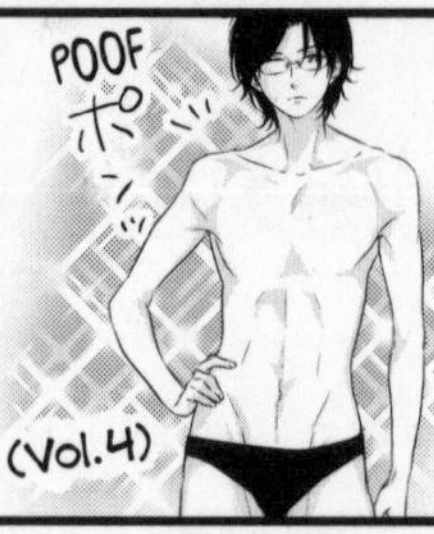
POOF
ポ
(Vol.4)

Easy to draw because he's so expressive

★ Rui ★

(Reason)

He's just always winking or sticking out his tongue or doing a peace sign.

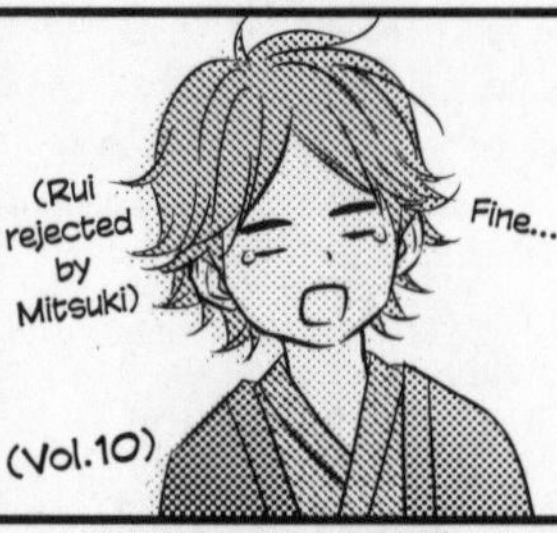
Fine...
(Rui rejected by Mitsuki)
(Vol.10)

Idiotic personality, and easy to draw, too

★ Ryūji ★

(Reason)

Short hair and small eyes are the best!

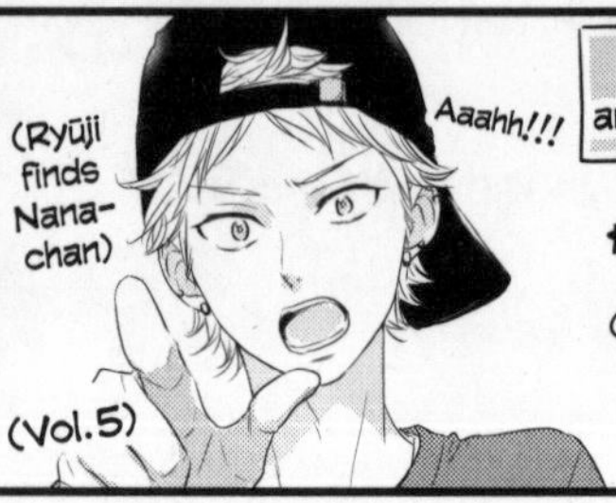
Aaahh!!!
(Ryūji finds Nana-chan)
(Vol.5)

The illustrations were selected from my favorite picture (or scene) of these characters.

Continues on the next page.

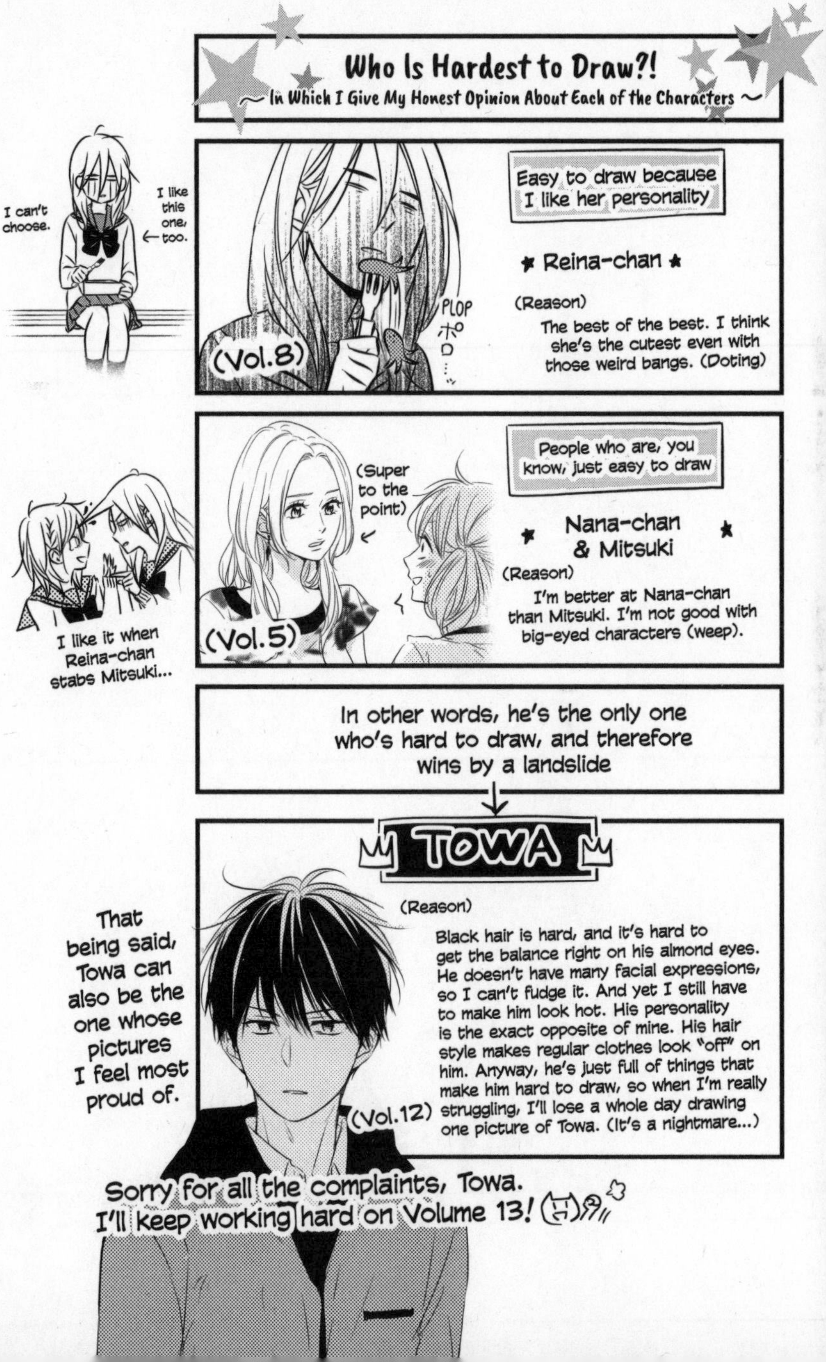
Who Is Hardest to Draw?!
~ In Which I Give My Honest Opinion About Each of the Characters ~
Easy to draw because I like her personality
★ Reina-chan ★
(Reason)
The best of the best. I think she's the cutest even with those weird bangs. (Doting)
PLOP
ポロ…
(Vol.8)
I like this one, too.
I can't choose.
People who are, you know, just easy to draw
★ Nana-chan & Mitsuki ★
(Reason)
I'm better at Nana-chan than Mitsuki. I'm not good with big-eyed characters (weep).
(Super to the point)
(Vol.5)
I like it when Reina-chan stabs Mitsuki...
In other words, he's the only one who's hard to draw, and therefore wins by a landslide
TOWA
(Reason)
Black hair is hard, and it's hard to get the balance right on his almond eyes. He doesn't have many facial expressions, so I can't fudge it. And yet I still have to make him look hot. His personality is the exact opposite of mine. His hair style makes regular clothes look "off" on him. Anyway, he's just full of things that make him hard to draw, so when I'm really struggling, I'll lose a whole day drawing one picture of Towa. (It's a nightmare...)
(Vol.12)
That being said, Towa can also be the one whose pictures I feel most proud of.
Sorry for all the complaints, Towa.
I'll keep working hard on Volume 13!

Waiting for Spring

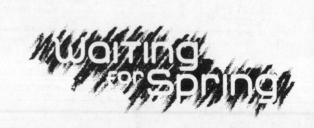

YOUR NEW FAVORITE ROMANCE MANGA IS WAITING FOR YOU!

THAT WOLF-BOY IS MINE!

A beast-boy comedy and drama perfect for fans of *Fruits Basket*!

"A tantalizing, understated slice-of-life romance with an interesting supernatural twist."

- Taykobon

WAKE UP, SLEEPING BEAUTY

This heartrending romantic manga is not the fairy tale you remember! This time, Prince Charming is a teenage housekeeper, and Sleeping Beauty's curse threatens to pull them both into deep trouble.

A picture-perfect shojo series from Yoko Nogiri, creator of the hit *That Wolf-Boy is Mine!*

Mako's always had a passion for photography. When she loses someone dear to her, she clings onto her art as a relic of the close relationship she once had... Luckily, her childhood best friend Kei encourages her to come to his high school and join their prestigious photo club. With nothing to lose, Mako grabs her camera and moves into the dorm where Kei and his classmates live. Soon, a fresh take on life, along with a mysterious new muse, begin to come into focus!

LOVE IN FOCUS

Love in Focus © Yoko Nogiri/Kodansha Ltd.

Praise for Yoko Nogiri's *That Wolf-Boy is Mine!*

KC KODANSHA COMICS

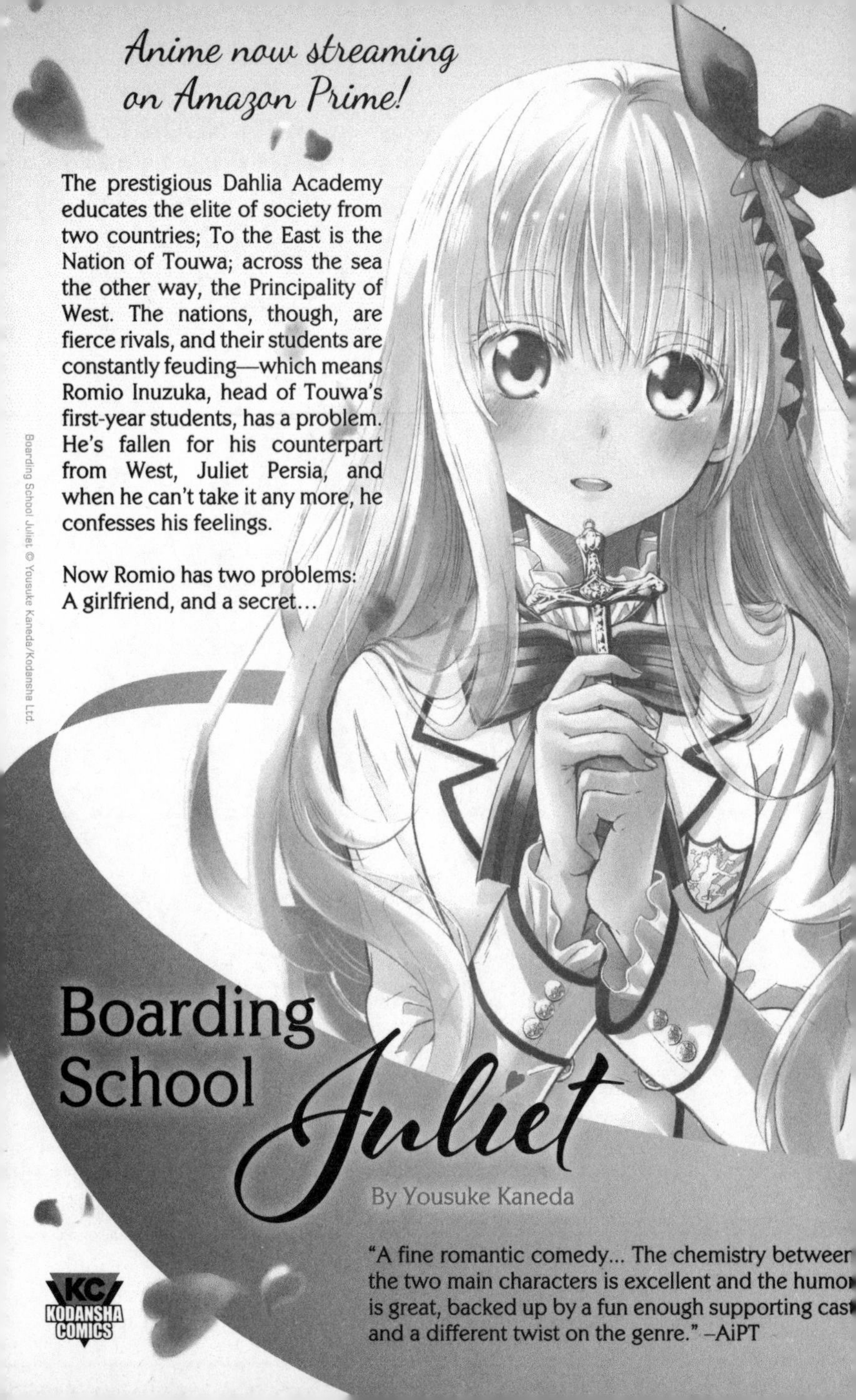

Anime now streaming on Amazon Prime!
The prestigious Dahlia Academy educates the elite of society from two countries; To the East is the Nation of Touwa; across the sea the other way, the Principality of West. The nations, though, are fierce rivals, and their students are constantly feuding—which means Romio Inuzuka, head of Touwa's first-year students, has a problem. He's fallen for his counterpart from West, Juliet Persia, and when he can't take it any more, he confesses his feelings.
Now Romio has two problems: A girlfriend, and a secret...
Boarding School Juliet
By Yousuke Kaneda
"A fine romantic comedy... The chemistry between the two main characters is excellent and the humor is great, backed up by a fun enough supporting cast and a different twist on the genre." –AiPT
KC KODANSHA COMICS
Boarding School Juliet © Yousuke Kaneda/Kodansha Ltd.

Yuri Is My Job!

miman

Acclaimed screenwriter and director Mari Okada (*Maquia, anohana*) teams up with manga artist Nao Emoto (*Forget Me Not*) in this moving, funny, so-true-it's-embarrassing coming-of-age series!

When Kazusa enters high school, she joins the Literature Club, and leaps from reading innocent fiction to diving into the literary classics. But these novels are a bit more... *adult* than she was prepared for. Between euphemisms like fresh dewy grass and pork stew, crushing on the boy next door, and knowing you want to do that *one thing* before you die—discovering your budding sexuality is no easy feat! As if puberty wasn't awkward enough, the club consists of a brooding writer, the prettiest girl in school, an agreeable comrade, and an outspoken prude. Fumbling over their own discomforts, these five teens get thrown into chaos over three little letters: S...E...X...!

Anime coming soon!

O Maidens in your Savage Season

KC KODANSHA COMICS

Mari Okada   Nao Emoto

Futaro Uesugi is a second-year in high school, scraping to get by and pay off his family's debt. The only thing he can do is study, so when Futaro receives a part-time job offer to tutor the five daughters of a wealthy businessman, he can't pass it up. Little does he know, these five beautiful sisters are quintuplets, but the only thing they have in common...is that they're all terrible at studying!

The Quintessential Quintuplets © Negi Haruba/Kodansha, Ltd.

THE QUINTESSENTIAL QUINTUPLETS

negi haruba

ANIME UT NOW!

My Little Monster

OPPOSITES ATTRACT...MAYBE?

Haru Yoshida is feared as an unstable and violent "monster." Mizutani Shizuku is a grade-obsessed student with no friends. Fate brings these two together to form the most unlikely pair. Haru firmly believes he's in love with Mizutani and she firmly believes he's insane.

A Kodansha Comics Trade Paperback Original
Waiting for Spring 12 copyright © 2019 Anashin
English translation copyright © 2019 Anashin

Published in the United States by Kodansha Comics, an imprint of Kodansha USA Publishing, LLC, New York.

Publication rights for this English edition arranged through Kodansha Ltd, Tokyo.

First published in Japan in 2019 by Kodansha Ltd, Tokyo.

ISBN 978-1-63236-859-1

Printed in the United States of America.

www.kodanshacomics.com

9 8 7 6 5 4 3 2 1
Translation: Alethea and Athena Nibley
Lettering: Sara Linsley
Editing: Haruko Hashimoto
Kodansha Comics edition cover design by Phil Balsman

Publisher: Kiichiro Sugawara
Managing editor: Maya Rosewood
Vice president of marketing & publicity: Naho Yamada

Director of publishing services: Ben Applegate
Associate director of operations: Stephen Pakula
Publishing services managing editor: Noelle Webster
Assistant production manager: Emi Lotto